ARTHUR BROWN JR.

Progressive Classicist

C.1 (*preceding page*). Arthur Brown Jr., "A Vitrine for a Precious Object," study for the Prix Rougevin, February, 1903. Drawing, Arthur Brown Jr. Collection, Bancroft Library.

C.2. Arthur Brown Jr., terminal for AT&SF Railroad, San Diego, 1913, entry and tower.

C.3. Bakewell & Brown, Filoli, Woodside, 1917, cupola over garage and sunken garden.

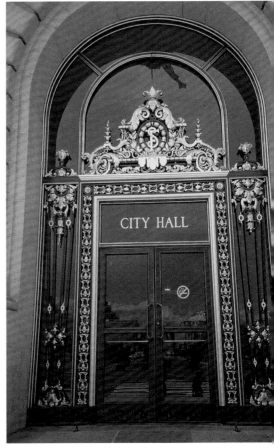

C.4. Bakewell & Brown, San Francisco City Hall, 1912–16, corner pavilion.

C.5. Henri Crenier, San Francisco City Hall, c. 1915, term.

C.6. Bakewell & Brown, San Francisco City Hall, 1912–16, entry door with ornamental ironwork. Photograph courtesy of Christopher VerPlanck.

C.7 (*opposite*). Bakewell & Brown, San Francisco City Hall, 1912–16, rotunda stair.

C.8. Bakewell & Brown, San Francisco City Hall, 1912–16, view into dome.

C.9. Bakewell & Brown, San Francisco City Hall, 1912–16, rotunda, north wall.

C.10. Arthur Brown Jr. and G. Albert
Lansburgh, War Memorial Opera House,
San Francisco, 1932, Van Ness Avenue
elevation.

C.11 (*opposite above*). Arthur Brown Jr. and
G. Albert Lansburgh, War Memorial Opera
House, rendering of section looking to
proscenium, c. 1928.

C.12 (*opposite below*). Arthur Brown Jr. and
G. Albert Lansburgh, War Memorial Opera
House, San Francisco, 1928, auditorium as
restored in 1997.

C.13. Arthur Brown Jr., San Francisco Federal Building, 1935, view from United Nations Plaza.

C.14. Diego Rivera, *Making a Fresco, Showing the Building of a City*, 1931, fresco, San Francisco Art Insitute, gift of William Gerstle. The three "patrons" under Rivera are Timothy Pflueger, William Gerstle, and Arthur Brown Jr. Photograph courtesy of San Francisco Art Institute.

C.15. Bakewell & Brown and Sylvain Schnaittacher, Temple Emanu-El, 1925, courtyard view to main door to sanctuary.

C.16. Bakewell & Brown and Sylvain Schnaittacher, Temple Emanu-El, 1925, view from balcony to bema.

C.17 (*opposite*). Bakewell & Brown,
Pasadena City Hall, 1927,
view from Holly Street.

C.18 (*left*). Bakewell & Brown,
Pasadena City Hall, fountain.

C.19 (*above*). Bakewell & Brown,
Pasadena City Hall, 1927,
stair at corner towers.

C.20. Arthur Brown Jr., Labor–ICC Group, Washington, DC, view from National Mall.

C.21. Arthur Brown Jr., Labor–ICC group, Andrew W. Mellon Auditorium, dais.

C.22. Arthur Brown Jr., Coit Tower,
San Francisco, 1933. Photograph courtesy
of Steven Kyle Weller.

C.23. Bakewell & Brown, Cecil H. Green Library, 1917 and Hoover Tower, 1941, Stanford University.

C.24. Bakewell & Brown, Cecil H. Green Library, Stanford University, 1917, view into former receiving hall.

C.25. Arthur Brown Jr., Sproul Hall,
University of California, Berkeley,
1942.

C.26 (*following page*). Arthur Brown Jr., Tower
of the Sun, GGIE, San Francisco, c. 1937. This
drawing was the last rendering done by Brown
himself. Arthur Brown Jr. Collection, Bancroft
Library. Photograph of drawing by Moulin
Studios.

ARTHUR BROWN JR.
Progressive Classicist

JEFFREY T. TILMAN

in association with
THE INSTITUTE OF CLASSICAL ARCHITECTURE
AND CLASSICAL AMERICA

W. W. NORTON & COMPANY

NEW YORK · LONDON

For information about permission to reproduce selections from this book,
write to Permissions, W. W. Norton & Company, Inc., 500 Fifth Avenue,
New York, NY 10110

Composition and book design by Abigail Sturges
Manufacturing by Friesens
Production manager: Leeann Graham

Illustration Credits
The illustrations are numbered by chapter and referenced by source; complete citations for these materials can be found in the bibliography. Most
primary source material credited to the papers of Arthur Brown Jr. has been
recently donated to the Bancroft Library. No attempt has been made to cite
the specific folder or item number of the Bancroft materials because the
collection has not yet been formally cataloged. Photographs not credited
to a source or a photographer are by the author.

Library of Congress Cataloging-in-Publication Data

Tilman, Jeffrey T.
    Arthur Brown, Jr. : progressive classicist / Jeffrey T. Tilman.
       p. cm.
    Includes bibliographical references and index.
    ISBN 0-393-73178-2
    1. Brown, Arthur, 1874-1957—Criticism and interpretation. 2.
Classicism in architecture—United States. 3. Ecole nationale supérieure
des beaux-arts (France)—Influence. I. Brown, Arthur, 1874-1957. II. Title.

NA737.B695T55 2005
720′.92—dc22
2005051297

W. W. Norton & Company, Inc., 500 Fifth Avenue, New York, NY 10110
www.wwnorton.com

W. W. Norton & Company, Ltd., Castle House, 75/76 Wells Street,
London W1T 3QT

0 9 8 7 6 5 4 3 2 1

CONTENTS

ACKNOWLEDGMENTS

In a project as extensive as a monograph, the author naturally owes a debt of gratitude to a large number of family, friends, and professional colleagues. I have received assistance from an unusually large number of people in the course of the past ten years, and wish to give these supporters a small portion of their due here.

I wish to thank first my family for their unswerving support. My parents, Ted and Nancy Tilman, made the research for this book possible not only through their hospitality and many airline tickets, but through their love, reassurance and boundless faith in me. Having grown up in a house full of popular histories, I suppose it was inevitable that my writing would take on a historic cast. My sister Jennifer also lent her support (and at times her computer) in encouragement of what has become a family enterprise. A whole host of other relatives should also be thanked for their patience during this process; I'm certain that they all have heard quite enough about Mr. Brown.

I have been quite fortunate to place this book with W. W. Norton. My thanks must go to Stephen Salny for his suggestion that I bring to manuscript to New York. Nancy Green has done a superb job of managing the production of this volume, and of managing the author. In places she gave the manuscript much-needed shape, and in others she politely suggested that brevity might be in order. Without her enthusiasm for this project, it might have been several more years in the creation. I also wish to show appreciation to Abigail Sturges for her great design—she gave this book order and style.

I would like to express my appreciation to all those at the University of Virginia, where this project started. The faculty of the Department of Architectural History and the Department of Art History taught me how to read and write architectural history from something more than the technical perspective. Lisa Reilly, Kevin Murphy (now at the City Univeristy of New York), and Paul Barolsky all asked me the hard questions I didn't have an immediate answer to and taught me how to formulate hard questions of my own. My co-workers at the University's Office of Real Estate and Space Management took up the slack when I was off on many month-long research trips during the preparation of the dissertation that preceded this monograph. Melanie Besio, Bill Bohn, Mark Webb, Tracy Tanner Bond, and Bill Bond all lent me their encouragement and limitless understanding.

I have also found a great deal of support for this project at the University of Cincinnati, where Gordon Simmons and Michaele Pride-Wells ensured that I would complete the manuscript of this book in a timely fashion. The University's Faculty Research Council provided a very generous stipend that allowed me to spend a summer in San Francisco just when the need was most critical. My friend and colleague Elizabeth Riorden read the entire manuscript and offered edits that have made the text much clearer and informative; she also lent her talents to the drafting of the plans of the San Francisco War Memorial. Likewise, Patrick Snadon offered many helpful suggestions for strengthening the conclusion of the book. Several of my new friends in Cincinnati have also lent me their "non-specialist" perspective—Jimmie Sanford and Randy Ryan both kept me in line when my prose threatened to become a bit too technical, while Alben Roland kept me laughing through the re-writes.

Several friends in the San Francisco Bay Area have also assisted with the research and publication phases of this book. Christopher VerPlanck has offered his home and unique architectural insights to me on countless occasions since he became San Francisco's most enthusiastic defender of its vernacular architecture some years ago; his photographic skill is also represented in an image in the color insert. Bridget Maley provided me with copies of the Architectural Resources Group's extensive documentation on Pasadena City Hall and has remained a champion of this project throughout its long gestation. Wayne and Cheryl Renshaw, Brady and Francis Keys, Randy and Karla Nubling, and Mark and Lisa Kobayashi all offered me their extended hospitality and the use of their computer equipment whenever I asked; my gratitude to these long-standing friends is truly limitless.

Brown's papers have been preserved in several repositories on both coasts; a great number of archives specialists have assisted me while using these materials. At the Bancroft Library at the University of California, Berkeley, Bonnie Hardwick, Richard Ogar, William Roberts, Carola Derouy, Teresa Salazar, and Susan Snyder have all assisted me with the Brown papers whenever required. Waverly Lowell has shared her unparalleled knowledge of Bay Area architectural resources with me at crucial points in the project; her staff at the Environmental Design Archives of the University of California, Berkeley, has likewise been knowledgeable, efficient and quick to offer a smile. University Archivist Margaret Kimball was a great help at Stanford University, where I also received assistance from Laura Jones of the University Architect/Planning Office and Kristina Seyer Smith of Facilities Operations. Jeff Gunderson, Librarian of the San Francisco Art Institute, performed heroically on my behalf both in the library and out on Jones Street, where he summoned AAA when all hope was lost. Bill Callan spent several days with me at the Olympic Club as we sorted out the various building campaigns the Club sponsored. Closer to home, Jennifer Masengarb of the Chicago Architecture Foundation and Julia Bachrach of the Chicago Parks Foundation found for me the rare images of the Century of Progress Exhibition that accompany my discussion of that important event. On the East Coast, C. Ford Peatross and Marrisha Battle both showed me the ropes of the Library of Congress's research apparatus, while down Independence Avenue, Cynthia Field was extremely generous with the material under her care at the Smithsonian Institution. Not only has she become a close colleague and collaborator, Dr. Field has become a great friend as well.

Several prominent architectural historians shared their knowledge and insights about Brown's work with me over the past several years. Harold Kirker proved to be an invaluable resource when fitting Brown into his early San Francisco context. The late Joan Draper very generously lent her materials on the Federal Triangle to me and directed me to the correct files at the National Archives. Michael Corbett graciously arranged for me to visit Brown's first work in the Bay Area, and has become a faithful correspondent. Richard Chafee shared with me his important collection of records from the Ecole des Beaux-Arts, enriching the first chapter of this book immeasurably. Bruno Giberti reviewed the material on San Francisco City Hall and offered important suggestions for focusing the text there. Paul Turner has discussed with me his understanding of Brown's place in the campus-planning tradition at Stanford and has since become a friend as well as a colleague. Finally, Richard Longstreth constantly challenged me to infuse my enthusiasm for Brown's architecture into my prose; he has offered his expertise and encouragement every step of the way, and I hope this book meets his expectations.

Members of Brown's inner circle were extremely supportive of this undertaking. The late George Livermore sat for several interviews and delivered an insider's view of the workings of Brown's office in the 1930s, as well as an architect's perspective of how Brown studied his designs. Victoria Brown Polk enthusiastically described her family's life in the first half of the twentieth century, and provided an insight into her father's character as only a daughter can. Brown's younger daughter, Sylvia, and her husband, Rollin Jensen, photographed Brown's work throughout the 1950s and 1960s. Once married, they mounted the first exhibition of Brown's work and preserved the bulk of his papers for decades at great personal inconvenience and expense so that they would be available for public study. Their daughter, Margaret Jensen, proved to be an equally worthy steward, and worked tirelessly after her father's death to ensure that her grandfather's papers would become part of the Bancroft Library's collections. Ms. Jensen's measureless kindness in granting me the publication rights to her father's drawings and her parents' photographs has made this volume a much richer visual document.

This book is the result of the extraordinary generosity of two parties. The Jensen's contribution has been described above. But I would not have met the Jensens, nor known what to do with their archive, nor understood the importance of Arthur Brown's architecture, were it not for the mentorship of Richard Guy Wilson. Always giving of his time and ideas, Mr. Wilson backed me for admission to the doctoral program at the University of Virginia when others would not. Through his patient instruction I discovered the social and intellectual significance of what we architects do, and by his example I learned to express some of this to a wider audience. Although he himself had planned to write a monograph on Arthur Brown, Mr. Wilson set me to work on Bakewell & Brown the moment he learned of my interest. Ten years later, I hope this book might serve as partial substantiation of such generosity and confidence.

In recognition of the debt I owe them both, this book is dedicated to the Rollin Jensen Family and to Richard Guy Wilson.

Arthur Brown Jr. at drafting table in Montgomery Street Studio,
c. 1914. Photograph, private collection, San Francisco.

INTRODUCTION

Arthur Brown Jr.'s story begins with the transcontinental railroad and ends with the atomic bomb. His life and career spanned the critical years and events that saw California rise from a far-flung outpost of the American West to a wellspring of American civilization. At the same time the American nation itself recovered from its near-extinction in the Civil War to make itself a superpower whose military, political, and economic power extended to nearly every corner of the globe. Brown's architecture, employing the classical architectural tradition that had been born in ancient Greece, extended in Rome, and reinterpreted in the Italian renaissance, celebrated and embodied this dual transformation of nation and state. His masterpieces, the city halls for San Francisco and Pasadena, the Temple Emanu-El, and his Labor–ICC block of the Federal Triangle, continued the American classical tradition that had begun with Thomas Jefferson and Benjamin Henry Latrobe and was sustained by William Strickland and Thomas U. Walter and renewed by Richard Morris Hunt and Charles Follen McKim.

At its best, architecture does more than simply house day-to-day life; it provides the setting for the rituals and defining events of a civilization. A great work of architecture represents the values of its patrons and, at the same time, informs the human condition, in both its personal and corporate states, and ennobles both the institutions it houses and the individuals who inhabit it. In a fast-changing society such as the America of the early twentieth century, architecture was often used to emphasize continuity with the past, rather than to celebrate a contemporary break with it. Public building in the late nineteenth and early twentieth centuries utilized the forms of past European civilizations, particularly those of Imperial Rome and Bourbon France, to argue that the United States was the logical successor to the great empires of the West, except that its rhetoric proclaimed that the great power of emperors and kings now rested with the American people.

Yet, if the architectural expression of the public building was rooted in the past, the construction of these edifices was as technologically advanced as possible. The building industry mechanized in the years after the Civil War as rapidly as the rest of the economy. New materials, such as steel and concrete and plate glass, revolutionized how architecture was achieved, even if it did not initially change the formal language architects employed in their work. During the course of the first half of the twentieth century that language would be reformed, and a new, sparer grammar of glass and steel would come to dominate public building in the United States. This new idiom would be called modernism, and it would challenge and supplant the Latinate forms of the classical tradition, at least for several generations. To Brown this new architecture, whose champions insisted on an absolute break with the past, was anathema; to him, architecture was an evolutionary art, not a revolutionary one. To Brown and many of his generation, the modern movement denied architecture its voice. Without its rich set of historical associations, its symbolic ornamentation, or its role in coordinating the other visual arts, architecture could only speak about itself and articulate no additional meaning.

During the years Brown and his generation matured, the 1890s, three American architects stood above all others as exemplar artists and men: Daniel Burnham, Charles Follen McKim, and Henry Hobson Richardson. Brown's work combines the salient qualities of all three.[1] From Burnham, Brown learned to value the architectural ensemble. In collaboration with Burnham's associates and successors, Willis Polk and Edward H. Bennett, Brown explored the potential of grand design in scales as intimate as the garden for a country house and as monumental as the District of Columbia. Like McKim, Brown became a master of architectural proportion and one of the few American architects able to precisely detail the classical orders. Brown would worry over the slightest proportional problem, knowing that the extra effort would be rewarded in a more perfect building; this perfectionism demanded that he periodically leave his practice to go on sabbatical, to regain perspective on his career. Finally, Brown sought to infuse his buildings with the power and presence of those of Richardson. Though Richardson died in 1886, Brown knew many of his works by the time he was fifteen years old. Indeed, he seems never to have forgotten Richardson's use of simple geometric solids, the integration of the architectural elements into the whole, and his love of the big motif. Within the context of his own generation, Brown was the West Coast counterpart to his contemporary, John Russell Pope, with whom he collaborated on the Federal Triangle. But whereas Pope's classicism is polite and deliberate, Brown's is strong, massive, and at times aggressive. This dialectic is extended by the two architects' choice of orders— most of Pope's major classical buildings are Ionic or Corinthian, whereas Brown designed most often in a muscular Doric. The bold quality of Brown's work is distinctly American and may have developed after close study of those who came before him.

This book owes a great debt to the resurgent interest in the French Ecole Nationale Supérieure des Beaux-Arts and American classicism of the past thirty years. In the two decades following Brown's death in 1957, only a few inveterate apologists for American classicism found Brown a subject worthy of architectural ink.[2] However, Arthur Drexler's 1975 landmark exhibition of drawings from the Ecole des Beaux-Arts at the Museum of Modern Art in New York inaugurated a new interest in French academic design methods. The publication in 1977 of an edited volume of essays by Drexler, Richard Chafee, Neil Levine, and David Van Zanten brought a renewed appreciation of the Beaux-Arts as a source for American modernism, even if the essays were largely concerned with the mid-nineteenth-century history of the school.[3] Two years later the Brooklyn Museum sponsored an exhibition, The American Renaissance 1876–1917, that examined the American application of Beaux-Arts planning and architectural theory in the remaking of the nation's urban centers at the turn of the twentieth century.[4] In conjunction with this rising interest in the Beaux-Arts in America, a parallel series of investigations were undertaken into the origins and implementation of the National Mall and Federal Triangle in Washington, DC. Sally Kress Tompkins's research into the life of Charles Moore focused on his involvement with the design of the Triangle, and George Gurney's study of the sculpture of the group, pub-

lished as *Sculpture and the Federal Triangle* in 1985, also contributed a great deal to our understanding of the design of the buildings themselves.[5] Two journal articles have since highlighted Brown's civic work. Richard Guy Wilson's reintroductory article of Brown in *Progressive Architecture*, "Precursor: Arthur Brown, Jr., California Classicist," established Brown's place in the canon of twentieth-century American architects and expertly analyzed a few of Brown's most important works. David Gebhard's article, "Civic Presence in California Cities: Where and How?," placed the San Francisco and Pasadena Civic Centers in the context of other such City Beautiful planning efforts in California, such as Los Angeles's partially realized municipal scheme.[6]

This book emphasizes Brown's role as a designer of representational and institutional buildings for the Bay Area as well as for California and the nation. The first chapter describes the three main influences in Brown's early life and his development as a designer: his family, the artistic circle surrounding the California Institute of Fine Arts and the University of California, and the Ecole des Beaux-Arts. The even-numbered chapters outline Brown's architectural output with Bakewell & Brown and on his own. Chapter Two examines the founding of Bakewell & Brown and the partnership's work until the firm's hiatus at the First World War. Chapter Four picks up the history of the practice from 1920 until its dissolution at the end of 1927. Chapter Six describes Brown's sole proprietorship, which lasted until his effective retirement in 1950. Although some supporting background information is included in this material, these chapters do not constitute a definitive biography, nor do they represent a comprehensive *catalogue raisonné*, because many works, particularly residences, are not discussed in any detail. Instead, Brown's principal works are discussed in the context of their geographic and temporal location and within the framework of grand design.

The remaining odd-numbered chapters are thematic; each focuses on a particular site or set of sites for which Brown contributed work over a period of time. The third chapter examines the work at the San Francisco Civic Center in depth and gives particular attention to the social and political forces that shaped this most complete of City Beautiful civic centers. Brown's design response to this context is also explored, and a few of the many other architects and artisans who worked on the project are profiled in brief. Chapter Five recounts Brown's involvement with the reshaping of the monumental core of Washington, DC, and explores Brown's role within the design team of the Federal Triangle. The design of his buildings for the Department of Labor, the Interstate Commerce Commission, and the Departmental Auditorium (now the offices of the Environmental Protection Agency and the Andrew W. Mellon Auditorium), is analyzed with particular attention to the critical part these structures play in the composition of the Triangle group. Chapter Seven explores Brown's role as supervising architect at Stanford University and the University of California at Berkeley. At both universities Brown revived existing master plans, extending them and attempting to incorporate nonconforming facilities into the overall fabric. At Stanford, Brown brought back the courtyard and arcades that had made the initial construction so successful; at Berkeley he continued the work of John Galen Howard to regularize the haphazard development of the university. Finally, the Conclusion attempts to assess Brown's contribution to American architecture within the context of the emergence of the modern movement, just as Brown himself often did in the last years of his life.

Each of these chapters demonstrates that like Burnham, McKim, and Richardson, Brown believed the greatest calling of the architect was to design the settings for public life. Several themes unify the varied strands of Brown's career; these are taken together to define his place in our understanding of American architectural history. The first of these is the influence of the Ecole des Beaux-Arts and French cultural life on Brown's development. Brown was a lifelong devotee of French design; it is not inappropriate that he is chiefly known for his use of French architectural forms and motifs. In his lifetime Brown was one of the most decorated American architects in France since Richard Morris Hunt, and he was recognized in the middle decades of the last century as the American most closely associated with the French architectural establishment. However, although Brown did make several lasting French friends in Paris, he spent much of his time with fellow Americans and always regarded himself as the archtypical American in Paris. Brown also spent considerable time touring the rest of Europe, traveling as far east as Constantinople, where he viewed antique and Islamic architecture firsthand. Like many California architects, Brown thought the buildings of the southern Mediterranean and the Levant as particularly suited to the warmer regions of the state, and he never hesitated to use Moorish or Byzantine forms where the program and context warranted it.

The second theme is Brown's conscious decision to practice in the West, specifically in California. Like his *patron*, Victor Laloux, Brown hoped to practice primarily in his hometown and yet participate in the architectural life and culture of the capital. With the Federal Triangle commission he got the opportunity to do this, despite the distance between San Francisco and Washington, DC. In choosing to practice in California, Brown did not limit himself to architectural expressions that were manifestly regional, just as Bernard Maybeck, Julia Morgan, and Willis Polk felt no need to eschew classical forms when they were most suited to the problem at hand. In his monumental public architecture

Brown used a traditional classical language because it bespoke the state's fairly recent "civilization" and linked California to both the western European heritage of the majority of its citizens and to the public architecture of the eastern United States, particularly of the federal government in Washington. Except in his work in Southern California, regional identity in Brown's official architecture, rather than being evident in materials or relationship to site, was largely limited to ornament and public art. In the residential, recreational, and commercial work, however, a wider, more "Californian" palette of materials was employed, and a more intimate siting and informal disposition of parts marked the massing. Whether walking the Champs-Elysées or designing the Federal Triangle thirty years later, Brown never ceased to remain first a Californian.

A third theme follows from Brown's roots in California: his association with the people and institutions of the progressive wing of the Republican Party. Upon his return to San Francisco in 1903, Brown was confronted by a city in the throes of political corruption and chaos, the likes of which even "Boss" Tweed's New York barely approached. The reform of the city political system took almost eight years to accomplish and left few politicians or businessmen unsullied. Brown knew many of the leaders of the reform movement (and their targets) through associations with his father, an executive civil engineer for the Southern Pacific, and later through his residence in Hillsborough and membership in several social clubs. The Civic Center is the most tangible success of the reform movement in San Francisco, which was closely allied with the statewide progressive movement of Hiram Johnson and Teddy Roosevelt's Bull Moose party. The Civic Center, like the Panama-Pacific International Exposition, was the concrete manifestation of the gains made by the people of the San Francisco in reestablishing control over their polity. Brown was quite aware of this meaning, and scrupulously administered the construction of San Francisco City Hall to ensure that it would be completed on time, at budget, and wholly within the law.

The overriding formal theme of Brown's architectural work is his commitment to the realization of the American Renaissance grand design—that is, the formal arrangement of representational buildings and landscape according to a predetermined, often collaboratively generated, master plan. The American Renaissance architects—Burnham, McKim, Stanford White, the landscape designer Frederick Law Olmsted, and others—first determined to elevate the public taste and to reorder the American urban environment at the World's Columbian Exposition at Chicago in 1893. Their efforts culminated in the restoration and expansion of the L'Enfant plan for the nation's capital, which continues to develop according to principles they laid out in the famous Senate Park Commission Plan of 1902. Throughout the years between the Columbian Exposition and the Great Depression, scores of American cities adopted redevelopment plans for the city centers; among these were Chicago, Cleveland, Denver, Philadelphia, and San Francisco. While some architects planned and theorized more vociferously, perhaps no other American architect had the opportunity to execute more buildings within the context of the grand design than Arthur Brown, who contributed buildings to three civic centers, three world fairs, several university campuses, and the monumental core of the District of Columbia.

Brown constantly worked within the long-term framework of the master plan, usually in association with other architects and design professionals; he often revived or expanded the initial scope of the master plan to accommodate new programs and conditions. For example, Brown's War Memorial complex enlarged the Civic Center precinct across Van Ness Avenue and at the same time refocused architectural interest on his city hall. And although Brown employed the classical language, he likewise updated and expanded the architectural tradition it represented, incorporating the latest in engineering and construction technology into his work, and producing novel and at times unexpected combinations of elements and motifs to make a statement about the work and the institutions that work embodied. Thus, Brown's design for Pasadena City Hall might borrow elements from three or four Mediterranean cultures and render them in reinforced concrete, but the resulting monument is so closely identified with its community that one cannot imagine the building being located anywhere else. To Arthur Brown, the classical tradition was not a sacrosanct, unchanging body of knowledge; it was an expanding and evolving set of ideas about architectural design that permitted, and even demanded, change as new conditions and technologies were developed.

It is in the grand designs where all of these themes come together in a vision often described as being particularly characteristic of progressive-era America. Theodore Roosevelt's demand that government ensure the public health, safety, and general welfare paralleled efforts in other western democratic societies to mitigate the consequences of unregulated industrialism. In America this expanded governmental role was accompanied by a corresponding expansion in private institutions, many of which provided some sort of public accommodation. At the same time, a swelling number of immigrants and the spreading suffrage movement enlarged the polity and redefined the appearance of the voting citizen. Architects, newly professionalized, seized the opportunity to shape a civic environment scaled to this new social, economic, and political order. Architecture was to serve the public by housing the institutions of liberal government and religion within a planned architectural context. Like others of his generation, Brown expected civic architecture to firmly claim the institutions of American government for western civilization, no matter what the background of the population the institution served. In bringing this ideal to California, he hoped to better politically, socially, and aesthetically the nascent society. He also, not incidentally, hoped to develop a personal architecture that would extend the classical tradition into the modern age, an architecture that would be as deliberately evolutionary as American politics of the time seemed to be. He achieved this and more.

ARTHUR BROWN JR.

Progressive Classicist

1.1. Arthur Brown Sr., c. 1870.
Private collection, San Francisco.

1.2. Victoria Adelaide Runyon Brown,
c. 1870. Private collection, San Francisco.

CHAPTER ONE

THE EDUCATION
OF THE ARCHITECT

Arthur Brown Jr.'s career can be viewed as the product of one fortunate occurrence after another, as that of a man in the right place at the right time. Brown's life had very little dramatic content to it, and his professional life was a long catalog of successes, broken only at an age when most men of his generation had long since retired. However, the success Brown enjoyed with his professional partner, John Bakewell Jr., and on his own was due to years of preparation and academic training. Brown was not a prodigy (no architect ever has been) but an individual focused, even obsessed, with mastering the art of building over the course of several decades.

Three distinct societies shaped Brown's development and career: his family, particularly his father, Arthur Brown Sr.; the artistic community Brown found at Berkeley and the Mark Hopkins Institute of Art in San Francisco, which centered on Bernard Maybeck and Charles Keeler; and the students and faculty with whom Brown worked in Paris at the Ecole des Beaux-Arts. Often persons from each of these spheres interacted with Brown and each other at the same time. Throughout his years in Paris, for example, Brown lived and studied with members of his immediate family, with many of his classmates from Berkeley, and of course with his confreres at the Atelier Laloux. Brown maintained close professional and social ties with his earliest mentors and fellow students throughout his life and collaborated with several friends whom he had first met as a teenager. Likewise, many of his commissions came from long-term friends who directed important institutions in the Bay Area with ambitious post-earthquake building programs; these

patrons would remain with Brown throughout his career, often returning to him over the span of thirty years or more. Thus, Brown's life is marked more by its continuity than by tumult, and it demonstrates that the wrenching dislocations of the lives of a few well-known twentieth-century architectural figures were not a necessary ingredient in forging a successful artistic career for all.

THE FAMILY

The prominence of Arthur Brown Sr.'s engineering and architectural career has faded over the years (fig. 1.1). Yet no one individual made "Sonny" Brown's architectural career more possible than his father, who provided technical education, financial backing, and social connections. Arthur Brown Sr. (neither father nor son had a middle name) was born in Kentore, Aberdeenshire, Scotland, in 1830.[1] Brought to Canada as a child by his widowed mother, he was raised in Ottawa. He was apprenticed as a civil engineer and construction superintendent to his uncle, Alexander Christie, who contracted with the engineering companies of several fledgling railroad companies in New York, Pennsylvania, and Missouri. In the 1860s he and his uncle went west to the Frasier River country of British Columbia, and then found work at Victoria, where Brown designed the Wharf.[2] Brown made passage to San Francisco in 1864, after the Sacramento financiers of the Central Pacific had decided to replace the line's trailblazing general engineer, Theodore Judah, who had died late the previous year. Brown arrived in San Francisco to

1.3. Arthur Brown Sr.'s sketch for the lighting fixture at the newel post of the Mark Hopkins residence, c. 1877. Drawing in an untitled sketchbook, Arthur Brown Jr. Collection, Bancroft Library.

was called upon to solve numerous crises in order to keep the work trains moving toward the Union Pacific railhead to the east. Brown controlled every facet of these engineering jobs; he not only designed the structures, he hired and oversaw the construction crews and even guided the production of the timber and the procurement of the iron required to build his designs. At the height of the construction campaign, Brown was managing over twenty-five hundred laborers and craftsmen, all working in parallel to the equally massive army of men grading the roadbed and laying the track.[3] Brown would train his son to manage this kind of integrated construction campaign years later; thus the younger Brown would undertake the creation of one of his most important works, San Francisco City Hall, in a similar integrated manner.

Brown's most lasting innovation on the Central Pacific was the snowsheds constructed over the tracks at Donner Summit, which enabled work to continue through the winter.[4] With the laying of the final gold spike in Promontory Point on May 10, 1869, work on the Central Pacific settled down to the improvement of the structures that negotiated the terrain and the construction of permanent passenger and freight depots and engine facilities along the line. Few of these early works survive, but the earliest Sacramento station has been reconstructed as part of the California State Railroad Museum. These early stations were invariably wood framed, clad in either clapboards or board-and-batten siding. Other important design and architectural projects would eventually flow from Arthur Brown Sr.'s drafting table, mostly at Charles Crocker's behest. The most important of the railroad terminals was the Oakland Mole, which provided a viaduct connection between the San Francisco Bay ferry system, owned and operated by the Central Pacific, and the railroad itself.[5] Shortly thereafter, Brown designed the car ferry *Solano* to complement the new interchange facility.

The less peripatetic work of the 1870s allowed Brown to think of settling down, and on September 28, 1870, he married Victoria Adelaide Runyon (fig. 1.2).[6] Little is known of his wife except that she was born in the 1840s in the Midwest. The family moved westward, eventually arriving at Sacramento, where her father apparently had a commercial enterprise, and thus was known to Brown and his employers. The Browns' marriage would prove to be a happy and durable one, lasting forty-six years until their deaths in 1917. The newlywed couple moved to a moderately sized house in the western flats of Oakland in 1871 and celebrated the birth of their only child, Arthur Brown Jr., three years later, on May 21, 1874. The Browns and their son would remain especially devoted to each other for the remainder of their lives.

In 1871 the Central Pacific purchased the California Pacific Railroad and thus extended the transcontinental line all the way to Oakland and, by ferry, to San Francisco. The railroad moved its headquarters to the "city by the bay" and

organizational chaos as the Big Four (Charles Crocker, Mark Hopkins, Collis P. Huntington, and Leland Stanford) identified the roles they would play in the reformed enterprise, and as various contractors attempted to organize the huge undertaking. Brown was a valuable commodity in 1864—a civil engineer with considerable railroad experience; as a British subject he was exempt from the Civil War draft. He was appointed the superintendent of the Bridge and Buildings Department, a post he held until his semiretirement in the late 1890s.

During the early years of the construction of the Central Pacific, Brown was responsible to Charles Crocker for the design and construction of every bridge, culvert, and viaduct on the line from Sacramento, California, to Ogden, Utah, and soon the Big Four were building mansions on the heights of Nob Hill, the better to survey their growing domain. While the Big Four looked to San Francisco's developing architectural community for the design of their homes, they asked Arthur Brown Sr. to manage their construction. The erection of Charles Crocker's house, completed in 1876, afforded Brown his first opportunity to construct high-style architecture. The "early renaissance" Crocker house combined Second Empire and Italianate motifs in a vast pile, culminating in a 76-foot-high mansarded tower, which allowed Crocker to view the city from above the rooftops of his partners' equally lavish homes. The house was long the largest in San Francisco, with over 12,000 square feet of living space that included a theater, a well-appointed library, and a billiard room.[7] The elder Brown also coordinated the construction of the Stanford and Hopkins mansions in the following years. With the Mark Hopkins house he took on a design role alongside architects Wright & Saunders, as he engineered the introduction of gas lighting fixtures, indoor plumbing, and advanced heating systems (fig. 1.3). A sketchbook dating from the time of this project demonstrates that Brown designed the lighting fixtures himself and also engineered the famous stone wall along Pine Street, which today serves as the base of the Hotel Mark Hopkins.

Arthur Brown Sr.'s most extensive exercise in high-style architecture was the original Hotel Del Monte in Monterey (fig. 1.4). The hotel was the pet project of Charles Crocker, who was anxious to develop a passenger trade on the Central Pacific south of San Jose. It was constructed in 1880 in one hundred days, and soon became the most fashionable resort on the West Coast.[8] As travel writer William Henry Bishop described the place in 1882, "The Hotel del Monte is a beautiful edifice, not surpassed in its kind by any American watering place, and not equaled, I think, at any of them in its charming groves of live-oaks and pines, the profusion of cultivated flowers by which it is surrounded, and the air of comfort existing at the same time with its elegant arrangements."[9]

Almost everything concerned with the Del Monte was designed by Brown and two junior architects on his staff. The

1.4. Arthur Brown Sr., supervising architect, Hotel del Monte, Pacific Grove, California, 1880. *Harpers Monthly* Magazine, October 1882.

1.5. Arthur Brown Jr. at age fourteen, c. 1888. Private collection, San Francisco.

main building was described as being "Queen Anne or Eastlake" in architectural style, but really was a mix of Italianate and Gothic elements characteristic of resort hotels all over the nation at this time. The hotel was 370 feet long, 100 feet deep, and four stories high, its main block terminating in five-story towers. It was surrounded by a deep verandah, from which guests could view the Pacific or the Del Monte forest. The interior appointments of the hotel were no less sumptuous and apparently adhered closely to the Eastlake mode; Brown intended the Del Monte to offer the sort of public rooms that defined grand hotels in New York City or San Francisco. The central wing of the original Del Monte was destroyed by fire in 1886 and rebuilt in a Swiss chalet mode, probably also by Brown, and was then totally consumed by fire in 1924 and replaced by the present structure, now the Naval Postgraduate School, designed by Lewis P. Hobart and Herbert Tantau.[10]

Arthur Brown's position with the Central Pacific Railroad had a greater importance for his son's future career than this brief catalog of major works suggests. As a senior officer of the railroad, the elder Brown came into daily contact with the line's owners, particularly with Charles Crocker and Mark Hopkins.[11] Of these associations, none was stronger than that between the Browns and Mark and Timothy Hopkins. "Uncle Mark" Hopkins was the most well-liked of the Big Four and the only one of them to remain unaffected by his incredible wealth. Brown and Hopkins developed a friendly and successful working relationship that continued on a social basis once Hopkins retired from his daily duties. Brown was with Hopkins at his death in Yuma, Arizona, in 1878.[12]

Hopkins's adopted son, Timothy, replaced his father as the chief financial officer of the railroad and kept close ties with the Browns. Over the next several decades, as Hopkins married, endured his adopted mother's remarriage and rejection of him, and fought for his share of the family fortune, he relied on the friendship and counsel of his father's friend. At times Brown served as a sort of surrogate father.[13] Arthur Brown Jr.'s travel diary records how close the families were in 1889; in the six-month span of time recorded in the diary, the families arranged to travel together in Paris and Brussels and also spent most of Christmas week together at the Hopkins's Peninsula estate, the former Latham mansion, which they renamed Sherwood Hall. Their relationship was so close that Brown notes, nearly parenthetically, that on December 29 he "stayed around [Sherwood Hall] all afternoon and broke a vase."[14] Such horseplay notwithstanding, Timothy Hopkins would prove to be Brown's most important private client, because through him Brown would receive close to twenty commissions at Stanford University as well as numerous residential and institutional projects.

The Browns also benefited financially from their association with the railroad, not only from the large blocks of stock they acquired in the early days when the railroad was cash poor and awash in shares, but also from side investments in real estate and other ventures into which Arthur Brown Sr. was invited. As a result of these investments, the Browns were quite comfortable by the late 1880s and were able to provide their son with enriching travel and the best possible education (fig. 1.5). The most conspicuous of the Browns' efforts to raise their son as a gentleman particularly attuned to the arts was the family's journey to the East Coast and Europe, which commenced on May 19, 1889, the eve of "Sonny's" fifteenth birthday. The ostensible aim of this trip was the Centennial Exposition in Paris, where the Browns stayed for over a month. However, this nearly seven-month journey through Europe and North America encompassed almost all of the major artistic sites in the western world, excluding only Central Italy and Greece. In each city the Browns viewed the principal engineering and architectural sites and the art museums, where it fell to Mrs. Brown to instruct her son in the appreciation of art. Often the two would return to view a work that was supposed to be especially superior, and one can sense some exasperation in Brown's tone as he describes his tenth or twelfth sortie through the Exposition's Palais des Beaux-Arts.

Nonetheless, Brown did get to see much that interested him between the trips to unfinished bridges and interminable shopping excursions with his mother and Mrs. Hopkins. Although the younger Brown did a bit of sketching on his trip and was taking painting lessons back home, his interests in Europe were those of any teenage boy of the period (fig. 1.6). He was fascinated by all things military, by the diverse sports he saw practiced on the Continent and by the spectacle of the European monarchies (he managed to see the Shah of Persia, the German Kaiser, and the Prince and Princess of Wales on his trip), and by the sensational news stories occurring at the time, such as the search for Jack the Ripper. Brown did not seem to be overwhelmingly devoted to architectural studies; he only noted those landmark structures that his father told him were important, such as the Galerie des Machines at the Paris Exposition or Charles Garnier's Opera House.

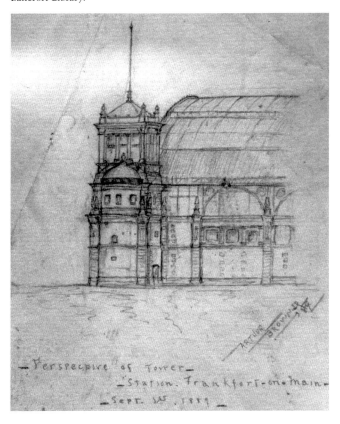

1.6. Arthur Brown Jr., travel sketch of tower at railroad station, Frankfurt-am-Main, Germany, September 1, 1889. One of the few travel sketches to survive from Brown, and the only known extant sketch from his 1889 world tour. Arthur Brown Jr. Collection, Bancroft Library.

BERKELEY, OAKLAND, AND SAN FRANCISCO

The Oakland of the 1880s was small, quiet, and family-friendly, in contrast to its larger neighbor across the bay. The town that sprang up between the Alameda estuary and the east foothills was composed of neat Italianate and Queen Anne houses on quarter- and half-acre lots surrounding a prosperous commercial district. There was a lively port and a certain amount of industry in the southern and western sectors of the city, but the newness of the place—less than twenty years old at that time—infused the citizenry with a sense of anonymity. Yet the community seems to have nurtured the talents of its youngest members; among Brown's contemporaries were Gertrude Stein, Isadora Duncan, Julia Morgan, and Jack London.

Apart from a friendly acquaintance with the Morgans, however, the teenage Brown did not keep company with such strong personalities. The most enlightening portion of his travel diary may be the three weeks that Brown recorded upon returning to Oakland, for it is within these entries that he revealed details of his everyday life. His existence was unknowingly privileged and contentedly commonplace. For example, Brown describes Christmas at Sherwood Hall, but also notes a number of less exclusive charitable events that marked the holiday season. Other entries speak to Brown's interest in an artistic life—he took drawing lessons from the faculty at the San Francisco Art Institute, and frequently dropped in on William Keith, the great California landscape painter, at his studio on Montgomery Street. Brown's association with Keith was not a casual one. His father was one of Keith's earliest champions and collectors. Keith's biographer records that Arthur Brown Sr. bought some Keiths, including *King's River Cañon*, in the 1870s; it is possible that it was through Brown that Keith came to the attention of Huntington and Crocker, whose collections of Keiths became renowned.[15] Throughout the ensuing decades, the Browns were inducted into the artistic and literary circles that centered around Keith's legendary soirées at his Berkeley home. Arthur Brown Sr. remained Keith's close friend until his death in 1911, at which time Brown served as Keith's pallbearer. The Reverend Joseph Worcester officiated.[16]

Worcester, the pastor of the Swedenborgian Church at Washington and Lyon streets, was the spiritual guide for a generation of the city's leading artistic figures, among them Keith, Bernard Maybeck, Bruce Porter, Ernest and Almeric Coxhead, Willis Polk, and Charles Keeler. The church adhered in theory to the tenets of the eighteenth-century Swedish cleric Emmanuel Swedenborg, but most people came to hear the engaging sermons and personal philosophy of Worcester. The Browns were friendly with Worcester, although they were never formal members of his church.

They did, however, participate in the cultural milieu of the church, and many of the congregation played important roles in Arthur Brown Jr.'s architectural development.

The defining moment in the development of the artistic community surrounding Worcester was the construction of the Lyon Street church in 1894. Swedenborg himself considered architecture to be a divine art, and Worcester was something of an amateur architect, having designed his cottages in Piedmont and on Russian Hill.[17] Thus, careful attention was given to the design of the building, which was commissioned to the architectural office of A. Page Brown and designed by A. C. Schweinfurth. Inspired by a Bruce Porter sketch of a Lombard village church, Schweinfurth's design transcended its immediate source and responded to Swedenborgian theology, which emphasized the manifestation of the Holy Spirit in nature. In particular, the church integrates a large meditative garden into the sacred precinct through which one travels to the sanctuary, which was paneled in pine and roofed with rough-hewn rafters and sheathing supported by madrone posts with preserved bark. The art program inside the church continued the natural themes; Bruce Porter's stained-glass oculus above the pulpit illustrates a dove at rest, and William Keith's cycle of four paintings along the sanctuary's north wall depicts the seasons of California.[18]

The Swedenborgian church is often cited as one of the first institutional buildings to exhibit the nature-inspired sensibilities of the Bay Area arts-and-crafts movement; it is almost emblematic of what came to be understood as a native California architecture. Yet all who worked on the enterprise—Worcester, Schweinfurth, Maybeck, Porter, and Keith, were born in the East—and only Keith had been in the state as long as twenty years. All were striving to define the California exceptionalism they expected to find in the Golden State in both their work and their lifestyles. This effort was most intense in Berkeley, where the intellectual and artistic circles associated with the University of California joined forces to create a rather self-conscious Arcadian community north of the campus.

The one man who perhaps did most to define the mode of living that emphasized the unique qualities of the California environment was Charles Keeler, the young naturalist, poet, and architectural writer who would become a protégé of Worcester, Keith, and Maybeck. Like many others in the artistic circle around Worcester, Keeler became enthralled in 1892 with the reverend's philosophy of a life attuned to Creation.[19] At about this same time, Keeler met Bernard Maybeck on the ferry into the city.[20] The two immediately became friends, and within a year, Keeler was exploring the possibilities of an architecture that would elevate the mind and body through a closer association with nature. In 1893 Keeler sponsored the construction of Ernest Coxhead's Beta Theta Pi Fraternity House on Dwight Way. Two years later he commissioned Maybeck to build his home on Highland Place, which became the general prototype for hundreds of rustic houses in the Berkeley Hills and the ideal "simple home" to Keeler and his fellow Hillside Club members.

Upon entering the University of California, Keeler had colonized a chapter of Beta Theta Pi, and soon the chapter became the haunt of several budding architects and engineers. John Bakewell Jr., Loring P. Rixford, and Frederick Ransome (the concrete pioneer Ernest L. Ransome's son and future geologist) were also founding members, and Arthur Brown pledged at his arrival in 1892.[21] By 1893 the community had enough prospects to build a house, for which Keeler commissioned Coxhead & Coxhead to prepare plans (fig. 1.7). The house, which the brothers no doubt helped in part to construct, was modeled after the half-timbered postmedieval houses of northern European towns. Each of the four sections of the building read as an individual structure and housed a distinct function, the most striking of which was the three-story stuccoed dormitory tower.[22] Yet the parts also made up a convincing whole in the continuity of materials and the uniform pitch of the roofs.

Although Brown knew the Berkeley circle well from his visits to the Keiths' home south of Bancroft Way, he became a full participant in the life of the city only after enrolling in the university in September 1892. Initially Brown was as undirected in his future career at Berkeley as he had been in 1889; he did not declare a major until his junior year, when he enrolled in the College of Engineering, where he intended to study sanitation engineering.[23] Over the course of several years, however, he met several important personalities who would become friends, mentors, and colleagues for the rest of his life. Their commitment to architecture as a means to improve the environment would propel Brown into the profession, and his determination to learn all aspects of the art would, in turn, bring him artistic success.

Brown's primary mentor at the University of California at Berkeley was Bernard Maybeck, then an eccentric drawing instructor and architectural theorist with little built work and an uneven employment history. Born and raised in New York City to a furniture carver, Maybeck was a transplanted easterner, like many of his fellows in the Worcester circle. In the early 1880s Maybeck was sent to Paris to apprentice in the furniture studio of his father's employer's brother and in short order found his way to the Ecole des Beaux-Arts, intending to become an architect.[24] Maybeck was trained at the Ecole to appreciate the classical architectural tradition. Although classicism was not unchallenged as the official style for French state architecture, it was the primary architectural language of instruction at the Ecole. Maybeck was equally captivated by the medieval world, and much of his residential work would reflect his fascination with all things

1.7. Ernest Coxhead, Beta Theta Pi House, Berkeley, California, 1893, early view from Hearst Avenue and Dwight Way. Sepia-tone print, Arthur Brown Jr. Collection, Bancroft Library.

Gothic.[25] Yet in the atelier Maybeck learned the catechism of the French method: that drawing was the communicative medium of the architect; that the plan generated all else in a work of architecture, and that sections and elevations must be derived from the plan; and that the plan and elevations must possess *caractère*, an unmistakable expression of the building's function and place in the urban and social context of its milieu. All this he brought to the San Francisco Bay Area after brief stays in New York with Carrère & Hastings and in Kansas City.

Maybeck's first forum for his brand of architectural education was the San Francisco Art Institute, which had been founded in the 1870s as a museum and school for the fine arts. At the institute Maybeck taught freehand drawing and architectural drafting, and presented courses on the history of architecture. When in 1894 the institute became affiliated with the University of California, Maybeck began to teach in Berkeley as well, and many of his students attended courses at both sites in these years. As demand for more architectural instruction grew, Maybeck began a series of Saturday morning classes in design at his home. Julia Morgan, Edward Bennett, Harvey Wiley Corbett, and Brown took part in these classes, which taught the fundamentals of classical design, presumably in order to prepare the students for the Ecole or an American school modeled on it. Only one drawing of Brown's survives from these classes, a small watercolor rendering of a garden loggia in the Italian renaissance mode (fig. 1.8). In this early student design Brown used architectural elements much like a child overusing a newly learned word and he mastered the language only after experimentation and gentle correction. Maybeck did not have any kind of regional orientation to his architectural assignments. Although he was discovering his arts-and-crafts vocabulary for the Bay Area, he taught his students the kind of academic architecture that would be expected of them in the East and at the Beaux-Arts.

1.8: Arthur Brown Jr., "A Loggia in a Garden," student project drawing for Bernard Maybeck's design course at the University of California, c. 1895. Drawing, Arthur Brown Jr. Collection, Bancroft Library. Image courtesy of the Bancroft Library.

Through their associations with Maybeck and Keeler and their work with the Beta Theta Pi House, both John Bakewell and Arthur Brown were directly involved with the formation of the Bay Area mode of residential architecture while, at the same time, being educated by one of its founders in the rudiments of the classical tradition. The two modalities of building were not seen as antithetical by them or by Maybeck and Keeler (or the Coxheads or Willis Polk, for that matter). Rather, these building forms both expressed the *caractère* of the institution they housed. This ethic would be demonstrated by the citizens of Berkeley a decade later, when the same devotees of the arts and crafts who built their redwood cottages in the Berkeley Hills would commission Bakewell & Brown to design a French neo-baroque city hall. The architectural language of the home and that of the state simply reflected two contrasting aspects of civilized life.

THE ECOLE DES BEAUX-ARTS

Although several promising American schools of architecture had been founded on the eastern seaboard by the late 1890s, the Ecole Nationale Superieure des Beaux-Arts in Paris was still the school of choice for most serious architectural students in the United States at the end of the nineteenth century. To those at Berkeley who had heard Maybeck's humorous anecdotes and been trained by him in the school's preparatory curriculum, there must have seemed to be no other choice but the Ecole. They were not alone. Over three hundred fifty Americans studied at the Ecole in the twenty years from the close of the 1893 World's Columbian Exposition to the beginning of the First World War. They came not only for the school's two-hundred-year-old tradition but because it offered the most rigorous and professionally challenging architectural curriculum in the world.

The Ecole des Beaux-Arts had its beginnings in the Royal Academies instituted by Colbert during the reign of Louis XIV. Clarity of form, axiality, and monumentality—principles of design espoused by the institution's founder, Jacques-François Blondel—would become the foundation for two centuries of architectural education, and would be the hallmark of an architecture called the Beaux-Arts tradition in the United States.[26] The search for an architecture appropriate to a modern, industrial society dominated the discourse of French architecture from the mid-nineteenth century on. Beginning in the 1880s and accelerating under the leadership of Julien Guadet, professor of theory from 1894 to 1908, the Ecole prepared its pupils for multifaceted careers in which state architects ever more valued technical as well as artistic competency. Guadet was uniquely positioned to lead the Beaux-Arts into the twentieth century; he maintained the school's traditional stylistic orientation while introducing into the curriculum modern methods of construction and architectural practice. His theoretical program for reconciling these two sometimes opposing architectural currents—the traditional and the contemporary, or as some understood it, the artistic and the scientific—became a primary model for Brown as he adapted the classical architectural tradition to twentieth-century California.

Guadet was installed as professor of theory in 1894, at a time when the ideological struggles of past decades were largely settled. By the 1890s the battle between the medieval and the classical traditions seemed passé, and the controversies surrounding ferrous construction had quieted. Released from past agendas, Guadet was free to set his own. He further accentuated the professional orientation of the curriculum, an emphasis that had been a part of the Ecole's teaching since the 1880s. Guadet shaped the pedagogy of the school and wrote the programs for the *concours d'émulation*, or juried competitions, which were the mainstay of the design program. The programs and winning designs of these competitions demonstrate a shift in emphasis by Guadet from the propagation of a narrow, court-centered official architecture to a broad-based professional education that highlighted contemporary architectural problems. Guadet used these programs to connect the community of the Ecole to the real world; many programs directly confronted political or social events of the time in which they were written, and others drew on social trends that had been apparent for decades.

Guadet's politics were staunchly Liberal-Republican, and he often used his architectural programs to communicate his party's social message to his students. A liberal social agenda often pervaded the Ecole competition programs during Guadet's tenure. The *Concours Labarre*, a seventy-two-hour sketch problem, was sometimes used to explore new urban building typologies that addressed the needs of the working class. The program for 1902 described a "Palais d'Enfance," a

recreational and educational facility for working-class children in which exhibits illustrating the happy lives of children living under the new social economy and attending the new schools would be contrasted with the life of children living in poverty or at work in sweatshops. Brown's entry was quite well received and published (fig. 1.9). The forecourt in this design, which contained the playgrounds for the complex, is bounded by a colonnaded walk. This cloister-like device is punctuated at the corners by pavilions and entered through a triple-arched gatehouse (a device Brown would use again at his railroad terminal at San Diego). The plan of the palace itself focused on a large vaulted hall and contrasted circular chambers with the basilican main hall.

1.9. Arthur Brown Jr., "Palais d'Enfance," Concours Labarre, 1902, competition entry. Heliograph by Armand Guérinet, Les Medailles des Concours des Beaux-Arts: 1901–02.

The life of the average student at the Ecole des Beaux-Arts is well documented. In fact, reminiscences of one's student days there became a staple of American architectural journals in the years before World War II. The Americans who entered the school in the Third Republic had to meet the same eligibility requirements as French nationals; they had to be between eighteen and thirty years old, and until Julia Morgan's groundbreaking entrance in 1898, they were exclusively male. Students would study for a year or two within the *atelier préparatoire* just to pass the entrance examinations and earn the right to call themselves *élèves* of the Ecole. The entrance examinations were held twice a year, in July/August and December/January, and through each about fifty students were admitted, of whom one-quarter could be foreign nationals.[27] These *nouveaux* would then study for two to four years in the second class until they had won enough medals in the bimonthly *concours d'émulations* in design and construction to merit promotion to the first class. The primary preoccupation of the curriculum in the second class was the exacting course in construction, which culminated in a set of details of a building of the student's own design. The technical curriculum of the Ecole gave as much emphasis to iron as to wood and masonry, and students were required to master iron detailing in the second class and to use this mastery in their designs within the first.

In the first class, design skills were honed for the *diplôme*. Students competed in the monthly design juries and for the endowed prizes while attending classes in building law and serving apprenticeships in the offices of their patron or another practicing architect. The most senior students, by now in their late twenties, competed for the Grand Prix de Rome, which was only open to French citizens. Only a select corps of highly successful designers was allowed to compete for one of the eight *loges* used for the *projets rendu* of the final Grand Prix.[28] Thus the Ecole was structured much like a pyramid—many students toiled at the bottom levels of the hierarchy, while only one man a year could reach the apex and win the Prix de Rome. The enrollment figures for 1894–95 illustrate this point well. Nearly eight hundred students were enrolled as officially accepted *élèves*. Of these, perhaps one-third had been elevated into the first class. Fifty of these competed for the final eight spots; one, Auguste-Rene-Gaston-Antoine Patouilliard-Demoriane, a student of Paul-René-Léon Ginain, actually went to Rome for his design for an exposition hall.[29]

One made the transition from school to practice with the *diplôme*, which signified the termination of one's studies and intensified the professional orientation of the curriculum. The degree program, which had languished since 1867, was thrust into importance in 1887, when the Ecole granted its *diplôme* to all living recipients of the Prix de Rome. By the mid-nineties the degree was the goal of all who studied at the Ecole, for it was the official certification granted by the government. The *diplôme* required a thesis project, to be defended in front of an examining review board, and a year's full-time apprenticeship to a qualified architect.[30] Although those receiving the degree could call themselves DPLG, "*diplômé par le gouvernement*," it was not a legal prerequisite to the practice of architecture. Nonetheless, more and more students decided to make the effort to become DPLG, which became recognized by public and private clients alike as the signifier of minimal competence.

While lectures in construction, history, and building law were given at the Ecole's compound on the Rue Bonaparte, the student's true education in architecture took place within the ateliers scattered around the northern Left Bank. The selection of an atelier was the most important decision a student made at the Ecole. One had to have rapport with the *patron* and subscribe to his personal philosophy of architecture in order to succeed, but one also had to feel comfortable with the other members of the atelier, in whose service the *nouveau* was inevitably placed. This servitude was the crux of the organization of the atelier—the younger students learned more from assisting the older students with their enormous *projets rendus* than they did directly from the *patron*, who usually spent only a few hours a week with the younger students. In exchange for their service, the *nouveaux* received criticism and instruction from the *anciens* and learned to negotiate the customs of the school.

The *esprit-de-corps* of the ateliers was legendary and often the most memorable aspect of the Ecole experience, particularly when viewed through the filter of old age.[31] This sense of community was built through a paramilitary system of rank and discipline, in which the *anciens* held supreme dominion over the time and well-being of the *nouveaux*, and in which the least infraction could be punished with a fine or some form of public humiliation. This tense structure was tempered with the rambunctious late-night antics common to any organization composed of unsupervised young men. At odd times in the night someone might demand a chorus or two of a favorite song or play a practical joke on a hapless friend (the most memorable of these seem to have always involved either fire or nudity, though rarely both at the same time). The loyalty to one's atelier was intense. As Charles Collens reported of his time at the atelier Pascal at the turn of the twentieth century: "When you once entered an atelier, it was like entering a secret society—you were never allowed in the sacred precincts of another atelier, and your whole aim was to build up the fame of your atelier by helping to win more medals and mentions at the monthly exhibitions."[32]

American students at the Ecole had a dual loyalty; they cared deeply for their atelier, but they never lost their collec-

1.10. Group photograph, American football demonstration, Paris, November 26, 1897. Sitting, fourth from left, Brown; to immediate right, Robert Farquhar; reclining, second from right, Frère Champney; standing third from right, John Bakewell; standing, far left, James Gamble Rogers; to immediate right, Clarence Zantzinger; standing, sixth from left, Joseph Howland Hunt. Photo reproduced from sepia-tone print, Arthur Brown Collection, Bancroft Library.

tive American identity. Thus they often socialized with each other outside of the atelier culture, particularly on American holidays. Brown participated in one of the more noteworthy of these social events when the American contingent at the Ecole played the first American football game on French soil on Thanksgiving Day, 1897 (fig. 1.10). The demonstration, which was covered by the French press and well attended by curious Parisians, did not convert multitudes of Frenchmen to the religion of the wishbone offense, but it did its part to cement friendships among the participants that would last their entire professional careers.[33]

The Americans were set apart from many of their French confreres in other ways than their nationality; they were older, most having already earned bachelor's degrees in civil engineering or some other discipline before arriving in Paris.

Many had also worked in architectural firms, or had experience managing construction sites; some, such as James Gamble Rogers, had worked for several years with what we perceive now to be the most progressive firms of the day.[34] These Americans came to Paris not only for the cachet of the French experience and an extended grand tour, but to receive a graduate architectural education that would best prepare them to build the great American city of the twentieth century.[35] From the mid-1890s on, many Americans stayed the full course of the program and earned the *diplôme*, but others stayed for just a year or two to absorb what they felt was most significant about the school's theory.

Brown stayed longer than most, six years, and won a great many prizes, a source of pride to his mother, who shared much of this time with him. For Brown, Paris was preor-

1.11. Arthur Brown Jr., "A Portal," student project drawing for the Atelier Godefroy-Freynet, Ecole des Beaux-Arts, October 13, 1886. Arthur Brown Jr. Collection, Bancroft Library.

dained not by his artistic gifts, which were still under development, but by his mother's will. As early as the European tour of 1889, the Browns toured the studios of the Ecole in anticipation of their son's eventual residence there.[36] In 1895 the family again made plans to go to Paris, this time in order that Arthur might spend a semester abroad. Julia Morgan was to accompany Mrs. Brown and Sonny and stay with them until she could find suitable accommodations near the Ecole. Just before sailing, however, Mrs. Brown took ill and had to cancel the trip; Morgan went on to Paris with another friend the following year.[37] Once the Browns did make it to Paris, they set up house at 8 Rue Bonaparte. There many of the Berkeley grads took rooms, along with several other American architectural students, such as John Russell Pope and Lawrence Butler. All were welcome in Mrs. Brown's salon, where she acted as a sort of genteel housemother to her artistic charges. Victoria Brown took special care of Julia Morgan, who needed a female companion from time to time. When her brother Avery left Paris and Morgan was forced to

live in smaller quarters, Mrs. Brown offered her salon; when no Frenchman would work for her, *nouveau* or not, Mrs. Brown assisted Morgan in rendering her watercolor elevations *en charette*.[38]

In addition to Brown and Morgan, six of Maybeck's students from his early years at the University of California went to Paris. Edward Bennett went over first, in 1895, but had to interrupt his studies and return to his relatives in London for a few years due to financial difficulties. The following year John Bakewell Jr. and Harvey Corbett were accepted into the school.[39] Brown made the second class in 1897, Julia Morgan in 1898. After several years of military service, Loring Rixford arrived in 1899. Two other students of Maybeck's, G. Albert Lansburgh and Lewis Hobart, would come to Paris by the time Brown left in 1903. The extraordinary record of students from the University of California in Paris was made possible as much by one woman's beneficence as by the faculty's instruction. Phoebe Apperson Hearst, mother of William Randolph Hearst, became the primary sponsor of most of these students' careers at the Ecole. In return for a $25 per month stipend, they were expected to finish their studies in a timely manner, see as much of Europe as possible, write dutiful letters back to San Francisco, and, when successful, return the favor for another promising student. All of Hearst's benefactors abided by her stipulations and thus a substantial revolving fund of scholarships was established that sent students to Paris well into the 1920s.

Arthur Brown arrived in Paris in September 1896 and enrolled in the *atelier préparatoire* of Godefroy and Freynet (fig. 1.11). Brown's first attempt at the entrance examinations, in February 1897, was not successful, presumably due to a failure in one of the history or literature examinations.[40] This was hardly uncommon; few students were received into the Ecole on their first attempt. Once better acclimated to the language and the examination itself, Brown fared much better. He placed twenty-sixth in the July exams and became a member of the second class on July 23, 1897.[41] The same month he entered the atelier of Victor Laloux (fig. 1.12), who had a reputation for being one of the most progressive *patrons* at the Ecole, and was the favorite of the Americans. Usually, a meeting was arranged between the *patron*, the aspirant, and, if available, his parents. Although the Americans typically met the *patron* on their own, in Brown's case it is conceivable that his parents did meet Laloux that July, because they both spent considerable time in Paris while Brown was there (his mother lived with him on the Rue Bonaparte or the Rue de la Chaussée for much of the seven years he was there). Laloux was designing the Gare d'Orsay at the time and may have been interested in Brown for his railroad heritage; his father was well known to a select company of railroad officials at the time, and Laloux may very well have wanted to meet him. Laloux would become more than Brown's mentor, as he would actively promote Brown's career in France and sponsor him in the Academie des Beaux-Arts. In return, Brown would visit his *patron* at every opportunity, name Laloux his daughter's godfather, and arrange a fitting tribute at his death in 1937.

1.12. Group photograph of the Atelier Laloux, 1900, at the Arc de Gaillon, Ecole des Beaux-Arts. Front center, with long gray beard, Victor Laloux; second row, eleventh from left, Arthur Brown Jr.

1.13. Victor Laloux, "A Cathedral," Grand Prix de Rome, 1878. Heliograph by Armand Guérinet, Ecole Nationale des Beaux-Arts: sLes Grands Prix de Rome de 1850 à 1900.

VICTOR LALOUX

Victor Laloux was born in Tours in 1850 and remained a resident in the Touraine his entire life. Laloux was a successful product of the regional system of art schools in France. After graduating from the gymnasium in Tours, he attended the local Ecole Municipale des Beaux-Arts, from which he went to Paris in 1869 to enter the atelier André, later the *patron* of Bernard Maybeck.[42] Laloux's career at the Ecole was highly successful, although it was interrupted by the Franco-Prussian War. A student of Jules André, like Guadet, Richardson, and Maybeck, Laloux took the *diplôme* in 1877. He then started competing for the Grand Prix, which he won in 1878 on his third attempt.[43] The winning project, for a cathedral for a principal city, was dominated by a dome modeled on that of St. Peter's Basilica in Rome (fig. 1.13). As if to compensate for the screening effect Maderno's west facade has on Michelangelo's work, Laloux expanded his dome to enormous proportions, dwarfing the portico at its base.

Nonetheless, this composition was effective because the dome appears to rest on the solid abutments on either side of the portico, conveying a sense of strength to the whole.

The work for which Laloux is now most remembered was his principal preoccupation while Brown was in his atelier. The Gare d'Orsay was constructed on the banks of the Seine in Paris to bring the public as close as possible to the grounds of the 1900 Exposition. This fair had an unusual plan; it occupied both the old Champs-de-Mars site of the 1889 Centennial Exposition and new facilities on the Right Bank south of the Champs-Elysées. Laloux's station was to serve as the monumental nexus between these two sites as well a representational structure heralding the steel-and-glass twentieth century.

It is Laloux's skills as a teacher of design and his commitment to his students that won him a lasting importance to American architecture. Laloux guided over one hundred Americans through his atelier, among them William Lawrence Bottomley, William Adams Delano, John Galen Howard, George Howe, and William Van Alen. He stressed the art of composition, especially in plan. As William E. Parsons recalled at his death, Laloux's last words to him were, "Do not forget that every work of architecture, however small or unimportant, must be a composition." Charles Butler remembered Laloux stressing the primacy of the plan to him thusly, "You can put forty good facades on a good plan, but without a good plan you can't have a good facade."[44]

Laloux's atelier no doubt retained its popularity with both the French and the Americans for its success at winning the Ecole's juried competitions. Sixteen members of the studio won the Prix de Rome in the forty-seven years of its existence, by far the most successes of any atelier.[45] Laloux emphasized drawing as the vital skill of an architect, and his atelier was known (and sometimes resented) for its ability to win prizes with superior draftsmanship or "painterly" effects. Laloux's students also excelled at ornament and interiors, frequently winning the endowed competitions that concentrated on these specialties, such as the Prix Godeboeuf and Rougevin.[46]

Laloux was highly honored both in France and in the United States. He was elected to the Institut de France in 1909, and presided over that body in 1923.[47] As a well-placed member, he arranged to have two of his former students, William A. Delano and Arthur Brown, installed as corresponding members of the Academie des Beaux-Arts; he was equally instrumental in Brown's election as a full Membre Etranger of the Institut in 1926.[48] In partial recompense for his generosity to his American students over many years, Laloux was awarded the AIA Gold Medal in 1922 at the Institute's annual convention in Chicago. While all of Laloux's students revered him, few felt as great a debt to him as Arthur Brown. To Brown, Laloux embodied the continuity of the classical inheritance, and his work demonstrated the adaptability of the Beaux-Arts method to modern needs and materials. Brown described Laloux's convictions and character this way: "He was completely imbued with the Classic tradition and his whole career was devoted to expanding that influence and handing on the torch to others. . . . He believed in rational change and progress in harmony with the needs of the epoch, but stood sturdily for his profound convictions as to the essence of architectural design. . . . In keeping with his temperament, he expressed himself with exuberance controlled by a fine sense of measure and taste, and an extraordinary eye for proportion. He delighted in noble forms."[49]

ARTHUR BROWN IN PARIS

Brown's initial work in Laloux's atelier was not remarkable, yet by the time he left Paris he was considered to be the most talented American of his decade (fig. 1.14). The transformation of Brown's talent was due to his exemplary work ethic and the instruction of Victor Laloux. In Laloux's atelier Brown found his artistic self, and the *patron* responded by lavishing an increasing amount of attention on him. By 1900 Brown was placing high in the juried competitions; he won the Prix Godeboeuf and placed second twice for the Prix Rougevin. Laloux asked Brown to stay on for a year or two and work through more competitions; in the end Brown won more *valuers* (competition points) than any other American. In Laloux Brown found a role model and lasting friend whose lessons regarding design were only matched by his lessons in life.

1.15. Arthur Brown Jr., "A Campanile for a Town Hall," Concours Godeboeuf, 1900. Heliograph by Armand Guérinet, Les Medailles des Concours des Beaux-Arts: 1900–1901.

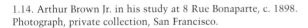

1.14. Arthur Brown Jr. in his study at 8 Rue Bonaparte, c. 1898. Photograph, private collection, San Francisco.

Brown's resumé of work for the second class gives no hint of the success he would find in the first. None of his design work earned more than the perfunctory *mention* given to those who completed the assignment. Brown did shine, however, in the construction sequence, winning a medal in stereotomy (the shaping of stone for construction), and he did very well in the drawing competitions. The routine of the second class must have also been broken by the arrival of Maybeck in Paris in 1897 to conduct the competition for the University of California master plan. Maybeck stayed abroad for several years, during which time he mentored a few of his former students and greatly assisted Julia Morgan in her bid to win formal admission to the Ecole.[50] William Keith also visited the Browns in Paris in 1899 and stayed a few days with them on the Rue Bonaparte.[51] By the summer of 1899, Brown was elevated to the first class, where he immediately improved his design skills.

Brown's greatest triumph was the Prix Godeboeuf in December 1900, a competition that challenged the entrant to design a fragment of a building, in this case a campanile for a *hôtel-de-ville*, or city hall (fig. 1.15). The Godeboeuf was considered the second most prestigious of the annual competitions, subordinate only to the Prix de Rome itself. Brown's entry referenced the composite late Gothic and early renaissance architecture of the sixteenth century, which evoked both the formation of the municipal corporations in the medieval period and the consolidation of a centralized royal authority under the Valois and Bourbons. The overall design rose in stages above the roof; the tribunal platform was enclosed by arches, which were in turn surmounted by an open oculus (treated ornamentally as a wreath of victory), upon which rested the pinnacle and finial. Laloux liked this form so much that he adapted it for his *hôtel-de-ville* at Roubaix in 1906.[52]

1.16. Arthur Brown Jr., "Episcopal Throne," Concours Rougevin, 1901. Heliograph by Armand Guérinet, *Les Medailles des Concours des Beaux-Arts: 1900–1901.*

Brown's successes in the Prix Rougevin were equally impressive. The Rougevin was an exercise in ornamentation but was not always architectural in its focus. Brown's best showing in this competition came in February 1901, when his design for an episcopal throne was judged second best in the show (he lost to Paul Cret, who would better Brown several times over the ensuing thirty years). This design again combined early renaissance detail with medieval forms, in this case after the twelfth-century Romanesque (fig. 1.16). Brown's other second-place showing came in 1903, when he designed a lavish "vitrine for a precious object." With this competition, Brown put far more effort into the Louis XV setting than into the design of the case itself, presenting a lavish interior in blues and golds that likely caught the jurors' eyes with much greater force than the ostensible subject of the competition (fig. C.1).[53] The Rougevin for 1902 was one of the more unusual, as it asked the competitors to design a frontispiece for a memorial folio dedicated to Charles Garnier. Brown received only a second medal for his effort, but it was published in a *cahier* of student work for the year.[54]

One must not underestimate the impact Brown's victories in the Prix Godeboeuf and Rougevin had at the Ecole. No foreigner had ever won the Godeboeuf before, and no one had ever won the Godeboeuf and Rougevin in the same year. These prizes carried with them large monetary awards as well as the prestigious medal. The fact that a relatively well-off American won these awards, which were designed to be scholarships, caused an uproar among the faculty of the school, who immediately passed a decree that denied Brown, and any other foreigner, any monetary award. Once the students learned that Brown was to be deprived of his prizes, they stormed the school's administrative building and demanded that Brown be paid. This conflict put Brown in a very uncomfortable situation—he naturally wanted what was due him, but he did not wish to be the center of a *cause célèbre*. In the end, Brown got his check, with which he bought several rare and expensive architectural folios for the Atelier Laloux, and the administration enforced the new regulation from 1901 onward.[55]

By May 1901 Brown had enough *valuers* to submit a thesis project for the *diplôme*, which he received on June 21, 1901.[56] Although he originally wanted to design a monumental bridge, the proposal was denied for being not "architectural" enough. With just weeks before the deadline, Brown turned to his second-choice project, a *Caisse d'Epargne*, or savings bank.[57] Unfortunately, many of the formal renderings of this project were destroyed in 1906, and only an elevation survives (fig. 1.17). This drawing shows Brown's skill in planning stone construction in its presentation of a three-bay French renaissance facade. Much of the design interest is concentrated at the main entry, where Brown effectively placed an elaborate cartouche above a broken segmental ped-

FAÇADE SVR RVE

CAISSE·NATIONALE·D'EPARGNE·

Echelle 0.02 p.M.

1.17. Arthur Brown Jr., Diplôme Project, "Une Caisse d'Epargne," 1901, principal elevation. Drawing, Arthur Brown Jr. Collection, Bancroft Library. Image courtesy of the Bancroft Library.

iment; however, other aspects of the design suggest that the project could have benefited from more study.

More evidence remains of a project for a market, which may very well be his construction demonstration, which was completed in 1899. This project, fragments of which survive in the Brown Collection at the Bancroft Library, demon-strates the amount of study that Brown put into his work. His initial response to the problem was to design a three-hinged structure of a very wide span, in which the steel arch-es were lifted one story above the floor on high stone abut-ments. After some reflection, Brown incorporated a second sales floor into the design and extended the steel arches to the floor. The additional square footage gained by these maneuvers allowed him to narrow the span of the main shed and to articulate the main facade with three tall arches that were carefully integrated into the ornamental program of the building (figs. 1.18, 1.19).

After receiving the *diplôme* Brown traveled in Europe. He accompanied Edward Bennett to London, arriving just before the coronation of Edward VII, and then may have traveled to the south of France.[58] By December 1901, however, he was doing extracurricular work at Laloux's atelier and again residing at 8 Rue Bonaparte. The following March Brown joined Bennett and another student on a grand tour to Italy, Greece, and Turkey.[59] By April the trio was in Rome, where they paid their respects to the great monuments of antiquity and the Italian baroque. Contrary to common perception, the baroque style was known to the senior students at the Ecole, though discussed with the *patron* in hushed tones when within earshot of the *nouveaux*.[60] While Bennett returned to Paris to wrap up his scholastic career and to begin his work with Daniel Burnham in Chicago, Brown was asked to stay in Paris and study privately with the *patron*. This was an unusual high honor indicating that Laloux considered Brown

a student of rare talent. In a letter to his father, Brown described Laloux's program:

> I went to show my studies to M. Laloux last night at his office and he gave me a long talk. . . . He says that I was now going to start what he called the "etude supérieure" of architecture—the most difficult and at the same time the most interesting and one that would give me a great superiority over my confreres in America because it was little understood by any of the graduates, even of the Beaux-Arts. It is the study of big dispositions. He cites the Opera of Garnier as showing how the details so out of style but the genius of the man showed the great dispositions. He said that it was the study of getting the maximum effect with the resources at hand. He also said that he preferred we go to his office instead of the atelier which was flattering. My work will then consist of my working at my rooms, at the library, and going to see the great buildings to study them—and discussing my work in private at the Master's—a very seductive program—isn't it?[61]

Brown remained with Laloux until the summer of 1903, sometimes traveling, sometimes working through problems assigned to him, such as programs that Laloux intended to be

1.18. Arthur Brown Jr., presumed project in construction: an urban market, 1899, study of main facade. Drawing, Arthur Brown Jr. Collection, Bancroft Library.

1.19. Arthur Brown Jr., presumed project in construction: an urban market, 1899, rear facade. Drawing, Arthur Brown Jr. Collection, Bancroft Library.

used for the Prix de Rome. Several of these, including a faculty of sciences and a maritime museum, were subsequently used in the competition. Brown also assisted the atelier's competitors in preparing their drawings. Ostensibly, competitors were allowed to receive drafting and watercoloring assistance from the *nouveaux*, because by the turn of the twentieth century the drawings for the competition had grown so large that one person could not execute them even in two months. Brown's assistance to Paul Bigot and Ferdinand Janin was suspected of making the difference to their prize-winning entries. In 1903, after Léon Jaussely won the Grand Prix for his design for an urban square and bourse, the Academie des Beaux-Arts announced that henceforth the finalists for the Prix de Rome would work alone, locked into their loges, and that any outside assistance would be grounds for disqualification. Of course, Brown himself was not eligible to compete for the Prix de Rome, but he was honored in 1902 with the annual medal of the Societé des Architects Diplômé par le Gouvernement, which recognized the best student of the preceding academic year. This honor, never before awarded to a foreigner, was a singular means by which the French architectural establishment sought to recognize Brown's extraordinary scholastic career.[62]

Most of Brown's student work was not for the special competitions but for the common monthly exercises. This work is interesting for its variety as well as its relevance to Brown's later work. Whereas the Ecole des Beaux-Arts has been criticized for the seeming obsolescence of its programs, the programs on which Brown worked at the Ecole strangely

foretold his later work as a professional architect. Brown won his greatest prize for his city hall designs—a building type for which he would become renowned—but competition programs as unusual as the synagogue, the scientific laboratories of 1903, and the circa-1902 conservatory were all preparatory to projects Brown later built in San Francisco. Likewise, the more mundane programs, such as those for schools, commercial structures, and residences, prepared Brown and his fellow students for their professional careers.

As grandiose as some of the Prix de Rome and other competition programs seem, America was building on this scale in the first half of the century in projects as diverse as the Mall in Washington, the University of California, and the San Francisco Civic Center. In each case, Ecole-trained American architects were brought together in collaboration to meet the challenge. For the San Francisco Bay Area the lessons in cooperative urbanism taught at the Ecole were especially relevant, and it was indeed fortuitous that a large number of Bay Area architects had completed their studies in Paris in the years before the earthquake and fire of 1906. When the need arose to rebuild all of the urban core of San Francisco and many of the institutions in her satellite communities, Brown and his classmates from Berkeley and Paris were equipped with the academic spirit and professional skills required of the task. In concert with architects trained in the East, they designed a new urban framework for modern life that visually tied the city to the architectural traditions of the American nation as well as to the cultural heritage of the entire western world.

2.1. San Francisco City Hall in the aftermath of the earthquake
and fire, April 1906. Photograph, author's collection.

CHAPTER TWO

BAKEWELL & BROWN
1905–1919

Arthur Brown returned from Paris eager to build in the grand manner; however, after over six years in Paris his architecture was more Gallic than American in spirit and detail. Like many of his fellow compatriots before him, Brown initially failed to distinguish between French modes of architectural expression and the method of design that underlay them. In time he found his own way and produced works comprehensive in their understanding of the classical tradition and regional in their unmistakable evocation of their California settings. Although modernist critics claimed that the Ecole des Beaux-Arts failed to prepare its students for twentieth-century practice, Brown's built commissions strongly paralleled in program and scope the academic projects he designed in school; he designed city halls, opera houses, scientific laboratories, and even synagogues in Paris long before he built them on the Pacific Coast.

Arthur Brown's active architectural career spanned more than forty years, from his apprenticeship in Washington to his final works for the University of California, where his architectural studies had begun. About half of this time Brown worked in association with John Bakewell Jr., with whom he did the civic buildings that cemented his reputation as a great American classicist. From 1905 to 1927 the firm of Bakewell & Brown completed well over one hundred commissions, ranging from simple memorial headstones to San Francisco City Hall. The work of the partnership can be divided into three periods: the time of establishment, from the firm's founding to its success in the San Francisco City Hall competition of 1912; the postcompetition expansion of the practice, which ended with the suspension of architectur-

al work in 1918 resulting from American participation in World War I; and the final corporate period, which began about 1920 and lasted until the firm's dissolution in 1927.

Brown practiced under his own name for the second half of his career, although his long-time associates continued to work with him in important roles. This second career is divided into two parts: the first, governmental, period lasted from 1928 to 1935 and was characterized by Brown's large commissions for the Labor–ICC (Interstate Commerce Commission) block of the Federal Triangle in Washington, DC, and the San Francisco War Memorial Group and Federal Building; the second, institutional, period encompassed the end of his active work from 1936 to the last of his projects at Berkeley. Each of these five periods demonstrates a characteristic set of architectural concerns and values. Although Brown's commitment to the classical tradition remained constant throughout his lifetime, his definition of what constituted a classical architecture appropriate to modern life broadened as his work matured.

THE BEGINNINGS OF BAKEWELL & BROWN

Arthur Brown Jr. and John Bakewell Jr. did not immediately go into practice together upon Brown's completion of his work in Paris. In fact, both Bakewell and Brown worked for East Coast firms for a short while before returning to San Francisco. Bakewell practiced in Pittsburgh in the first years of the century as an associate with Thorsten E. Billquist, a Norwegian-born architect who had worked for McKim, Mead

& White while that firm designed the Boston Public Library. After a brief visit to California in late 1903, Brown moved to Washington, DC, to work as a project designer with Hornblower & Marshall, where he designed elevations for the Smithsonian's Museum of Natural History on the Mall (this work is recounted in chapter 5). While in the East, the two friends found their first opportunity to collaborate together on the competition for the master plan of the Carnegie Technical Schools (now Carnegie-Mellon University), eventually won by Palmer & Hornbostel.

Over the summer of 1904 Bakewell and Brown had become restless in their respective positions. They realized that their potential as practitioners would be slowed if they remained in the well-established architectural community in the East, and so they began to consider returning to San Francisco to set up practice. For Brown this was a significant decision; while working for Hornblower & Marshall he had received employment offers from George Post and Carrère & Hastings, among others, and could thus have made his mark in New York if he had wished.[1] Brown suggested to his father in late July that he would like to return to the Bay Area, and they discussed the possibility of his working with either John Galen Howard (who had offered him a job six months earlier) or Henry A. Schulze. At this point Brown believed that he still needed some time in an established office before striking out on his own, so he did not consider Bakewell's overtures for a partnership seriously.[2]

Brown entered into partnership with Henry Schulze, who was probably a friend of his father.[3] Schulze, son of Washington, DC, architect Paul Schulze, was serving as president of the San Francisco chapter of the AIA at this time. His most significant client during the partnership was J. A. Folger, the coffee magnate. In 1904 and 1905 Brown and Schulze designed for Folger a large roasting plant and office complex, the Folger Building, and a large home in Woodside. The Folger Building, located south of Market at the foot of Howard Street, was probably designed by Schulze before Brown's arrival. It still stands, a survivor of the earthquake and fire of 1906 and the 1989 Loma Prieta earthquake, a tribute to its carefully fireproofed steel frame and heavy masonry walls. Brown was more directly involved in the design of the Folger house, his first residential commission. Brown and Schulze's other significant work was a three-story addition to the Olympic Club, which housed the swimming pool and attendant locker rooms.

Brown was a whirlwind of energy in his first years as a practitioner. While working with Schulze, Brown also became involved with the "Burnham Plan" for San Francisco, which was being developed by his friends Edward Bennett and Willis Polk. Brown moonlighted for the two and executed many of the drawings for the plan.[4] As work on the plan concluded, Brown found himself with too much time on his hands, for at the same time Schulze departed for an extended tour of Europe. It happened that once again John Bakewell was looking for a design partner. Upon Schulze's return Brown gave his notice, and the two friends established the new firm of Bakewell & Brown in late in 1905. At the time, the partnership must have seemed like a foolhardy proposition, given that the two had few, if any, commissions lined up.

As the earth shook early on the morning of April 18, 1906, everyone in the Bay Area must have believed some sort of judgment was at hand (fig. 2.1). Many hundreds of Californians were killed by the temblor, which caused widespread damage from Santa Rosa to Monterey. Yet while there were significant pockets of devastation, particularly at Stanford University and at Agnew State Hospital in Santa Clara, where over one hundred inmates and staff died, the greatest part of the destruction centered on San Francisco. Over the next three days, twenty-eight thousand buildings were destroyed, almost all by the firestorms that raged over the northeast districts of the city. Nearly one-half billion dollars worth of property was destroyed by the earthquake and fire, of which about half was recoverable from insurance claims.[5] The entire commercial center of the city was destroyed, over one-half of the city's housing stock was gone, and every civic building of importance, except the Ferry Building and the United States Mint, lay in ruins. Yet these facts could not have been completely disheartening to a pair of young architects. Once Bakewell and Brown recovered from the shock of the city burning down around them, they must have realized that their careers were now assured.

The immediate effect of the earthquake and fire was unfortunate. The partners lost everything in their office, including whatever work was on the boards and their portfolio pieces, including their *diplôme* projects from the Ecole des Beaux-Arts. Moreover, whatever projects they were scheduled to build in 1906 were unlikely to be constructed in the post-fire inflationary economy of San Francisco. The kind of commissions that Bakewell & Brown most sought—the grand house or the elaborated commercial building—was suddenly something of an anachronism, too. It would be several years before San Franciscans built anything that was not fairly utilitarian in character, capable of quick and efficient construction. Because of the fire, almost nothing is known of the first few months of the firm's existence, other than that they published a notice of association in the January 1906 edition of *The Architect and Engineer*.

Of course, Bakewell and Brown were competing in what became a crowded market, and they were not the only Beaux-Arts–trained architects in San Francisco—by the time of the fire over a dozen architects with some education at Paris were practicing in the Bay Area. The most well-established of these practitioners, Albert Pissis, for example, had grown up in San Francisco (he was born in Mexico) and attended the Ecole in the 1870s, a full generation before Brown. Pissis practiced for thirty years in the city, producing such landmark structures as the Emporium Building on Market Street and the Hibernia Bank Building at the corner of McAlister and Jones Streets.

The larger share of the big commercial projects went to just a few architects, most of whom had practiced in the Bay Area for some years before the earthquake and fire. Nearly all of these architects claimed some training in Paris, but their actual matriculation in the Ecole des Beaux-Arts is not confirmed by any French source. The Reid Brothers, James and Merritt, had arrived in California from Evansville, Indiana, in 1886.[6] While James designed the Hotel del Coronado in San Diego, Merritt set up a practice in San Francisco, which James joined the following year. The brothers, sometimes joined by younger brother Watson, designed many landmark buildings in the city, including the Fairmont Hotel, the Call Building, the new Cliff House, the Hale Brothers Department Store on Union Square, and the band shell in Golden Gate Park.[7] Willis Polk also received a number of important post-fire commissions, including the rehabilitation of many of the buildings he had designed or supervised with Daniel Burnham & Company, such as the Mills Building and the Merchant's Exchange. Polk also designed many important post-fire office buildings, including the Chronicle Building, the Hobart, and most famously, the Hallidie Building, his last major commercial building. He also displayed a rare sensitivity with his restoration work at Mission Delores, which retains its integrity a century later, and with his rehabilitation of the James Flood House on Nob Hill for the Pacific Union Club.[8]

The most successful architects in the immediate post-fire period may have been Walter D. Bliss and William Faville, who had met at MIT and had both worked at McKim, Mead & White before they opened their practice in San Francisco in 1898. The pair was fortunate to become acquainted with Charles Crocker, who commissioned the very young architects to design his Hotel St. Francis on Union Square. Bliss & Faville repaired the damaged hotel in 1907 and then designed a large number of important commercial buildings, such as the Bank of California Building on California Street, the Masonic Temple, the Geary Theatre Building, and the Southern Pacific Headquarters Building at the foot of Market Street. At several points in their careers Bakewell & Brown and Bliss & Faville clashed over commissions and aesthetic vision. They both made much of their livelihood from their associations with the Big Four and their children. Faville, in particular, resented some commissions that Brown received through his connections with the younger Crockers and Hopkinses. Brown, in turn, became annoyed at Faville's artistic independence—he often insisted on a Mediterranean or Italian expression within an ensemble that was otherwise stylistically unified. Although the two firms often found their work adjacent, the distaste the two designers felt for each other's aesthetic preferences grew into a true enmity on several occasions, and they would remain rivals their entire lives.

Like many architectural partnerships, Bakewell & Brown fell into established roles in getting out the work. From the beginning Brown was the designing partner of the firm, whereas Bakewell wrote the specifications and managed the construction sites. In the early years there was not enough work to justify a staff. In time draftsmen were hired whenever the construction documentation for a larger project had to be produced; it is likely that the Berkeley Town Hall was the earliest project to require outside help. As at many architectural firms, the number of employees swelled and shrank as the work demanded. By early 1912 there was little work in the office, and the firm may have had no staff at all. Immediately after the fire the firm worked out of a small building at 1860 Webster Street, but in the summer of 1907 it moved to 417 Montgomery Street, where Bakewell & Brown would stay for five years, until the San Francisco City Hall and Palace of Horticulture projects demanded larger quarters. The firm then moved to 251 Kearney Street, to the Charleston Building (designed by Albert Pissis), where they would occupy the seventh and eighth floors in whole or in part for the next forty years.

In light of their later success, it is tempting to assume that Bakewell & Brown had an easy time of it in the immediate post-fire years. However, because the two architects were untried in the Bay Area at the time of the fire, they really were not able to compete for the big reconstruction jobs commissioned to the Reid Brothers, Willis Polk, or Bliss & Faville. Much of the firm's early work was either replacement structures for small commercial buildings destroyed in the fire, or residences in the western neighborhoods of San Francisco or in the East Bay for friends and relatives—the kind of work typical of fledgling architectural firms. Some drawings of these early projects survive, although the collections held by the family and the Bancroft Library are incomplete. Photographic evidence is slight because the firm used glass negatives to archive portraits of their built work until World War I (few of these plates are identified as to the project they represent). The earliest houses were largely designed in a restrained Queen Anne form (with cross gables and towers), in the colonial revival, as found in the city's western residential districts, or in an arts-and-crafts mode that liberally employed pergolas, trussed gables, and cantilevered balconies. A number of these houses were published in 1909 and demonstrate that Bakewell & Brown were not seeking a "corporate look" in their residential architecture. As the article in *The Architect and Engineer* relates, the young firm took

2.2. MacDonald Residence, Oakland, c. 1908. Glass negative, Arthur Brown Jr. Collection, Bancroft Library.

each commission as an independent problem in which the client's needs and predilections were most important.[9]

Several of these houses were built at or near the intersection of Vernon and Perkins Streets in Oakland, where a developer friend of Brown's father had platted a small subdivision of moderately sized building lots. Brown became the street's architect and built at least four houses there between 1907 and 1910. The houses hardly appear to have been designed by the same architect. The A. S. MacDonald House resembles an English arts-and-crafts house after the manner of Charles F. A. Voysey (fig. 2.2). Its stucco finish, steep, prominent asymmetrical gables, and massive chimney stacks suggest both an English inspiration and a careful look at the cottages of Ernest Coxhead and Bernard Maybeck of the partners' university days. The rear of the house, which had an exceptional view at one time, is dominated by a glazed porch that is framed in heavy timbers that tie the space to the prominent woodwork on the interior. The neighboring S. B. McKee House is much more formal and references seventeenth- and eighteenth-century French sources with its lucarne dormers, colonnaded porch, elaborate entry, and broken pediment ornamented with an oversized baroque shell. The George Hammer Residence, up the street a bit, owed its forms to the arts-and-crafts bungalow. It featured low, spreading eaves supported on brackets and purlins that shel-

tered its stucco walls from strong sun. Access to the grounds was marked by pergolas, which became a feature of many early Bakewell & Brown houses.[10] The final house on Vernon Place came a few years later and was a house for Brown's parents, who finally had had enough of living at the Metropole Hotel downtown. This house reflected the character of the client, in that it is a nearly unornamented hip-roofed box of a fairly severe character. The only architectural elaboration on the exterior occurs at the entry, where a Doric porch is crowned by an extremely simple wrought-iron balcony rail, into which was set the elder Arthur Brown's monogram.

The earliest extant residence by Bakewell & Brown is 16 Presidio Terrace, which was built for E. C. Hutchinson, president of the Kennedy Mining and Milling Company (fig. 2.3). This house, one of the very earliest built on the Terrace, and located just north of Temple Emanu-El, dates from either 1905 or early 1906, and may be the one pre-earthquake building by Bakewell & Brown that survives.[11] The design of the house is interesting in that Bakewell & Brown adapted the colonial revival forms popularized on the eastern seaboard to San Francisco building traditions. The house is a hip-roofed Georgian revival box, ornamented with a few classical motifs, such as the modillions at the eaves and the balustrade around the widow's walk at the top of the roof. The entry is

2.3. Hutchinson House, Presidio Terrace, San Francisco, c. 1906. Glass negative, Arthur Brown, Jr. Collection, Bancroft Library.

aggrandized with a Doric door surround (here Brown used an Ionic entablature over his Doric columns) and an elegant set of stained-glass side lights with fan transom. Yet the house's most prominent feature is its pair of full-height octagonal bays on the street elevation, which resembles the Italianate town houses of the 1870s and 1880s for which the city is now so famous. Thus the house's design attempts to update the "bay window" vernacular of the city with borrowings from federal New England and contemporary eastern practice.

Brown was particularly keen to establish a practice designing branch banks, the subject of his *diplôme* project at the Ecole des Beaux-Arts. However, his conception of the type, as he understood it from his French education, did not initially square with the needs of the banking community in the Bay Area; his work was simply too fussily ornamented and "architectural" for the serious-minded bankers who would have been his clients. He entered three competitions for branch banks in the first years of the practice and lost every one of them. Bakewell & Brown did build a number of commercial structures in the years after the fire, including the Buckingham & Hecht warehouse building for the University of California. Few of these structures survive (many were in the South-of-Market and have succumbed to rounds of urban renewal), and few photographs of them exist. However, the images that do remain suggest that these struc-

tures were two- and three-story loft buildings typical of those constructed in San Francisco following the fire, and deviate from the standard pattern only in detail.

BERKELEY TOWN HALL

Throughout this early period, Bakewell and Brown hoped for a prominent civic commission that would fully challenge their design abilities and bring some notoriety to their fledgling firm. This big break came with their successful entry in the competition for Berkeley Town Hall. With this project Bakewell & Brown became a regionally known firm and attracted a wider circle of clients.

The town of Berkeley lost its second purpose-built town hall to fire in 1904, just four years after it had been constructed. After two years, the town resolved to build a new town hall on an expanded site, so that the building would face a park on Grove Street and become the primary structure of a small civic center.[12] A bond issue for $100,000 was passed in March 1907, and an architectural competition commenced the following month. Bakewell & Brown topped ten other entrants with an interpretation of a seventeenth-century French *hôtel-de-ville*, obviously modeled on Victor Laloux's

2.4. Arthur Brown Jr., Berkeley City Hall, early schematic design
sketch, c. 1907. Drawing, private collection, San Francisco.

city hall for Tours, and crowned with a tower adapted from
Brown's Godeboeuf campanile (fig. 2.4). Although this classical civic building may seem incongruous among Berkeley's
shingled homes and experimental structures, such as
Florence Boynton's Temple of the Wings, it actually demonstrates that at the time both Beaux-Arts classicism and the
arts-and-crafts were understood as appropriate architectural
forms for their respective spheres of community life, the
civic and the residential.

The constructed building differs greatly from the first
sketches and from its French models, not only in size, but in
materials, decorative treatment, and function (figs. 2.5, 2.6).
The building grew into a shallow U-shape, with a five-bay
main block now flanked by three-bay wings. The basement
or ground floor, reached directly from the rear on the sloping
site, housed the police, fire, and medical departments, which
needed to be accessible at all times. Above, on the first floor,
Brown placed the business departments, including the financial, clerical, and engineering offices. Like the early sketch,
the upper floor of the building housed the mayor's suite, the

council chamber, and the offices of the school board. The
architectural detailing of the building was a bit more subdued from the first sketches. The roof pitches were brought
down to reasonable slope, and the window openings were
regularized—all openings on the first floor are arched, unifying the elevation, whereas the tall French doors on the second floor open out to balconies.

As might be expected of a building in the Bay Area in
1907, municipal officials insisted that its new city hall be
constructed of a fireproof material, and this became a mandate for reinforced concrete. Several architects were working
in concrete even before the earthquake and fire, most notably
Ernest Ransome, who pioneered the use of reinforced concrete in the United States, and who had constructed several
major buildings in the new material in San Francisco and at
Stanford University in the 1890s.[13] Brown knew of the material from working with his father, who used it in the
Southern Pacific dock works, and he observed firsthand the
development of reinforced concrete in Paris, particularly at
the Exposition Universelle of 1900, where the reinforcing

2.5. Arthur Brown Jr., Berkeley City Hall, May 25, 1907, presentation sketch demonstrating effect of campanile. Drawing, Arthur Brown Jr. Collection, Bancroft Library.

system of François Hennebique was used to construct many of the exposition buildings.[14] Brown's challenge was to adapt the classical detailing he desired for the building to this relatively new material. He did this by employing chunky, over-scaled elements, such as the giant-order engaged columns and projecting reseaux on the main block, which could be easily formed and poured in place; originally these columns were to be Corinthian, but they became Ionic in deference to the material and the budget.

Other elements were also dramatically interpreted in concrete. The balconies on the second floor, for example, are supported only by the keystones of the arches below at the main block, giving them a cantilevered effect, whereas at the wings the balconies rest on pairs of six-foot-high consoles, suggesting a play with the issue of structural support. At the center of the composition Brown placed a round tablet above the entablature, which was intended as the setting for a municipal clock. The newspapers reported that the clock was to be "a gift of various public-spirited citizens"; these benefactors apparently never came forward, and the tablet

remains blank to this day.[15] The interior of the building was fitted out rather simply, in order to meet the budget and the general American desire for efficient, businesslike civic office space. However, the stair hall and council chambers were given a more ornate finish. The council chambers have been renovated several times, but the stair hall preserves the original color scheme and the sensuous curving forms of the steps themselves, which seem to spill like liquid from one floor to the next. Both of these features establish Brown's interest in the rich tertiary colors and the sinuous organic curves of the art nouveau.

The most controversial part of the Berkeley Town Hall project proved to be the tower: many of the town's trustees as well as architectural advisor John Galen Howard thought it was an unnecessary adornment. Bakewell and Brown were, in fact, ordered to draw up plans for the building without the tower in July 1907 as a precondition to acceptance of their design, and these were used for the cost estimates of the building. Nevertheless, images of the building with the tower were exhibited and circulated throughout Berkeley,

2.6. Bakewell & Brown, Berkeley City Hall, 1908, view from civic plaza. Photograph by Sylvia Brown Jensen.

and the campanile gathered a constituency and the support of the newspapers. By October the tower was again a part of the project and was incorporated into the construction drawings prepared for the contractors.[16] Ground was broken for the Berkeley Town Hall project in early 1908. Construction went surprisingly quickly and was completed in October of the same year. The building was widely admired for its artistic use of a relatively new material, as Berkeley Town Hall was one of the first reinforced concrete civic buildings in California. In the context of Brown's career, the Town Hall is more of a promise of greater things to come than a landmark work. Within the next two decades Bakewell & Brown would build two more city halls: one, in San Francisco, the finest adaptation of French architectural traditions to any municipal building in the United States; the other, in Pasadena, an internationally renowned masterpiece of construction in reinforced concrete.

THE CITY OF PARIS DEPARTMENT STORE

Bakewell & Brown's next large undertaking was perhaps an even greater success from a public relations standpoint than Berkeley Town Hall. And although the firm's early adherence to French architectural modalities was a handicap in procuring some commissions, its affinity for all things French was the primary qualification needed for its next big job. In 1909 Bakewell & Brown was commissioned to outfit the rebuilt City of Paris department store on Union Square in San Francisco. The proprietors, Félix and Gaston Verdier, *père et fils*, were extremely successful importers and retailers whose company dated back to Félix's arrival in San Francisco in 1850. By the 1880s the City of Paris set the standard for high-end merchandising in San Francisco.[17] The Verdiers also supported the Amitiés Français, a local French-American cultural association that sponsored a number of social and artistic events each year, and of which Bakewell and Brown were members.

The commission was strictly an interior design problem. Architect Clinton Day had already reconstructed his department store building at Stockton and Geary, which he had first seen through to completion in 1896, but which had been gutted in the fire. Freed of responsibility to San Franciscan urban sensibilities, Brown was able to execute an unabashedly French interior in the manner of the department stores of the East Coast, such as Daniel Burnham's building for Wanamaker's in Philadelphia. The display cases and storefronts were exuberant and yet neutral enough to effectively showcase the objects within them. The same reserve cannot be considered characteristic of the primary interior space. Brown chose to light the store with an elliptical court, skylit by a glass dome, into which the emblem of the Verdier family was set (fig. 2.7). The various levels of the store were unified by Corinthian columns and marked out by wrought-iron railings, each floor receiving a distinct design. The white interior was enlivened by the profuse use of gilded architectural ornament, the program and design for which was devised by Jean-Louis Bourgeois, Brown's close friend and fellow student from the Atelier Laloux in Paris.[18] This spectacular interior became a meeting place for San Francisco's shopping citizenry and a focal point of the Union Square retail district (fig. 2.8).

In fact, the reconstruction of the City of Paris symbolized the return to Union Square of the retail district, which had been moved to temporary quarters along Van Ness Avenue after the fire. The Verdiers insisted on returning to the exact location the store had previously occupied, even though that meant a delay in reopening. Newspaper accounts of the new store lavished praise on the interiors, and spread Bakewell & Brown's name to many who only visited San Francisco perhaps once or twice a year. The San Francisco *Chronicle* gushed that the store was "fashioned after and combining the best features of the leading stores of Paris, [and] is a model among modern dry goods stores. . . . [I]t is a pride and ornament and enhances the attractions of the now famous shopping district of San Francisco, of which it forms the center."[19] The Verdiers were equally effusive in their praise of the building, and they used Bakewell & Brown's rendering of the grand court as the centerpiece of their reopening campaign, and kept Bakewell's, Brown's, and Bourgeois's names front and center in their advertising and press releases.[20]

2.7. Arthur Brown Jr., City of Paris Rotunda, 1909, perspective sketch. Drawing, Arthur Brown Jr. Collection, Bancroft Library.

2.8. Bakewell & Brown, City of Paris Rotunda, c. 1920. Library of Congress, Prints and Photographs Division, Historic American Buildings Survey, CAL.38.SANFRA.135-78.

2.9. Bakewell & Brown, Burlingame Country Club, 1910, presentation rendering. Drawing, Arthur Brown Jr. Collection, Bancroft Library.

Seventy years later, the City of Paris again became the symbol of a changing Union Square when the Neiman Marcus company purchased the landmark building and hired Philip Johnson to design a new store for the site.[21] Preservationists from around the Bay Area rallied around the building and demanded its conservation. The Foundation for San Francisco's Architectural Heritage launched a press offensive and letter-writing campaign, and hundreds of citizens demanded that the building be retrofitted for modern use rather than demolished.[22] In the end, the activists lost, and the building was destroyed in the late summer of 1980.

Neiman Marcus was not interested in any kind of retrofitting scheme. But pressure from these activists forced Neiman Marcus to reconsider the rotunda and dome, and by the time of the hearings Johnson had incorporated these elements into his design. In fact, although Johnson did not think much of the shell of the City of Paris (he called it "a travesty of its former self"), he was thoroughly charmed by the rotunda.[23] He termed it "one of the finest pieces of 1910 Beaux-Arts design anywhere in the world," and insisted on saving not just the dome but the entire room. He moved the assembly to the corner of the building, wrapped in glass, "clasped as in a setting for a precious jewel."[24] This move was in itself highly controversial. Much of the fabric of the rotunda was lost or altered with the reconstruction, and many preservationists decried the exercise, believing that the

rotunda's meaning was changed in its transformation from atrium to entry. Yet without Johnson's insistence, most of the rotunda would be landfill by now, and the space would not exist in any form.

BURLINGAME COUNTRY CLUB

The City of Paris project made Brown a household name among the smart set of the Bay Area. Many who associated French design with quality and distinction sought Bakewell & Brown for their residential and institutional work; this popularity led to the firm's most important early commission, the Burlingame Country Club. Within ten years, Brown would not only ingratiate himself with the membership of the club, the very highest social strata of California, he would become one of their own, and build his own house in Hillsborough, the club's neighboring community.

Founded in 1893 by Francis Griffith Newlands, United States Congressman from Nevada, Burlingame Park was one of the first planned residential suburbs in California and decidedly the most exclusive in the first half of the twentieth century. The property was originally part of a vast estate on the mid-peninsula successively owned by William Ralston and Newlands's father-in-law, William Sharon. In the early 1890s Newlands sponsored two very successful real estate developments: he laid out Chevy Chase, Maryland, outside of Washington, DC, and began to construct Burlingame Park, fifteen miles south of San Francisco. Newlands himself had little practical knowledge of town planning or architecture—he hired what he needed. He commissioned Richard Pindell Hammond Jr. to lay out the plat of Burlingame, which was wrapped around a golf course and a polo field, its winding tree-lined streets intended to emulate the great suburbs of the East, such as Merion outside of Philadelphia or Tuxedo Park, New York.[25] The social center of the community was the country club building, a Tudor-revival half-timbered structure designed by A. Page Brown to reinforce the English country theme of the development. The clubhouse was accompanied by five rental "cottages," homes leased by Newlands to those wishing a prolonged stay in the new suburb.

The benign climate and recreational amenities offered at Burlingame Park enticed many of San Francisco's elite to settle there in the 1890s, among them hardware magnate Francis J. Carolans and William H. Crocker, son of the Southern Pacific's Charles Crocker. These families and others built large estate houses of an increasingly formal character. By the time of the earthquake and fire several dozen of the city's wealthiest citizens had built country places at Burlingame, and the country club had become the center of the city's social scene in the warmer months. In the years following the fire the mid-peninsula became more densely developed, as displaced San Franciscans looked for places to relocate. To ensure continued quiet and exclusivity, the residents of the neighborhoods surrounding the country club incorporated as the Town of Hillsborough. At the same time,

the president of the country club, George A. Pope, sought to build a new, expansive clubhouse that would better reflect the scale and formality of the new municipality.

Bakewell & Brown's French classicism fit the aspirations of the Burlingame Club perfectly, and yet even this institution found Brown's first designs a bit overly ornamented and historically minded for its tastes. The presentation rendering of the clubhouse depicts a two-story main block on a raised basement, terminated by twin end pavilions and capped by high hip roofs that backed into a long, narrow suite of dining rooms and sunrooms (fig. 2.9). The ornamentation was elaborate; the end pavilions were fitted with frontispieces built up with pilasters, projecting balconies, and lucarne windows, and wrought-iron balcony rails fronted nearly every French door and window. The entry projected from the center of the block and was covered by an elaborate iron-and-glass fan-like canopy reminiscent of Hector Guimard's canopies for the Paris Métro. The constructed building presented a much simpler front to the street. The projecting entry and canopy remained, with a sculptural pediment. The pavilions, however, were greatly simplified; the lucarne dormers were abandoned, and French doors were placed within pilastered surrounds. The roofs were much less steeply pitched and were not broken at the eaves with dormers. Two one-story wings filled in the front corners of the building, making a much more graceful transition from the clubroom block to the dining and sunrooms behind.

The glories of the building were the skylit court and porches. The large square court, defined by a Doric colonnade that wrapped around its edges, originally open to the sky, was

2.10. Bakewell & Brown, Court, Burlingame Country Club, c. 1955. Photograph by Sylvia Brown Jensen.

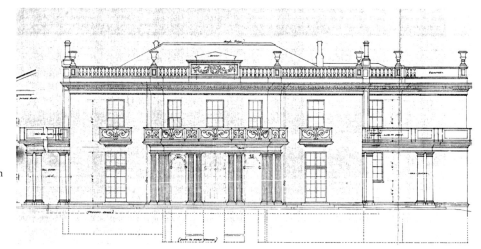

2.11. Bakewell & Brown, Truxtun Beale Residence, 1909, construction drawing, bayside elevation. Arthur Brown Jr. Collection, Bancroft Library.

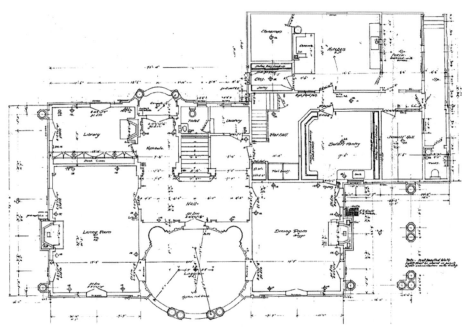

2.12. Bakewell & Brown, Truxtun Beale Residence, 1909, plan. Arthur Brown Jr. Collection, Bancroft Library.

lit from above throughout its entire extent. Dramatic by day, this space took on an ethereal glow when artificially lit in the evening, when it was frequently used as a ballroom (fig. 2.10). Beyond lay the porches, which were long corridors of space lighted on three sides by floor-to-ceiling windows fitted between Doric columns and pilasters. The room was entirely rational; each column or pilaster in the exterior wall was reflected on the interior wall with a corresponding structural element. The suite was vaulted with a plaster ceiling that was faced with latticework, reinforcing Brown's suggestion that the porches were an extension of the garden, rather than an annex to the clubhouse. The other interiors of the building were less inventive, rather practical applications of Edith Wharton and Ogden Codman's *The Decoration of Houses*

(1897). The interior woodwork was a restrained yet canonical presentation of the orders, painted white to minimize its presence. The furniture was generally French in inspiration, but upholstered in American chintzes and rattan.

Brown's work for the Burlingame Country Club paid big dividends for Bakewell & Brown and for Brown personally. The firm won commissions from many of the club's members, and Brown himself was elected a member on April 3, 1912, just days before the commencement of the San Francisco City Hall competition. The Burlingame Country Club retained Brown's headquarters building for many years. However, in 1954 the club sold forty acres of its property in order to purchase the late William H. Crocker's New Place, designed by Lewis Hobart in 1910 and remodeled it in the same year for use as a new clubhouse, obscuring its original domestic scale and character.[26] Brown's building was subsequently demolished in the reworking of the golf course layout that attended the acquisition of the new property.

WORK BEFORE THE SAN FRANCISCO CITY HALL

Bakewell & Brown's triumphs at Berkeley Town Hall, the City of Paris, and Burlingame Country Club increased the firm's profile among potential clients. The firm also enjoyed a presence in the local architectural press and was featured in a generous retrospective article in the February 1909 issue of *The Architect and Engineer*.[27] Such publicity introduced potential clients to the modern academic design vocabulary Brown was most interested in employing. The later residen-

tial commissions from this period are more boldly French in planning and effect and demonstrate the growing acceptance of Gallic forms by the upper classes. Senator Truxtun Beale's house is a case in point (figs. 2.11, 2.12). Brown designed this house in San Rafael, Marin County, for his good friend Marie Beale, in 1909. The house's central feature is a large elliptical loggia set so deeply into the block that it served as an outdoor living space, its columns framing a spectacular view of San Francisco Bay. The colonnade also formed the central feature of the primary elevation, which is crowned by a heavy cornice and balustrade that is punctuated by a series of decorative urns. Brown also used the ellipse in his proposed ballroom addition for George Pope, president of the Burlingame Country Club. In this scheme, a new entry gallery at the corner of Divisadero Street and Pacific Avenue would have led through a double column-screen to a large elliptical ball-

2.13. Bakewell & Brown, design for a ballroom for George A. Pope, Webster Street Residence, San Francisco. Drawing, Arthur Brown Jr. Collection, Bancroft Library.

PRINCIPAL ELEVATION (PINE ST·)

·· UNITED · STATES · SUBTREASURY ··
·· SAN · FRANCISCO · CAL ··

2.14. Bakewell & Brown, competition entry for the subtreasury of
San Francisco, 1909, principal elevation. Drawing, Arthur Brown Jr.
Collection, Bancroft Library.

room, which would have been ringed by Ionic columns and pilasters (fig. 2.13). A trompe-l'oeil ceiling that simulated a balustraded mezzanine would have been further decorated with an illusionistic mural that depicted a host of drunken gods and goddesses cavorting in a sea of fluffy clouds. This project was never executed; Pope devoted more of his time to his peninsula estate, and the house itself burned to the ground in 1929.

Despite the relative success of Bakewell & Brown's initial years, the firm was not receiving a large number of commis-

sions by 1910. As the post-1906 rebuilding effort concluded, it found itself with very little paid work. As architects often do in these circumstances, Brown busied himself with a house for his parents, and Bakewell also did work for family members. In addition, the partners entered a number of architectural competitions. In 1908 the firm had entered the competition for the statehouse for Puerto Rico in San Juan, but had not met with much success. In 1911 the firm won the right to compete for the federal Subtreasury for San Francisco. This was a national event, and fifteen firms were

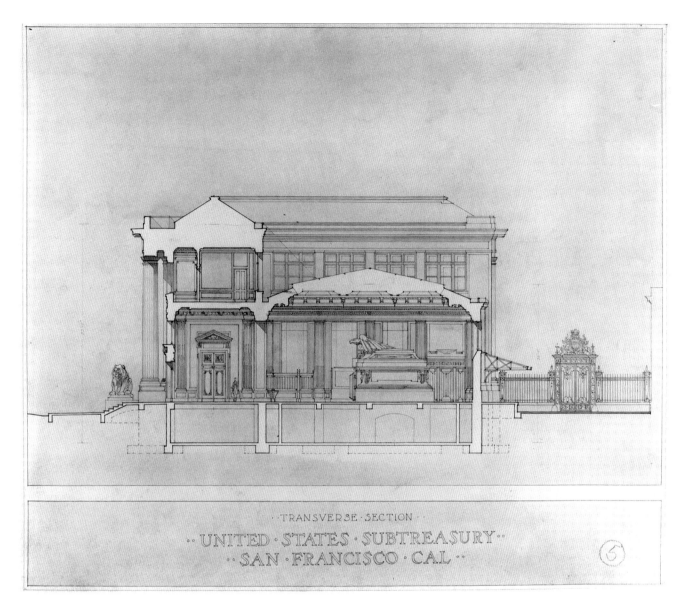

· TRANSVERSE · SECTION ·

·· UNITED · STATES · SUBTREASURY ··
·· SAN · FRANCISCO · CAL ··

2.15. Bakewell & Brown, competition entry for the subtreasury of San Francisco, 1909, transverse section showing banking lobby and vault. Drawing, Arthur Brown Jr. Collection, Bancroft Library.

short-listed to submit design entries. Bakewell & Brown's entry was a sober Doric neoclassical block (fig. 2.14). The principal elevation on Pine Street was flanked by granite guardian lions and aggrandized by an octastyle portico that gave onto three ceremonial doors. Inside, a public lobby led to teller's cages and the banking floor proper, dominated by the cash and gold reserve vaults, which Brown designed as an oversized sarcophagus guarded by a five-foot-high eagle perched on its lid (fig. 2.15). Bakewell & Brown's entry was not chosen to receive recognition by the jury, but it was illus-

trated in *The Architect and Engineer*, and it did receive approbation from the winner, Cleveland architect J. Milton Dyer, a former classmate of Brown at the Ecole des Beaux-Arts.[28]

The most significant of Bakewell & Brown's early competitions was held in 1910, when the city of Oakland decided to build a new city hall; this was the moment for which the partners had been waiting, and they worked hard to be among the thirty architectural firms invited to compete for the commission. With their success at Berkeley, both Bakewell and Brown

WASHINGTON STREET ELEVATION

OAKLAND CITY HALL COMPETITION

2.16. Bakewell & Brown, competition drawing for Oakland City Hall, 1910, Washington Street elevation. Arthur Brown Jr. Collection, Bancroft Library.

were convinced that the Oakland commission would be their big break. This was not to be the case—in fact, the Oakland press pointedly noted that the system by which the jury was to be selected—by vote of the competing firms—nearly guaranteed an East Coast–based jury and a win for an eastern firm.[29] Still, Bakewell & Brown labored on its designs for the competition, trusting that with their Beaux-Arts pedigree and eastern office experience they would procure some award for their work. They were also buoyed by the fact that John Galen Howard, the advisory architect to the city, was a close colleague of theirs, and that Frère Champney, Brown's roommate in Paris and Washington, had been named to the jury.

In many ways this design was a hybrid of the firm's city halls for Berkeley and that which they would design for San Francisco. Like the Berkeley design, the Oakland competition entry derived from the French *hôtels-de-ville* Bakewell and Brown both knew from their Paris education. The building was visually raised on a high basement that supported a piano nobile, on which Brown located the council chamber and mayor's suite. This floor was identified on the elevations with a colossal Doric order, whose pilasters were doubled at the ends and center to create the illusion of a main block and flanking wings (fig. 2.16). The ceremonial central entrance of the building was marked with a frontispiece that carried freestanding columns up to an attic story crowned by a sculptural group. An elaborate iron campanile and belvedere rose above the six floors of office space, reminiscent of the tower at Berkeley Town Hall.

Yet for all the debt to the Berkeley project, the Oakland City Hall entry contains the genesis of the San Francisco City Hall in its planning. As he would do at San Francisco, Brown designed a double-court building in which the circulation is concentrated at the center of the building. Unlike the San Francisco design, the Oakland entry does not permit this central circulation to be expressed as a volume within the building (fig. 2.17). Several floors were carried through the

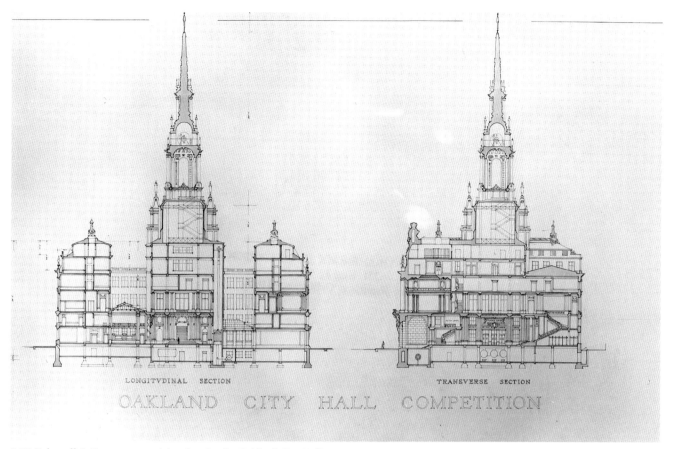

LONGITVDINAL SECTION   TRANSVERSE SECTION

OAKLAND CITY HALL COMPETITION

2.17. Bakewell & Brown, competition drawing for Oakland City Hall, 1910, longitudinal and transverse sections. Arthur Brown Jr. Collection, Bancroft Library.

rotunda zone, and these severed what connection might have been made between the entry space and the tower. Brown also experimented with the distribution of functions within the Oakland program; he placed the council chambers on the piano nobile over the principal entry, and he experimented with the use of the skylit courts as a sort of banking hall for the collections and recordation groups. Even the corners were chamfered on the front of the building, as Brown would be forced to do at San Francisco.

As circumstances developed, the Oakland competition did not lead directly to the big breakthrough commission. However, Bakewell & Brown did not fare poorly—they did win one of the ten second-place mentions and a $1,000 award for their efforts.[30] Palmer & Hornbostel of New York, winners of the Carnegie Institute competition, also won the Oakland City Hall contest and saw their design for a ten-story skyscraper city hall through to construction in 1911. John Galen Howard lauded the innovative winning design

as a "work of extraordinary brilliancy and beauty. The distinctive and dominating idea underlying the design is that the city hall of today is of a dual character; first, official and second, utilitarian. To give perfect architectural expression to these dual functions was the task which the designers have set themselves and they have realized their purpose."[31] Clearly, Brown remembered Howard's words when, two years later in the spring of 1912, he designed yet another city hall in a competition adjudicated by the same John Galen Howard. Again, there was little work in the office. Bakewell & Brown entered the competition hoping to make a few more rent payments on their office—instead, by following Howard's direction to separate the official from the utilitarian, they won not only the competition but a host of private and institutional clients that would keep them busy for the next fifteen years. The development of the San Francisco Civic Center and its city hall is discussed in the next chapter.

Post-Competition Consolidation

Within weeks of the announcement of their success in the competition for San Francisco City Hall, Bakewell & Brown had become the most highly sought-after architects in the San Francisco Bay Area. Several important commissions came to the firm because of their victory, among these the terminal depot for the Atchison, Topeka, & Santa Fe Railroad at San Diego. Bakewell & Brown's new-found fame, too, allowed their friends and allies to procure work for them at the institutions with which they were associated—this led to more work at Stanford University, for example. Before Bakewell and Brown could turn their attention to these new clients, however, they had to complete their commission at the Panama-Pacific International Exposition.

The Panama-Pacific International Exposition

The Panama-Pacific International Exposition (PPIE) was a long-held dream of many San Franciscans who were expecting the city to become the major trade center of the Pacific Rim with the realization of the Panama Canal. As early as 1904, while St. Louis was hosting the Louisiana Purchase Exposition, San Francisco merchant Reuben B. Hale proposed a similar great world's fair to mark the completion of the Panama Canal. The idea remained a dream as the canal project was beset by delays and as San Francisco rebuilt from the earthquake and fire. However, Hale's dream took a step toward realization in October 1909, when President William Howard Taft declared in San Francisco that the canal would be open for business on January 1, 1915. For the next two years, boosters of the fair organized an exposition company and raised over $6 million in subscriptions toward the funding of the venture. The State of California supported the initiative as well. Governor James Gillette had proposed, and won passage for, a constitutional amendment that permitted the company to issue $5 million in construction bonds, and he had the state legislature levy a like amount in new taxes that were earmarked specifically for the exposition.[32]

This tremendous show of financial support for San Francisco's bid impressed the House of Representatives, which voted on January 31, 1911, to award an exposition franchise to the San Francisco Exposition Company over a competing bid from New Orleans.[33] This was an act of faith on the part of the House. Certainly there was considerable pressure to locate the exposition in San Francisco to accentuate the Pacific empire acquired by the United States since 1898. Yet much of San Francisco's municipal government was in shambles, given the indictments and trials of the graft prosecutions of 1907–10, and although much of the city had been rebuilt since 1906, the public infrastructure lagged well behind the reconstruction of private interests. The local directors of the exposition were prominent men of business and governmental affairs who knew little of architectural or planning matters; they relied heavily on first local, and then national, design professionals to locate and design the fair's physical environment. The Board of Architects included many famous names, including McKim, Mead & White, Henry Bacon, and Thomas Hastings of New York, and Chicago architect Edward Bennett, author of the "Burnham Plan" for San Francisco. The balance of the board was composed of California architects and included Robert Farquhar, Louis Christian Mullgardt, George Kelham, Willis Polk, William Faville, and Clarence Ward. Brown was active on the Board of Architects from its inception, named to the board by its initial chair, Willis Polk.[34]

Brown and Polk had worked together the previous year on a proposal to locate the exposition in four precincts around the city, which would have been joined to one another by grand boulevards. This scheme, devised by Brown, Polk, Ernest Coxhead, Frederick H. Meyer, and George Howard, attempted to incorporate many of the sites debated among the public and the directors for the exposition, and to mitigate the enormous impact the fair would have on any one district. Once the Harbor View site was identified as the principal location of the exposition, the Board of Architects met to outline a master plan for the facilities. They chose to develop Ernest Coxhead's so-called Court Scheme, which best unified the various exhibition buildings and controlled the cold winds that blew off the bay to the north by placing most of the exhibit palaces behind a high buffer wall.[35] Patrons would move between the palaces through courtyards that were designed around specific themes, such as The Court of the Four Seasons, or The Court of Abundance. In meetings in August and December 1912, the Board of Architects (later called the Architectural Commission to include its nonarchitect members) adopted Edward Bennett's refinements of the ground plan and developed their assigned exhibition palaces.

The most significant structure of the PPIE was, without doubt, Bernard Maybeck's Palace of Fine Arts (fig. 2.18). Maybeck, once a celebrated architect and educator, was working in Willis Polk's office as a draftsman when Polk held an interoffice competition for the building. Maybeck produced a charcoal sketch that captured the mood of sadness and introspection that he felt was essential to the proper appreciation of art. In the drawing, a decayed but noble domed rotunda rose in front of a reflecting pool. To either side, a curved colonnade held the rotunda within it and related the dome to the landscape around it. Polk took one look at the drawing and proclaimed it the design of the palace. He presented the drawing to the Architectural Commission, which immediately ratified the design; Polk

2.18. Bernard R. Maybeck, Palace of Fine Arts, Panama-Pacific International Exposition, San Francisco, 1915. Photograph, author's collection.

then revealed Maybeck as the designer and asked that he be given the commission for the building.[36]

By October 1912 the schematic designs of structures such as Maybeck's had already been established.[37] Each architect was free to design his building as he wished; however, every structure was to be subordinate to the whole in some way. Taken as a whole, the board thought of the complex as a sprawling Islamic citadel, "an Alladin's Palace, facing the azure harbor and the mountains beyond." As Polk put it, "the serene goddess of harmony" was to be given her due by imposing a strict architectural unity on the exterior of the general exhibition buildings—color, texture, and landscape were all to be tightly controlled.[38] Divergent architectural expression was confined to the interiors of the courts, where smaller-scale deviations from the palette would emphasize the larger unity. Thus, although the theme structure, Carrère & Hastings's Tower of Jewels, nearly 435 feet high, appeared from afar to resemble a shimmering Buddhist stupa, its details were Imperial Roman, as it led to McKim, Mead & White's Court of the Universe, an elliptical plaza entered

through triumphal arches and framed by Corinthian peristyles. In fact, it would appear that the exoticism described by Polk was not universally subscribed to—nearly all of the East Coast architects on the board worked within the Beaux-Arts Roman classicism to which they had been accustomed. The structures most evocative of the Middle and Far East were produced by the Bay Area architects. Louis Christian Mullgardt's Court of the Ages, for example, was based on the Alhambra, the renowned Moorish palace of Grenada, Spain.

Like Maybeck's Palace of Fine Arts, Arthur Brown's Palace of Horticulture was also intended to strike a mood. But whereas Maybeck sought the sublime and introspective, Brown was charged with creating a joyous, festive building that celebrated overwhelming abundance. The most exuberantly ornamented structure at the PPIE, the Palace of Horticulture brought the full fruits of California's agricultural bounty under its enormous dome, which was larger than that of St. Peter's in Rome. The palace stood on the west side of the South Gardens, the primary entrance plaza of the complex, and directly opposite Robert Farquhar's Festival Hall

2.19. Panama-Pacific International Exposition, San Francisco, 1915.
Photograph, author's collection.

(fig. 2.19). Both buildings were designed with complementary massings in order to frame the gardens, which were quite formal *tapis verts* organized along long rectangular pools. The center of the gardens was dominated by A. Stirling Calder's Fountain of Energy, which prominently presented a heroic "superman" astride a horse, pushing apart the great continents of the Americas, and incidentally emphasizing the correspondence between Brown's greenhouse and Farquhar's concert hall. Brown and Farquhar consulted each other frequently about the design of each other's buildings; indeed, Farquhar finished the drawings for his Festival Hall in Brown's office. Brown's building attempted to fuse the primary architectural elements of the South Gardens complex—Farquhar's dome and Hastings's tower—into a harmonious composition that captured the energy and optimism of the exhibition itself.

The Palace of Horticulture owed a great debt to a design for a conservatory and spring house Brown had designed in 1902 at the Ecole des Beaux-Arts; these were drawings undertaken shortly after Brown and Bennett had returned to Paris from a trip to Istanbul. Like Mullgardt's Court of the Ages, Brown's Palace of Horticulture also had an Islamic source and was modeled, in part, after the Blue Mosque of Ahmed I in Istanbul. Brown's glass dome rose above a sea of semi-domes and swelling skylights, a skylit peristyle, and soaring

pinnacles that were intended to recall minarets (fig. 2.20). And like the Carrère & Hastings tower, the detail employed at the Palace of Horticulture was rather more western in its references than eastern. The building was a study in the "free" French baroque and displayed coupled orders, mansard roofs, and a profuse variety of ornamental garlands, cartouches, and statuary. Most of this ornament was designed by Jean-Louis Bourgeois, who emphasized the festive nature of the building. Particularly charming was the use of John Bateman's caryatids along the colonnades flanking the entry pavilion and the crown of the dome, whose compression ring was resolved into an enormous fruit basket. Although some critics found its profusion of ornament too exuberant, the constructed building was considered second only to Maybeck's Palace of Fine Arts in architectural quality, and it was very well received by the public. William Woollett, who would be much more reserved about the use of ornament in San Francisco City Hall, proclaimed the Palace of Horticulture to be "a tour-de-force of exposition architecture . . . without exception the most electric, the most expressive, effervescent, playful bit of joyous architecture."[39]

The Palace of Horticulture was designed in analogy to a railroad terminal. Just as the polite and ornamented head-house of a major station was appended to a functional steel-and-glass train shed, the great domed main pavilion of the

2.20 (*above*). Bakewell & Brown, Palace of Horticulture, PPIE, 1915, entry concourse. Photograph, author's collection.

2.21 (*below*). Bakewell & Brown, Palace of Horticulture, PPIE, 1915, dome and greenhouse shed. Photograph, author's collection.

palace was affixed to a long steel-trussed exhibition building (fig. 2.21). Most of the horticulture exhibits were housed in this shed and alongside it in the exhibition garden, rather than in the main pavilion, which housed the tropical gardens. The domed hothouse was also distinctive in that it was the only exhibition building to be exempted from Director of Color Jules Guerin's official palette. Brown kept the exterior subdued, limiting the color in the building to a series of greens, as befitting a conservatory. At times the building was described as an iridescent soap bubble; in fact, the main dome was to have been fitted with opalescent glass that would have shimmered in the sun. Inside the great dome, however, W. D'Arcy Ryan, the PPIE's director of lighting, had a bolder concept: dozens of revolving colored lights threw images of heavenly bodies across the spherical surface in what he called an "electric kaleidoscope."[40] This lighting effect dazzled the viewers at the exposition. As Edwin Markham wrote: "I looked at the dome of the Palace of Horticulture and saw strange colors at play within its dark green depths. Circles and clefts of blue and red and green shifted, faded, and returned like hues within a fiery and living opal. It was the workshop of a maker of moons, who cast his globes aloft in trial flights."[41]

The Palace of Horticulture was not the only structure that Brown designed for the PPIE; he also designed complementing refreshment stands for Welch's Grape Juice and the Ghirardelli Chocolate company (fig. 2.22). These little jewel-like circular buildings stood at one edge of the main concourse as twin gatehouses to the amusement area called "the Zone." With these concession buildings, Brown continued his exploration of the florid French baroque—each was designed with as much attention to detail as a piece of cloisonné enamel work. The architectural features of the other buildings along the Zone were not quite as studied, but proved quite popular. The Sante Fe and Union Pacific Railroads, for example, produced stirring dioramas of the Grand Canyon and Yellowstone Park, respectively. The featured attraction of the Zone, however, was L. E. Meyer's scale model of the Panama Canal, which visitors viewed from a moving platform nearly half a mile long.

At its close, the PPIE was deemed a financial success that made its shareholders a $1 million profit after all expenses. The fair was also an artistic success, garnering praise for its innovative architectural planning and imaginative landscapes. Although the unbounded optimism that San Franciscans had intended to present to the world was chilled by the outbreak of the First World War, the PPIE was a successful community-building effort as well. More than a collection of plaster buildings and commercial presentations, it was a tangible representation of the city's pride in its reconstruction and its nearly unlimited confidence in its future. San Francisco believed itself to be the hub of an ever-expanding American empire of the Pacific, and the exposition gave the city the opportunity to demonstrate its continued domination of the eastern Pacific Rim while extolling the virtues of the region's economic, social, and political development.

2.22. Bakewell & Brown, Ghirardelli Chocolate Pavilion, PPIE, 1915. Photograph by Cardinell–Vincent Company, author's collection.

THE SANTA FE RAILROAD STATIONS AT REDLANDS AND SAN DIEGO

Coming from a railroading family, Brown was naturally interested in designing railroad stations. He had little luck, however, in procuring work from his father's firm; the structures group at the Southern Pacific did all of the design work in-house and therefore did not need Bakewell & Brown's services. The Atchison, Topeka, and Santa Fe (AT&SF) however, did employ local architects to design many of its facilities, and in fact promoted a unified architectural presence along the line. This corporate mission revival became a hallmark of the railroad and was even used in places where no Spanish settlement ever existed, such as on the Plains or in the Midwest.

2.23 (*above*). Bakewell & Brown, terminal for AT&SF Railroad, San Diego, 1915: view from downtown business district. Photograph by Passmore Photography, author's collection.

2.24 (*below*). Bakewell & Brown, terminal for AT&SF Railroad, San Diego, 1915, plan.

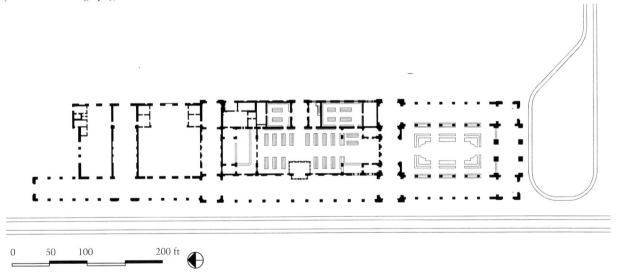

0   50   100   200 ft

Brown's first station for the Santa Fe was for the town of Redlands, in San Bernardino County. In 1909 the railroad required a new station to replace an earlier 1890 depot; Bakewell & Brown were given the job by W. B. Storey, vice president of the railroad and a personal friend of Brown's father.[42] Brown designed a small baggage room, ticketing office, and waiting room, all tucked within the shelter of a long colonnade whose coupled Tuscan columns march sever-

al hundred yards along the track. Each end is terminated with a simple pediment that carries the name of the town on its frieze. Behind each end twin monitor skylights rise several feet above the roof; these clerestories light the center of the platforms and provide some vertical counterpoints to this long, low composition.[43]

The Redlands depot is largely constructed of concrete, a material Brown used with ever-greater confidence after

2.25. Bakewell & Brown, terminal for AT&SF Railroad, San Diego, 1915: interior of waiting room. Photograph by Passmore Photography, author's collection.

Berkeley Town Hall. At Redlands the concrete simulated stone, and Brown carefully detailed the building to avoid any noncanonical elements. He studiously avoided the mission revival look of the railroad's earlier passenger stations, largely to emphasize the town's relatively recent, non-Hispanic origins. As Redlands was at the center of the citrus lands, Brown thought the analogy to the Franciscans friars who founded the California missions seemed forced. By contrast, he chose to emphasize the town's Mediterranean climate, and so he produced a building that both linked the site to the origins of the railroad and employed the classical language in a fresh interpretation. Brown was able to use concrete because the cost of the structure was underwritten by a group of civic boosters—the railroad paid little of the cost of the new facility. The

depot hosted its last passenger train many decades ago, but it is still an important landmark in its community.

Brown's second job for the AT&SF was the terminus at San Diego (fig. 2.23). As the gateway to the Panama–California Exposition, the building was to evoke a holiday spirit while providing a permanent embellishment for its city and serving as the surface transportation hub for downtown. The exposition, a companion of the greater PPIE in San Francisco, was intended to be a regional celebration of the West's development over the previous half-century and the high promise held by its future. The San Diego fair served as a second destination for the throngs of fairgoers from the East who toured California after viewing the PPIE. Indeed, it was many an easterner's first personal experience of Southern

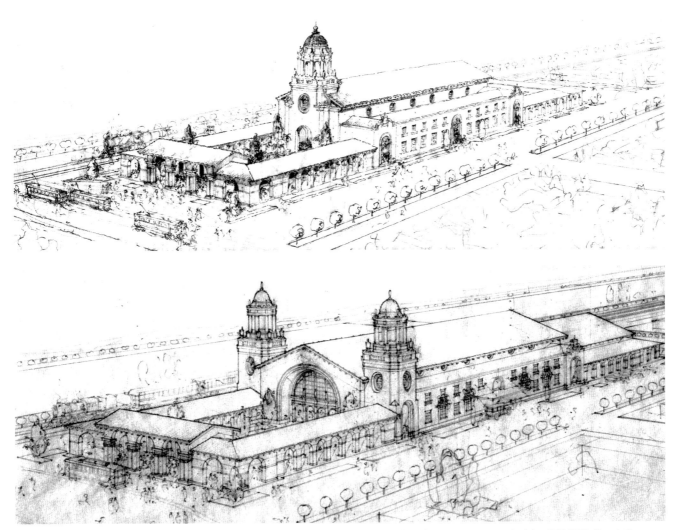

2.26 (*top*). Arthur Brown Jr., terminal for AT&SF Railroad, San Diego, 1913, cartoon for presentation drawing: single-towered alternative design. Arthur Brown Jr. Collection, Bancroft Library.

2.27 (*above*). Arthur Brown Jr., terminal for AT&SF Railroad, San Diego, 1913, cartoon for presentation drawing: double-towered alternative design. Arthur Brown Jr. Collection, Bancroft Library.

California. Bertram Grosvenor Goodhue's exposition buildings in Balboa Park are commonly credited with popularizing the Spanish colonial revival in California, and later in the rest of the Southwest and Florida. Goodhue's structures, particularly his California Pavilion, employed Plateresque and Churrigueresque ornamental devices at the focal points of the structures, and explored the potential of ceramic tile work and wood carving in exposition buildings. Brown's railroad terminal was several miles away from the exposition grounds in Balboa Park, between San Diego's downtown and the harbor, on the site of the Santa Fe's former station. Nonetheless, Bakewell & Brown felt it was important to tie the architecture of the building to that of the exposition and to the corporate identity of the Santa Fe, which at this time made extensive use of the mission style for its trackside structures.

The AT&SF terminus at San Diego incorporates motifs of both Californian and more sophisticated Latin American architectures into a building unified by an extended analogy to traditional sacred design and the functional requirements of a modern railway terminal (fig. 2.24). Like many of their contemporaries, Bakewell & Brown did not seek to duplicate the California missions but to borrow from them forms associated with Hispanic California. Bakewell described their strategy in an article for *The Architect and Engineer*: "The station is decidedly not an archaeological replica of one of the old missions. In its design an honest attempt has been made to build a building that appears to be what it is, a railway station, and yet which has the characteristics of the early California architecture; in other words, it was the aim of the of the architects to design a station as one of the Franciscan Fathers would have designed it had railway stations been built in his day."[44] This last is a rather large supposition! And yet, although Bakewell & Brown employed the most modern of materials—concrete over a steel frame—they started the design process with prototypes that would have been familiar to a Franciscan father. In particular, the parti of the building, with its gatehouse, atrium, narthex, and basilica, follows extant forms as old as S. Ambrogio in Milan, and ultimately dates back to Old St. Peter's. At San Diego, Brown transcended the French architectural vocabulary typically associated with the Beaux-Arts and demonstrated his mastery of Guadet's theory of typological composition—that the architect should interpret past architectural solutions in forging new typologies for the modern age. He adapted a prototypical

2.28. Arthur Brown Jr., terminal for AT&SF Railroad, San Diego, 1913, design-development drawing for western towers. Arthur Brown Jr. Collection, Bancroft Library.

form, the basilica, to a new building type, the railroad station, which by then had its own typological conventions, while employing the architectural motifs of Hispanic America; the result is one of the most original railroad stations in the nation.

Travelers entered the station precinct from the municipal trolley stop in front of the gatehouse. Beyond the triple archway, surrounded by an arcade, was a large outdoor waiting room, a desirable amenity in a city with weather as temperate as San Diego's. The station proper was entered through the yawning arch of the narthex, which led to the vaulted indoor waiting room. To the left, the arcade of the atrium continued through the western tower over 500 feet to form the train-side concourse. To the east of the waiting room Brown placed retiring rooms, rest rooms, and access to the second-floor railway offices; beyond, to the north, was the Harvey House, the station restaurant. The waiting room continued the ecclesiastical analogy (fig. 2.25). The space is formed around deep semicircular concrete arches, each bay twice the width of the arcade bay in the "aisles." The space was lighted by paired arched-top clerestories in the bays and a thermal window on the end that filled the entire wall. The walls were lined with a high wainscot of Moorish-style ceramic tiles, produced in San Diego to Brown's design. The counter furniture is as high as this wainscot, and from the end of the room these fixtures give the appearance of choir stalls.

From the evidence left in his papers, Brown worried most over the design of the towers that flanked the front of the building. Three perspective drawings from December 1913 survive in Brown's papers, each delineating a different scheme for the building (figs. 2.26, 2.27). All three were presented to Santa Fe executives, who apparently preferred the most elaborate alternative: the one with a pair of baroque towers. Brown explored many alternatives for the design of the towers and examined the arcaded second stage in detail—one late design presented an arcaded upper chamber, which was ornamented with wrought-iron balconies and flower boxes. In addition, the finials have been transformed into pinnacles, and the domes are tiled. Finally, Brown arrived at the constructed design in a drawing that graced the cover of the April 1912 issue of *The Architect and Engineer* (figs. 2.28, C.2). In this final design, the arches in the second stage are framed by pilasters and guarded by a balustrade, the finials above the entablature are transformed into urns, and small columned lanterns top the domes. These features, through rarely found in the California missions, are characteristic of the more sophisticated architecture of Mexico, South America, and Spain itself. In fact, Bakewell and Brown traveled to Mexico to see this Spanish baroque architecture for themselves sometime before the design of the San Diego terminal.

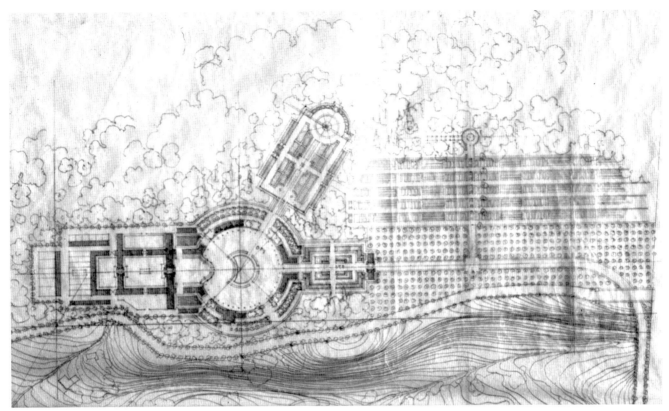

2.29. Bakewell & Brown, Filoli, Woodside, c. 1916, plan of extended farm complex, with orchards and vegetable terraces to the south and the ornamental garden and spring to the west. Drawing, Arthur Brown Jr. Collection, Bancroft Library.

FILOLI

Work at Stanford became the mainstay of Bakewell & Brown's office between the completion of San Francisco City Hall in 1916 and the end of World War I. However, one project from this period deserves mention for its employ of the grand design in large-scale domestic architecture and for the firm's collaboration with Willis Polk and Bruce Porter. William Bowers Bourn's Filoli illustrated the fusion of a large-scale architectural ensemble with an equally ordered landscape characteristic of planning in the grand manner. The talents of many design professionals were brought to bear on the property, but it fell to Bakewell & Brown to orchestrate the completion of the house and the schematic design of the extensive formal gardens.

Bourn, owner of the Empire Mine consortium, president and majority shareholder in the Spring Valley Water Company, and later a director of Pacific Gas & Electric, had commissioned two other residences from Willis Polk before he asked Polk to design a country estate for him on a large plot of land south of the Crystal Springs Reservoir, thirty

miles south of San Francisco. Polk first designed a house for Bourn in Presidio Heights, on Webster Street. Polk also designed the Empire Cottage at Bourn's Empire Mine, outside of Grass Valley in Nevada County. But the city house soon became confining to Bourn and his wife Agnes, and in 1915 Bourn asked Polk to draw up plans for yet another house. Polk designed a Georgian manor house that would offer the Bourns a suite of large formal rooms enfilade at the rear of the house. The following year Bakewell & Brown was hired to design a large farm complex to be located about one-half mile north of the house along Old Cañada Road.

Two schemes are known for this gentlemanly agricultural endeavor.[45] The first organizes the agricultural structures around a gated *cour d'honneur* to the south, reminiscent of Versailles, and a large square court to the north, which is accessed through a domed pavilion, like the court of the Luxembourg Palace. In the second scheme, more ambitious in scope, entry was on axis from a rigidly organized orchard through a formal gatehouse to a monumental *rond-point*, the center of which was marked with an ornamental pool (fig. 2.29). This space was bounded by auxiliary staff quarters

2.30 (*above*). Bakewell & Brown, Filoli, Woodside, c. 1916, isometric cartoon of farm buildings. Drawing, Arthur Brown Jr. Collection, Bancroft Library.

2.31 (*below*). Bakewell & Brown, Filoli, Woodside, November 26, 1919, design for the formal gardens. All of the essential elements of the Filoli gardens are in this drawing, although some details were altered or omitted in execution. Arthur Brown Jr. Collection, Bancroft Library.

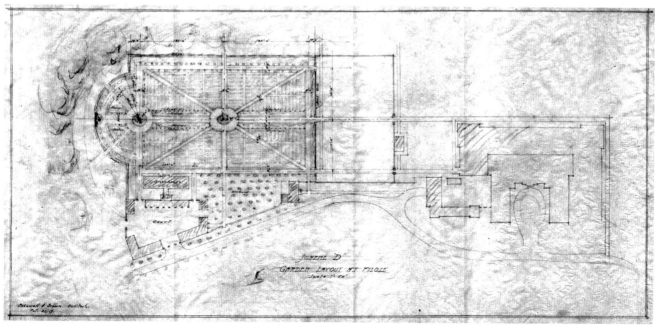

and the farm complex proper, which was doubled in size about the square court, the subsidiary barnyards having been moved beyond a second pavilion. In axonometric drawings of this scheme, these buildings are worked up in a rustic Norman vernacular, with steep thatched roofs and clipped dormers (fig. 2.30). In this second scheme, Brown struck a secondary, oblique axis radiating from the circular court, which ran to a cleft in the hills and a spring. Along this axis he arranged a formal flower garden and a nymphaeum, which repeated the circular forms of the larger court to the southeast.

Had Brown's schemes of 1916 and 1917 for Filoli been executed, they would have resulted in a garden complex that would have rivaled any in North America for size and audacity of design. As it happened, however, the sobering social and economic climate that accompanied America's entry into World War I denied Brown and Bourn the opportunity to build this model farm. Bourn radically altered his plans for Filoli as difficulties arose in completing the main house; in the end he asked Bakewell & Brown to oversee the completion of Polk's design and to plan a more manageable garden next to the house.[46]

In late 1917, Bakewell & Brown designed the garage and servant's quarters for the estate. Brown integrated this service structure into the garden, setting the structure on axis with a sunken water garden. He marked this axis on the roof with a cupola that recalls a domed version of Willis Polk's Sunol Water Temple; this incidental detail has become the hallmark of the entire estate (fig. C.3). Brown also proposed that a walled garden be set to the south of the house, its central axis to be struck just to the west of the large terrace that faced the formal rooms of the main house. As this garden scheme was realized, Brown prepared designs for the garden house to be set into the north wall, at first in a rusticated Cinquecento mode, and then in a lighter eighteenth-century Palladian style more in keeping with the Georgian architecture of the manor house.

Toward the end of 1919, Brown once again drew up plans for structures at Filoli, this time the gardener's sheds and greenhouses. More importantly, he was also asked to plan the rest of the garden to the south of the walled garden. In a plan surviving in the Brown Papers, a drawing labeled "Scheme D" demonstrates that Brown devised the form of these gardens and calculated the necessary dimensions (fig. 2.31). The garden was divided into four quadrants, through which diagonal paths were to be struck (these were not carried out). An allée of trees along the primary longitudinal axis led to an apsidal colonnade at the "High Place," from which a view of the entire estate was to be had. While Bakewell & Brown superintended the construction of the hardscape of the grounds, Bruce Porter and Isabella Worn chose the plant materials and accent pieces. Throughout the 1920s, Brown

was also consulted on the decoration of the house, particularly for the ballroom, for which he received nominal fees as late as 1927. Although Filoli is a later manifestation of the country house movement, it rightfully takes its place alongside the estates of the eastern seaboard as an expression of this influential mode of living.

MARRIAGE AND ACADEME

World War I devastated the building industry in California. By the end of 1916 Bakewell & Brown had very little work in the office, although a few projects at Stanford and a few houses on the peninsula were still under construction. The partners used the lull in business to tend to aspects of their lives that were postponed during the four-year "charette" that was the San Francisco City Hall project. Foremost on Brown's agenda was his marriage to Jessamine Garrett of Seattle (figs. 2.32, 2.33). Born in 1884 in New Orleans to a Louisiana family, Garrett considered herself something of a southern lady, although she was raised almost entirely in Seattle, where her father and brothers ran successful manufacturing concerns. She was an elegant and beautiful young woman, with light skin, dark hair, and sparkling, commanding eyes.

Brown met Jessamine in Seattle through Frère Champney's mother, Elizabeth, who was a prominent member of the congregation of St. Mark's Episcopal Cathedral, where the Garretts also worshiped. It appears that the introductions were first made in 1909, when Brown traveled to Seattle to visit Champney and see the Alaska–Yukon–Pacific International Exposition. "Jazz" and "Arturo" were betrothed as early as 1914 but delayed their wedding until completion of San Francisco City Hall; they were married on July 19, 1916, in Seattle, with Frère Champney acting as Brown's best man. Upon their nuptials the newlyweds leased the Avenali House, a residence on Russian Hill Brown had designed some years earlier.[47] This setting permitted him time to enjoy the company of his immediate neighbors, the Livermores, the Polks, and Rev. Joseph Worcester, and allowed him easy access to the firm's offices on Kearny Street.

In these early years Jessamine made Brown an ideal architect's wife. She possessed a formidable intelligence and a quick wit, and was dedicated to the promotion of her husband's career. The two considered themselves equal partners in their relationship, perhaps signified by their identical height (both stood 5 feet 6 inches tall), and each possessed characteristics that complemented the other. Arthur had an easy sociability and an obvious creative temperament, but he could be overly trusting and was loath to publicize his accomplishments. Jessamine saw the bigger picture and cultivated relationships that would be advantageous to her or

2.32. Brandon Johnson, Portrait of Arthur Brown Jr., pastel on paper, early 1920s. Private collection.

2.33. Brandon Johnson, Portrait of Jessamine Garrett Brown, pastel on paper, early 1920s. Private collection.

Arthur; her socializing often had a purpose behind it. She was fiercely protective of her husband and would notice any slight or disadvantage that might come his way and move to rectify it. This sometimes caused Arthur some embarrassment, as Jessamine could be quite direct, but usually her efforts ensured that Arthur received the notice his work deserved.

The Browns shared one personality trait: they were both careful with money. Each found parting with a dollar nearly painful, and they spent only what was absolutely necessary for their needs, and then only after extensive negotiation. This tendency to conserve the family purse became something of a joke among Brown's friends; fortunately it did not extend to Brown's employees, who were generally well paid. But many of his acquaintances noted that although he could be extremely generous with his praise, his talents, and his time, Brown rarely volunteered to pick up a check.

Brown's contentment with his newly married life was short-lived. Nine months after his wedding, in March 1917, his father died of old age; his mother died the following

August, a victim of that year's influenza epidemic. Brown was now burdened with the task of settling both his parents' affairs at once. He was devastated by the loss of his parents and longed for a change of scenery and purpose. Fortuitously, he was offered a teaching post at Harvard University.

This interest in an academic career did not come to Brown as a momentary convenience; he had been teaching young draftsmen the rudiments of architectural design for years. Soon after forming Bakewell & Brown both architects had become involved with the San Francisco Architectural Club, an organization of architectural drafters, construction clerks, and students that provided practical training and theoretical instruction in architecture outside of the university setting. The club sponsored a biannual exhibition and a number of teaching ateliers based on the French model that provided instruction in architectural design and criticism of student work. The students generally worked problems taken from the Ecole itself, or from programs written by the Beaux-Arts Institute of Design, a New York body that coordinated a nationwide system of architectural clubs and smaller univer-

2.34 (*above*). Edward Frick, elevation, design for a hydroelectric dam, c. 1912, Atelier Bourgeois & Brown, San Francisco Architectural Club. Glass negative, Arthur Brown Jr. Collection, Bancroft Library.

2.35 (*below*). Edward Frick, plan, design for a hydroelectric dam, c. 1912, Atelier Bourgeois & Brown, San Francisco Architectural Club. Glass negative, Arthur Brown Jr. Collection, Bancroft Library.

sity programs. Students attended lectures and critiques in the evening, after the day's work was done, and could prepare themselves for an academic degree in architecture or for a state registration exam.

Brown ran an atelier with Jean-Louis Bourgeois. The students met in rented rooms near Brown's office, eventually settling in the Charleston Building when Bakewell & Brown relocated its offices there. Many of Brown's students were, or became, draftsmen in his office, and many returned to the firm upon their graduation from an architectural program on the East Coast or even in Paris. All of Brown's junior associates, including Edward Frick, Ernest Weihe, Lawrence Kruse, and Carl I. Warnecke, attended Brown's atelier. As students they designed a series of architectural projects that progressed from the simple to the very complex. Some of the introductory course work consisted of overtly historical studies, such as a "Romanesque Chapel" or an "Egyptian Rock-Cut Tomb," but many of the design projects of the upper grades were surprisingly contemporary, such as Edward Frick's design for a hydroelectric dam, executed in 1913 (figs. 2.34, 2.35) or the "Aeronautical School" of January 1917.

The most advanced of Brown's students competed for the Paris Prize, which entitled the winner to study at the Ecole des Beaux-Arts. Although several of Brown's students did well in this national competition, Ernest Weihe did the best: he won first place in the 1919 competition with his design for a great cathedral, obviously modeled on Victor Laloux's Prix de Rome project of 1878 (fig. 2.36). Weihe stayed at the Ecole until 1923 when his scholarship expired.[48] Weihe was not the only Bakewell & Brown employee to study in Paris. As described earlier, John Chandler left for Paris in 1908. Edward Frick traveled to Paris in 1914, only to see his studies cut short by the war.[49] As late as the 1930s, Brown continued to send students to Paris; his most successful student of that period must be Edgar Preston Ames, who became a leading set designer for MGM.[50]

Brown's decision to go to Harvard was not a casual expediency. Harvard had been relentlessly recruiting him since the departure in 1914 of E. J. A. Duquesne, chief design instructor in the Architecture Department. Although Brown was tempted by the offer of a chaired professorship and the cultural life of Boston, he had repeatedly declined Harvard's overtures, citing his work on San Francisco City Hall and the need to stay close to his parents.[51] By late 1917 both of these constraints were in the past, and Brown agreed to a trial semester in Boston. It did not go well because only a handful of students remained in school by the spring term of 1918—most had joined the service or were involved in defense work. Moreover, wartime conditions dampened the cultural life Brown and his wife had anticipated.[52] Despite these travails, Harvard again offered a full professorship to Brown, which he once more politely refused, having made up his mind to remain forever a Californian. Although a split-year arrangement was discussed for another several years, Brown formally severed his ties to Harvard in 1918.

In the fall of 1918 Bakewell left the firm for an extended period. In September he joined a Red Cross unit in eastern France and served for nearly a year. In his absence Brown tended to the office (a part-time occupation in 1919) and temporarily filled another academic position at the University of California, when John Galen Howard took a sabbatical in the spring of 1919. Although the student body at the University of California was also reduced by the war, Brown was able to guide a few seniors through their thesis projects, among them was William Wurster.[53] With Howard's return later in the year, Brown's formal academic career as a professor of architecture ended, although he continued the sponsorship of his atelier at the San Francisco Architectural Club into the 1920s.

The revival of the building industry in the years after World War I afforded Bakewell & Brown a second phase of their partnership. In their seven years together after Bakewell's return from France, they would design and construct some of their most noteworthy and innovative works of architecture. At the same time the growing acclaim Brown was receiving for his design talents emphasized the disparity between the two partners' talents and ambitions. Although this strain would eventually cause Brown to disassociate himself from Bakewell, he was always mindful of the professionalism and friendship Bakewell brought to the partnership, and he would always look back with pride on their greatest accomplishment: the design and construction of San Francisco City Hall.

2.36 (opposite). Ernest Weihe, Paris Prize entry for a metropolitan cathedral, 1919, Atelier Brown, San Francisco Architectural Club. Glass negative, Arthur Brown Jr. Collection, Bancroft Library.

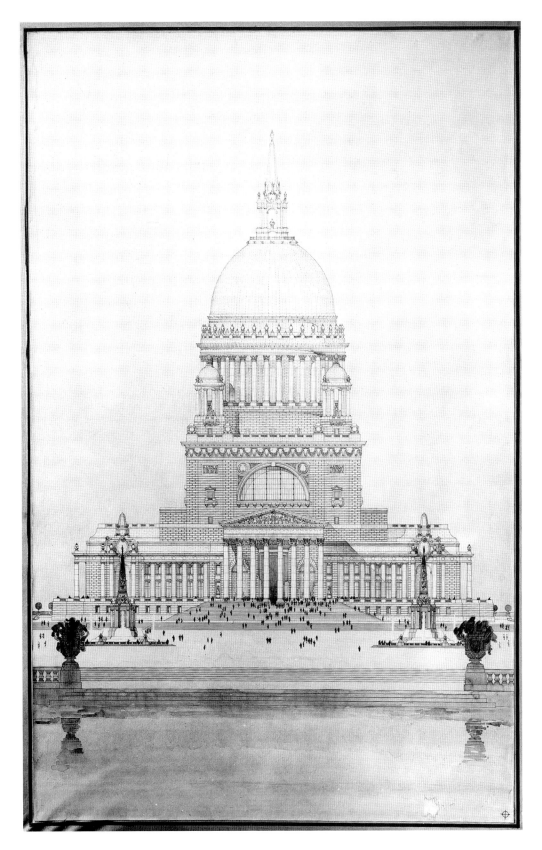

3.1. Bakewell & Brown, San Francisco City Hall, 1916, view
from the civic center plaza. Photograph by John Channing for
The Architect and Engineer, author's collection.

CHAPTER THREE

THE SAN FRANCISCO CIVIC CENTER

*Floating in the fog, the perfect dome of the City Hall rises in sharp outline against the sunny Mission,
its contours as noble as St. Paul's in London or St. Peter's in Rome. On a quiet Sunday, you can see
the great building for what it is—cold and clean, far above the little people who clutter its halls,
gather in scheming knots on its wide stairs, and plot their little plots in its timeless shadows.*[1]

—HERB CAEN

The San Francisco Civic Center is acknowledged as one of the masterpieces of the American renaissance. The most complete and vital of the many City Beautiful civic centers proposed and begun in the decades between the World's Columbian Exposition of 1893 and the Great Depression, the twelve buildings that surround the city hall and its plaza constitute one of the finest municipal groups in the nation. Planned in several phases between 1899 and 1912, the original civic center blueprint has been extended to encompass a far richer variety of civic institutions than originally contemplated. Despite this programmatic diversity, the buildings are unified in their adherence to planning guidelines developed at the beginning of the project and in their deference to the focal point of the ensemble, the great dome of Bakewell & Brown's city hall (fig. 3.1).

Most interpretations of the San Francisco Civic Center have concentrated on its planning history.[2] While the formal aspects of the civic center's design most overtly recall the ideals of the American renaissance and the City Beautiful movement, the array of institutions represented within the group and the history of the center's design and construction demonstrate the close parallels between these ideals and the political and social aims of the Progressive movement. At its initial completion in the 1920s, the center confirmed to San Franciscans not only the resurrection of the city from the inferno of the earthquake and fire of 1906, but the return of its municipal government to the people from both the Southern Pacific Railroad and a series of corrupt political bosses.

PLANNING THE SAN FRANCISCO CIVIC CENTER

As a city that grew from a collection of shacks to a world metropolis in less than two decades, San Francisco has always been keenly aware of its own development, and has often attempted to solve political and economic problems through architecture and urban design. San Francisco first attempted to plan systematically its urban form at the turn of the twentieth century. By the late 1890s San Francisco was no longer the teeming boom town of the mid-nineteenth century; its gangly youth had given way to middle-aged spread. The Second Empire commercial and financial district of the city was punctuated by the West's first skyscrapers; these prominent structures were built by the robber barons of the 1860s and 1870s, whose precious metals from the Sierra Nevada and the Comstock Lode were funneled through San Francisco, from which they were shipped east on the Central Pacific Railroad.[3] As in many an entrepôt, the profits in this lucrative trade were displayed in bricks and mortar.

Yet the building boom the city experienced at the turn of the century masked an uncertainty about the future. In comparison to the boom years of the 1860s and 1870s, the last twenty years of the nineteenth century cast a sort of malaise over the city. Civic boosters were concerned that San Francisco's growth and economic prosperity were lagging behind that of Los Angeles. In particular, the city's infrastructure was viewed by many as a serious impediment to further development. Examples of the city's civic inadequa-

3.2. Arthur Brown Jr.?, designs for the Burnham Plan for
San Francisco, 1905, the amphitheatre, Daniel Burnham et al., *Report
on the Improvement and Adornment of San Francisco*, unpaginated.

cies abounded—the sewers were spewing filth into the bay at
over 125 locations along the shore; the public health facilities counted only 500 hospital beds for the population of
350,000; and the waterfront had not been modernized for
decades.[4]

By 1899 the situation was bad enough to prompt several
independent efforts at civic beautification, all of which
focused on the creation of some sort of grouping of institutional buildings on the upper (southwestern) end of Market Street.
These efforts would eventually meld into a workable plan for
the present civic center. However, between 1899 and 1912, the
year of the plan's adoption by the electorate, the city's economy was rocked by general strikes, the downtown business district burned to the ground, and many municipal officials were
indicted on conspiracy and bribery charges. The volatile conditions of these years gave those advocating a civic center time
to perfect the eventual plan and earn support.

The first champion of a civic center for San Francisco
was James K. Phelan, a successful banker and three-time
mayor who sponsored and ensured adoption of the
Burnham Report for San Francisco of 1905. He was converted to the City Beautiful aesthetic and its progressive
political tenets while managing the California exhibit at
the World's Columbian Exhibition in Chicago. Determined
to bring the White City to San Francisco, Phelan was the

first politician in the city's history to attempt to salve the
city's ills with urban design. He was elected mayor in 1896
on a reform platform that called for a new city charter and
a program of civic improvements modeled on those of
Athens, Paris, and Vienna. Phelan faced several structural
obstacles to achieving his vision. His full program of parks,
hospitals, utilities, and street widenings would have
required a very large bonded indebtedness, which was limited by state law to 15 percent of the city's assessed property value. He also tried to extend the Golden Gate Park
panhandle to Market Street, but this project was derailed
when a general strike of teamsters and dockworkers forced
him out of office in the fall of 1901. This same election
brought Union Labor Party boss Abraham Ruef and Mayor
Eugene Schmitz to power.[5] Much of Schmitz's early terms
were spent quelling labor unrest and building an elaborate
political machinery that institutionalized graft. Watching
on the sidelines as his years of good government and con-
sequent civic improvements were undone by blatant
bribery and kickback schemes, Phelan organized an independent effort to save the city by political and urbanistic
means: he initiated an investigation that led to Schmitz's
indictment on conspiracy charges in October 1906, and he
pushed through the adoption of the *Plan for the
Improvement and Adornment of San Francisco*.

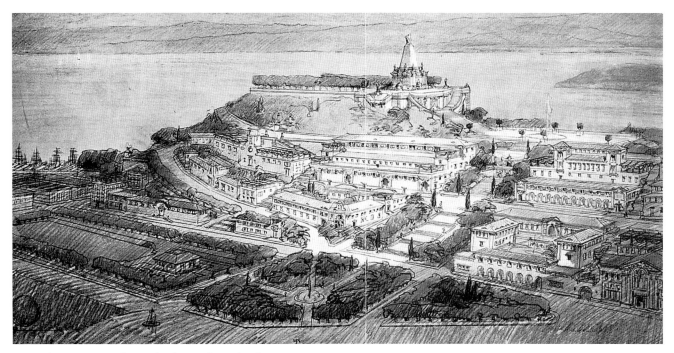

3.3. Arthur Brown Jr.?, designs for the Burnham Plan for
San Francisco, 1905, Telegraph Hill, looking east, showing suggested
architectural treatment. Daniel Burnham et al., *Report on the
Improvement and Adornment of San Francisco*, unpaginated.

Phelan began the planning process with a call in the San
Francisco *Bulletin* for a general plan for the city, to be "prepared by a competent person or commission, as has been
done recently for the city of Washington, D.C., and
Cleveland, Ohio."[6] Phelan invited a group of "representative
men" to meet with him and other leaders at the Merchant's
Exchange Building to discuss the future of the city. At this
meeting twenty-six such citizens ratified Phelan's suggestion
to ask Daniel Burnham to create a master plan for San
Francisco.[7] Burnham had not yet been given the opportunity
to redesign an entire city—the San Francisco commission
offered him just that. He thought of San Francisco as the perfect Mediterranean-type setting for the City Beautiful and
was anxious to see this dream realized.

Burnham sent Edward Bennett to San Francisco to lead
the firm's effort on the plan. Bennett in turn arranged for the
assistance of Polk, who built the company a small house and
studio on Twin Peaks, a double-crested hill in the geographic center of the city, from which much of the city could be
surveyed.[8] By late September 1904, Bennett and Polk were
constant occupants of the place. As the study gave way in
1905 to design and drafting, local assistance was required.
Bennett acknowledged Arthur Brown along with Willis Polk
and John McLaren as having assisted "in the study of various
architectural problems."[9] Several sections of the plan were

illustrated by Brown, including the "Playground North of
Washington Square," the Amphitheater, the "Atheneum,"
and redeveloped terraces for Telegraph Hill (figs. 3.2, 3.3).[10]

The plan of 1905 derives its proposals and form from
Burnham's conceptual view of the ideal city. Such a city (he
used Paris as his primary example) is built around a set of
monumental civic buildings, from which radiate grand diagonal streets and concentric boulevards. Buildings of particular importance to the life of the city are placed at the inter-
sections of these avenues, on prominent topography.[11] In a
gesture to San Francisco's hope of becoming the capital of an
American–Pacific empire, Burnham asked the citizens of San
Francisco to conform to this ideal by constructing monumental boulevards and civic structures, despite the rather
severe topography and the fragmented nature of the San
Francisco urban form (fig. 3.4).

The civic center of the 1905 plan was largely designed by
Bennett, with assistance from Polk. It took the form of a
landscaped ring-road rather than that of one unified urban
set-piece (fig. 3.5). Specifically, the intersection of Market
and Van Ness was to become the "Central Rond Point,"
from which nine grand boulevards were to radiate. At some
distance beyond this central point were subsidiary squares,
at which Burnham located important structures, including
the existing city hall. These monuments were linked to

3.4. Edward H. Bennett, plan of San Francisco, showing system of circuit and radial arteries, and its communication with San Mateo County, 1905. Daniel Burnham et al., *Report on the Improvement and Adornment of San Francisco*, unpaginated.

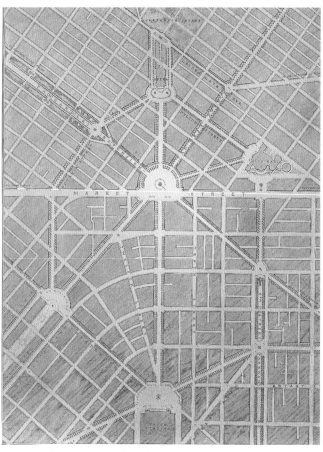

3.5. Edward H. Bennett, "Plan of Civic Center," 1905. The radial form of this civic center, with its widely spaced monuments, recalls Paris and Vienna rather than the "courthouse square" typical of American civic centers and as adopted at San Francisco. Daniel Burnham et al., *Report on the Improvement and Adornment of San Francisco*, unpaginated.

each other through tree-lined boulevards, some of which were existing streets, widened, whereas others were completely new diagonal thoroughfares. Although the plan specified the plantings and cross sections of the boulevards, it did not identify the architectural character of the new monuments.

At the same time B. J. S. Cahill offered his unsolicited opinion on the matter of a civic center. He drew up a plan for a civic grouping around a two-block central square, which would be bounded by a library, Mechanics Pavilion, and old city hall; this scheme is the origin of the realized civic center. Cahill had a drawing of his idea published in the newspapers and personally sent copies of the plan to Phelan in New York and Burnham in Chicago (fig. 3.6). However, Bennett was more interested in parks and boulevards than a civic center, and did not feel compelled to

include Cahill's schemes in the final report. Cahill felt betrayed by Burnham's and Bennett's indifference to his plan, and thus began a campaign to frustrate any civic center campaign based on the 1905 plan. His efforts would succeed, and in the end his plan of 1904 became the model for the civic center. However, in recompense for his obstructionist position, Cahill had no official role with the Civic Center Commission, nor did he receive any credit for his contribution to the design.[12]

THE EARTHQUAKE AND FIRE AND THEREAFTER

Burnham's plan was enthusiastically received at its completion in September 1905. The Board of Supervisors accepted the plan within the month and arranged to have over two thousand copies printed as soon as practicable.[13] Before anything more could be done, however, one-third of San Francisco burned to the ground on April 18–21, 1906. The fire gave the city's planners a near tabula rasa on which to work; only thirty or so buildings survived completely intact within the 2,600-acre burned district.[14] Ironically, Augustus Laver's city hall was one of the few buildings that was destroyed by the earthquake rather than by the fire. For a short time in 1906, San Franciscans united to reestablish control over their urban environment and forgot the political divisions that had characterized land-use policy before the calamity.

Despite this tempting opportunity to adopt the Burnham plan, the citizens of San Francisco found it too radical a reworking of the city's street infrastructure to be implemented. Almost every change Burnham proposed involved structures that had survived the fire, and the public was in no mood to spend its scarce resources on the civic improvements Burnham detailed. Those structures merely damaged in the fire were quickly rehabilitated, while the rest of the burned area was rebuilt much in the previous manner, but taller and better constructed. Few of these buildings conformed in any meaningful way to the 1905 plan. The reconstruction of San Francisco's municipal infrastructure lagged behind the rebuilding of private interests. A series of bond issues proposed for this reconstruction was defeated at the ballot box, including the 1909 effort to appropriate funds for a reduced version of Burnham's civic center.[15] The city's failure to make the civic improvements so obviously required was primarily due to the collapse of the municipal government during the graft prosecutions of 1906–9.

The graft prosecutions were part of the more encompassing reforms of the California progressives, an amalgamation of small business, agricultural, and professional interests dedicated to liberating state and municipal governments from the stranglehold of the Southern Pacific Railroad. For the first forty years of its existence, the railroad had simply bought the government it required, arranging for the election or appointment of local, state, and federal officeholders, regardless of political party. In the last decades of the nineteenth century details of the corporation's manipulation of government officials and its unfair rate structures encouraged Californians to nominate, if not actually to elect, non-railroad politicians to statewide and national office.[16] Cheered by these near victories and Theodore Roosevelt's reforms on the federal level, progressives such as Phelan attempted to purge the cities of corruption in preparation for a reform of the state and federal governments under the Progressive Republican banner.

The graft prosecutions began with a sensational newspaper story on September 11, 1906, which claimed that Abraham Ruef had received $20,000 from the Southern Pacific's William Herrin for delivering the city's votes for the railroad's candidate in the Republican gubernatorial primary the previous summer. The ensuing investigations of the San Francisco city government led to the indictment and prosecution of seventeen of eighteen supervisors, the mayor, and Ruef on various bribery and jury-tampering charges.[17] The political divisions fueled by these prosecutions led to unprecedented violence, including the kidnapping of one witness, the bombing of a supervisor's home, the murder of the former police chief, and the attempted murder of the lead prosecutor, Francis J. Heney, in open court. Before the prosecutions ended in 1911, nearly every municipal official was forced to resign, and many of the city's leading citizens were suspected of collaboration with the deposed regime. The graft prosecutions took on a statewide importance as several members of the prosecution achieved notoriety and eventually higher office, including Hiram Johnson, who was elected governor in 1910, and who instituted the most sweeping reforms in the state constitution's history the following year.

Ironically, the tide of public opinion that swept the reformers to statewide office turned against the prosecutors in San Francisco as men of capital were indicted in 1909 and 1910. The public grew uneasy at the thought of its most prominent citizens under threat of prosecution, and became outright hos-

3.6. B. J. S. Cahill, "Civic Center Plan of 1904," redrawn in 1909. Published in the San Francisco *Examiner* in 1904 and 1909, reprinted in *The Architect and Engineer 54*, no. 2 (August 1918): 72.

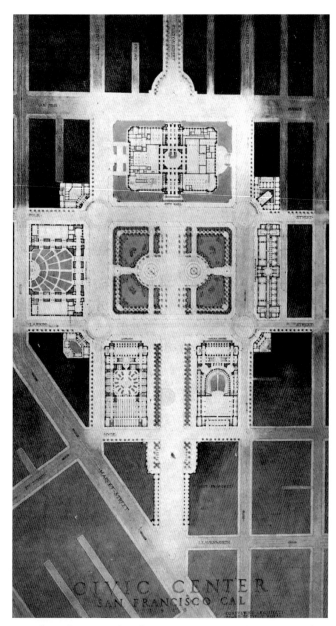

3.7. John Galen Howard et al., San Francisco Civic Center, 1912, plan. Engraving reproduced in program for the groundbreaking ceremony for San Francisco City Hall, April 5, 1913.

tile when several of Ruef's associates, including Mayor Schmitz, had their convictions overturned on appeal. In the end, only Ruef went to prison for any length of time.[18] Despite rising public sentiment against the graft prosecutions, they were just the cathartic collective experience necessary to spur the electorate to long overdue civic improvement. The civic center became the expression of this new-found community spirit.

PLANNING THE CIVIC CENTER

The civic center is a primary legacy of San Francisco's reform mayor, James P. Rolph, first elected to office in 1911 on a civic-improvement platform. His first achievement was to secure fair labor agreements for the city's most important unions, without whose support no large-scale construction would be possible. He then initiated the installation of a city-owned streetcar line down Market Street and into the outlying districts of the Mission, Richmond, and Sunset, thus breaking up the Southern Pacific's monopoly on public conveyances within the city.[19] These works underway, Rolph then turned his attention to the civic center.

Rolph began the planning process for the civic center even before his inauguration by asking the architects of the city for their suggestions as to the location and planning of the municipal group, which at that time included only a city hall and the exposition auditorium.[20] Over fifty architects responded, including Bakewell & Brown, and as one might expect, these suggestions largely fell into two camps: those that supported a group at Van Ness and Market, following the Burnham Plan, and those that supported a group centered on the ruins of the old city hall.[21] An advisory committee of several architects was consulted further about the plans, and these again split into two factions: the majority favored the old city hall site, and the minority, namely Willis Polk and Edward Bennett, defended their work on the Burnham Plan. On January 29, 1912, the Board of Supervisors formally adopted the former site, called for a special election for the approval of a bond issue for the civic center, and charged the mayor with selecting a three-member Board of Advisory Architects to assist the Public Buildings Committee of the Board of Supervisors in the planning of a civic center and the erection of a new city hall.[22]

The advisory architects, later employed by the city to head the city architect's office and given the title of "consulting architects," included chair John Galen Howard, professor of architecture at Berkeley and master planner of that campus; Frederick Meyer, president of the San Francisco chapter of the American Institute of Architects; and John Reid Jr., a young architect and former student of Howard, who was also the mayor's brother-in-law. This triumvirate prepared a site plan of the civic center to accompany the bond election materials.[23] This plan was very close to that of Bernard J. S. Cahill's published proposals of 1904 and 1909, in that a formal group of buildings was distributed about a two-block green bounded by Larkin, McAllister, Polk, and Grove streets and organized about a central axis on Fulton Street (fig. 3.7).[24] Unencumbered by the existing conditions of 1904, however, the advisory architects were able to bring together a more comprehensive range of state and municipal services than was possible before

3.8. John Galen Howard et al., "San Francisco Civic Center," 1912, bird's-eye perspective. Ink and watercolor drawing, collection of the Department of Public Works, City of San Francisco.

the fire, and they were able to specify programs for each contributing facility (fig. 3.8).

Once a suitable design was determined, Mayor Rolph pushed for its realization with great zeal. Rolph called for a special election on March 28, 1912, on which day the citizenry was to vote on an $8.8 million bond issue to cover the costs of acquiring the land in the civic center district and of constructing a $4 million city hall. Rolph and the city's many civic improvement groups undertook an unprecedented media campaign in support of the bond, arguing for the civic center on aesthetic, financial, and practical grounds. Significantly, women's groups were particularly active in the campaign, because the bond election was the first in which women were allowed to vote in California. The bond won approval by an overwhelming eleven-to-one margin, the largest victory for any ballot issue in the city's history.[25] This mandate for the civic center was more than a demand for municipal bricks and mortar, although the city desperately needed permanent quarters; the vote was also a resounding endorsement of the Rolph administration, which promised the first stable and clean government the city had seen in over a decade, and a signal that the city might finally find the collective spirit that would make it a true community. As the *Call* editorialized on the morning after the election:

> [City] Hall, auditorium, opera house, state building, library, museum—these, with the spacious grounds and the broad Avenues about them, will make the home and lodging place of the municipal conscience and municipal pride. They will be evidence that at last we learned how to do collectively what had been long before accomplished by individual initiative and effort—learned how to labor together, as apart, for the general as well as the private good. . . . The Call congratulates the citizens of San Francisco on this outcome—congratulates the women voters upon their part in bringing it about, and especially congratulates Mayor Rolph and his colleagues in office upon the success that has crowned their unselfish efforts.[26]

Mayor Rolph wasted no time in proceeding with the development of the civic center. Despite his other reforms, he knew that the success of his administration would be established by the realization of the two great Cities Beautiful planned for his municipality: the ephemeral "Evanescent City" of the Panama-Pacific International Exhibition and the permanent "People's Center" two miles south on Van Ness Avenue. While the Exposition Company was seeing to the fair and fronting the money for the cost of the Exposition Auditorium in the civic center, the mayor and his fledgling civil service would have to manage the design and construction of a new city hall with one-half the budget and in one-eighth the time of its predecessor.

THE ARCHITECTURAL COMPETITION FOR SAN FRANCISCO CITY HALL

The day after the election Rolph proposed the reorganization of the Bureau of Architecture, so that the advisory architects would have full control of the architectural plans for the civic center. The same day Rolph and Howard announced the terms of the architectural competition for city hall. All architects who maintained an office in San Francisco as of January 1, 1912, were eligible to compete.[27] A dossier outlining the regulations of the competition, delimiting the project site, and describing the program for the building was distributed to each competitor on April 6, 1912. The entrants were given just over two months to complete their submissions, which were to be sealed in anonymous packages and presented to the Board of Public Works on June 15, 1912.

Although no architectural mode was advocated by the consulting architects, their competition program was quite detailed in its description of the desired massing of the working portion of the building and the spaces required of each department.[28] The program specified a rectangular four-story building enclosing no more than 8 million cubic feet of volume, which would house twenty-five distinct departmental groups in 236,000 square feet of useable space. The prescribed massing block was chamfered at the corners to accommodate the oblique frontage of Marshall Square and Market Street at the southeast corner of the site. Contestants were guided as to the jury's aesthetic sense only by the statement that "a dominating monumental feature may be introduced at the intersection of the street axes [of Fulton and Eighth streets]."[29] The specifications for the drawings were as meticulous as the building program, and led some to charge that the competition favored those trained in Paris or on the East Coast. Although these restrictions forced many of the competitors to work in a manner to which they were unaccustomed, they also guaranteed a uniformity among the entries and some anonymity among the entrants. The competition generally ran smoothly, despite one significant change in the brief made in early May. Sensing that the old city hall site would not be cleared in a timely fashion, the consulting architects polled the competitors about swapping the sites of the city hall with those of the opera house and library—that is, moving the building to the blocks bounded by Van Ness, Grove, Polk, and McAllister. The new site was deemed superior by the architectural community and adopted.[30]

By June 15, seventy-three submissions had been received at the Board of Public Works. The consulting architects uncrated the drawings, numbered them in order of their receipt, and hung them together in a large room in the Bankers Investment Building on Market Street. Not surprisingly, a central dome dominated a number of the submitted designs, as it recalled the old city hall and also suggested a county seat. Other competitors took a cue from the Oakland City Hall competition of 1910 and accented their designs with a tower that was either strictly ornamental or functional, such as Ralph Warner Hart's design, which was large enough to accommodate a dozen or more floors of office space. A smaller group of designs employed no overtly monumental accent at all and, like Bernard Maybeck, screened their entries with long colonnades.[31] For four days the jury deliberated over the submissions, gradually eliminating them, until design thirty-three, Bakewell & Brown's, was declared to merit the $25,000 first prize and the presumed right to design the city hall.[32]

The selection of Bakewell & Brown was popular with the public, the press, and the architectural establishment. The two youngish architects were truly all things to all people—they were local boys making good, as well as foreign-educated and

WEST ELEVATION

SAN FRANCISCO CITY HALL COMPETITION

3.9. Bakewell & Brown, San Francisco City Hall, 1912, competition
drawing for west elevation. Arthur Brown Jr. Collection, Bancroft
Library. Photograph of drawing courtesy of Moulin Archives.

eastern-trained, thus belonging to both the "native" and the "academic" factions of the Bay Area architectural profession. The newspaper coverage stressed the simplicity in the planning of the design, that the architectural effect of the structure would be "obtained by well distributed masses rather than by an attempt at originality of composition or ornamentation."[33] The drawings, too, were considered a notable achievement in their own right (fig. 3.9). As B. J. S. Cahill described them, "they have the lightness and daintiness of the etcher's needle." In his review, he commented: "The great fault most generally felt with most of the drawings was in the planning. Most of the competitors seemed to have been too soon satisfied; to have spent much too little time on small scale sketches and full scale studies. The plans of Bakewell & Brown give all evidence of exhaustive study."[34] Bakewell & Brown could devote "exhaustive study" to their entry because there was hardly any work in the office at the time; within weeks of their winning the San Francisco City Hall competition, however, they entered the busiest period of their professional lives.

Designing San Francisco City Hall

Bakewell and Brown were perhaps not quite as surprised by their victory as the public believed. The young firm had some recent experience in designing city halls, and Brown had begun to study the old city hall in 1911, when it was suggested that the building be salvaged. A drawing from that year, now in the Library of Congress, shows Brown's first attempts to crown the awkward remains of the structure with a large dome (fig. 3.10).[35] Brown's efforts to manipulate the dome continued once the competition for the city hall was announced. On the back of a letter Brown sketched out several initial ideas for the building, including a tower design (fig. 3.11). The most fully realized of these ideas described a staged tower-dome, in which a high, domed central space on a piano nobile would itself be surmounted by an open domed belvedere. Although the wedding-cake massing of this design was quickly abandoned, the controlling parti of the plan, the grand hall surrounded by functional office space, survived.[36]

3.10. Arthur Brown Jr., schematic design for a new city hall, San Francisco, 1911. Note the assemblage of architectural motifs that populate Brown's later works. Drawing, Library of Congress, Prints and Drawings Division, Arthur Brown Jr. Collection.

Once Bakewell and Brown received the competition program, the specifics of the design began to form in their minds. The high dome remained the focal point of the composition, not only for its symbolic function and potential for monumental elaboration, but for its ability to control the entire civic center. Bakewell confirmed this intent when asked about the firm's winning design strategy: "The central

feature was clearly indicated by the program, whether it be a dome or tower. And not only by the program of this building, but by the larger program of the whole civic center. This group of buildings should be crowned by a dominating central feature, and the importance of the City Hall as well as of the buildings that will flank it seems to call for the noblest of all Architectural forms, the dome. Then, too, the interior

3.11. Arthur Brown Jr., sketches for San Francisco City Hall, March 1912. These doodles are on the back of a letter and probably represent Brown's first responses to the competition program for San Francisco City Hall. Arthur Brown Jr. Collection, Bancroft Library.

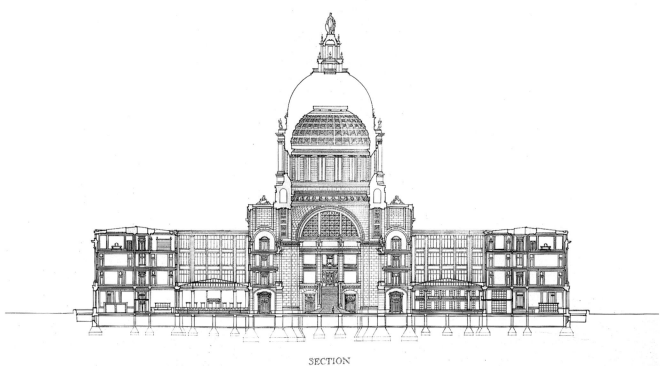

SECTION

SAN FRANCISCO CITY HALL COMPETITION

3.12. Bakewell & Brown, San Francisco City Hall, 1912, competition
drawing for longitudinal section. Arthur Brown Jr. Collection,
Bancroft Library. Photograph of drawing courtesy of Moulin Archives.

effect of a monumental dome running up through the various
stories serves to unify the whole building."[37]

Bakewell and Brown thus intended the rotunda to be the
focal point of the interior as well as the exterior (fig. 3.12).
The monumental stair directs the visitor to the piano nobile,
on which the legislative chamber and chief executive offices
are located. Through galleries set in front of the great thermal
windows that light it, the rotunda also binds the two halves
of the building together through all four floors, ingeniously
simplifying the circulation of the upper floors, which housed
the sheriff's office and the municipal and superior courts.

Although Brown may have been experimenting with
domes even before the release of the competition documents,
Bakewell & Brown certainly inferred from the program their
other great creative leap—the decision to group the financial
and recording departments in separate wings of the main
floor (figs. 3.13, 3.14). This critical decision, which combined
the assessor, tax collector, treasurer, and controller on the

south side of the building and the Department of Elections
and Recorder on the north, simplified the composition into
comprehensible halves—which, incidentally, reinforced the
American dialectic of taxation and representation. These
departmental areas would be businesslike in their character,
in clear distinction to the monumental treatment of the
rotunda. Two spacious light courts flank the rotunda, allowing all the offices on the inner side of the double-loaded corridors of the office blocks ample light and ventilation. On the
ground floor great skylit lobbies serve as public antecham-
bers to the recorder's offices and the finance group.

On the exterior, the same distinction was made between
the monumental central core and the functional office wings.
Bakewell & Brown was nearly unique among the competitors
in choosing to raise the architectural order of the building
above a high basement (three other placing designs do this),
and theirs is the only entry to employ two separate architectural systems to distinguish the ceremonial spaces from the

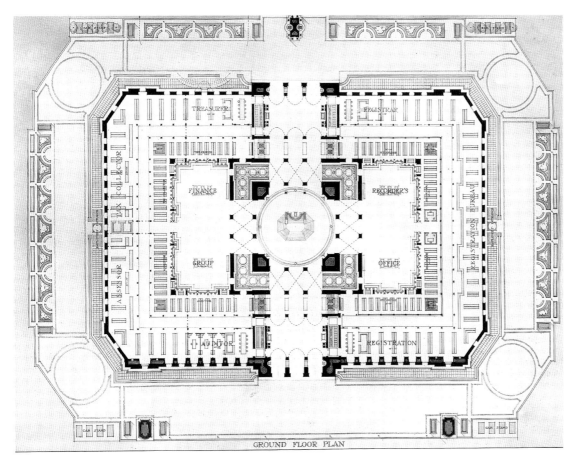

GROUND FLOOR PLAN

3.13. Bakewell & Brown, San Francisco City Hall, 1912, competition drawing, ground-floor plan. Arthur Brown Jr. Collection, Bancroft Library. Photograph of drawing courtesy of Moulin Archives.

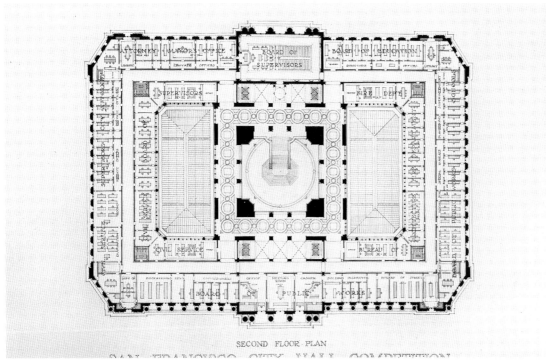

SECOND FLOOR PLAN

3.14. Bakewell & Brown, San Francisco City Hall, 1912, competition drawing, second-floor plan. Arthur Brown Jr. Collection, Bancroft Library. Photograph of drawing courtesy of Moulin Archives.

3.15. Arthur Brown Jr., schematic design for City Hall, San Francisco, spring, 1912. Brown explored the parti of the United States Capitol in working up his design for San Francisco. Drawing, Arthur Brown Collection, Bancroft Library.

common ones. The functional advantages of this arrangement were many, but the jurors most appreciated the lighter, two-story order that controlled the elevations of designs with such a basement; these orders could be set closer to the wall of the office wings and thus admit far more light than a full three-story colossal order could.

Brown reserved the big column for the porticos on the entry facades. Although he wisely decided to forsake the pyramidal massing of his initial studies, Brown knew that he would need to build up interest to the dome in the horizontal mass of the main block. He seems to have initially thought of the United States Capitol, which employs three pediments to emphasize the points of interest in the composition (fig. 3.15). However, the clipped corners of the office block required by the program precluded this arrangement. Consideration was also given to detaching the central block from the rest of the building with a recessed bay (a device Brown would use in the Federal Triangle), but this seemed to require pavilions at the ends of each office wing, which then crowded the central composition. A sketch illustrates one form this approach might have taken; in this scheme the central portico would have been crowned by a high

attic and the city clock (fig. 3.16). Of more lasting significance, Brown raised the entablature of this pediment and employed the dual orders that would bring him success. After considerable study he combined features of all of these sketches in his final elevations, but imposed upon the elevation the same functional logic as the plan. The resulting composition is, diagrammatically, two buildings superimposed: a functional four-story office block whose ends terminate in pavilions with coupled Doric columns and chamfered corners, and the ceremonial *corps-de-logis*, whose dome and lantern soar above a tetrastyle Corinthian portico (the ends again coupled) and a high, peripteral drum.

Bakewell & Brown's competition design stood out to the jury, and most other observers, as the most carefully considered and best presented of the entries, if not the most architecturally adventurous. In his review of the competition in the July 1912 issue of *The Architect and Engineer*, B. J. S. Cahill declared the winning design the most conservative possible solution: "Surest encouragement and victory itself went to the perfectly obvious, the two-court plan, even the four-court plan, and the inevitable dome—the dear old com-

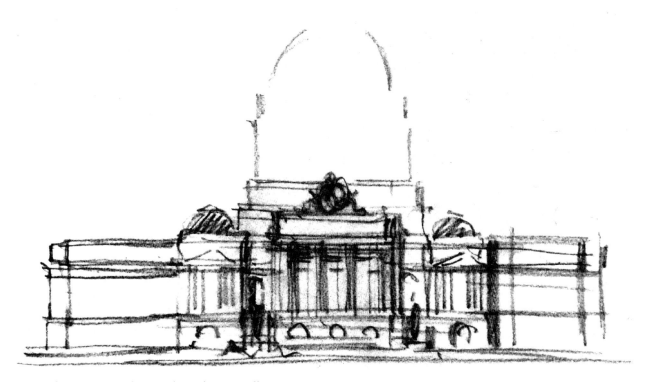

3.16. Arthur Brown Jr., schematic design for City Hall, San Francisco, spring, 1912. Drawing, Library of Congress, Prints and Drawings Division, Arthur Brown Jr. Collection.

fortable fat familiar dome! It may be that in this instance the safe conservative thing offered was so attractively served up that it won out over fresher offerings not so well served up."[38] Cahill justified the jury's decision, however, by reminding the profession that the jury's duty was to interpret the community's expectations as to representative architecture and to select the best design that met that standard: "The progressives in the profession who lament that the chosen design is a generation behind the times might take consolation in the fact, too, that public work must almost necessarily be behind the general line of march. It indicates the architectural status of the community en masse, rather than the standard of the cultivated few. It should please the people rather than the profession."[39]

DEVELOPING THE DESIGN

Whereas many in San Francisco may have believed that the design that won the competition was ready for construction, the architects knew that most of the design work was ahead of them. For most of the ensuing year Brown refined the com-

petition design and began to develop the ornamental program for the building. While most accounts of San Francisco City Hall claim that the constructed building is nearly identical to the competition drawings, significant changes contributed to the success of the finished structure. Refinements were made to the overall massing and the architectural elements of the building for much of the year following the competition. The interior architecture was also carefully studied and improved as the details were identified.

Brown was particularly concerned with optimizing the relationship between the dome and the porticos. He made numerous studies of both elements at a variety of scales and commissioned a plaster model at the end of October 1912 (figs. 3.17, 3.18). The model shows an intermediary stage of the dome's development; by this time Brown had agreed with some critics of the competition drawings that the dome was not large enough to control the civic center plaza, despite its enormous size. In the model, the drum and dome were enlarged to the full width of the base, which corresponded to the galleries below. The columns were coupled in the manner of the Dôme des Invalides, much as Victor Laloux had done on his Grand Prix–winning design for a cathedral.[40]

3.17 (*top*). Bakewell & Brown, study model of
San Francisco City Hall, autumn, 1912. The model
was used to check the three-dimensional qualities
of the dome and the end pavilions.

3.18 (*above*). Bakewell & Brown, study drawing of
San Francisco City Hall, autumn 1912. Note that
the columns on the drum are coupled and that end
pavilions are present at the wings. Arthur Brown Jr.
Collection, Bancroft Library.

Some months later, Brown made the final refinement that
truly integrates the dome with the pediment. He realized
that with the increased diameter of the dome, it was possible
for the intercolumniation of the drum and the portico to be
identical. In this arrangement, the lines of the columns
would "flow" from the portico to the drum (fig. 3.19).[41] The
desire for more unity between the dome and portico also

drove the decision to change the order of the main porticos from the Corinthian to the Doric.

Brown abandoned the great statue on top of the dome, opting to design a lantern instead. His lantern takes on a Greek cross plan in its lower stages, which is resolved into an octagonal spire. Although the specific forms are novel, Brown borrowed the framed-arch motif for the second stage from his

3.19. Bakewell & Brown, study of the dome, San Francisco City Hall, early 1913. This rendered study of the dome was featured in the program for the cornerstone laying ceremony later in 1913 and demonstrates the consideration Brown gave to the flow of the upper columns in the drum to those of the lower portico. Drawing, Arthur Brown Jr. Collection, Bancroft Library. Photograph of drawing courtesy of Moulin Archives.

Prix Godeboeuf design, which in turn had been inspired by the lantern of the Dôme des Invalides. The ornamentation used on the lantern celebrated San Francisco's recovery after the earthquake and fire—triumphal trophies crowned bound fasces, which rose above flaming urns and lamps—and the city's monogram was worked into the shields at the base (fig. 3.20). More important to the effect of the lantern and the dome was the gilding scheme, which was carefully worked out to contrast the structural and ornamental elements of the dome and lantern with burnished and bright finishes. While fresh, the gilding dazzled viewers in fine weather (fig. C.5).

In the winter of 1913 Brown decided to give added prominence to the central block on the Van Ness elevation; this volume contained the council chambers and faced the widest street in the city. To this end he used a number of architectural devices to elevate this *corps-de-logis* above the Polk Street side and to communicate the importance of the council chamber. Brown advanced the block 10 feet beyond the line of the adjacent colonnade using a hollow chamfer that carried the entablature behind wings to the dome base (fig.

3.20. Edward Frick, lantern for San Francsco City Hall, 1914. This presentation drawing detailed the gilding plan for the lantern as well as the intended ornamental scheme. Arthur Brown Jr. Collection, Bancroft Library. Photograph of drawing courtesy of Moulin Archives.

3.21. Arthur Brown Jr., "Preliminary Sketch Study of Central Motif," San Francisco City Hall, 1912. Crenier's terms have been designed by the architect, and only detail was left to the sculptor. Drawing, Arthur Brown Jr. Collection, Bancroft Library.

3.22. Bakewell & Brown, rendering of central pavilion, San Francisco City Hall, 1913. This was a presentation drawing to detail the Van Ness elevation for the mayor and advisory architects. The same drawing was the basis for the stereotomy details of the pavilion. Photograph, Arthur Brown Jr. Collection, Bancroft Library.

3.21). The entrance at Van Ness was given particular emphasis with a series of atlases (terms) that support the balcony at the council chamber. This room itself was marked by three arched French doors, over which overscaled cartouches signified the double-height room behind (fig. 3.22). As with the architectural emphasis Brown gave the council chamber in plan and in the *marche*, the primary sequence of movement

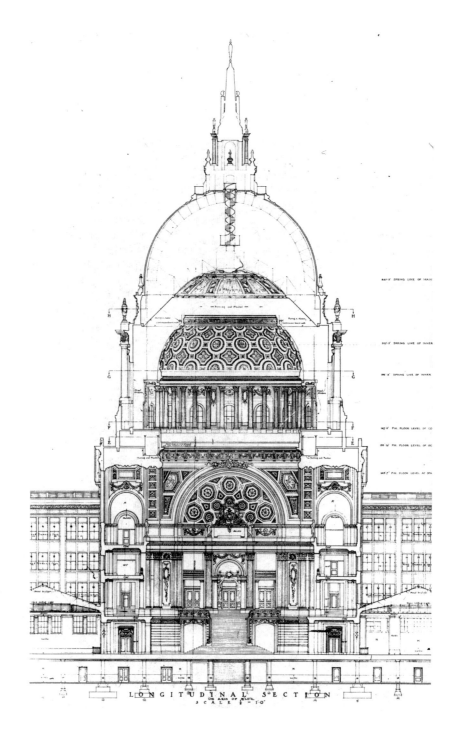

LONGITUDINAL SECTION
ON AXIS OF BLDG.
SCALE ⅛" = 1'0"

3.23. Bakewell & Brown, longitudinal section,
San Francisco City Hall, 1914. Construction drawing,
Arthur Brown Jr. Collection, Bancroft Library.

through the rotunda, these exterior refinements served to
remind visitors that in the reformed San Francisco political
power resided in the Board of Supervisors rather than with a
boss and his hand-picked mayor.

Although Brown had outlined the basic volumes of the
rotunda in the competition drawings, the true proportions of

3.24. Bakewell & Brown, rotunda, San Francisco City Hall, 1916. Photograph by John Channing, *The Architect and Engineer*, author's collection.

the space and the specific details were not finalized until the exterior proportions of the elevations and dome were fixed. In fact, the enlargement of the dome allowed Brown to reassess the architectural qualities of the interior and introduce a certain amount of complexity into the articulation of the central core. The rotunda became conceived as two shells: an inner shell that aligned with the original plan of the dome in the competition drawings, and an outer shell brought out to the line of the light courts (fig. 3.23). These two systems, each consisting of dome, drum, and walls, one inside the other, were separated by galleries that circumscribed the rotunda proper. The interplay between these two

3.25. Arthur Brown Jr., development of rotunda, San Francisco City Hall, 1913, preliminary outline sketch. Arthur Brown Jr. Collection, Bancroft Library.

3.26. Arthur Brown Jr., development of rotunda, San Francisco City Hall, 1913, scaled elevational sketch. Arthur Brown Jr. Collection, Bancroft Library.

systems gives the space its spatial character and architectural interest.

Brown had approached the design of the rotunda with several ideas in mind. He wanted the *marche* to lead the visitor through the space and up the ceremonial stairs to the supervisors' chamber, but he also wanted to give the room, which was square in plan and essentially static, a sense of dynamism. He accomplished both by framing the north and south sides of the rotunda with the galleries that connected the two office wings on each floor, whereas on the east and west he allowed the space to flow beyond the great arches to the outer shell and the supervisors' chamber and mayor's suite (fig. 3.24). Additionally, the gallery on the third floor is supported by an interpolated suborder, which further screens the north and south elevations from view and directs the gaze to the focal point of the space. All around the rotunda, Brown suppressed the second-floor level by 40 inches, increasing the apparent height and thus the sense of a piano nobile. Despite these visual tricks, the structural clarity of the rotunda is never lost, thanks to the simple treatment of the enormous corner piers that support the dome and the unornamented frames of the pendentives and drum ring. The dome itself is visually disengaged from its supports by a girdle of thirty-six Corinthian columns that line the inner drum. This screen filters the light from the great windows on the exterior to bathe the space in a muted glow.

The interior design of the rotunda and council chambers was more of a collaborative effort than any other part of the project. Whereas Brown created the architectural framework of these ceremonial spaces, the inspired ornamentation that overlays their surfaces and sets the celebratory mood of the building came from the pencil of Jean-Louis Bourgeois. (Brown designed the ornamental ironwork, lighting fixtures, and hardware himself.) Many of Brown's architectural studies and Bourgeois's sketches for the ornament survive and can be analyzed in sequence to demonstrate how the rotunda was designed and codified into working drawings. The following discussion examines just one portion of the rotunda: the west wall at the top of the monumental stair and the adjacent lobby to the Board of Supervisors' chamber.

The main features of the composition were roughed out in a series of quick sketches done shortly after Brown decided to suppress the floor elevation of the gallery. The parti is clear—the stair will lead the visitor through an arch framed by Corinthian columns to the Board of Supervisors' chamber (fig. 3.25). Overhead, the entablature of the colonnade carries a high attic festooned with swags and an enormous sculpted cartouche. The next sketch firms up the proportions of the design and places the colonnade and third-floor gallery in proper relationship to the entire wall. In the next drawing this group is placed into the entire elevation of the rotunda (figs. 3.26, 3.27). At this point, Bourgeois began to work on

3.27. Arthur Brown Jr. development of rotunda, San Francisco City
Hall, 1913, scaled and drafted interior elevation with drum. Drawing,
Arthur Brown Jr. Collection, Bancroft Library.

3.28. Bakewell & Brown, construction document drawing of west wall of rotunda, San Francisco City Hall, 1913–14. Arthur Brown Jr. Collection, Bancroft Library.

the details of the composition. First he studied the design and sought out harmonious geometries for the ornament that would complement the architecture. Once a suitable geometry was discovered, Bourgeois then worked up the ornament in detail, at first to a small scale, such as with his sketch of the intrados of the great arch above the west wall, and then in full-size details. The west wall of the rotunda, given added attention, was modeled at quarter-scale in the architect's offices (the mock-up was over 5 feet high). Finally, the design was drafted into the working drawings, both in the sections and elevations, and in larger-scale stone-laying diagrams, which detail the dimensions and sectional layout of each course of masonry (figs. 3.28, C.8). The construction documents for all of Brown's major works carefully detail the masonry work. Brown considered himself an authority on stone construction; the one medal he won in the construction sequence at the Ecole des Beaux-Arts was for stereotomy: the layout, dimensioning, and cutting of stone.

THE DESIGN REALIZATION TEAM

The development and construction of Brown's design required more resources than any one architecture or building firm in San Francisco had on staff. To add to the challenge, there was no time to prepare a formal bid set of construction documents for the project, because the building was scheduled for completion by the 1915 Panama-Pacific International Exposition. Thus construction was to begin before the drawings were formalized, and much of the detailed design work would barely anticipate the building crew's needs. To meet the tight schedule and shrinking budget of this mammoth task, Bakewell and Brown hired the engineering and construction management expertise they themselves did not have and proposed to oversee the construction contracts and materials procurement in-house. In this sense Bakewell & Brown became something like the modern design–build contractor, if only for the limited life of the project. The construction of the exposition, in contrast, was organized so that each building was designed and detailed in full before any contracts were let, and most of the architects did not superintend the work.

At first, it was assumed by the consulting architects that they would act on behalf of the city as contractors, and that Bakewell & Brown would simply present the Board of Public Works with a complete set of bid documents before construction began. For this more limited scope of services, it was expected that Bakewell & Brown would be paid about 4.5 percent of the cost of constructing the building. This was not Bakewell & Brown's understanding of the language of the competition program nor of their subsequent appointment as "Architects of the City Hall." No professional architect

3.29. Principal designers of San Francisco City Hall, c. 1914; from left, John Bakewell Jr., Arthur Brown Jr, Jean-Louis Bourgeois, John Baur. Note the eighth-scale maquette of the west rotunda wall to the rear. Photograph, Arthur Brown Jr. Collection, Bancroft Library.

would have agreed to summarily relinquish control over his designs in such a fashion. Bakewell & Brown presumed that they would be employed throughout the construction period, and would therefore receive the full AIA standard fee of 6 percent of the construction cost. This disagreement caused some in the San Francisco chapter of the American Institute of Architects to call for the removal of the consulting architects, and particularly John Galen Howard, from the organization. A series of contentious meetings resulted in the expulsion of the consultants and many other members left the AIA chapter in protest, including Bakewell and Brown. These defecting members formed their own organization, the San Francisco Society of Architects. The two organizations coexisted until the following year, when the San Francisco chapter expunged all records of the "trial" of John Galen Howard and welcomed all to return to the AIA.[42]

After threat of lawsuit, it was agreed on September 25, 1912, that Bakewell & Brown would receive the full fee if they also superintended the construction of the works.[43] For this task they hired George Wagner, a former employee of Frederick Meyer, and the consulting architects' intended general contractor. Wagner proved to be a critical member of the project team. A supervising construction manager for a large building concern in Seattle, Wagner returned to San Francisco in 1912 intending to form his own construction firm, but agreed instead to work for Bakewell & Brown on the city hall.[44] Afterward, Wagner went into business for himself and became Brown's most trusted contractor, respon-

3.30. C. H. Snyder, structural framing of dome at San Francisco City Hall, c. 1914. Photograph, author's collection.

sible for executing the War Memorial complex, Temple Emanu-El, and many buildings at Stanford. He joined the firm in October 1912 and initially prepared construction estimates and reviewed and amended the specifications. Wagner advocated the use of separated, segregated contracts, a strategy that saved the city thousands of dollars in additional construction expenses. Although Wagner became the general contractor for the job, the consulting architects still served as the city's representatives and verified the quality of the work and builders' legal conformance to the contracts.

Other members of the architect's team also had to be assembled (fig. 3.29). John Baur, a friend from the Ecole, was hired to assist in writing the construction specifications. J. S. Gould, a member of Bakewell & Brown's staff for several years before the competition, became the job captain of the drafting office and directed the efforts of twenty draftsmen. Gould coordinated the many floor-plan changes required by the various city agencies and reviewed all of the numerous

plans and construction details throughout the three-year project. He stayed on to become a senior member of the firm, retiring from Brown's practice during World War II.[45] Edward Frick, Ernest Weihe, and Lawrence Kruse also joined the firm as draftsmen during the city hall project, although Frick would leave before completion to study in Paris and to serve in the United States Army.

Bakewell & Brown's staff had to work quickly to develop the working drawings and specifications to the point that construction could begin in mid-1913. The office's first task was to confirm the actual space required by each of the departments to be housed in the building. Because the program had been derived from Newton Tharp's studies of 1909, there were considerable adjustments to be made in the space required in the building. Members of the Board of Supervisors demanded entrances on the Grove and McAllister Street elevations, disrupting the financial and recording office suites on the first floor (these entrances were eventually incorporated into the basement floor plan). By mid-January 1913, Bakewell and Gould had confirmed floor-plan layouts with all of the major departments and were able to turn their sketches over to the draftsmen to complete the working plans. George Wagner used these design-development plans, from which the final contract drawings were derived, to confirm his cost estimates and then sent them to the various engineering consultants for the development of their systems designs.[46]

The structural engineering was done by Brown's close associate, Christopher H. Snyder. Snyder was a true architect's engineer, willing to make the architect's vision a reality without imposing untried solutions on the project. Snyder's design for San Francisco City Hall adhered as closely as possible to the standards set for steel-framed class-A office space at the time. Eight thousand tons of steel were employed in the structure, primarily for the framing of the floors and roof; all was encased in a lightweight concrete fireproofing composed primarily of crushed brick salvaged from the old city hall. The steel columns supporting the floor and wall loads carried their loads down to four hundred sixty piers in the foundation. The dome and drum were designed as an isolated structure analogous to a gas tank frame. The drum was framed in sixteen radial bays, which were stiffened with five rings of horizontal bracing, and the inner and outer domes were framed with thirty-two radial trusses joined at the top by a large circular gusset plate and restrained at the spring-line by a tension ring. The entire dome structure was supported by four great piers, composed of five steel columns each and tied into the main structure at the second-, third-, and fourth-floor levels (fig. 3.30).[47] Snyder also carefully considered the structure's seismic performance and intentionally omitted any shear bracing on the first floor of the building, theorizing that a "soft" first floor would give way in an earthquake, and absorb the shock of the temblor, saving the rest of the structure from harm. Although this is hardly recommended practice today, the structure behaved largely as Snyder predicted it should in the 1989 Loma Prieta earthquake.[48]

CONSTRUCTING CITY HALL

Construction formally commenced on April 5, 1913, with a groundbreaking ceremony that had all of the progressive-era pageantry one would expect of such an event. The mayor and eighteen supervisors excavated one truckload of dirt (the mayor using a silver shovel) while the municipal band played and four hundred children sang "San Francisco" and "The Star-Spangled Banner."[49] That summer, George Wagner and his assistants moved to the on-site office and workshop, the Park-Hartford Automobile showroom at the corner of Van Ness Avenue and McAllister Street. This building would become the nerve center for the entire construction operation. Wagner's first challenge upon letting the grading contract was to cut the budget of the remaining work by 10 percent, because the city found it had to buy more land for the civic center and required an additional $400,000 from the bond appropriation. He compensated for much of this reduction by breaking down the steel work into separate fabrication, shipping, and erection contracts, allowing the marketplace to drive down the price of the work. The foundation costs, too, were much less than originally budgeted, only $40,000, because the absolutely ideal subsoil conditions allowed for a minimal amount of excavation and concrete work.[50]

The stone used in the construction also came at a discount. Brown hoped to use light gray Sierra granite for the exterior of the building but realized that the quantities necessary for such a large structure would tax the production capacities of the state's entire industry. The two granite companies in San Francisco were so anxious to have the city hall job that they got into a bidding war that dropped the price of the stone by 60 percent, to $3.50 a cubic foot.[51] The interior of the dome is Indiana limestone. The Home-Industry league of San Francisco objected to this use of non-local material, but in truth, no light-colored fine-grained stone was available in California (the sandstones suggested by the league are quite dark in color).[52] George Wagner specified that this limestone be set in plaster rather than mortar, so that the stone would not be stained by Portland cement. A wide variety of marbles was used for the floors and wainscot, including stone from Vermont, Georgia, Utah, Alabama, and California. The installation of the stonework actually delayed the completion of the building, because a long statewide strike by the quarry workers caused the masons in San Francisco to strike in sympathy on the first of June 1915; work resumed on November 19, 1915.

The ornamentation of the city hall was a significant and highly visible part of the construction process. Although preliminary plans for the ornament were drafted into the construction documents, changes were made throughout the construction process. In fact, the ornamental work done at San Francisco City Hall was created by a group of craftsmen and designers organized more like a medieval guild than like a modern construction firm. Hundreds of skilled artisans from around the world converged on San Francisco in anticipation of work at the Panama-Pacific International Exposition, so there was no shortage of talent willing to execute any design in almost any imaginable material. Bourgeois, Brown, and the chief sculptor, Henri Crenier, would sketch out their ideas at a large scale. These drawings were passed on to model makers, who created plaster casts. Once the models met approval with the design team, they

3.31. Henri Crenier, terms at Van Ness portico, San Francisco City Hall, 1915. Ironwork design by Arthur Brown Jr. Photograph by Sylvia Brown Jensen.

3.32: Bakewell & Brown, Polk Street portico, San Francisco City Hall, 1916. This photograph illustrates Brown's concept of flow. Photograph by John Channing, *The Architect and Engineer*, author's collection.

were sent on to the fabricators, who would recreate the piece in plaster, wood, iron, or stone. Every aspect of this work, from initial design to installation, was done on site in the high bays of the construction office on McAllister Street.

This centralized administration of the craft work permitted Bourgeois and Crenier to test ideas quickly before finalizing their designs. Whereas Bourgeois worked closely with Brown, Crenier demanded more autonomy, at times not to the project's benefit. Although his atlases on the Van Ness elevation are successful, the pedimental sculptures on the principal elevations are not especially inspired (with the exception of the figure representing San Francisco, in the center of the Polk Street pediment, which does display some dynamism (figs. 3.31, 3.32, C.7). The medallions on the pendentives of the rotunda, representing liberty, equality, learning, and strength, are perhaps a bit out of scale with the other figural sculpture in the space.[53] Bourgeois's plaster and cast-stone ornaments, executed by Paul Denville, more closely realized the architect's intentions. Some repeated elements,

such as the garlands on the entablatures and the urns over the colonnades, were cast in the shop and installed, but other ornament was cast in place and detailed in situ (fig. 3.33).

The supervisors' chamber represents another example of the team's frugal opportunism. The entire room was designed around a shipment of rare Manchurian oak that was bought for a fraction of its value in a bankruptcy auction. The heavily carved paneling of the supervisors' chamber was designed by Brown as soon as the bid was successful and executed by yet another Frenchman, M. La Roulandi. This room has a distinctly different character from the rotunda; its deeply coffered ceiling recalls Italian forms (fig. 3.34). Other details, especially the door surrounds and the arch-topped windows, relate the room to the French sources of the rest of the building. The lighting fixtures in the chamber are of Brown's own invention. Other foundry work, such as the iron and bronze railings around the rotunda and the balconies on the exterior porticos, was fabricated in San Francisco by the Rudgear–Merle Company.[54]

Although the quarry workers' strike delayed the completion of the city hall beyond the closing of the Panama-Pacific International Exposition, Mayor Rolph was able to keep his promise that he would move into the building in 1915. On December 28 Rolph dedicated the new building in front of a rain-soaked crowd. In his address, the mayor lauded the new structure, declaring: "I love that building. It is marvelous how it has risen. It has been built without a breath of scandal and on time. I am proud to be the first Mayor to occupy it, and I thank you, my fellow citizens, for honoring me as no other man has ever been honored. It is the finest public building in the world."[55] Rolph then invited the public to view the building and to greet him in his new office, which he occupied that morning. Arthur Brown also spoke briefly, expressing his gratitude as architect to all involved with the project for fulfilling his vision "smoothly and without needless difficulties to distract and delay."[56] By the middle of March 1916, just four years after the bond election of 1912, the city hall was fully occupied and open for regular business. Equally important, George Wagner's cost-saving measures limited the city's total expenditure on the building to just over $3.4 million, 15 percent under the original appropriation and $100,000 less than the revised budget.[57]

3.33. Bakewell & Brown, rotunda looking toward supervisor's chambers, San Francisco City Hall, 1916. Photograph by John Channing, *The Architect & Engineer*, author's collection.

3.34. Bakewell & Brown, San Francisco City Hall, 1916, board of supervisors' chambers. The ceiling focuses attention on the president's podium at the back of the room. Photograph by John Channing, *The Architect and Engineer*, author's collection.

CRITICAL RECEPTION OF
SAN FRANCISCO CITY HALL

The importance of the city hall to the people of San Francisco was immediate and obvious; the building symbolized their struggle to progress beyond the natural and political disasters of the previous decade. B. J. S. Cahill identified this sense of civic pride in his review of the building. In Cahill's opinion, San Francisco City Hall transcended stingy programmatic requirements and its diverse sources to amply serve both utility and beauty.

Cahill praised the exterior of the dome (fig. 3.35): "The sheer beauty of the new City Hall dome transcends anything of the kind I have ever seen. Its proportions are perfect, its glistening granite lifts up like an apparition and the triumph and joy of its gilded finials as they gather in the glory of the sun to the final pinnacle of flame stirs the senses as do chords of music and moves the soul like beacon flashes that proclaim some mighty victory!" Cahill also recognized the larger movement the building represented and placed San Francisco City Hall in the context of the American renaissance, the City Beautiful movement, and the Progressive Republican reforms. He wrote:

> All over the United States today our cities are renewing them-selves in splendid structures of admirable design. A veritable army of architects has been in hard training for some decades and has now taken the field. . . . Ours is a Renaissance more nearly comparable with that of Italy, inspired by ideals of this world rather than by ideals of the next. . . . In our time and in our land the modern use of steel . . . pervasive prosperity, swift growing urban communities, universal education, and the admirable organization of the profession of architecture are all of them prime elements in explaining the origin of this American Renaissance, in defining its drift and, perhaps, in indicating its goal.[58]

Although Cahill's assessment of the city hall was widely shared (and his review reprinted in several East Coast journals, such as *The American Architect*), there were some aspects of the design that were less well received. The ornament of the rotunda was particularly controversial. In his response to Cahill's article, William L. Woollett, a Los Angeles architect, questioned the relevance of the ornament to the people served by the city hall:

> In Athens, Rome, in Venice and in old Florence, these carv-ings and tablets and statues and busts always meant some-thing to the contemporaneous populace. What do these orna-ments mean to us? . . . The whole range of western spirit could have been here idealized. The naive Bohemia that San Francisco was and in part still is should have been expressed. And the great men who have gone before, like Stephenson and O'Henry and Huntington, and the deeds of Mackay, Fair,

Flood, and O'Brien, and the romance of the still earlier Spanish time—all these and more should speak from the walls.[59]

Of course, from the present-day perspective, nothing would have made the rotunda a politically unacceptable white elephant faster than monuments to robber barons such as Fair, Flood, and Huntington! Yet the underlying criticism of the rotunda was valid—in the true spirit of the renaissance the rotunda should have become a record of the community's collective experience. The restoration of the city hall completed in 1999 recaptured space for such a record. Now a history room in one of the light courts tells some of the city's rich past, and a veritable army of mayoral busts greets the visitor; as is tradition, the current mayor's favored predecessors stand guard astride his office door. Yet, no matter how the city's past is commemorated within the walls of the city hall, the building itself is the chief record of its designers and builders. As J. C. Branner, president of Stanford University and client of Bakewell & Brown, wrote: "When the last echo of the chisel has resounded through its spacious corridors, and the toilers have reluctantly depart-ed, they will leave behind them an immortal monument to the architects, whose *chef-d'oeuvre* shall be the joy and pride of city and state and nation for generations to come."[60]

BUILDING THE REST OF THE CIVIC CENTER

The city hall was just one of the four major structures con-structed in the first building campaign at the San Francisco Civic Center. The Exposition Auditorium, designed in 1913 by consulting architects John Galen Howard, Frederick Meyer, and John Reid Jr., was completed in January 1915, in time to serve as the primary in-town venue for the Panama-Pacific International Exposition. The general massing and materials followed the precedent set by the city hall. George Kelham's main library was completed in 1917, and again was designed to honor the regulating lines of the city hall. Its plan was widely admired for its efficient circulation and accommo-dation of the library function. The Larkin Street elevation, however, was controversial, because it was based on Cass Gilbert's design for the Detroit Public Library, and Gilbert was on the competition jury.

However, no structure in the civic center caused more fury than the State Building on McAllister Street. Once

3.35 (*opposite*). Bakewell & Brown, San Francisco City Hall, 1916, general view from south side of civic center plaza. Photograph by John Channing, *The Architect and Engineer*, author's collection.

3.36. Willis Polk, Civic Center Opera House, San Francisco, 1913, proposal for the Marshall Square site. Photograph of drawing, author's collection.

again, a competition was the source of the discord. In March, 1917, Bliss & Faville won the competition with an Italian renaissance design completely out of scale and character with the rest of the civic center.[61] Many in the San Francisco architectural establishment were outraged by the design, particularly because Faville was one of the instigators of the trial of John Galen Howard in 1913 (see note 42), and was actively hostile to the consulting architects and their civic center.[62] With the delays brought about by this controversy and World War I, the cornerstone of the building was not laid until 1920, and the structure was not occupied until 1926, a full decade after its design.[63] By then, plans were well underway to build the first of the corner buildings, Samuel Heiman's Public Health Building, and to expand the civic center beyond its original boundary at Van Ness Avenue with the San Francisco War Memorial group.[64]

THE WAR MEMORIAL

Imagine the following as an excerpt from the program of a Grand Prix de Rome project:

A monumental but functional memorial to those who fell for the greater glory of their nation is to be built in a great western metropolis. The people of this city have decided that this memorial should take the form of a cultural and recreational center, but that it should also serve the social and organizational needs of the veterans of the recent war and their living predecessors. To this end, it is required that this memorial complex contain the following:

* 4,000-seat opera house
* Military Hall of Valor
* Municipal Symphony Hall
* Museum of the Visual Arts
* Veterans Posts and Offices
* Memorial Garden
* 1,500-seat theater
* Ballroom and retiring rooms
* Cafe or restaurant
* Gymnasium & bowling alley

3.37. Arthur Brown Jr. and Willis Polk, San Francisco War Memorial, autumn 1922, presentation rendering for the board of trustees. Photograph of drawing, Private Collection, San Francisco.

A site on the principal boulevard of the city, two blocks in extent, has been purchased for this endeavor; the site directly faces the city's great Hôtel-de-Ville. The project is being managed by a Board of Trustees composed of members of the municipal music society and several veterans organizations—no preference is to be given to either of these groups. The funds available for the work will be determined once the complex has been designed.

Such a program would have been considered outlandish even within the walls of the Ecole des Beaux-Arts, yet this is exactly the challenge that faced Arthur Brown in designing the San Francisco War Memorial Opera House and Veterans Building.

An opera house had always been a part of the civic center ideal and was prominent in the civic center proposed by the Burnham Plan in 1905. The destruction of the opera company's former home in 1906 heightened the need for a proper opera house, and such an institution was incorporated into

the advisory architects' plans for the center in 1912. Willis Polk drew up plans for a municipal opera house in 1913, which would have been used to carry a bond election to create a public–private partnership to manage the building's construction and operation (fig. 3.36). The intended site, the block bounded by Larkin, Fulton, Hyde, and Grove streets, was part of the site of the old city hall, and was cleared of that building's remains as Bakewell & Brown's City Hall rose across the plaza. Before the bonds could be approved, the California Supreme Court ruled that the city's partnership with the Musical Association of San Francisco was contrary to the city's charter and to state law, and that no joint venture could be commenced.[65] This ruling effectively killed the project for the time being.

The opera house project did not die in the hearts of its supporters, who were unimpressed with the acoustical qualities of the Exposition Auditorium and with its inadequate backstage accommodations. By 1918, the Musical Association raised over

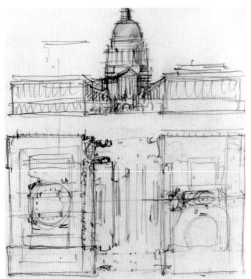

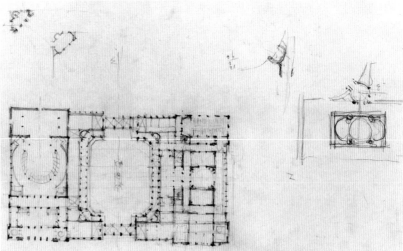

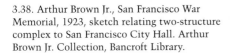

3.38. Arthur Brown Jr., San Francisco War Memorial, 1923, sketch relating two-structure complex to San Francisco City Hall. Arthur Brown Jr. Collection, Bancroft Library.

3.39. Arthur Brown Jr., San Francisco War Memorial, 1923, plan sketch exploring linking devices across Fulton Street to enclose the memorial garden. Arthur Brown Jr. Collection, Bancroft Library.

$1.6 million toward an opera house to be located two blocks west of the auditorium, the site of today's Davies Symphony Hall. With the conclusion of the First World War, it was decided that the project would be enhanced if it were combined with efforts to construct a war memorial to those who had served in the nation's armed conflicts; together, the Musical Association and the American Legion raised another $1 million toward the project.[66]

On October 11, 1922, as the funding drive was proceeding, the trustees for the War Memorial appointed an Architectural Advisory Commission, composed of many of the city's most prominent architects.[67] At first the commission attempted to work within the confines of the single block owned by the trustees. The ambitious program, which already included a memorial arch, an opera house, a symphony hall, an art museum, and veterans' quarters, proved to be too much for the site. Sketches by Brown and Polk that survive demonstrate the crowded nature of the proposal (fig. 3.37). Within a month of their appointment, the advisory architects recommended relocating the site of the project to a larger plot of land. The board of trustees proposed that the two blocks directly west of the city hall be used for the memorial group, and offered to donate one-half the cost of the purchase of these two blocks to the city in return for the right to erect the complex there. The city agreed to this action and, through a series of resolutions, condemned and purchased the land in question over the next three years.[68]

The advisory architects then redesigned the project to accommodate the larger site.

Because Brown was expected to ensure that the complex would harmonize with City Hall, he was intimately involved with the planning at this early stage. Sketches surviving in his papers demonstrate his concern for the design of the space between them and for how the two new buildings would frame City Hall from this open plaza (figs. 3.38, 3.39). In late 1923 the advisory architects presented their preliminary drawings to the trustees in a series of plates (fig. 3.40) that describe two nearly identical buildings on either side of a large memorial court. The southern building housed the opera house and symphony hall, the northern the veterans' auditorium, American Legion posts, ballroom, and museum of art. The memorial court, entered through long arcades that flanked each building, was dominated by a victory column modeled after that of the Place Vendôme in Paris. Polk designed the elevations of the buildings, presumably in a loose collaboration with Brown (fig. 3.41). The Van Ness Avenue facades, entered through arched doorways punched through a high, rusticated basement, adhered to the established vocabulary of the civic center. Above, a double-height colonnade of coupled Doric columns supported a very high attic, into which a lengthy inscription was set.

These drawings further whetted the interest of the public and the board of trustees for the full scope of the War Memorial project. On April 25, 1924, the trustees contracted

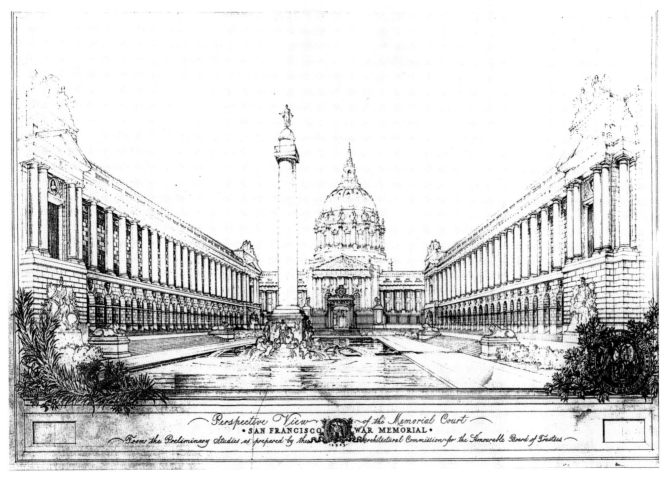

3.40 (*above*). Consulting Architects, San Francisco War Memorial, 1923, presentation drawings of War Memorial complex, "Perspective View of the Memorial Court." Drawing presumably held by the Building Superintendent, San Francisco War Memorial. Photograph, author's collection.

3.41 (*below*). Consulting Architects, San Francisco War Memorial, 1923, presentation drawings of War Memorial complex, elevation of Opera House by Willis Polk. Drawing presumably held by the Building Superintendent, San Francisco War Memorial. Photograph, author's collection.

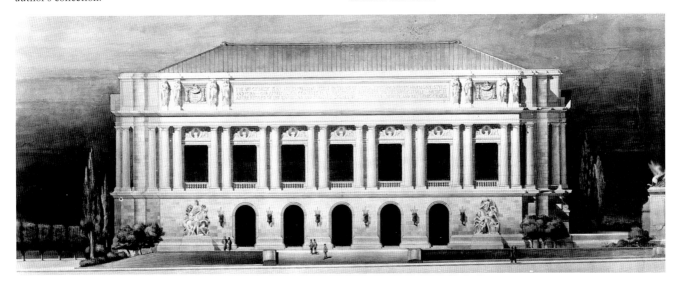

3.42. Arthur Brown Jr., War
Memorial Opera House and
Veterans Building, San Francisco
War Memorial, 1932, view from
Van Ness Avenue. Photograph
courtesy of Moulin Archives.

3.43. Arthur Brown Jr., John
Bakewell Jr., and G. Albert
Lansburgh, War Memorial Opera
House and Veterans Building,
1932, plan. Illustration by
Elizabeth Riorden.

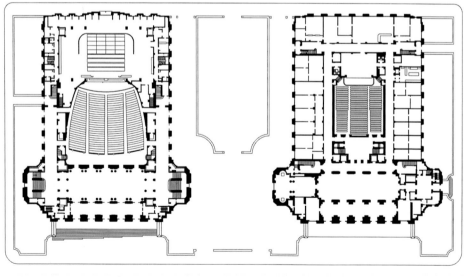

0 25 50   100 ft

with Willis Polk, G. Albert Lansburgh, and Arthur Brown to prepare detailed plans of the 1923 proposal. It was agreed that Polk and Lansburgh would collaborate on the opera house, and that Bakewell & Brown would design the Veterans Building and memorial court. Before work could begin, however, the entire project was thrown into disarray with the death of Willis Polk on September 10, 1924, and the realization that the trustees would need at least $4 million more capital to build the proposed scheme.

The project was suspended for over two years, until February 1927, when a bond campaign was undertaken to furnish the additional funds required.[69] Brown was asked to take over the design of the opera house by John S. Drum, the president of the trustees. This appointment confirmed the importance the trustees placed on harmonizing the memorial group with the city hall and the rest of the civic center. In the autumn of 1927, the architects set up an independent drafting office, where Alexander Wagstaff managed the production of the design development and construction documents. Wagstaff also acted as liaison between the architects and the engineering consultants. At the peak of production, in the latter half of 1928, the drafting office employed, in addition to Wagstaff, six designers, six architectural draftsmen, eight engineers, two specifications writers, and a stenographer.[70]

The design of the Van Ness Avenue elevations of the group changed only in detail from Brown and Polk's earlier conceptions; the coupled orders in the colonnades and rusticated basement and arcading remained a part of the design throughout the project's development. Brown did adjust some aspects of the edge conditions to better harmonize the group with the city hall (figs. 3.42, C.9). For example, he introduced the chamfered reentrant corners he had used on the Van Ness portico across the street, and he employed many of the same materials, including gilded bronze railings at the balconies and lead-covered copper on the roofs. Small ornamental touches, such as the lion's heads in the keystones over the entry arches and Brown's signature lighting fixtures, were introduced into the design to lighten the severity of the facades.

The memorial court and the building elevations bounding it underwent significant alterations due to budget constraints that made the realization of the complete scheme impossible. By August 1927, it had become apparent that the $6.5 million construction cost of the initial project would not be raised, even with the city's participation. Well over $1 million was cut from the budget in the ensuing year. From an architectural perspective the most significant cost-saving measure was the decision to substitute terra cotta for granite on all elevations of both buildings. In addition, an entire suite of facilities, the width of the stair pavilions, was removed from the buildings in the design-development stage

of the planning. This alteration allowed Brown to substitute arcaded windows across the side elevations in place of the more expensive colonnade originally considered. In some ways, these revisions benefited the project because the twin buildings more effectively framed the memorial court, which in turn became less linear in its proportions (fig. 3.43).[71] A simple design for the court by the well-known Bay Area landscape architect Thomas Church accommodates the ceremonial traffic of gala-night celebrations well and leaves the view to the city hall dome as open as possible; the court was landscaped in 1936.

The programs and scope of both the opera house and the Veterans Building, drastically altered under financial and political pressure, were the cause of considerable worry for the architect. Early in the second design campaign, it became clear that certain features, such as the independent symphony hall and the grand ballroom, could not be funded. Yet, additional programmatic elements had to be included in the project well after the schematic design stage. Although the Veterans Building and opera house were designed to appear as alike as possible, the problems faced by the architects with each were quite dissimilar.

THE VETERANS BUILDING

The building for the American Legion and other veterans' groups was the ostensible reason for the entire War Memorial project; the veterans never let the board of trustees forget this, asserting their considerable political and moral authority to ensure that their interests would be served. Although the architects were supposed to answer only to the board of trustees, their plans for the Veterans Building were openly debated in the press and often rejected by the very veterans groups the board supposedly represented. Although Brown's plans were consistently reviewed by the veterans' representatives on the board, a growing discontent with the building was developing in the veteran community. The fear that the Veterans Building would be subordinated to the opera house seemed to be confirmed when a large block of the northwest corner was removed from the proposed structure in the 1927 cost cuts. Brown attempted to quell this unease with the plans by inviting the veterans into the drafting room for informal discussions and design charettes. Many of the ideas generated in these meetings were adopted into the plans; other proposals proved to be impractical.[72] Although many of the veterans remained skeptical of the design process, Brown was able to demonstrate that the space allotted to the veterans was almost two-and-one-half times greater than that specified by the program of 1923.[73]

Because many of the veterans felt that Brown's work with them was mere window dressing, they appointed an advisory board to negotiate on their behalf with the board of trustees. The initial efforts of this body were not necessarily helpful to their cause. For example, in a program statement issued to the board from the veterans in February, 1928, they called for the inclusion of a 1,500-seat theater, a swimming pool, a twenty-lane bowling alley, and a replica of the U.S. Senate chamber to be used for national meetings of the United Veterans Council.[74] In March 1929, a committee representative of the rank-and-file veterans submitted to the board and Mayor Rolph a detailed program and report that objected to many features of the proposed design, including the irregular shape of the ground plan and the architectural treatment of the building. Many of these objections were somewhat architecturally naive. For example, the advisory board wrote: "The facade as set forth in existing plans for the War Memorial is, in our opinion, poorly designed. It contains neither dignity or detail and is inferior to a degree to the various public buildings now standing in the civic center. . . . Particular criticism is directed to the lowest story, particularly the entrances, which are very weak and unattractive and give one the impression of entering a basement rather than a building dedicated to the purposes for which this structure is intended."[75] The veterans threatened to walk out of the entire project and take their $4 million bond with them, unless the building was completely redesigned.

Mayor Rolph attempted to defuse this explosive situation by creating a reconciliation committee of nine members who would fairly distribute the cost reductions among the space allotted the three principal tenants. This committee recommended reconstitution of the board of trustees, which was accomplished in 1930 after much politicking. By this time, the composition of the board was altered enough to allow compromise, and both the opera house and veterans' building were built to the same, reduced ground plan. This compromise was possible largely because the capacity of the opera house was reduced to 3,300 seats, but it was also due to a more realistic assessment of the veterans' needs than in 1928. All three entities got most of what they wanted: the Music Association got its opera house; the veterans were allocated all the office and meeting space they needed and an auditorium, the 900-seat Herbst Theater; and the San Francisco Art Association received the fourth floor of the Veterans Building to house its museum. The rapid deflation of the Great Depression also assisted the architects in stretching the construction budget, which eventually reached $6 million. In the end, it became more important to the veterans and the general public that the building fund for the War Memorial be pumped into the economy than to squeeze an extra meeting room or two into the plans. By the time the cornerstones of the buildings were laid on Armistice Day, 1931, all sides were satisfied with both the program and governance of the War Memorial.

The Opera House

The War Memorial Opera House was to be the first opera house owned and operated by a municipality in the nation and would contain one of the first rooms scientifically designed for opera. It was to be the "people's opera"—popular, democratic, and underwritten largely by ticket sales. Exposed at an early age to opera of the highest caliber in New York and Paris, Brown well understood the importance of architecture to the opera-going experience. Shortly after he took over the development of the opera house, Brown realized that the size of the auditorium would drive the success of the building, from both the financial and acoustical perspective.

Throughout his development of the opera house, Brown lobbied for a reduction in the size of the house from its initial, "democratic" capacity of over 4,000 seats to a more manageable total of just over 3,300 seats. The 1927 schemes for the opera house were designed around one great sweeping balcony, modeled after the movie palaces of the time; the trustees were particularly enamored of this design concept precisely for the cinematic analogy. However, the great balcony posed architectural and acoustical challenges that could not be resolved. Brown was concerned about the acoustic problem because he had had trouble with the acoustics in the courtrooms at the city hall, and he and Lansburgh had just worked through similar questions at Temple Emanu-El.

Fortunately, he had an ally in his fight to put acoustics first. Arthur Upham Pope, a historian of Islamic art and curator at the Art Institute of Chicago, was a friend of Brown and of John Drum, who hired Pope as a "special advisor" to the board of trustees. Pope began his service to the board in November 1927 and immediately sought several leading acousticians.[76] Pope first consulted with Vern O. Knudsen, a Los Angeles–based consultant who had worked on over one hundred auditoria throughout the nation.[77] Meanwhile, Brown began a correspondence with Benjamin Wistar Morris, who was designing an opera house for the Metropolitan Opera. In March 1928, Pope called on Morris in New York and was introduced to his consulting acoustician, Clifford Swan, Wallace Sabine's chief assistant and successor.[78]

Swan became very interested in the San Francisco project and agreed to guide the design of the auditorium in conjunction with Knudsen. Swan arrived in San Francisco in late April 1928 and reviewed the auditorium plans under development, which had two balconies, seated 4,000, and featured a slightly domed ceiling over the orchestra (fig. C.10). In his official report to the trustees, Swan strongly urged a change in the ceiling design and a reduction in the seating capacity to about 3,500. He argued that only by reducing the overall dimensions of the auditorium could a satisfactory acoustic

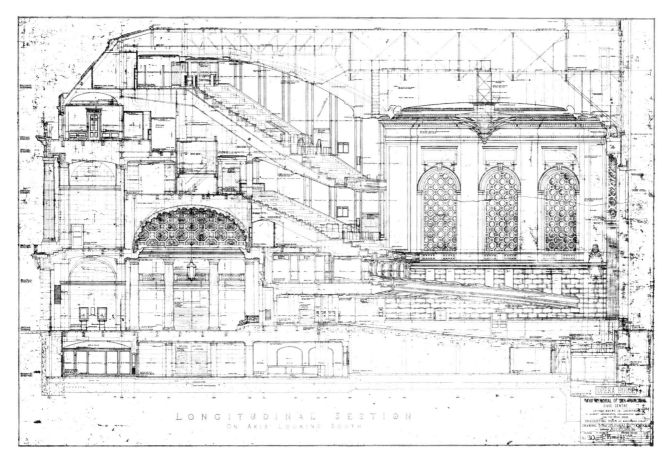

LONGITUDINAL SECTION
ON AXIS LOOKING SOUTH

OPERA HOUSE

3.44. Arthur Brown Jr. and G. Albert Lansburgh, War Memorial Opera House, San Francisco, 1930, section through auditorium from the construction documents. Arthur Brown Jr. Collection, Bancroft Library.

result be guaranteed, and that if the house could be yet smaller, an even better design could be realized.[79]

Swan's suggestions were adopted by the board of trustees after several tumultuous meetings. The final design was something of a compromise; the seating was divided between an orchestra and two relatively shallow balconies, but covered by two ceilings. By October 1928, Brown believed that the auditorium needed to be reduced yet further.[80] Providentially, within days the Chicago Civic Opera announced that it was reducing the size of its house, then well advanced in construction, from 3,750 seats to 3,250, primarily out of concern for the questionable acoustic properties of the larger auditorium. This announcement removed the last impediment to agreement on a smaller facility in San Francisco. Pope lobbied William Crocker and John Drum for the smaller house and prevailed by the end of the year.[81] In December 1928, Swan reviewed the final plans for the auditorium and deemed them satisfactory except for a

few key details. Over the ensuing year, Swan continued to review the specifications and construction details to ensure acoustic fitness.

In early 1927 Pope arranged for the hiring of Christopher Snyder as chief structural engineer, no doubt at Brown's urging.[82] The trustees originally had hired a Mr. Silverberg, a structural engineer with theater experience. It soon became apparent that he overdesigned his projects, resulting in the copious use of nonstandard sections and details, thus driving up the cost of construction. Snyder eventually took over the entire project, but was asked to incorporate Silverberg's design for the balconies, which were cantilevered on enormous rolled sections, arranged fan-like along the axis of the building; these beams were directly supported at the back wall of the auditorium on steel columns (fig. 3.44).[83] Snyder also reviewed the specifications for the War Memorial group and examined the structural soundness and installation of the stage rigging and equipment. The stage complex was the

3.45. Arthur Brown Jr. and G. Albert Lansburgh, War Memorial Opera House, San Francisco, 1928, rendering of column scheme of the auditorium, following Polk's interiors from 1923. Drawing, Arthur Brown Jr. Collection, Bancroft Library. Photograph, author's collection.

largest in an American opera house at the time it was completed and was considered a technical marvel, fully equipped with multiple fly galleries and gridirons, bridges and traps, and electrically controlled lighting and sound systems.[84] All of these technical features were consistent with the opera company's desire to merge the very successful technical achievements of Wagner's Bayreuth experiment with its own largely Latinate repertoire.

Arthur Pope also interceded on the behalf of Brown regarding the design of the interior elevations of the auditorium and, in fact, did a bit of designing himself. Brown had designed several alternative schemes for these elevations and allowed the staff to consider them while he was in the East working on the Century of Progress buildings and the Federal Triangle. While Brown was away, however, Lansburgh usurped control of the design and unilaterally advanced his favorite scheme, one that framed the proscenium with giant engaged columns (fig. 3.45).

Pope, aware that Brown favored a scheme that hid the organ grilles with large relieving arches, wrote scathing letters to Drum and Lansburgh, advising the former that the latter was acting beyond the scope of his contract.[85] To Lansburgh he was much more direct, reminding him that "Mr. Brown had left orders upon going East that he wanted several of those schemes transferred so that he could do some of the colored drawing himself. I was, of course, working on some ideas for the ornamentation of some of these various schemes. Mr. Brown does not remember saying that he preferred the column scheme. All of the schemes are his, and it is my own feeling that he would prefer the arch scheme, if further study showed it to be advisable."[86]

Brown's arch scheme prevailed and allowed him to simplify the interior and introduce the curves of the proscenium, ceilings, and balconies to the side elevations (fig. C.11). With the smaller seating capacity, Brown was also able to remove

3.46. Arthur Brown Jr. and G. Albert Lansburgh, War Memorial
Opera House, San Francisco, 1932, main foyer. Photograph courtesy
of Moulin Archives.

the front two rows from the balconies and improve the architectural qualities of the auditorium, for with this excision
the ellipse in the ceiling controlled the plans of all the balconies and boxes. The ellipse was further accentuated by the
great aluminum sunburst chandelier at the center of the
composition.

Simplicity was Brown's theme throughout the building,
not only for cost considerations but because he firmly
believed that the character of a people's opera demanded it.
For this reason, he applied very little ornamentation to the
architecture. With the exception of Edgar Walter's reliefs in
the spandrels of the proscenium and his tragic and comic
masks at the sides, no sculpture was employed in the project.
Rather, Brown used the Doric order and a consistent color
scheme to unify the interiors with the War Memorial as a
whole. The foyer, for example, acts as a collector not only for
the patrons of the opera, and by extension, San Francisco

society, but also for the architectural elements employed in
the building (fig. 3.46). The space is ordered by a series of coupled stone columns, which set out the bays of the building
but also recall the paired columns in the colonnade above it.
The vault, too, is reminiscent of the rusticated arches of the
entry and the lower zone of the auditorium, and its octagonal
soffits are used again in the grilles in the main space. The
gilding in the ceiling prepares the opera goer for the main
auditorium, where the architectural details are picked out in
gold, the walls are painted in deep gold, and the draperies and
curtain are a deep gold brocade.

The War Memorial was officially inaugurated on October
15, 1932, when the opera house opened with a performance
of Puccini's *Tosca*. At the introductions following the performance, the trustees, donors, financiers, company admin-
istrators, and performers were all acknowledged. The architect was forgotten, despite the fact that Brown was in atten-

3.47. San Francisco Civic Center with War Memorial Group, c. 1936. Photograph courtesy of Moulin Archives. Library of Congress, Prints and Photographs Division, Historic American Buildings Survey, CAL.38.SANFRA.71-8.

dance with his wife and daughters—such is the fleeting fame of architects. Still, the musical and architectural presses were unanimous in their praise of the buildings and, in particular, of the opera house's acoustics. In the end, Brown's years of struggle to achieve a musically driven design were vindicated.

The primary importance of the War Memorial complex to the history of American architecture does not lie with the individual buildings. Rather, the group is noteworthy for its urban design (fig. 3.47). For one of the few times in American urbanism, a monumental group of buildings was extended beyond its original scope and continued in the future. Brown had a nearly unique opportunity to provide the ideal architectural setting for his acknowledged masterpiece, the dome of San Francisco City Hall. As if by the command of a renaissance pope or a Bourbon monarch, Brown's buildings and formal plaza were inserted into the existing context to better glorify the city and its institutions. Yet no such decree was issued; rather, the will of the people and the moral authority of the democratic process ensured the construction of the War Memorial and the rest of the civic center. In his keynote address at the laying of the cornerstone of the War Memorial group, Richard M. Tobin, Brown's neighbor and director of the Hibernia Bank, declared the War Memorial "in the widest sense a popular work. In the cornerstones are contained the names of 65,000 contributors to the fund in sums ranging from the princely gifts of $50,000 to the pennies of the school children. . . . Our pride in the work is augmented by the consciousness that its execution has been wholly in the hands of San Franciscans. San Francisco's distinguished architect, Mr. Brown, has made a . . . new contribution to the beauty of his native city, and dedicated a lasting monument to his own gifts and acquirements. It will be said of him as of another great monument, 'If you seek his monument, look about you.'"[87]

The Continuation of the Civic Center Ideal

Brown made one last contribution to the civic center with his Federal Building on United Nations Plaza. Although a federal building was planned from nearly the beginning of the civic center, the federal government did not approve the site and the project until 1930.[88] By this time, Brown was well established with the department of the treasury and had served on the Board of Architectural Consultants for three years; thus Brown was already in federal service when he got the commission. The design of the building went very quickly, and construction documents were prepared for bidding by the end of 1932. Construction was delayed until the following year, but the building was completed by 1936.[89]

The architectural vocabulary used at the Federal Building is a combination of forms and motifs Brown had developed earlier at the city hall, the War Memorial, and the Labor–ICC block of the Federal Triangle (fig. 3.48). The building's massing is simple—the facility is essentially a five-story block surrounding a large light court. As in all of the civic center structures, the building's piano nobile rests upon a high, rusticated basement, into which arcaded entries are set along Fulton Street. Visual interest is built at the corners of the building through the use of the reentrant corner, similar to the city hall. At the Federal Building these corners are enlarged to take in an entire bay (fig. C.13). The interior of the building is strictly functional, although there is one ceremonial entry hall at the center of the Fulton Street elevation.

The Federal Building reaffirmed the city's commitment to the civic center and to the continued use of traditional architectural forms in its development. In the late 1950s a new steel-and-glass federal office building was erected on Golden Gate Avenue, which challenged the prevailing classicism of the civic center. The Office of the City Architect also had plans to construct a large International-style office complex on Marshall Square, but this project never got beyond the planning stage. In fact, financial constraints prevented any further development of the civic center until the early 1980s, when Skidmore, Owings & Merrill made a seamless addition to the opera house and designed two new buildings on Van Ness Avenue in a manner considered by many to be complementary to the civic center: the New California State Building and the Louise M. Davies Symphony Hall.[90] The Loma Prieta earthquake forced a massive $1.2 billion investment in the civic center. The completion of Pei-Cobb-Freed's new library and the Superior Court Building, the seismic upgrade of the city hall, the Civic Auditorium, and the old State Building, and Gae Aulenti's conversion of the old main library into the Asian Art Museum are demonstrations of San Francisco's commitment to its municipal heart. Eighty-five years after its inception, the civic center is still the primary unifying force in this most politically and culturally diverse city.

3.48. Arthur Brown Jr.,
San Francisco Federal Building
and City Hall, c. 1936.
Photograph courtesy of Moulin
Archives.

4.1. Arthur Brown Jr. in his first automobile,
inherited from his mother. Brown displays
his characteristic disdain for driving—
whenever possible, he was a passenger,
not a driver. Photograph, private collection,
San Francisco.

CHAPTER FOUR

BAKEWELL & BROWN
1920–1927

Arthur Brown's life became much more settled after the First World War (fig. 4.1). After his stint with the University of California in 1919, he revived his architectural practice with John Bakewell, who returned from his relief work in France in 1920. During the 1910s public institutions and quasi-public ventures such as the exposition companies and Stanford University provided the partners with much of their work; in the 1920s private interests would also request their services. Brown's social connections gave him access to clients who were building country homes, large commercial structures, and religious monuments. The firm's prewar clients also renewed their building projects. And, fittingly, the life of the firm of Bakewell & Brown concluded with the inauguration of their final civic commission, Pasadena City Hall.

RESIDENTIAL ARCHITECTURE

Many of Bakewell & Brown's clients in the 1920s were friends from the Burlingame Country Club. Although Brown did not consider himself a residential architect, he did not turn down such commissions from his friends, and, in fact, he was happy to have these jobs during the post-war recession. Usually Brown employed a French classical vocabulary much like that at the Truxtun Beale house. Occasionally, however, the client's desire or the site demanded a different mode of expression; when required, Brown could design excellent houses in a variety of modes. Two examples of this versatility are the Van Antwerp house in Burlingame and the Clark villa in Carmel.

Brown turned to English Tudor sources for the William Van Antwerps in order to provide the proper setting for their nearly unparalleled collection of late-medieval and renaissance antiques. His approach was more archeological than most such efforts in the 1920s, and the house is framed with hand-adzed oak timbers and carries over one hundred tons of slate on the roof (fig. 4.2). The interiors were designed to complement the furnishings, but they also attempt to perpetuate the forms found in late-medieval manor houses. Thus the great hall is entered through a paneled screen, lighted from an enormous lead glass–paned bay window, and features a deep paneled alcove for the Van Antwerps' pipe organ (fig. 4.3). When completed, Danvers House was considered by many critics to be one of the finest Tudor houses in the nation.

Brown's villa for Celia Tobin Clark at Pebble Beach makes an early statement on indoor–outdoor living in coastal California while referencing Italian seaside homes. The main rooms of the house are disposed about a large open atrium and fronted on the seaside elevation by an open loggia as large in area as the public rooms put together. Much of the architectural elaboration in the house is focused on the loggia, which sports a ceiling decorated with sgraffito and a Tuscan arcade (fig. 4.4).[1]

Of course, for Brown the most important house of the decade was his own. The Browns had decided to remain in San Francisco in the early 1920s and rented the Ettore Avenali house (now demolished) on Green Street while the artist and his wife worked in France and Italy; thus Brown was able to live in a house of his own design before he built his own home. While in residence on Russian Hill the Browns became fully integrated into its artistically inclined society and

4.2. Bakewell & Brown, Danvers House, William Van Antwerp Residence, Hillsborough, 1921. This is Brown's most extended essay in the Tudor mode, expressly designed to accommodate the Van Antwerp's collection of early Renaissance antiques. Photograph by F. M. Fraley, author's collection.

4.3. Bakewell & Brown, Danvers House, the William Van Antwerp Residence, Hillsborough, 1921. Interior of Great Hall. Photograph by F. M. Fraley, author's collection.

renewed their friendships with Joseph Worcester and the Norman Livermores, who lived up the street. At this time the Browns welcomed a daughter, Victoria, born in December 1921, followed by her sister Sylvia in late November 1923.

With a family of four, Brown became much more anxious to build his own home. He found himself increasingly split between his friends in San Francisco and his social connections at the Burlingame Country Club. When choosing where to build Brown eventually decided on the suburban idyll of Burlingame, where his daughters could play in a large yard and where the social opportunities so valued by his wife would be most plentiful. Brown bought a one-and-one-half-acre lot in the Irwin tract of Hillsborough. He called the estate Le Verger, the orchard, because it was the site of the fruit orchards of the estate from which the tract had been subdivided. There Brown built a large but not overwhelming two-story house that melded his French and American design sensibilities into one structure (fig. 4.5).

4.4. Bakewell & Brown, Mrs. Celia Tobin Clark Residence, Pebble Beach, 1921. The loggia extends across the entire bay front of the residence. Photograph by F. M. Fraley, author's collection.

4.5. Arthur Brown Jr., the architect's house, Le Verger, Hillsborough, 1925.

4.6. Arthur Brown Jr., the architect's house, Le Verger, Hillsborough, 1925. Photograph by Rollin Jensen, c. 1968.

Le Verger was a formal but not pretentious house, composed of a nearly square three-bay main block and two projecting pavilions, the east containing the kitchen and services, and the west, a grand library. With its steeply pitched mansard roof, quoining, and segmental lucarne dormer windows, the house was distinctively French, yet the rear opened onto an extensive terrace, through a suite of French doors, that took advantage of the California climate. This terrace was centered on a reclining statue of Apollo, Greek god of the sun, in celebration of the warm afternoons spent there. The gardens were a chief feature of Le Verger. The site was divided into outdoor rooms with high cypress hedges that bounded a formal *tapis vert* and rose garden as well as a kitchen garden on either side of the rear terrace and lawn. The rose garden was one of the largest in Hillsborough and a special point of pride for Jessamine Brown (fig. 4.6). To the rear of the yard remnants of the fruit orchard provided the family with pears and oranges.

Entry to Le Verger was through a circular foyer, which led to the library to the right and a large drawing room straight ahead. To the east of the drawing room Brown planned an elliptical dining room, which communicated with the kitchen and services in the wing. These principal entertaining rooms were decorated in the French provincial style, with cane-backed chairs, plush upholstered divans, and painted furniture. The library was the glory of Le Verger and the room in which Brown most often received visitors. Brown was always buying architectural books; indeed, in his prime he had one of the most comprehensive architectural libraries in private hands. Many of these volumes were folios of French architectural work of the nineteenth and early twentieth century, but Brown also collected most of the important works on American and British architecture of his own time as well. His collection of older treatises was fairly impressive and included first editions of Blondel, Daviler, Durand, and the entire *Vitruvius Britannicus*. Perhaps Brown's rarest book was a 1560 edition of Serlio's *Third Book of Architecture*, which included the famous engravings of the Pantheon and other ancient Roman monuments. Many of these treasures were irrevocably damaged in 1950 when a neighboring house caught fire; in an effort to protect Le Verger, the Burlingame fire department drenched the library wing with water.

COMMERCIAL BUILDINGS

Brown's friendships with the smart set of Burlingame had lasting benefits for Bakewell & Brown. Throughout the building boom of the 1920s, Brown won commercial work from companies controlled by friends from the peninsula. For example, Richard Tobin hired Brown to design a series of bank branches for the Hibernia Bank in the early 1920s; these simply ornamented corner buildings created a corporate identity for the bank in the outer neighborhoods of San Francisco (fig. 4.7). But although Brown certainly encouraged

this kind of work, he was most interested in the archetypal building of the 1920s: the skyscraper. Most of the tall buildings in San Francisco went to other architects, most notably, to Lewis Hobart, George Kelham, and Timothy Pflueger. However, Brown did design several tall buildings in the 1920s that allowed him to develop his notion of a classically correct skyscraper. Although many of these designs remained projects, Brown did have the opportunity to construct one: the headquarters for the Pacific Gas & Electric Company.

As noted earlier, Brown's very first work experience in San Francisco was the Folger Building in the South-of-Market district, and many of Bakewell & Brown's early commissions involved replacement buildings after the earthquake and fire. One of these projects, dating from 1910, was for a commercial building for Eugene Gallois on Sutter Street (fig. 4.8). This design merits consideration for its bold use of skeletalized

4.7. Bakewell & Brown, Hibernia Branch Bank, 22nd Street and Valencia, San Francisco, 1925. Photograph by Sylvia Brown Jensen, c. 1968.

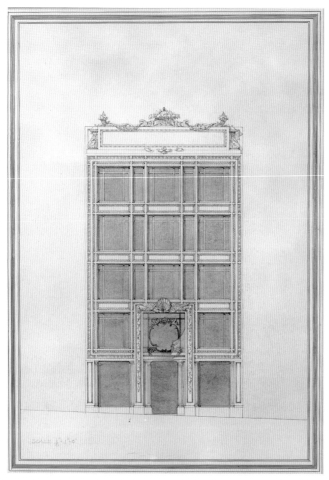

4.8. Bakewell & Brown, project for Gallois Building, San Francisco, c. 1910. With this project Brown comes close to designing an all-glass facade. Drawing, Arthur Brown Jr. Collection, Bancroft Library.

and seventh floors. In a building for Selah Chamberlain, a real estate developer, Brown created a building that was *all* fire escape.[3] Constructed in 1925, the Chamberlain Building is only 23 feet wide but ten stories high; the fire escapes stretch across the entire facade of the upper floors, their slightly bowed iron balustrades creating the dominant aesthetic statement of this concrete-and-glass building (fig. 4.9).

Brown's first design for a true skyscraper came in 1922 with the Chicago *Tribune* competition. In an effort to boost interest in the paper and to enhance its reputation for civic engagement, the *Tribune* and its executive editors, Joseph Patterson and Robert McCormick, sponsored the largest and most lucrative architectural design competition ever held to that time. Two hundred sixty-three architects competed for $100,000 in premiums by designing the "world's most beautiful office building" for the *Tribune*'s North Michigan Avenue site.[4] The paper hyped the competition throughout the six months the architects prepared their drawings, and generated great anticipation in the public for the judgment. The winners, Raymond Hood and John Mead Howells, produced a Gothic design based on the Tour de Buerre at the Cathedral of Rouen; it was built by the Tribune Company and occupied in 1925.

Although ten architectural firms were invited to participate in the competition, any registered architect was eligible to enter. Bakewell & Brown submitted an entry that compares favorably with the winning design as representative of the "traditional" entries of the competition (fig. 4.10). By the 1920s, a formula had long been worked out for the design of the skyscraper. As identified by Louis Sullivan, the tall building was analogous to a classical column and had a base of one or several stories that related the building to the street; a number of identical floors that composed the middle, or "shaft" of the building; and an ornamented crown that gave the building a distinctive silhouette against the sky.[5] There was less consensus about the architectural dress of the tall building. Early skyscrapers had been nearly invariably classical, but recent tall buildings had exploited the Gothic for its inherent vertical expressiveness. Brown attempted to fuse the prevailing Gothic paradigm, made popular with Cass Gilbert's Woolworth Building, with his own predilection for the forms of the French renaissance. The three-story base of the building features a rusticated triple portal and works in the regulating lines of the printing house behind the tower. Above a deep pedestal, Brown carries the middle floors of the building in a continuous visual sweep to an executive penthouse, which takes the form of a triumphal arch. As in Hood's design, Brown's features a vertical tower, that carries the major and minor piers of the structure through most of the building's height; Brown terminated these piers at the ornamental crown with flyers and ornamental urns.

Brown's design was not awarded any particular notice in the competition, which may be the result of his attempt to

construction and its role as a possible precursor to Willis Polk's famous Hallidie Building down the street. Designed for a 30-foot-wide lot, the five-story facade of the Gallois Building was nearly all glass; only the narrow spandrels at each floor and the frame around the edge of the building are solid. The panelized windows are set behind a thin grid of steel superstructure, which was accented with vegetal ornament indicative of the owner's vocation (Gallois was an upscale grocer).[2]

Although Brown never used a glass curtain wall in his office buildings, he did take another design feature from the Hallidie Building. Polk's building is one of the few in San Francisco to make a design element of the twin fire escapes, which by necessity are located on the front elevation of the building. The pair are composed of ornamental ironwork that is integrated into the facade; the diamond pattern of the railings is echoed in the balcony railings on the second, third,

4.9. Bakewell & Brown, Chamberlain Building, San Francisco, 1925. Brown treats the fire escape as the primary architectural element in this ten-story building that measures 23 feet wide.

create a hybrid building. As Katherine Solomonson demonstrated, the jury favored Gothic forms not only for their verticality but because they expressed the structural nature of the steel frame (a point still debated today). The jury also made associations to a spiritually centered past that, at least in myth, emphasized the individual within the context of community and reminded the *Tribune*'s coeditors of their efforts to defend Western Europe against German aggression in the recent war.[6] In addition, each of the three award-winning designs was created by architects known to the members of the jury in one way or another. Brown's design, although competent and interesting, simply did not have a look that the *Tribune* could make its signature, unlike Hood & Howell's winning entry, nor did it advance the aesthetic presentation of the tall building in the way that Eliel Saarinen's design did.

4.10. Bakewell & Brown, entry for the Chicago Tribune competition, 1922, presentation perspective. The firm's entry contains many elements that would be later used in the Pacific Service Building. Competition drawing, Arthur Brown Jr. Collection, Bancroft Library.

PACIFIC GAS & ELECTRIC BUILDING

Although Brown did not get to construct his ideal office building in Chicago, he was able to build a version of his design as the corporate headquarters of the Pacific Gas & Electric Company, commonly known as PG&E. This utility controlled nearly the entire power grid for Northern California and Nevada, and it has not always been regarded as a public beneficence by either scholars or the public. However, at its inception, the company's founders considered it a reformative institution, because it consolidated the generation and distribution infrastructure of the region's energy industry into a more efficient, integrated system. Born of the merger of William Crocker, Frank Drum, and Eugene deSalba's California Gas and Electric Corporation and William Bowers Bourn's San Francisco Gas and Electric Company in 1906, PG&E was able to wed the first company's hydroelectric plants along the Yuba, Mokelumne, and Tuolumne Rivers with the second's distribution infrastructure within San Francisco. The company also merged the interests of two great families that would become some of Brown's staunchest clients. Brown knew William Crocker, of course, because his father had worked for Crocker's father, building the Central Pacific. And although the Crockers habitually hired kinsman Lewis Hobart for many of their building projects, Brown proved his worth to the family with the PG&E building, and designed several houses for the family in the 1920s. The Bourns were already clients of Brown, and he likely owed the PG&E commission to Bourn more than anyone.

The Pacific Service Building at Beale and Market streets was the initiative of Frank Drum, who had been president of PG&E from 1907 to 1920. As the PG&E empire grew, the need to consolidate the legions of administrative workers that ran the company became an imperative. Bakewell & Brown received the commission in late 1921 or early 1922, and extensive drawings of the projected building were published in the PG&E corporate magazine in November 1922.[7] These drawings are very close to the constructed building and reveal that Bakewell & Brown cooperated closely with Bliss & Faville to unify their building for PG&E with the latter firm's building for the Matson Navigation Company, then under construction. The two buildings share a number of architectural features: a uniform base and cornice height was established, both employ arcaded crowning motifs, and both suppressed the vertical elements of the structure in the shaft behind lightly rusticated terra-cotta cladding (fig. 4.11). Behind their imposing facades, both structures carry L-shaped towers that are lighted from adjacent light courts. Brown had a composite photograph of the Matson Building and a plaster model of the PG&E Building created in order to verify the compatibility of the two structures; from this study a number of details of the crown were modified.[8]

Despite all of this neighborliness, Bakewell & Brown wanted to ensure that its building would get most of the block's attention. The crowning motif, which takes the arcade idea from the Tribune Tower design, contained the corporation's executive suites and asserts itself with great height and an aggressive broken cornice (fig. 4.12). Above this, a two-story attic both visually terminates the building and hides the mechanical penthouses. John Bakewell described the purpose of this overscaled crown at the building's completion in 1925: "An effort was also made to have a certain contrast to that building [the Matson Building] and to adopt a scale and mass which would by contrast show the semi-public character of

4.11 (*opposite*). Bakewell & Brown, Pacific Service Building (at *center*), San Francisco, 1925. Bliss & Faville's Matson Building is to the left. Photograph courtesy of Moulin Archives.

4.12. Bakewell & Brown, Pacific Service Building, 1925, working drawing with details of crowning motif. *American Architect*, November 20, 1925, pl. 310.

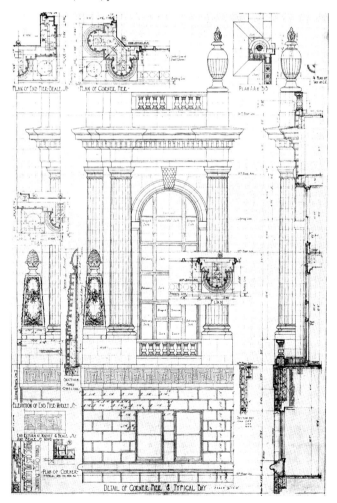

4.13. Bakewell & Brown, Pacific Service Building, 1925, main entry. Edgar Walter's allegorical and ornamental sculptural groups on the PG&E building are one of the few examples of overt regionalism in Brown's work.

treated more elaborately; the walls of the entrance hall and elevator lobbies, for example, were faced with a buff Bedford stone, and these rooms were punctuated with deeply coffered plaster ceilings. The executive offices on the fourteenth floor were paneled in oak and enjoyed spectacular views from the balconies that fronted on the principal elevations. Throughout the building, Bakewell & Brown's signature iron-work and lighting added a refined sense of detail to what was a fairly austere interior statement.

Designed in the early 1920s, the PG&E Building did not reflect the emerging concept of the modern skyscraper. Many of those reviewing the PG&E Building were conscious of the traditional, evolutionary aesthetic stance taken by the architects. These same writers also approved of the neutral form of the shaft of the building—the terra-cotta surface is only vaguely horizontal in effect and serves solely to counteract the vertical orientation of the fenestration. This design allowed the proportions of the block to dominate the particulars of its component parts, at least up to the arcade. From there upward to the cornice of the attic, the parts become disengaged from the body of the building and muddle the clarity of the cubic mass below. Those critics who advocated a less historicizing treatment of the skyscraper were troubled by Brown's French renaissance detailing. Irving Morrow, writing for *The Architect and Engineer*, criticized the schematic design for the manner in which it hid the underlying structure of the building, adding that the details were "unnecessarily, even unnaturally, stony."[11] Bakewell and Brown both revisited the PG&E Building at the end of their careers, in 1950, when they designed an extensive addition to the building in association with their successor firm, Weihe, Frick & Kruse. The team emphasized continuity with the original structure despite the twenty-five years that separated the two phases of the building. So although there is a slight recess in the Beale Street facade at the hyphen joining the original structure with the addition, the newer structure carries the same regulating lines across the facade and employs the same Granitex cladding and fenestration as the original structure, unifying the entire composition. The building no longer houses the executive offices of the corporation, but the Pacific Service Building remains in use by PG&E. In 1995 it was joined to the Matson Building and seismically upgraded and rehabilitated.

THE BOURN BUILDING

Brown's most interesting exploration of the skyscraper type may have been the series of buildings he designed for William Bowers Bourn between 1925 and 1930. Bourn approached Brown with his idea for a multi-block skyscraper development in late 1925. His goal was to build three large commer-

this public utility building."[9] This public character was also related to the viewer by the architectural ornament of the facade. Edgar Walter's sculptural group above the Market Street entrance intended to symbolize the "production and application of electrical energy"; an idealized powerhouse rests between these two allegorical figures (fig. 4.13). California agricultural products and native animals were also incorporated into the ornamental program to demonstrate the region served by the resident corporation. Thus a grizzly bear stares down at those entering the building, and ram heads decorate the keystones of the first-floor arcade.[10]

As one might expect, the interior of the building was not lavishly finished except on the executive floors. The simple, unarticulated surfaces of the exterior shaft of the building were carried inside to the office floors, where large, uninterrupted runs of space maximized the daylighting and ventilation of the interiors. The public areas of the building were cial office buildings that would move the center of the financial district a block or two north from Market and Montgomery streets. He already owned a six-story building on the gore block at the intersection of Pine, Market, and Front streets and was arranging for control of much of the blocks bounded by Front, California, and Market as well. Brown contrived a site plan that would employ the interior circulation of these buildings to link them together—that is, the lobbies and arcades in one building would align with their neighbor across the street; the group would have been a unified ensemble similar in concept to the Embarcadero Center that now occupies the blocks to the north.[12]

The Bourn Building was to be sited on a tight triangle of land whose leading corner was just over thirty degrees. The base of this building was to cover the entire block up to the eighth floor. From the ninth to the twenty-seventh floor, the building took on the form of a pentagonal tower, which was then set back to a penthouse. Entry to the building was at the narrow end, across a small triangular plaza that accommodated the foot traffic coming across Market and led to the other buildings in the complex across Pine Street. A number of elevational studies of the Bourn Building were created in order to identify an appropriate character for the entire development.

Brown's first impulse was to design another classicized tower. The earliest schemes applied thin pedimented pavilions to the centers of the facades and organized the elevations with fluted pilasters and a full classical entablature. The most compelling of these schemes, depicted in a rendering of August 1927, was as much a tribute to Willis Polk as a serious design statement; Brown terminated the tower with a very large circular temple, evocative of Polk's Water Temple at Sunol, designed for Bourn's Spring Valley Water Company fifteen years earlier (fig. 4.14). Later designs attempted a fusion of the medieval and the classic. In a 1929 design Brown eliminated much of the applied ornament of the previous drawings and gave the building a clean, spare, classical look, employing the semicircular Roman arch as a primary motif. He again terminated his tower with the arcade motif, this time in a set-back grouping of the upper office floors and an exaggerated form in the penthouse (fig. 4.15). Although some classical ornamental elements remain in the elevation, Brown attempted to work in the abstracted Gothic of the New York skyscraper architects, which had been brought to San Francisco the previous year by Timothy Pflueger in his building for Pacific Telephone.

Bourn's interest in the project waned in the latter years of the project, and eventually his worsening health forced him to abandon his skyscraper project in 1929 or early 1930. And although Brown remained interested in the design theory of commercial work throughout his career, he was forced by circumstance usually to leave the actual practice to others.

4.14. Bakewell & Brown and Arthur Brown Jr., proposal for Associated Oil Company (Bourn) Building "Water Temple" design, May 1927. Photograph courtesy of the Environmental Design Archives, University of California.

4.15. Bakewell & Brown and Arthur Brown Jr., proposals for Associated Oil Company (Bourn) Building, Modern Gothic design, c. June 1929. Photograph courtesy of the Environmental Design Archives, University of California.

Still, in his few commercial projects he attempted to integrate the office building into the urban form of the city. With the PG&E Building he sought to create a unified wall along Market Street that would catch the vista down Pine Street. With the Bourn complex, this unity takes on a third dimension and comes close to achieving the "skyscraper city" predicted in turn-of-the-century novels and realized a few years later at Rockefeller Center.

THE OLYMPIC CLUB

One of Bakewell & Brown's best clients in the 1920s was the Olympic Club of San Francisco, the first and one of the greatest urban athletic clubs of the nation. The club, founded in 1860, eventually purchased a large lot on Post Street, next to the Bohemian Club, and built several facilities there before the turn of the twentieth century. In 1905 the club commissioned Henry Schulze to design the swimming pool complex at the Post Street location; it was this project that first acquainted Brown with the club. The pool was apparently in construction at the time of the earthquake and fire, which destroyed the main club building and left the membership in disarray. Those members who remained launched a rebuilding campaign and soon commissioned Schulze to design a temporary clubhouse to adjoin his swimming pool. However, in 1909 the club suddenly announced that it would hold a design competition for a new principal clubhouse. The competition was won by Pfaff & Baur, but because Henry Schulze believed that he was still under contract to build a new clubhouse, he sued the club for enforcement of his contract. Schulze also asked members of the profession to support his claim for the commission.[13] This situation was particularly awkward for Brown, because Schulze had been his first partner, and Baur was his close friend and frequent associate. In the end, Pfaff & Baur's building was constructed and at its completion in 1912 it was hailed as one of the city's finest recreational facilities.

Brown did not become the club's architect until the 1920s, when he won the commission for the Lakeside Clubhouse. The Lakeside course and clubhouse were initially developed by the Lakeside Golf Club in 1917, when it purchased a 365-acre tract from the Spring Valley Water Company. By 1920 the golf club was forced into bankruptcy, so its directors offered the Olympic full use and control of its property for a two-year lease, with an option to buy outright the entire expanse between Lake Merced and the Great Highway at the end of the term. The Olympic Club made the most of the opportunity and purchased the parcel in 1922. The membership became so enthusiastic about golf during this time that it elected to build a second links course west of the Great Highway, which would capitalize on the ocean-front site.

4.16. Bakewell & Brown and John Baur, Associated Architects, Olympic Golf Club, Daly City, 1925, exterior view of clubhouse. Photograph courtesy Moulin Archives.

4.17. Bakewell & Brown and John Baur, Associated Architects, Plan of Olympic Golf Club as constructed, Daly City, c. 1925, plan as originally constructed by Jeffrey T. Tilman.

0 10 20   50 ft

4.18. Bakewell & Brown and John Baur, Associated Architects,
Olympic Golf Club, Daly City, 1925, principal lounge.
Photograph courtesy Moulin Archives.

This great expansion of the golfing facilities necessitated a larger clubhouse, and so the club asked John Baur to create an addition to the old clubhouse. This design was approved in plan but not in elevation, and the project languished. The following year the club asked Bakewell & Brown to design suitable elevations for Baur's project and to do the work in association with him. The resulting scheme applied French architectural motifs over Baur's massing.[14] However, just as in 1909, the club directors had a change of heart and decided to build an entirely new clubhouse, and just as in the past, they held a limited competition for plans for the new structure. Brown wished to ensure no repeat of the controversy of the earlier building campaign, and so he asked John Baur to join

him in entering the competition. One might wonder if it was pure happenstance that Bakewell & Brown and Baur won the competition, but as it happened, the associated architects demonstrated their understanding of the architectural program with their planning skills and their use of a Mediterranean vocabulary for the building (fig. 4.16).[15]

Like many of Bakewell & Brown's institutional buildings of the 1920s, and similar to the firm's Burlingame Country Club, the new Lakeside Clubhouse was designed around a courtyard (fig. 4.17). Access to the court was not direct, however; the principal axis led from the entry through a reception hall and into the lounge. The courtyard (now enclosed by a later addition) actually marked the secondary axis and was defined by the lounge, reception room, and a suite of service rooms, now the administration offices. The court's principal feature was Haig Patigian's sculpture, *Friendship*, which commemorated the life and passing of two directors of the club, John R. Hanify and Edwin A. Christenson; both men were killed in a yachting accident on the bay in 1922.[16] The lounge and the reception room were intended to evoke the character of a great villa in Tuscany or northern Spain. Each room was dominated by a large fireplace and mantelpiece and crowned with an impressive ceiling. In the reception room a stenciled beam ceiling adds warmth and color to the space; in the lounge a set of king-post trusses orders the room and adds a dramatic splash of volume and color to the space (fig. 4.18). All of the finishes in these rooms were intentionally faded and distressed to convey the impression that the rooms were old and well broken in. The large dining room was entered from both the lounge and the reception room, and it offered views of the golf course through a grand bay window and outdoor dining on a covered terrace. Of all the principal reception rooms on the first floor, none has undergone more change than the ladies' card room off of the main lounge—it was redesigned to become the club bar after the repeal of Prohibition and is now enjoyed by all members of the club late in the day.

The new Lakeside Club enjoyed a great reception upon its opening on October 28, 1925, receiving very favorable press and fully meeting the expectations of its members. After the old clubhouse was renovated for the needs of the club's professionals, the club was able to stage local and regional tournaments. Eventually the ocean course achieved the great distinction of being placed on the United States Open Championship *rota*, and the club has since hosted four United States Golf Open Championships—the last in 1998, when Lee Janzen won the event.

The expansion of the Olympic Club at Lakeside was accompanied by an effort to expand the facilities at the City Club on Mason Street, which was bursting at the seams with five thousand members on the club rolls. At first the board of directors envisioned a relatively modest addition to the club building; the swimming pool was to be demolished and relocated behind the existing clubhouse so that a new entry pavilion could be constructed in its place. Much of the existing club building was to be extensively remodeled and two new floors added—the first was to provide more hotel space, and the upper floor was to house an enormous skylit dining room and kitchen facilities. By 1925 the club had rejected this scheme and charged Baur and Bakewell & Brown with designing a completely new concept that could be self-funding. The architects designed a seventeen-story L-shaped tower at the corner of Mason and Post streets that contained several retail suites on the ground floor, a spacious new gymnasium on the second level, a dozen floors of leasable office space and hotel rooms, and social and recreational space on the upper three floors (fig. 4.19). Although the swimming pool was to be retained, much of the old clubhouse was to be leased to others, leaving only the basement level to be renovated for new locker and dressing room space.

The L-shaped tower was not accepted by the membership, and plans for the new clubhouse were revised several times between 1928 and 1930. The breakup of Bakewell & Brown occurred during this time, and Brown and Baur continued the design effort. Two main strategies emerged: in mid-1929 the team explored placing the swimming pool complex behind a seventeen-story tower that was to contain over two-hundred hotel rooms (fig. 4.20). This parti had its problems—although it presented the tower as an unbroken slab soaring up from the street, it set the pool in the middle of the block, beneath a cluster of fifteen-story buildings where it would receive no direct sunlight. A better scheme of late 1929 placed the tower in the center of the block and set the pool, hydrotherapy spa, and dining rooms in a ten-story block that fronted the tower along Post Street (fig. 4.21). The entire building was styled in the stripped classical mode with which Timothy Pflueger had much success in the late 1920s. Thin pilasters divided

4.19. Arthur Brown Jr., proposal for the Olympic Club city clubhouse, rendering of 1927 Corner Tower. Drawing, archives of the Olympic Club, San Francisco.

4.20. Arthur Brown Jr., proposal for the Olympic Club city clubhouse, mid-1929 design with plunge in back. Drawing, archives of the Olympic Club, San Francisco.

4.21. Arthur Brown Jr., proposal for the Olympic Club city clubhouse, late-1929 design with plunge along Post Street behind the arches. Drawing, archives of the Olympic Club, San Francisco.

the window bays of both the block and the tower, unifying the two elements of the building, and the chamfered corners of the tower were broken away from the crown to create a more complex silhouette at the skyline.

Like the L-shaped scheme, most of the ground floor of this second design was to be given over to income-producing uses: retail spaces and an auditorium accommodating one thousand spectators. All of these concessions had direct access to either Post or Mason Street, and they were supported by a parking garage in the basement.[17] A notable feature of this last scheme for the Olympic Club was the dramatic treatment of the entry lobby and the plunge rooms (figs. 4.22, 4.23). The center of the main block of the building was organized around three enormous four-story arches that fronted the plunge room, which was modeled on the great hall of the Baths of Caracalla in Rome and was dramatically roofed with three shallow domes. The dining room was located above the plunge and set back a bit from the building line, so that the large room opened up to a terrace.

Although this design underwent modifications over the course of 1930, the board of directors was sufficiently confident about the design to commission a large model and a full set of working drawings for the building.[18] However, as the directors negotiated the financing for the project, the value of the club's endowment and real estate assets dropped to the extent that the entire project was at first delayed and then abandoned. By 1933 the club had returned the drawings of the project to the architects and declared the project dead. Thus Brown's final opportunity to build a skyscraper in San Francisco was denied. Unfortunately, he did not handle the situation with all due grace—at the same time that the club terminated his architectural contract, Brown in turn resigned his membership. For Brown this was not a hardship, for he had been made a member of the Bohemian Club by this time, and he enjoyed the august company of that neighboring institution more as he approached his sixtieth year. But the action ensured that when the Olympic Club remodeled the City Club later in the 1930s, Brown was not considered for the work.

4.22. Arthur Brown Jr., proposal for the Olympic Club city clubhouse, early 1930, design for grand foyer. Drawing, archives of the Olympic Club, San Francisco.

4.23. Arthur Brown Jr., proposal for the Olympic Club city clubhouse, early 1930, design for the plunge. Drawing, archives of the Olympic Club, San Francisco.

4.24. Bakewell & Brown, San Francisco Art Institute, San Francisco, 1926. Photograph, Arthur Brown Jr. Collection, Bancroft Library.

THE SAN FRANCISCO ART INSTITUTE

The San Francisco Art Institute is one of Bakewell & Brown's most successful commissions, and an enduring landmark on Russian Hill. An independent college affiliated with the University of California, the institute has nurtured the aspirations of thousands of students over its 130-year history and graduated many notable artists, including John Gutzon Borglum, Chesley Bonestell, and Rube Goldberg.[19]

The Art Institute started as the art school of the San Francisco Art Association, a collection of artists founded in 1871. In the early 1870s the group sponsored a series of highly successful exhibitions that piqued the interest of a wide cross-section of San Francisco society and led to the demand for an art school in the city. The association founded the California School of Design in early 1874: within two years it was housed in rooms rented from the Bohemian Club over the California Market. The first school director, Virgil Williams, developed a highly structured coeducational curriculum that emphasized drawing and painting. The school

struggled to find stable leadership in the years after Williams's death in 1886, but in 1890 a new director, Arthur Frank Mathews, reinvigorated the curriculum and expanded the school's offerings.[20] In 1893 the school was given in trust the Mark Hopkins mansion on Nob Hill by Edward Searles, Mary Hopkins's young decorator/widower, and the school was renamed the Mark Hopkins Institute of Art. The school remained at the Nob Hill location even after the mansion was burned in 1906: it operated in temporary quarters on the mansion grounds until 1924, when it moved into its new building.

Arthur Brown first studied at the School of Art in the 1880s, when it was located over the market. He continued to take drawing and design classes at the Nob Hill location, even while he was a student at the University of California across the bay. He became a member of the Art Association as a practicing architect upon his return to the Bay Area in 1905 and remained a member and sometime officer until his death. Brown was a member of the board of directors in the early 1920s, when the association first began to look for another site for more permanent facilities, first at sites in Pacific Heights but then on Russian Hill, which afforded spectacular views of the bay and Fisherman's Wharf. In March 1923, the association sold the Nob Hill site to the developers of the Hotel Mark Hopkins.[21] It finally completed the purchase of the Chestnut Street site later in 1923. The site was purchased in trust by the University of California, which had also held title to the Nob Hill site, as per Searles's instructions.

The Art Association's executive directors, Walter Martin and Athol McBean, both requested Bakewell & Brown as the architectural firm for the new building. Because Brown was still a director of the association—and first vice-president, at that—he believed that there would be an inherent conflict of interest if his firm did the job, so he recommended that three of his associates, John Baur, Edward Frick, and Ernest Weihe, do the work, with Brown acting as an unpaid consultant.[22] Martin and McBean continued to insist on Bakewell & Brown, which led to the firm contracting for the commission in November 1924. It seems, however, that Baur, Frick, and Weihe did do preliminary schemes for the Art Institute in June 1924, while Brown was in Paris.[23] These preliminary sketches, now lost, may or may not have formed the basis for the final design. Upon his return later in the summer, Brown devoted a great deal of study to the design of the complex, and it is safe to attribute the design to both Brown and his associates. Bakewell & Brown presented a schematic design to the school's faculty and directors on January 27, 1925, and completed the construction documents the following November.[24]

The final design has many hallmarks of Brown's work in the 1920s. The building is styled in Mediterranean forms and consciously evokes the feeling of an Italian hill town (figs. 4.24, 4.25). Entry is on the high end of the site, on Chestnut, through a pedimented portal in a high wall, into a sunny arcaded courtyard that is dominated by a six-story tower. To the left, a double-height gallery space takes the form of a village church. Straight ahead, stairs lead past the administrative block to the library above, which originally offered inspiring views of the bay. To the right, two parallel wings of studios descend the hill along Chestnut Street to the block's intersection with Jones. Brown associated the hill-town imagery with artistic life in San Francisco, and certainly the steep slopes of Russian Hill and Telegraph Hill demanded small-scale structures that stepped down the hills on terraces, opening up unexpected views of the bay or the city every so often. But Brown may also have had in mind the Church of the New Jerusalem on Lyon Street as he worked on the Art Institute, because his building certainly shares several architectural motifs with the Swedenborgian church, including the frontal gable with a circular window and the bell tower. This influence would not be surprising, given that the first community of artists Brown knew was part of Joseph Worcester's congregation. The church demonstrates the coordination of the arts toward a single purpose; Brown had a similar aspiration for harmony within the walls of the Art Institute.

The program for the Art Institute buildings was relatively simple. Each department of the school required from two to twelve studios and a number of support spaces (fig. 4.26).

4.25. Bakewell & Brown, San Francisco Art Institute, San Francisco, 1926, presentation and study model. Photograph of model courtesy of Moulin Archives.

Three individual "master studios," a lecture hall (seating 350), exhibition gallery, and library were to serve the general student population, and an administrative suite provided office space for the Art Association, the school director, and two bookkeepers. In total, the program called for 45,000 square feet of space, arranged on three floors. The construction estimates for the building came in about 10 percent over the budget, and several changes were made to the scope of the project to bring the construction costs down to the board's available funds. The materials used at the Art Institute reflected both the association's budgetary constraints and the hard use the building was expected to sustain. The rough, unfinished, reinforced concrete walls, which clearly show the courses of the wood formwork, are nearly indestructible and give the complex a human scale and the impression of primitive stonework. Spanish tile and wrought iron reinforce the "primitive" qualities of the building, suggesting that the building is in the same state of rough formation as the students' emerging artistic talents. At the school's completion in 1926, most of the interior spaces were also left unfinished and only completed over time.

The most controversial of the decorating projects was Diego Rivera's mural, *Making a Fresco, Showing the Building of a City* (fig. C.14). From the first days of the new facility's operations, directors William Gerstle and Albert Bender, had been interested in bringing Rivera to San Francisco to paint a mural in its courtyard. For several years the idea remained on the back burner, primarily because Bender found that Rivera's radical-left politics made him unsuitable for a quasi-public commission in the United States. However, in mid-1929 the board's negotiations with

Rivera took on a renewed energy.[25] Senator (and former San Francisco Mayor) James Phelan and the American ambassador to Mexico, Dwight Morrow, arranged to have Rivera visit San Francisco in early 1930. Gerstle and architect Timothy Pflueger commissioned him first to paint the stairwell of the City (Stock Exchange) Club, a private commission for the Pacific Stock Exchange and sponsored by Pflueger. The resulting mural, *Allegory of California*, is a major work, unfortunately generally unavailable for public viewing.

Rivera's mural for the school was executed in mid-1931. Rivera was originally asked to paint the courtyard wall of the school gallery. This site proved too small, restrictive, and unimposing, so Rivera eventually selected the north wall of the gallery itself with its stairwell. Rivera's program for the painting seems clear: a great city is built by a host of skilled and unskilled workers, the most necessary of whom are often unseen and unheralded; these workers are depicted within a series of the spaces defined by a scaffold that alludes to the city's construction. But Rivera's mural is also self-referential. The artist himself, and his assistants, are featured prominently in the work, and they and others involved in the project are depicted in the act of creating the mural.

Many interpret Rivera's mural as a joke on San Francisco's artistic establishment. Rivera gives the viewer his backside and hovers over patrons Timothy Pflueger, William Gerstle, and Arthur Brown in an unmistakably crude manner. This image elicited ridicule in the press that put the directors of the Art Association on the defensive. If it was their intention to bring glory on themselves through the purchase of Rivera's talent, the joke was on them. Yet Rivera himself was utterly charming to his patrons. Brown had a friendly relationship

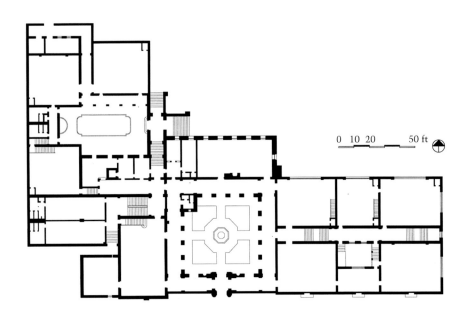

4.26. Bakewell & Brown, San Francisco Art Institute, San Francisco, 1926, plan as originally designed by Jeffrey T. Tilman.

with the painter and fully cooperated in sitting for the mural. We may wonder why Brown was grouped with Gerstle and Pflueger, particularly since Brown and Pflueger were professional rivals. Brown was not much involved in bringing Rivera to San Francisco, so he was not really Rivera's target—in fact, early cartoons for the mural show only Gerstle and Pflueger.[26] But Brown was the immediate past president of the Art Association, and the school facilities were built to his design. Someone at the Art Association apparently believed that Brown deserved to be included with the other patrons.

That "someone" may have been Jessamine Brown. Brown disliked self-promotion. His wife, however, promoted his career with such vehemence that occasionally she may have compromised his chances for a commission. She is said to have been anxious to ensure that Rivera did Brown's portrait right. According to the family oral history, upon being shown the painting Jessamine hunted up Rivera and insisted that he change Brown's hat—and then gave Rivera one of Brown's hats to use as a model![27] Apparently Rivera complied (one rarely defied Jessamine Brown), as there is clear evidence of an alteration to Brown's hat in the completed mural.

The surge in enrollment following World War II stressed the school's facilities, and in 1967 the Art Institute broke ground for Paffard Keatinge Clay's brutalist addition to the complex. Although this bold structure provided the Institute with much-needed teaching and student-life space, and included a specialized 250-seat auditorium, the placement and scale of the structure severely compromised the original building, particularly with regard to the lighting and views to the north once enjoyed by the library and several studios. Nonetheless, the Art Institute is flourishing in a competitive market, and its Russian Hill campus is a primary factor in its continued success.

TEMPLE EMANU-EL

The congregation Emanu-El dates to the very beginning of Jewish worship in San Francisco. It is one of two congregations founded after a highly successful Passover celebration in 1851 and nearly from its creation has been a leading congregation of the reform movement. The first temple, located on Broadway in North Beach, was constructed in 1854, even before the pioneer community had a rabbi.[28] The congregation soon outgrew this simple structure. Despite the Civil War and a schism within the membership, a magnificent new temple was constructed and dedicated on March 23, 1866. This Sutter Street temple was a landmark, its high, bulbous domes visible from all points in the city, and is said to have been the first structure visible from the bay when sailing through the Golden Gate. Architect William Patton's twin-towered synagogue combined a structural Gothic architec-

tural system with Judaic symbolism that was fully integrated into the design. Costing over $200,000 to build, the Sutter Street temple proudly demonstrated that the congregants of Emanu-El had achieved a full measure of economic, social, and political success.[29]

The temple was completely gutted by the earthquake and fire, but its solid stone construction ensured that it could be rebuilt. G. Albert Lansburgh, then a young member of the congregation, was commissioned to rebuild it. Lansburgh restored much of the temple's interiors, making only a few alterations, but he chose not to rebuild the tall onion-dome towers, drastically changing the appearance of the exterior.[30] In this modified condition, the Sutter Street temple continued to serve the Emanu-El congregation, even as the membership grew well beyond its capacity; within a decade of its reconstruction, the congregation was looking to relocate and build a yet larger temple building.

Rabbi Martin Meyer conceived of a multi-structure temple complex that would not only reconsolidate the temple proper and the congregation's educational facilities, but also include a host of recreational and social spaces. Although the First World War intervened, by 1920 Rabbi Meyer had refined his vision of a communitywide resource—a temple complex that would meet the spiritual, educational, social, and recreational needs of the entire Jewish community, and by extension, the entire population of San Francisco. Calling his vision the Temple of the Open Door, Meyer proclaimed that "community service is the word of the day. . . . We feel that any church or synagogue deaf to the possibility of social and community service is doomed. . . . One thing is certain, that just a house-of-prayer idea for weekly services and religious school instruction is apt to be barren."[31]

Notice that Rabbi Meyer did not restrict his statement to synagogues. This call for proactive, busy congregations was a nationwide, ecumenical phenomenon—religious groups all over America were building extensive physical plants that often combined schools, settlement houses, and recreational centers with their strictly sacred spaces. In 1922 the congregation was ready to transform Rabbi Meyer's exhortation into action. The building committee purchased a sloping L-shaped lot at the corner of Lake Street and Arguello Boulevard, just south of the fashionable Presidio Terrace subdivision. In the following year they hired an architectural team to translate the rabbi's vision into a constructed work of art. The building committee naturally called on one of its own first, Sylvain Schnaittacher, a member of the congregation and a leading architect in San Francisco. However, it was felt that Schnaittacher should collaborate with an office experienced in designing and detailing institutional buildings as large as the new temple complex. Because of their work for a number of Emanu-El congregants, including J. B. Levison and Walter Arnstein, and because of their great success with

San Francisco City Hall, the building committee chose Bakewell & Brown to join Schnaittacher as architect.

Although the partners apparently expressed some hesitancy about designing a religious structure outside their own personal traditions, they were reassured by the association with Schnaittacher. Born in 1874, he was a native San Franciscan who began his career as an office boy with A. Page Brown. Schnaittacher's early work was largely residential, but after the earthquake and fire, he did several important institutional buildings, including the Argonaut Club building on Powell Street.[32] Schnaittacher was an important member of the design team; he ensured that all parts of the design met the liturgical and cultural requirements of Jewish religious practice, and he is said to have designed much of the temple house.[33] The board of trustees also hired Bernard Maybeck to critique the plans, and employed fellow Emanu-El congregant G. Albert Lansburgh to suggest appropriate seating, lighting, and acoustical designs.[34]

The congregation also assisted the architects by presenting a spatial program for the building. The requirements included a main auditorium for seventeen hundred worshipers, a temple house containing a meeting hall for about eight hundred persons, twenty-five Hebrew school classrooms, social and recreational facilities, and an administrative wing.[35] Although Rabbi Meyer died under mysterious circumstances in June, 1923 (he was found dead of self-administered poisoning), the building campaign continued under his successor, Rabbi Louis Newman. Plans were approved on January 25, 1924, but construction was delayed while the congregation raised more money to cover the $1,280,000 cost of the building; by February 1925 construction of the sanctuary itself began with a cornerstone-laying ceremony.[36] The new temple was consecrated in April 1926 with a series of ceremonies and services (fig. 4.27). Prominent rabbis, musicians, and politicians celebrated with the congregation in dedicating the building, which Mayor James Rolph Jr. called "a towering monument to the Lord God of Israel."[37] Eight months later, in January 1927, the temple house was completed, bringing the Emanu-El complex to its full extent.[38]

The Temple Emanu-El project is one of those in Brown's oeuvre that seems predestined by his education. As students in Paris both Bakewell and Brown had worked up the *projet rendu* for October 1899, for which the first-class students were to design a large synagogue for Paris. Although neither of their entries survives, the prize-winning designs were published, and they demonstrate an interesting affinity to Temple Emanu-El—many were executed in the Byzantine style of the Levant and placed an emphasis on centralized forms, usually a dome. Julien Guadet's demand at the Ecole des Beaux-Arts that a work of architecture unmistakably express its function and place in the urban and social context

4.27. Bakewell & Brown and Sylvain Schnaittacher, Temple Emanu-El, San Francisco, 1926. The dome of the temple can be seen from much of the western half of San Francisco. Photograph courtesy of Moulin Archives.

and that the architect demonstrate both technical skill and artistry is evident in the design of Temple Emanu-El. It is a work of scientific construction adorned with the art of numerous painters, sculptors, metalworkers, and glassworkers, all controlled by a brilliant team of architects. The French method strove to destroy the Romantic myth of the architect as solitary genius, and considered the multidisciplinary collaborative effort as the supreme architectural accomplishment. For the raw power of its forms and spatial sequence, and for the stunning richness of its art program, Temple Emanu-El should be regarded as one such supreme achievement.

Temple Emanu-El is actually the most accomplished of a series of domed synagogues built in the 1920s, including Temple Tifereth Israel in Cleveland and Temple Beth Israel in Portland, Oregon. These religious structures were a response to a concern that the synagogue should become a recognized architectural type of its own in America, rather than a period-revival church with a Star of David affixed to the rear wall. Lewis Mumford, perhaps the most important architectural critic of the time, defined the synagogue problem for modern times in *The Menorah Journal* and he identified Temple Emanu-El specifically as a model for architects to follow. In his essay Mumford asked architects to identify "some unifying principle in Jewish culture and architecture" that would become the basis for the modern synagogue.[39] To Mumford that unifying principle was unity itself, expressed in architecture with the dome, and he thought that the dome could become symbolic of the Jewish tradition itself. "If it were possible for the dome to be used consistently in synagogue architecture in America," he wrote, "a very definite step would be taken towards a coherent architectural style, which would give the stamp of Judaism to a synagogue, as plainly as the Baroque gives the stamp of the Jesuit order to a church." Finally, he lauded Emanu-El's compositional technique, which allowed the support facilities of the complex to be expressed as independent masses, subordinate to, but independent of, the sanctuary: "the examples of Byzantine architecture from St. Sophia downwards are rich in honest precedents, which show how the dignity of the central mass can be combined with the more utilitarian necessities of its lesser parts. This has been very successfully done in the San Francisco temple."

Brown was quite familiar with the Byzantine—in fact, he may very well have been the only architect in San Francisco to have seen Hagia Sofia in person.[40] Brown chose to express Temple Emanu-El in what was termed a Saracenic mode, using forms borrowed from Levantine architecture tempered with Spanish colonial details and materials. The Byzantine satisfied Brown's aesthetic and historical sensibilities; the dome was, by far, Brown's favorite architectural form, and the Byzantine Empire had perfected it over many centuries. Moreover, Brown had seen many important examples of Byzantine architecture in his travels through Italy and Greece, and to Istanbul, and was interested in translating these forms to an American locale. The resulting building is both immediately identifiable as a Jewish house of worship and at home in its California context.[41] Writing about the project, Brown confirmed the significance of the dome to him: "Of all architectural forms yet imagined by the mind of man, the dome is, I feel very strongly, the most superb, the most noble and the most deeply inspiring. . . . It is most used when men wish to give material form to their most exalted sentiments. The Near East has many beautiful domes . . . and it was slowly developed in the lands about the Mediterranean until its culmination in Sancta Sophia."[42]

One of the geniuses of the temple complex is the spatial sequence from the street to the sanctuary—the faithful cross a number of thresholds on their way to worship and experience a number of spaces, each of which promotes an ever more prayerful state of mind (fig. 4.28). The first threshold is

the gatehouse on Lake Street, the entry to the sacred precinct; once up the steps and through the portal, the visitor enters the atrium, or courtyard. As he had at the Art Institute and the AT&SF terminal at San Diego, Brown organized the three units of the complex around a tiled courtyard, in the center of which he placed a fountain adorned with lions' heads (fig. C.15). This design simplified the circulation of the group and gave a cloistered feel to the whole, recalling the courts of King Solomon's Temple. The colonnade around the courtyard is constructed of formed concrete, with ornamental capitals detailed by hand; the roughness of these columns is purposefully contrasted with the highly polished antique verde marble columns of the interior. Two high pylons mark the junction between the arcade and the portals to the sanctuary. Almost without precedent, these solid masses of concrete are terminated by a peristyle of eight columns crowned by a highly stylized arched entablature, above which Brown placed a more conventionally arcaded second stage and vegetal finial. These pylons serve no purpose but to accentuate the portals; they also represent one of the very earliest examples of art deco found in San Francisco. From the atrium, entry to the temple building is from a deep travertine porch and through a high arcaded portal like an ancient triumphal arch. This triumphal spirit is enhanced by the presence of the Eternal Light and the Tablets of the Law.

The transition from the fairly monochromatic atrium to the rich, vividly colorful space of the narthex could not be more dramatic. The room has an otherworldly, submarine feel, which quiets the mind in preparation for worship. It is said that Bernard Maybeck worked out the color scheme for the narthex, with its strong cerulean blue ceiling, gold sten-

4.28. Bakewell & Brown and Sylvain Schnaittacher, Temple Emanu-El, San Francisco, 1926, plan by Jeffrey T. Tilman.

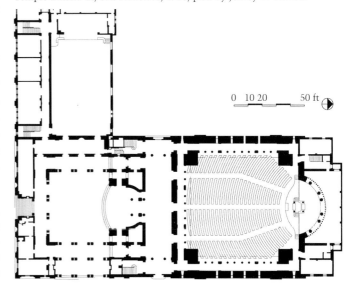

cil work, and leather doors. From the relatively low narthex, the worshiper enters the overwhelming space of the main temple (fig. C.16). A massive room, this sanctuary is defined by four vaults that rise unbroken from behind the balconies to meet the saucer dome of the ceiling. Three thermal windows, originally glazed with hundreds of pale amber panes, light the dome from the east, south, and west, and direct the eye toward the bema and the ark.[43] Architecturally, the space is ordered by the arcades of antique verde columns to support the balconies. These columns are also the primary architectural ornament of the room and present a set of unique, stylized Byzantine capitals designed by Edgar Walter and Richard Howard. Yet the columns do not distract from the one highly ornamented zone of the sanctuary, the bema and ciborium. The ciborium is particularly effective, as the stark, sharply chiseled forms of the pyramidal roof and arcaded sides contrast with the four marble columnar supports, the Eternal Light, and the richly enameled ark, the focal point of the composition, and indeed, of the entire building. The ciborium acts as a protective shelter for the ark, an ancient hut that shields the ark from direct exposure under the heavenly expanse of the dome.

The ark itself is one of a handful of outstanding works of sacred art in the United States (fig. 4.29). Its form, general dimensions, and essential iconography were designed by Brown in consultation with Schnaittacher. The specifics of the ornament and the unsurpassed artistry of the ark's realization belong to its creators, Los Gatos artisans George Dennison and Frank Ingerson, who revived several nearly lost ancient enameling and metalworking techniques to produce their masterpiece.[44] The form of the ark itself is significant—the architects insisted that the ark not be a cabinet in the wall, but a freestanding object modeled after the very first ark (although at 9 feet high and 3,000 pounds, no one will be carrying it through the deserts of the Sinai). This three-dimensional form emphasizes the ancient quality of the sanctuary, and also ties a number of ornamental and symbolic elements together to unify the space. For example, the lions' heads on the handles recall those in the courtyard, and the fish scales on the top of the ark echo the windows in the sanctuary as well as the belt courses in the courtyard and the tile roofs of the entire complex. The stylized Star-of-David on the front of the ark is precisely on axis with that above the main doors at the portal, communicating to the congregation that the truths promised at the entry to the temple are contained within the ark in the words of the Torah.

The ark was several years in the making. Dennison and Ingerson, already known for their jewelry, ceramics, and enameling, were asked to design the ark in early 1925 as a memorial to Marcus S. Koshland, an important contributor to the temple construction fund. The two artists traveled to Paris to study the Baron de Rothschild's collection of Judaica,

4.29. Bakewell & Brown and Sylvain Schnaittacher, Temple Emanu-El, San Francisco, view of bema, ciborium, and ark.

and then to London to consult the collections of the British Museum. While in London they located the A. B. Burton foundry, known for its traditional metal-casting techniques. The two artists set up their workshop nearby, in a Tudor building once used by Henry VIII as a hunting lodge. For fourteen months Dennison and Ingerson experimented with ancient enameling techniques, and eventually they crafted the six hundred jewel enamels that shimmer on the ark's exterior. Dennison employed the art of sculpted enamels, six of which adorn the top of the ark. Ingerson worked on the gesso-painted interior, whose stylized tree of life glows in vermilion, blue, and gold. Together, the couple also mastered bronze casting and leatherworking to enable them to craft the ark themselves as a total work of art. Their work caused a sensation in London at its completion; crowds gathered to view the ark before it was crated for transport, delaying its delivery to the temple in San Francisco.[45]

Response to the new Temple Emanu-El was extraordinarily generous. Rabbi Newman, usually fairly reserved, was overjoyed and wrote a lengthy description of his new temple for the architectural press: "There is a rugged and potent barbaric splendor in the edifice which is achieved with an almost too great simplicity of decoration. . . . The chief impression of the beholder is of vast and almost primitive power. Thus the heroic mood of the ancient Hebrew warrior is fused with the mysticism and rationalism of the modern Jewish worshiper."[46] Harris Allen, writing in *Pacific Coast Architect*, termed the temple "one of the great monuments of San Francisco—perhaps the greatest." He particularly praised the dome, which he thought appeared to float above the building: "to achieve such an effect, a great golden bubble, lofty, soaring in the sky, and still to preserve a feeling of architectural unity with the solid substance of its substructure, comes little short of being a triumph."[47] Brown's professional colleagues of the Northern California chapter of the American Institute of Architects thought very highly of the building, and awarded its architects the Distinguished Honor Award as the best building of the decade. The citation lauded the temple as, "a glorious building, placed most effectively upon a difficult site, beautifully planned and modeled, the utmost care and thought given to all of its details, it realizes to the highest degree the expression of its religious character."[48]

If one architectural criticism of the sanctuary is allowable, it is that it has no connection to the high outer dome overhead. The dome room, 100 feet above, enjoys unparalleled views of the western part of San Francisco from its ring of windows, but it can only be reached from a series of long and dusty staircases. One could question why Brown chose to set such a high dome above his sanctuary if this space would not be better utilized. It is with the dome, however, that the temple rises above mere functionalism to the realm of architecture. The dome acts as the congregation's gift to the urban form of the city, and as a landmark around which people set their mental maps of the surrounding neighborhoods. Equally important, the dome symbolizes the spiritual world and proclaims the acceptance and success the Jewish community has enjoyed in San Francisco's spiritual and civic life. High in the dome, one feels a rare sense of belonging to the community, both gentile and Jewish. The goodwill and respect the Jewish community has traditionally found in San Francisco has been reciprocated to the city by the Emanu-El congregation in many ways, not in the least by its decision to commission a team of leading artists and architects of many faiths to build this supreme house of worship. With the great dome, the associated architects, and Arthur Brown Jr. in particular, found a way to return the favor.

The Temple Emanu-El project was not Brown's only work for the Jewish community. Even a casual glance at his client list demonstrates that many of the Bay Area's leading Jewish families employed him as architect for their residences or commercial buildings. Many of these clients met Brown through his clubs, particularly the Cirque de l'Union, University, and Olympic Clubs, which did not bar Jewish membership. As prominent members of the Jewish community attained positions of authority within the city's art institutions, Brown found himself favored as architect for these projects—this is certainly the case with the War Memorial and the Art Institute. Yet Brown definitely moved in a different social circle from many of his Jewish clients, and he maintained a certain respectful separation between his world and theirs, at least when it came to familial relationships. Brown did count many Jews as personal friends, particularly those involved in the artistic community, such as Ernest Piexotto, Edgar Walter, and William Gerstle; his oldest Jewish friend may have been Emile Pontremoli, who became professor of theory at the Ecole des Beaux-Arts in the 1930s. Brown also collaborated with several younger Jewish architects on projects that warranted his assistance, such as the Jewish Community Center on California Street (now demolished), which he designed in association with Hyman & Appleton between 1931 and 1933.[49]

PASADENA CITY HALL

Bakewell & Brown's final important work, apart from its projects at Stanford University, was the municipal administration building for the City of Pasadena, which was dedicated just days before the formal dissolution of the partnership. Brown's design for Pasadena City Hall was intended to reinforce the town's identity as the quintessential Southern California community—and it does this brilliantly. The soaring open tower of this building has transcended the structure's specific program and locality to become a more universal symbol of the Southland. This is not unexpected. Like many of Pasadena's eastern founders, Brown was a romantic who imposed upon his city hall the architectural equivalent of an essay by Charles Fletcher Lummis—it was a mythical sun-drenched idyll that commented as much upon the present as on the past. Brown's tower harkened back not only to the days of the Spanish ranchero, but to Pasadena's fading literary and artistic prominence and to the region's well-established film colony. Now amplified by the entertainment industry, the mythic Southern California represented by Pasadena City Hall still holds currency for many Americans today.

The Pasadena of the 1920s was certainly not that of the Franciscan padres, but it was also not the Bohemian crafts

4.30. Bakewell & Brown, Pasadena City Hall, c. 1924, perspective view of refined bell-wall scheme. Photograph, Arthur Brown Jr. Collection, Bancroft Library.

community of Lummis or Greene and Greene, either.[50] No longer the solely residential enclave of wealthy industrialists it had been at the turn of the century, Pasadena had reached a demographic and economic maturity that demanded an expanded vision of its place in Southern California's constellation of communities. Great academic institutions, such as Caltech and the Huntington Library in nearby San Marino, both diversified the city's economic base and attracted a group of highly educated professionals committed to improving the city's well-being. One of these gentlemen, Caltech astronomer and future university president George Ellery Hale, worked harder than anyone to ensure that Pasadena had a first-class general plan and a vision for the buildings that would inhabit that plan.[51]

Hale began his campaign for a plan for Pasadena by making a presentation to the city's mayor, Hiram Wadsworth, the city board of directors, and leading city businessmen. Many of these civic leaders were, like Hale, sober, business-oriented Midwestern Protestants who expected to enjoy the benefits of progressive Republican government established in the previous decade. One of these benefits was an ordered

improvement of the city's urban form that would ensure that Pasadena would remain a "city of homes" while capturing its share of the ever-growing expansion of the region's commerce. Hale was given the green light to hire an urban planner to develop the plan; he immediately called Edward Bennett. In April of 1922 the City of Pasadena formally created a City Planning Commission, with Stuart French as chair. The following month the firm of Bennett, Parsons & Frost was commissioned to provide the city with a blueprint for its future development—a key feature of this plan was a civic center.[52]

Edward Bennett's civic center attempted to integrate a number of existing institutional buildings north of Colorado Boulevard into a civic district grouped around Garfield Avenue. At either end of this primary axis Bennett planned a new public library and a civic auditorium. A cross-axis was established on Holly Street, at the center of the group, where a new YWCA and YMCA (designed by Julia Morgan and Arthur Benton, respectively) offered a pair of compatible quasi-civic buildings. In Bennett's plan Holly Street would be extended to Orange Grove Avenue to create a site for an art

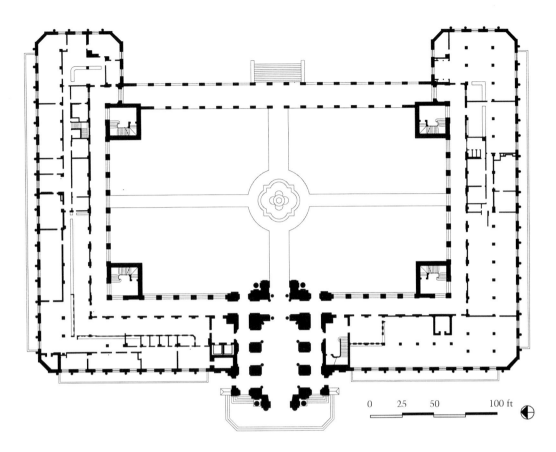

4.31. Bakewell & Brown, Pasadena City Hall, c. 1926, first-floor plan
by Jeffrey T. Tilman.

museum on the grounds of the Carmelita estate, now the home of the Pasadena Art Institute's Norton Simon Museum. At the intersection of these axes, at Garfield and Holly, Bennett proposed a grand plaza, before which was to rise a new city hall. Little attention was given to enlarging the city's commercial or industrial infrastructure; in fact, Bennett and his sponsors wished to be highly selective about which industries would be permitted in Pasadena. As Bennett stated, "Pasadena is a high class residential community and is not an industrial center, although it should welcome industries of the finer type. The quality of commerce and not quantity is the thing to be sought."[53]

Bennett introduced his plan to city leaders at a series of dinner meetings and official hearings in March 1923. At the same time, the city's legal team drafted a bond issue for $3.5 million that would support the costs of land acquisition and construction for the principal buildings of the new initiative. This bond issue passed with over 75 percent of the vote on June 7, 1923, causing the Pasadena *Star–News* to exclaim that the vote "betokens a new day in Pasadena—a day of harmony and unification in civic affairs; a day of dedication to virile policies of unintermitting advancement, along right lines."[54] In December the City of Pasadena announced that it was sponsoring an invitational design competition for the three new civic buildings: the library, the auditorium, and the city hall. Nine architectural firms, among them Bakewell & Brown, submitted drawings for each of the three buildings, from which winning designs were selected in late February 1924.[55] The jury, composed of both lay and professional members, considered three principal points in evaluating the entries: first, the general arrangement and composition of the plan with regard to function and operation; second, the adaptation of each building to its site; and third, the architectural character of the building, with particular reference to the unique climate and environment of Pasadena.[56] Myron Hunt, a well-known architect from Los Angeles, won the competition for the library with a Spanish renaissance design, while Edwin Bergstrom of Los Angeles and Bennett & Haskell of Pasadena prevailed with their Franco Italian proposal for the municipal auditorium. Bakewell & Brown won the city hall commission with a French renaissance *palais* to which a large mission-style bell–wall was appended (fig. 4.30).[57]

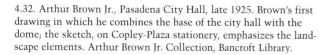

4.32. Arthur Brown Jr., Pasadena City Hall, late 1925. Brown's first drawing in which he combines the base of the city hall with the dome; the sketch, on Copley-Plaza stationery, emphasizes the landscape elements. Arthur Brown Jr. Collection, Bancroft Library.

4.33. Arthur Brown Jr., Pasadena City Hall, late 1925, schematic design sketches for dome and stair towers. Arthur Brown Jr. Collection, Bancroft Library.

It is not surprising that Bakewell & Brown won the city hall competition, despite the awkward appearance of the central motif of their design. One of Brown's closest professional friends, Robert Farquhar, served on the jury, and William Parsons, Brown's confrere from the Ecole des Beaux-Arts and Edward Bennett's partner, acted as professional advisor to the competition. Still, the design won on the merits of its circulation, flexibility, and integration into the civic center. The cortile form of the building, in which the circulation on all floors was open to the air and lined a landscaped courtyard, charmed the jury and celebrated Pasadena's exceptionally mild climate (fig. 4.31). The design also allowed the city to subdivide the interior in any way required of its departments. Finally, the idea of the overscaled focal element, if not the detail of the bell-wall, evidenced more than any other design an understanding of the role of the city hall in organizing Bennett's rather dispersed civic center.[58]

John Bakewell emphasized these points in describing the design to the press: "The entrance to the building is really an entrance to the patio, and from the patio one can proceed to the desired department directly. This makes the interior court an integral part of the plan, and every one entering the building passes through the court. . . . The exterior treatment of the building was designed to make a fine terminal effect for one of the principal vistas in the new civic plan. The belfry selected has a strongly appropriate character. The style of the belfry is used a great deal in the South of France and Italy in the Renaissance architecture of these countries."[59] Notice that Bakewell does not describe the building as Spanish. Bakewell & Brown intended the building to be Mediterranean, rather than evocative of just one nation. Nonetheless, the press in Pasadena at the time of the building's construction often termed the building Italian renaissance, despite the fact that the primary references made in the building's design were to structures in France and Spain.

Bakewell & Brown was awarded the commission in March 1924 and asked to submit a series of designs for the central motif over the next nine months. The bell-wall of the competition design was not acceptable to the city officials, nor was Brown particularly pleased with it. The evolution of the design to its final form demonstrates Brown's ability to refine an idea. At first, the changes to the bell-wall were minor. By the early fall of 1924, however, Brown was working on a more three-dimensional form of the motif. In this later version, the second stage of the wall opened up into an arcaded loggia, baroque in spirit, which was crowned by broken pediments over the flanking pilasters and a segmental pedimented third stage. Brown developed some plasticity in this later

4.34. Bakewell & Brown, Pasadena City Hall, view from Holly Street. The final design seamlessly integrates at least three independent compositions into the whole. Photograph by Rollin Jensen.

4.35. Bakewell & Brown, Pasadena City Hall, frontispiece.

the dome was placed upon the arcaded entry block Brown had salvaged from his competition design. Initially Brown considered placing the dome in the center of the building—the position it has at the Escorial. Wisely, he moved the entire composition to the front of the block, where the flow from base to dome is uninterrupted, and where this extraordinary assemblage of forms dominates the entire civic center.

The dome tower at Pasadena is really three buildings placed atop one another (fig. 4.34). The lowest zone of the composition, largely unchanged from the competition drawings, occupies the full height of the office blocks. The model for the frontispiece of the entry block is Salomon de Brosse's gatehouse for the Palais de Luxembourg. Whereas Brown used this rotunda in miniature for his stables at Filoli, at Pasadena he enlarged the lower floor of the street facade up to nearly twice its size to create the enormous entry arch. The flanking rusticated Doric columns, coupled in Paris, are set in different planes in Pasadena; this design permitted Brown to project the central pavilion forward to give the entry added prominence. The composition of the ornamental group over the entry arch was given particular attention (fig. 4.35). Brown pushed the voussoirs and keystone of the arch through the entablature. The richly carved pediment supports a pair of urns and fasces as well as a 16-foot-high cartouche on which the city insignia, a crown and keys, is carved. The cartouche actually projects above the balustrade that tops the attic of the lower zone, which was also modeled on the Luxembourg Palace, but this time on the upper floor of the end pavilions. The two-story base is open through its entire depth; only the main stair and an office for the building's concierge are accessed from the vaulted passage under the tower. The viewer is thus made immediately aware of the connection between the plaza and the garden court beyond.

The middle zone of the dome tower is roughly octagonal in plan, although the diagonal faces are actually concave segments of the circle described by the drum of the dome above. With this design Brown was able to build the open-air dome and observation tower he had had in mind since he sketched ideas for San Francisco City Hall in 1911 and 1912. The dominating motif of the elevations is that of the triumphal arch, as employed by many of the masters of the Italian baroque. The double-height primary arch (which repeats the arch of the entry below) is flanked by single-height arches on the diagonals, over which square openings are set. Both sets of openings are controlled by an Ionic order. The axial arches are set within coupled columns, which sit directly over the Doric columns below, thus providing the apparent structural continuity Brown valued in his domes. The upper zone of the tower, drum and dome, is an interpretation of the dome of the Escorial, in which the columns of the prototype are replaced with pilasters. The dome, over 200 feet above the street, is roofed with Cordova clay tile, originally multicol-

design, but the detailing of the segmental pediments was awkward; broken up as they were in plan and elevation, the entablatures seemed to serve no purpose.

In late 1924 Brown finally found the architectural device for which he was looking. He translated the open loggia of the intermediate design from a rectangular plan to an octagonal one. The result was the dome tower, without question the most audacious composition in all of Brown's oeuvre. One can see the idea come together in sketches found between the leaves of Brown's copy of Guadet's treatise: elements of several baroque buildings from France and Spain are sketched, particularly the towers and dome from the Escorial (figs. 4.32, 4.33). The western towers of the church were translated into the four corner stair towers at Pasadena, and ored but now red, which gives the surface the coarser texture required of an element that is commonly viewed from up to half a mile distant (fig. C.17).

The Garfield Street elevation of the city hall is dominated by the dome tower, but Brown was careful to introduce refinements into the long wings of the building to avoid monotony and to ensure the building's pleasing appearance from either end of the Garfield Street axis. The office wings were cast as two-story blocks, with a recessed attic at the third story; the Doric entablature of the entry block continued around the building to emphasize this interpretation of the building's section. The ground floor was given additional interest by encasing every other window with projected pedimented window surrounds. These aedicules established a rhythm across the facade of the 374-foot-long elevation and, with their rustication and mannerist ornamentation, referred back to the main block of the dome tower.

Although the budget for Pasadena City Hall was considerable (over $1.25 million was spent on its construction), a newly elected city government, under pressure to cut costs, demanded that significant parts of the city hall project be eliminated. The most startling proposal was to remove the dome tower from the building. Bakewell & Brown demonstrated with renderings what the building would look like without the second or third stage of the tower. The cost savings was determined to be minimal and the decapitated building looked weak and unappealing; they argued in the Pasadena press that the dome was essential to the visual and functional success of the entire civic center project.[60] Eventually, the city directors agreed and approved the construction of the entire dome.[61] Other cost-cutting measures were permanent. A three-story wing fronting Euclid Avenue, containing the council chambers and mayoral suite, was relegated to a later phase of the project and never constructed.[62] This wing was replaced with an arcade, which provided covered passage between the rear stair towers and continued the cloister walk around the courtyard. In many ways Pasadena City Hall cannot be considered complete without the rear wing, because all of the representational interiors of the building were planned for this structure. The present council chamber was a temporary expedient, and while well finished, was not considered by Brown to be representative of his interior architecture.

The dome tower dominates the courtyard, but other important elements make the scale appropriate for this outdoor room. Immediately visible is the burst of color from the landscaping—Brown intended the courtyard to be a showcase for the potential of gardening in Southern California, and to this day the courtyard is one of the most well-cared-for spaces in the Southland. The court itself is bounded by four stair towers, each rising four stories in two stages, and resembling in outline the towers of the Escorial (figs. 4.36, C.19).

As with the dome tower, the second stage of these stair towers is an open arcaded pavilion, framed by pilasters and set off by urns and cartouches. Above, the towers are roofed in lead and capped by belvederes identical to that on the dome. The centerpiece of the courtyard is an enormous fountain that fills the space with the sound of splashing water (fig. C.18). Similar to a fountain Brown designed to win one of his last *projets rendus* at the Ecole des Beaux-Arts, the fountain at Pasadena City Hall rises majestically from its quatrefoil basin to high bowl. Green men and sea monsters spit water down into four shell-shaped catch basins, complementing the generally grave ornament of the city hall itself with a whimsical touch.

Pasadena City Hall confirmed Brown's ability to compose diverse architectural elements into a unified whole, and the building was also a landmark in the use of concrete in traditional building. The entire building was constructed of rein-

4.36. Bakewell & Brown, Pasadena City Hall, garden courtyard and stair tower. Photograph by Rollin Jensen.

forced concrete except for the lower stories of the tower, which are framed in steel.[63] The somewhat crude detailing Brown had devised to build in concrete at Berkeley City Hall in 1907 gave way here to a refined architectonic system; this improvement reflected a growing confidence with concrete on the part of both the architect and the construction industry. By the 1920s concrete was seen as a material particularly suited to California. In 1928 Harry C. Allen wrote: "the flexibility of a material [concrete] which lends itself not only to broad surfaces but to highly ornamented areas as well, fitted it exceptionally to the style which can now fairly be called 'Californian.' Based on the traditional and appropriate Spanish Colonial architecture of early California and Mexico, and finding much of congenial inspiration on the Mediterranean shores of Italy, France, Spain, Africa, it has become a law unto itself."[64] Many viewed concrete as a modern-day adobe, a material possessing the mass and plastic qualities of Spanish colonial building, but with the strength and permanence of the industrial age. Bakewell & Brown achieved the fine detailing they did at Pasadena City Hall through the use of high-strength concrete. Construction by the Orndorff Construction Company went remarkably quickly. Ground was broken for the building on January 21, 1926, and the building was substantially complete by the fall of 1927.

The public responded enthusiastically to Pasadena City Hall, and the local press was equally positive, even if the Pasadena Star–News repeatedly termed the design "Italian renaissance."[65] The building was extensively illustrated in both The American Architect and The Western Architect, but neither journal published any editorial piece on the building.[66] The Architect and Engineer commissioned an essay by John Bakewell, in which he explained the building's design, giving particular emphasis to the dome tower, and defended the firm's eclectic stance with this design: "The expression of the architectural themes. . . . has been inspired by the work of the later renaissance architects and by more modern interpretations of the work of that school. The happy circumstance that the sunny climate of Southern California lends itself admirably to a modern development of the architecture of the Mediterranean has been kept in mind and makes the use of rich ornament particularly appropriate and effective."[67] Bakewell goes on to justify the apparent extravagance of the "functionless" dome tower. As at Temple Emanu-El, the dome tower at Pasadena City Hall relates the building to the city, and brings the city to the building. At Pasadena the spectacular landscape surrounding the city doubly justifies the tower. Bakewell makes this case, writing: "The dome becomes a great belvedere which commands a wonderful view of the city of Pasadena, with its beautiful gardens, and with the surrounding country and mountains as a background. These beauties are thus made an integral part of

the building itself to be enjoyed from this lofty terrace and give this feature great aesthetic value."[68]

Most critics of the building have agreed that the liberties taken at Pasadena City Hall were warranted, given the novel form of the tower, and many have even reveled at its fairy-tale-like fantasy. The first appreciation of the building in the modern period came with James D. Van Trump's glowing report in the Pennsylvania Journal of Architecture: "the great open arches of the tower-dome, pierced by light and air, surrounded by obelisks, garlands, and urns might be the dwelling place of Renaissance royalty costumed as Apollo or Aphrodite. Is this the golden breast of Juno or the divine phallus of Jupiter?" He affirmed the city hall as "an authentic document of southern California. . . . as a delight to the eye and the imagination there is nothing else like it in America."[69] David Gebhard described the building as a "marvelous confection" and proclaimed it superior to San Francisco City Hall, in large part because the building "reflect[s] the myth and fact of California's Hispanic tradition."[70]

Gebhard certainly identifies the fundamental truth of the building's appeal—it is a characteristically California building, despite making almost no reference to any one California structure. Pasadena City Hall is but one example of a number of Southern California civic buildings constructed in the 1920s that reinterpreted Mediterranean and Spanish colonial sources. The contemporaneous Santa Barbara County Courthouse, designed by William Mooser Jr., is perhaps closest to Pasadena in conception, and illustrates where Bakewell & Brown departed from their colleagues in the use of Hispanic sources for these buildings. By local ordinance the Santa Barbara County Courthouse had to reference only Spanish colonial architecture. Mooser's initial designs were heavily criticized by the city's architectural review panels as not being Spanish enough, so he went to Spain to acquire details for the project, such as the projecting oriels and the winding stairs. Much of the finish work at Santa Barbara was locally crafted by artisans active in Santa Barbara, who were given a generous amount of freedom in executing the work.

By contrast, every aspect of Pasadena City Hall was designed by the architects and executed by the contractors according to their drawings. This control was expected of them as architectural professionals. This professional mindset extended to the form of the building, because they believed that only the architect should determine the sources from which the building should draw. Bakewell & Brown approached the Pasadena job as a purposefully eclectic monument, whose design interpreted the classical architectural heritage of Mediterranean Europe, to which, by extension, Southern California belonged. When the California missions proved to be an inappropriate source for the central motif of the building, they did not hesitate to evaluate other, more canonical sources. The result of this investigation was a well-integrated tower, in which no one part overwhelms the whole, and an unforgettable building that then, as now, was perceived as quintessentially Californian.

THE BREAKUP OF BAKEWELL & BROWN

Bakewell & Brown had operated as a professional partnership for twenty-two years when Brown was appointed to the Board of Architectural Consultants in Washington in May 1927. The prospect of an individual commission in the Federal Triangle and the probability that the War Memorial Opera House would be contracted to Brown alone prompted Brown first to amend the partnership agreement and eventually to dissolve the firm. Both Bakewell and Brown restructured their practice with reluctance. They had the utmost respect for one another and continued to be friends as well as professional associates. However, the structure of the original partnership did not allow for independent work and demanded that profits be split evenly between the partners. By 1927 the partners may have outgrown the need for each other. Although Bakewell had always handled the business side of the office, written the specifications, and observed the construction on most of the partnership's work, it became evident to Brown that these services could be hired out at much less cost than 50 percent of the profits. Furthermore, Jessamine Brown was a primary lobbyist for breaking up the partnership. It is said by the family that she felt that her husband was due the lion's share of the credit and the profits for Bakewell & Brown's success, and she was not shy in letting her husband know this. According to the family oral history every day at breakfast she would ask her husband, "Is this the day we fire Johnny Bakewell?" After several years of this campaign, Brown finally relented.[71]

In June 1927, Brown began the dissolution process by hiring a new office manager, Tracy W. Simpson, who was charged with reorganizing the firm into two entities that could function independently as well as collaborate when required. In July 1927, the partnership published the following press release through *The Architect and Engineer*: "The firm of Bakewell & Brown, San Francisco, announces a change in their organization. Mr. Arthur Brown, Jr., and Mr. John Bakewell, Jr., will continue to carry on the work of Bakewell & Brown as associates or partners. However, the two members of the firm will, in certain new work, act as individuals, each conducting his own separate business. The present offices at 251 Kearny Street will be retained."[72] By the end of the year a formal dissolution was in place. The offices were split between Brown and the new partnership of Bakewell & Weihe, and work in the schematic design phase was assigned to each firm. Work at Stanford continued jointly, requiring that a third set of books be maintained. Other clients were given the opportunity to choose between the two organizations; as might be expected, over 80 percent of them chose to employ Brown.[73] Office staff members were given a similar choice and, knowing that most of the work would follow Brown, they too signed onto Brown's firm in disproportionate numbers. Edward Frick, J. S. Gould, and Lawrence Kruse remained with Brown and became senior associates within the new organization. On January 1, 1928, the new firms officially began.

While the office of Arthur Brown Jr. was poised to become a firm with a national clientele, Bakewell & Weihe remained an active regional firm. Bakewell assumed the same roles in his new partnership that he had in his old; Weihe did most of the design work, Bakewell wrote the specifications, observed the construction, and administered the firm. Bakewell & Weihe became best known for their academic and healthcare work, much of which was in association with Brown on the Stanford University campus. The firm's last work was at the Golden Gate International Exhibition, where the partnership designed the main entry, the Portals of the Pacific. The firm dissolved in 1941, when Weihe joined Edward Frick and Lawrence Kruse to form Weihe, Frick & Kruse.

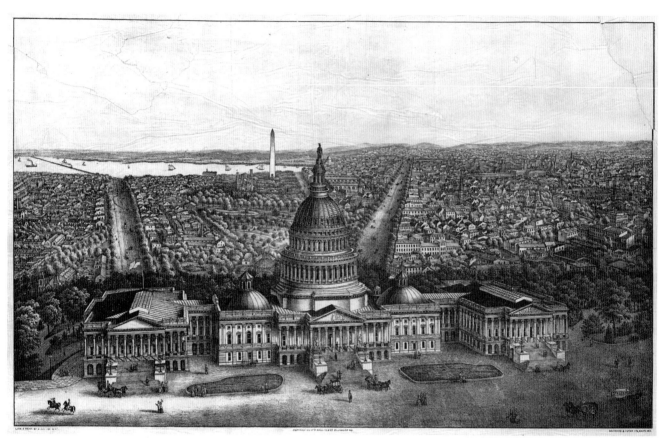

5.1. E. Sachse, View of Washington City, 1871. Engraving,
Library of Congress, Prints and Photographs Division.

CHAPTER FIVE

GRAND DESIGNS FOR THE FEDERAL REPUBLIC

Arthur Brown made the conscious decision to become a primarily Pacific Coast architect who at times designed buildings and ensembles for the national stage. In this respect he was emulating his revered patron, Victor Laloux, whose buildings in the Touraine responded to regional needs, yet who also built his most renowned work in the capital. Whereas Laloux easily sustained this dual practice, Brown had more difficulty in this because the travel between San Francisco and the major cities in the East and Midwest consumed a great deal more of his time. Still, Brown worked in Washington on three federal building projects; these mark the beginning, midpoint, and end of his career. The first project came in 1904, immediately upon Brown's return to America after his education in France, when he was hired by Hornblower & Marshall to design an alternative scheme for the Smithsonian Institution's new National Museum (now the National Museum of Natural History). At the height of his career, between 1927 and 1934, Brown was tapped by Secretary of the Treasury Andrew W. Mellon to serve on the Board of Architectural Consultants and to design facilities for the Department of Labor and the Interstate Commerce Commission (the Labor–ICC block) in the Federal Triangle. Finally, at his death in 1957 Brown was serving on an advisory panel evaluating the extension of the east portico of the Capitol.

PLANS FOR THE MALL

The span of Brown's career marks the transformation of the monumental core of the city of Washington from a primarily Romantic assemblage of many diverse and sometimes competing landscapes into the sweeping, unified Mall of today. From the late nineteenth century to the 1950s the Mall was under continual redevelopment; Brown was able to view this transformation at significant moments in the national capital's history and, at the end of his life, was able to offer a historical perspective to post–World War II modernization.

Brown first saw Washington in 1889 during his extended tour of Europe and North America. On November 19, 1889, he encountered the Capitol and the Mall for the first time. After a tour of the building and a glimpse of the Supreme Court in session, Brown and his family climbed up to the first colonnade of the dome.[1] There they surveyed a series of walled precincts landscaped in the English picturesque manner with thousands of specimen trees, all linked together with a series of curvilinear paths. At the base of Capitol Hill stood the National Botanical Garden, a series of greenhouses and terraces within a tree-enclosed compound. Several blocks to the south, at Fourth and B streets, NW, the Pennsylvania Railroad had constructed the terminal through which Brown entered the city, and behind which a high iron train shed on a viaduct cut across half the width of the Mall. A bit farther south, Brown saw the towers of James Renwick's Smithsonian Institution building, "the Castle," jutting above the trees, and the octagonal monitor of Adolph Cluss's National Museum, the newest addition to the precinct at that time. In the distance, the recently completed Washington Monument sat at the edge of the Potomac, its grassy earthen base jutting into the shoreline (fig. 5.1).

This wooded but visually chaotic parkland view largely resulted from the failure of the federal government to follow

5.2. F. L.V. Hoppin, Bird's-Eye View of General Plan from Point Taken 4,000 Feet above Arlington, 1901–02, watercolor rendering for the Senate Park Commission Plan, the McMillan Plan. *Ninth Report of the United States Commission of Fine Arts.*

through on picturesque designs envisioned by the nation's foremost landscape architects in the years between 1850 and Brown's visit to Washington. For the first half of the nineteenth century the lands now known as the Mall were pasture lands and waste heaps. Over the course of the second half of the nineteenth century Andrew Jackson Downing, Frederick Law Olmsted, and their successors implemented plans to create an American Hyde Park at the Mall—what Downing described as a "[t]asteful arrangement of parks and grounds."[2] Downing chose to celebrate that which all Americans could share proudly—the natural history of the newly continental nation. The Mall at the Washington Monument and Smithsonian grounds became a national botanical garden representative of the country as a whole. After his untimely death in 1852, Downing's scheme was only partially realized, largely on the grounds of the Smithsonian and at the Botanical Gardens. In the 1870s funds were authorized to commission Frederick Law Olmsted to design only the grounds immediately surrounding the Capitol.[3] The primary features of his design adhered to Downing's "naturalistic" landscapes further west, but contrasted formal allées of trees at the radial avenues with curvilinear drives that connected the many entrances to the precinct. Olmsted also constructed the large terrace at the west facade of the Capitol, providing the grounds with a cer-

emonial site facing the Mall.[4] This terrace refocused attention on the west end of the monumental core and reasserted a formal architectural relationship between the landmarks of the capital city and the river.

By the end of the century the growing national awareness of the nation's federal heritage and the lessons in formal urban design learned at the 1893 World's Columbian Exposition in Chicago created the context for the second great redesign of the Mall, the Senate Park Commission, or McMillan, Plan, in which political and historical metaphors would supersede the pastoral allusions of Downing and Olmsted. Members of the American Institute of Architects, inspired by the critical and popular success of the Court of Honor at the World's Columbian Exposition, felt that a similar order and dignity should be brought to the nation's capital. These first efforts were initially ignored by the government, but by 1900 the AIA was able to call for a comprehensive, multidisciplinary development plan for the District of Columbia at their national convention, held that year in Washington. The AIA won the enthusiastic support of Senator James McMillan of Michigan, who arranged in 1901 for the appointment of an expert commission to advise Congress on the physical improvement of the city. This panel, consisting of Daniel H. Burnham, Charles Follen McKim, Frederick Law Olmsted Jr., and Augustus Saint-

Gaudens, became the Senate Park Commission. After a whirlwind tour of the great European capitals and the most relevant colonial American communities, including nearby Annapolis and Williamsburg, the commission issued a report urging the restoration of the L'Enfant plan for the city of Washington, modernized to meet the expanded needs of the federal government.[5]

The McMillan Plan, named for its principal sponsor, ideologically melded reverence for federal America and Pierre L'Enfant's 1791 plan for Washington with the ordered splendor of baroque Europe, particularly Versailles, which was one of L'Enfant's primary models. Thus L'Enfant's great avenue, the vaguely described Mall, was to become an attenuated greensward, serving as a great prospect from the Capitol to the Washington Monument and as the ordering axis around which all else was reoriented (fig. 5.2). The Mall was to be extended to the Potomac to a new western memorial to Lincoln, the axis this time marked by a great cruciform reflecting basin; from there the axis was to be shifted to the southwest, to encompass a memorial bridge and Arlington House, physically and metaphorically linking North with South. On a less abstract plane, Downing's vestigial gardens were to be cleared and replaced with new regiments of elms, which would emphasize this shifted axis and the existing and planned monumental classical structures that anchor the core. Behind these trees museums and other cultural institutions, designed in a suitably chaste classicism, would likewise replace the unruly Smithsonian Institution and "temporary" governmental edifices. The Pennsylvania Railroad was to be housed in a new Union Station northeast of the Capitol, House and Senate office buildings were to form a formal group around the Capitol, and several federal office groups were planned around Lafayette Square and the blocks between the Mall and Pennsylvania and Maryland avenues.

The plan was presented to the president, Congress, and the general public at the Corcoran Gallery in the spring of 1902 in the form of two immense site models, at least a dozen atmospheric drawings, and a text written largely by Burnham and edited by Senator McMillan's aide, Charles Moore. The plan generated much popular support and professional acclaim, even if there were reservations about its overwhelming scope and tremendous cost. Although the McMillan Plan was never officially adopted by any federal agency, it did remain a guiding force in the capital's design. Despite McMillan's death in 1902, advocates for the plan succeeded in obtaining federal funding for the removal of the railroad terminal from the Mall to a new Union Station, and the reconstruction of a portion of the new Agriculture Department building to better conform to the plan. By 1905 the plan and its authors could count on the support of a wide cross-section of official Washington, including President Theodore Roosevelt. In that year the president decreed at the annual banquet of the AIA that future public buildings within the District of Columbia "should be erected in accordance with a carefully thought-out plan adopted long before, and that it should be not only beautiful in itself, but fitting in its relations to the whole scheme of the public building, the parks and drives of the district."[6]

THE NATIONAL MUSEUM

Although the relocation of the building for the Department of Agriculture in accordance with McKim's realigned Mall is usually regarded as the first instance in which the McMillan plan gained the force of executive mandate, the architectural language of this facility had been set previous to the plan and was constructed without intervention or modification to the plans of its architects.[7] The second structure to be designed for the new Mall, the new National Museum of the Smithsonian Institution, became the structure through which the "official" architectural style of the Mall was demonstrated by members of the Senate Park Commission, much to the discontent of the architects of record, the well-established Washington firm of Hornblower & Marshall. The course of the battle of wills between this local firm and the commission's august, well-intentioned outsiders was a lengthy one, and Brown found himself in the middle of the fight.[8]

Plans for another Smithsonian museum were underway in the waning years of the nineteenth century. The Smithsonian outgrew its first museum building (now the Arts and Industries Building), designed by Adolph Cluss, shortly after its completion. By 1898 proposals were in the works for a second museum, placed on the north side of the Mall, opposite the first. This second museum would house the anthropological, natural history, and technology collections, as well as a large auditorium. In 1901 Hornblower & Marshall was invited to begin studies of the project, having successfully completed renovation work in the Arts and Industries Building and at the National Zoo.[9] The museum was to be of the most up-to-date design, reflecting the high place the Smithsonian had achieved in American museum circles in the previous decades. The new structure was to be modeled on contemporary European precedents, with perhaps a nod to the Museum of Fine Arts in Boston and the American Museum of Natural History in New York, the only two American museums thought to be comparable institutions.[10] Although Hornblower and Marshall made several studies for the museum in 1901, they were asked to acquaint themselves with the museum type more fully through travel. At the request of Smithsonian staff, both Hornblower and Marshall traveled to Europe to study contemporary muse-

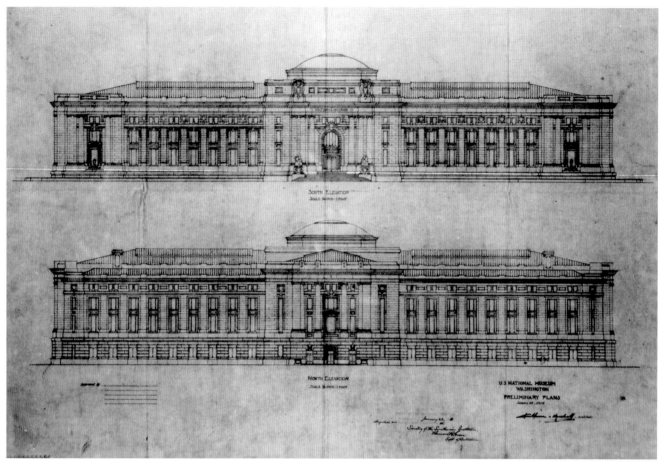

5.3. Hornblower & Marshall, proposals for the Smithsonian's second National Museum, January 12, 1904, principal elevations. Courtesy of the Smithsonian Institution.

ums, such as the Natural History Museum in Vienna and the Jardin des Plantes in Paris. Hornblower made the crossing three times between 1902 and 1908, and Marshall went on extended trips in 1902 and 1904.[11] Hornblower's and Marshall's travels intersected in Paris in September 1902, where they spent some time at the Ecole des Beaux-Arts, meeting the students and absorbing the latest in Parisian architectural fashion.[12]

Upon their return to Washington, Hornblower & Marshall completed several sets of design proposals for the museum, each presenting an imposing facade to Constitution Avenue in which a central entry pavilion was the dominant feature. These met with little enthusiasm from Smithsonian Secretary S. P. Langley, Assistant Secretary Richard Rathbun, and Supervising Architect Bernard R. Green, who was hired by Congress to act as the superintendent of construction on behalf of the Smithsonian. Eventually, on January 23, 1904, Green was able to transmit a "finalized" set of preliminary

drawings to Langley, who approved the concept four days later (fig. 5.3).[13] With this approval, Hornblower & Marshall began working drawings immediately, despite the fact that Rathbun expressed to Green that the regents were "still unsatisfied in particulars of the interior and even especially as to the design for the exterior of the building."[14] Unknown to Hornblower & Marshall, Langley and Green were getting architectural advice from the authors of the McMillan Plan. Burnham and McKim wished the new National Museum to more closely follow a more noble "Roman" architectural language, but they did not relate what that meant to Hornblower & Marshall very well. Instead, they used Green, who was not an architect, as their intermediary. Hornblower & Marshall's interpretation of Green's somewhat cryptic suggestions lacked force or meaning; they pleased neither the Smithsonian nor the architects.

It is at this point that Arthur Brown joined Hornblower & Marshall as "Chief Draftsman in Charge of Design" (fig. 5.4).

Brown was asked to produce a set of elevations that would satisfy the needs of both the firm and the client.[15] Brown had come to Hornblower & Marshall on the suggestion of McKim, whom he had met in December while in New York visiting Lawrence Butler and William Adams Delano.[16] Hoping to land a commission attached to the Mall redevelopment, Brown went to Washington knowing nothing about the firm for which he was to work. Similarly, Hornblower & Marshall knew nothing of Brown, except of his reputation in Paris; it was quite a leap of faith to give an untried architect such a position. Neither party was quite right for the other, and Brown's nine months in Washington proved frustrating—the firm had neither an architectural library nor a clear-cut organizational structure. Within weeks of arriving, Brown planned his departure.[17]

Brown's design is known from two sources: a set of four presentation drawings dated July 20, 1904, and a set of two pencil-on-tracing-paper cartoons for these renderings (fig. 5.5).[18] Brown's museum was a pastiche of free baroque architectural forms then fashionable in Paris, much in the spirit of the buildings for the 1900 exposition, and in fact borrowed liberally from Charles-Louis Girault's Petit Palais in its domed treatment of the entry pavilion. Sculptural groups flanked the entry block, and the end pavilions recalled the main block with deep niches set under broken pediments. The connecting wings returned somewhat to the 1903 scheme, as the windows and spandrels were deeply recessed behind the line of the pilasters, emphasizing the verticality of the bays. In most respects, however, Brown's design differed greatly from its predecessors, as it looked to French sources rather than to Italian or Roman precedents, and gave a greater prominence to architectural sculpture and ironwork. The proposal is overtly festive in its mood and positively radiates the exuberance of its young designer. This should be expected, as the design did not wholly originate in Washington but was brought there from Paris, where many of its essentials were in Brown's student projects of 1903. Adapting many of the motifs to Hornblower & Marshall's floor plans, Brown produced a design that remained the firm's intended scheme until September, 1905, almost a year after Brown's departure from Washington.

Brown's very French design was put forth to members of the Senate Park Commission even before it was submitted to the Smithsonian. According to Daniel Burnham's diary, he, Pierce Anderson, Frederick Law Olmsted Jr., and W. S. Eames met in Washington with Hornblower over July 11 and 12, 1904, to evaluate the proposal. All present realized that the architectural vocabulary of the entire monumental core of the city would be established by this one building. The assembled experts demanded revisions in order to subordinate the structure to the Capitol dome and to give it a more sober character. Despite these entreaties, Hornblower & Marshall made only minor, cosmetic changes to Brown's design for over fifteen months, even though Brown himself left the firm for San Francisco at the end of the summer, frustrated by the firm's unacademic culture and perhaps disheartened by the rough treatment his design received. The devel-

5.4. Arthur Brown Jr., in waistcoat, with drafting staff at Hornblower & Marshall's offices, spring 1904, with elevation drawings of Natural History Museum in the background. Photograph, Arthur Brown Jr. Collection, Bancroft Library.

5.5 (above). Frère Champney for Hornblower & Marshall, National Museum, rendering of Arthur Brown's design for the National Museum, July 23, 1904. Courtesy of the Smithsonian Institution.

5.6 (below). Frère Champney for Hornblower & Marshall, National Museum, revised design of February 1905. Courtesy of the Smithsonian Institution.

opment of the "French" design was continued, however, by Frère Champney, Brown's friend and roommate in Paris and Washington, who had been formally attached to the office of the architect of the Treasury before coming to Hornblower & Marshall (fig. 5.6).

By July 1905, work had stopped on the museum project until a suitable elevation could be designed. Hornblower & Marshall made several more proposals, but none met with approval from the Smithsonian. In January 1906, a representative of Hornblower & Marshall's office, probably Morris Leisenring, later the municipal architect for the District of Columbia, went to New York and was handed a drawing,

now lost, that described the kind of elevation Burnham and McKim desired for the Mall. Following this prescription, Leisenring designed the more "Roman" exterior for the building that was finally constructed by 1911 (fig. 5.7). In almost every aspect this revised design is more severe and controlled than its predecessors. The dominant feature of the building is still a dome over the entry hall, but this low dome only makes its presence known at some distance from the building.[19] The central pavilion on which it rests takes the form of a gabled Greek cross, into which semicircular thermal windows are cut. The end pavilions are eliminated entirely, replaced by paired pilasters in very low relief to give further emphasis to the central pavilion and to stress the more mural quality of the stripped architectural forms.

The revised design for the National Museum became a model of federal design for the next twenty-five years and was repeatedly held up as an ideal by the successor of the Senate Park Commission, the Commission of Fine Arts. Founded in 1910 by legislation sponsored by President William Howard Taft and initially chaired by Daniel Burnham, the Commission of Fine Arts was charged with reviewing all public building within the District of Columbia for design quality; this meant, in essence, that the commission could pressure governmental agencies to comply with the McMillan plan and, later, the plans of the National Capital Park and Planning Commission. Charles Moore, former aide to Senator McMillan and textual editor to Daniel Burnham, succeeded Burnham and Daniel Chester French as chair in 1915. Moore would oversee the commission's actions for over twenty years, guiding the architectural quality of the next wave of federal building in the monumental core, the building campaign of 1926–1937, which included Brown's Labor–ICC block in the Federal Triangle.

THE FEDERAL TRIANGLE

The Federal Triangle is a significant example of the grand design in American architecture, flawed perhaps only in its overreaching ambition and incomplete execution. Although no one designer's vision became the dominant one, Brown played a decisive role in translating the initial program prepared by Supervising Architect of the Treasury James A. Wetmore and Commission of Fine Arts Chairman Charles Moore into a master plan for a monumental architectural set piece unified by a spare but communicative classicism. The complex was both praised and condemned in its day, though nonetheless considered emblematic of the architectural credo held by the generation of architects and artists that created it. At its inception the ensemble was celebrated by its sponsors as a crucial element in the restoration of the L'Enfant plan, its classical dress linking the past to the present and its monumental scale proclaiming the future of Washington as a capital of international stature. As the modern movement dominated the American architectural establishment in the years after its completion, the Triangle was

5.7. Morris Leisenring for Hornblower & Marshall, National Museum, 1906, final, constructed design, reflecting Charles Follen McKim's design suggestions. Courtesy of the Smithsonian Institution.

sometimes despised for its traditional forms but more often found to be simply irrelevant. Joseph Hudnut's characterization of the Triangle as a series of "innocuous imitations of Gabriel" is indicative of the indifferent attitude many critics and historians had to the complex upon its completion on the eve of the Second World War.[20] Arthur Brown's role in shaping the Triangle has not been well studied, yet he made decisive contributions in the conceptual planning that set the unified framework for the architectural consultants to place their buildings, including Brown's own Labor–ICC complex, along Constitution Avenue.[21]

The more familiar history recounts how the Triangle, pre-ordained by the McMillan Plan, was resurrected in 1925 when Calvin Coolidge called for the construction of a long-term building program to house the expanded post–World War I federal government. With the passage of the Public Building Act of 1926 an appropriation of $50 million was made to construct facilities for the departments of Commerce, Labor, Agriculture, and Justice, as well as additions to the congressional office buildings and a new Supreme Court building. This law also allowed for the commissioning of architectural services for some of these buildings—the first time since the repeal of the Tarnsey Act in 1912 that governmental facilities would not be designed by the Office of the Supervising Architect (fig. 5.8).[22]

THE BOARD OF ARCHITECTURAL CONSULTANTS

The job of procuring the design and overseeing the construction of this enormous public building program fell to the Treasury Department, under the leadership of Andrew W. Mellon for most of the 1920s. Mellon's right-hand man, Charles S. Dewey, was charged as early as May 1926 with finding an architect who could assist Supervising Architect of the Treasury Louis A. Simon with implementing the Capital Improvement Program.[23] He chose Edward Bennett, who since Burnham's death had become his successor in the field of city planning in the grand manner. Bennett prepared a preliminary site plan for the Triangle by August 1926, based on the McMillan Plan and the program for an aborted building campaign for the base of the Triangle from 1910 (fig. 5.9). In this early plan the various buildings were arranged on either side of a longitudinal mall, which ran from Fourteenth to Tenth Street through the center of the Triangle, while a tree-lined allée ran perpendicular to Constitution Avenue to connect the group to the greater Mall. This scheme placed great importance on the National Archives building, which would have been placed at the head of the internal spine.

Bennett's plan was simply a straw man used to implement the Triangle legislation and to obtain approval from the newly created Public Buildings Commission, the legislative

5.8. Commission of Fine Arts, "Map Showing Progress on Commission Plan for Public Buildings on the Mall," September 1921. *Ninth Report of the United States Commission of Fine Arts.*

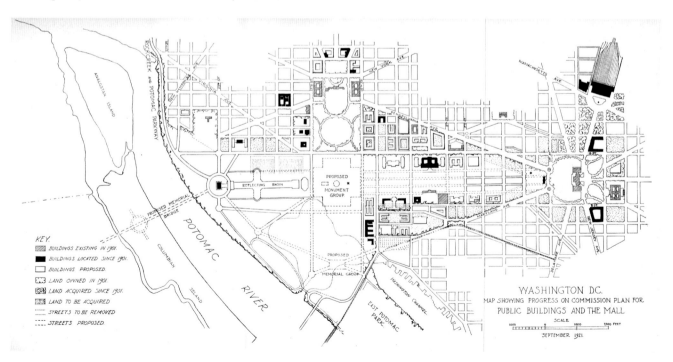

5.9. Edward H. Bennett, schematic plans for the Federal Triangle, December 1926, isometric rendering of central mall. Print of drawing, Arthur Brown Jr. Collection, Bancroft Library.

equivalent of the Commission of Fine Arts. Bennett's plan was put before the commission in December 1926 and approved in its general outlines. However, the architectural members of the commission lobbied for a more unified and monumental composition reminiscent of the Louvre. To this end Charles Moore drafted a letter suggesting that the entire Triangle be planned as one unit in the grand manner of Paris, the buildings enclosing large landscaped courts of monumental dignity; included was a tentative sketch plan prepared by Moore, commission member Milton B. Medary, and former member Louis Ayres, who was designing the Commerce Department building.[24] Upon receiving this letter, and noting that the AIA would be holding its annual convention in Washington in mid-May, Mellon agreed to form a Board of Architectural Consultants to undertake the supervision of the design of the Triangle and represent the nation's architectural establishment.

Mellon himself went to Paris in the early spring of 1927 to visit his daughter, and so was able to evaluate great monuments of French classicism as prototypes for the Triangle on his own. Meanwhile, Bennett realized that his initial scheme

was lacking in force, and so he turned for assistance to Arthur Brown, a trusted friend.[25] Bennett visited Brown in San Francisco in March 1927, and the two men reviewed Bennett's linear scheme for the Triangle. In Brown's papers are copies of Bennett's presentation drawings of the 1926 scheme, on which light pencil sketches are overlaid, suggesting the form the open spaces of the Triangle might take. Bennett also left Brown with blank grid maps of the Triangle on tracing paper, on which the preliminary schemes of the complex were drawn.

Returning from San Francisco to Washington, Bennett wrote Charles Dewey of his trip.[26] It was probably Bennett and Dewey who suggested a Board of Architectural Consultants to Secretary Mellon as a way of creating an entity within the Treasury Department that could include members of the Commission of Fine Arts and yet allow for the participation of leading traditional architects, such as Brown, who were not commission members. This supposition is supported by the fact that Bennett was allowed to nominate to Mellon the board's members and serve as chair. Mellon's letter of appointment to Brown, dated May 13, 1927, affirms

5.10. Board of Architectural Consultants, 1929. From left, John
Russell Pope, Clarence Zantzinger, Louis A. Simon, Louis Ayres,
Arthur Brown Jr., William A. Delano, Edward H. Bennett.
Photograph, Arthur Brown Jr. Collection, Bancroft Library.

both Bennett's advisory role in creating the Board of
Architectural Consultants and his meetings with Brown in
San Francisco. Analogous letters of appointment were sent to
the other members of the board: Louis Ayres, William Adams
Delano, and John Russell Pope, all of New York, Milton B.
Medary of Philadelphia, and Louis Simon, supervising architect of the treasury, who was overseeing the design of the
Internal Revenue Service Building at the time of his appointment and was to act as secretary to the board. Certainly all
these men were well known to Bennett and Dewey and at the
peak of their development as classically oriented architects.
Coincidentally, all but Simon claimed birthdates in 1874,
and thus they were all in their early fifties—fertile years for
an architect (fig. 5.10).[27]

Ayres, a former member of the Commission of Fine Arts,
was a principal of the architectural firm of York & Sawyer,

and was already working on the Department of Commerce
Building at the base of the Triangle, a commission won seventeen years earlier and explicitly reserved by legislation for
that firm. Delano was a current member of the commission,
known best for his lavish mansions on Long Island's north
shore; he also had close connections in Washington. Medary
too was a member of the Commission of Fine Arts, but, more
importantly, he could assure the support of the AIA for the
planning and procurement process.[28] Although John Russell
Pope was considered for the board from the very start, he did
not respond to Mellon's letter of appointment, initially
offending his most significant future patron. Upon a second
request, Pope joined the board in 1929 to design the National
Archives Building.

Brown was obviously selected by Bennett because of
their close personal friendship and the work the two had

done together in San Francisco. Bennett counseled Brown, however, that Mellon and Simon were concerned as to whether Brown would be able to participate fully in the project, since his office was four days' journey from Washington.[29] Brown was not the only school chum of Bennett's on the board. Delano was Brown's classmate in the Atelier Laloux, and Pope enrolled in the same year as well. Upon Medary's death in 1929, his partner, Clarence C. Zantzinger, was installed on the board, bringing the total alumni of the turn-of-the-century Ecole to five of the seven members. One can only imagine the excitement members felt at the opportunity to design a monumental governmental project larger than even the most ambitious Prix-de-Rome program. Many may also have been moved by an element of patriotism, viewing the Triangle as their generation's contribution to the development of the nation's capital. All approached their assignment with the utmost seriousness; their discussions over the seven-year course of the project emphasized modern construction techniques and budgetary concerns, the efficient planning of the nonceremonial aspects of the program, and the sociological and technical requirements of modern urban design. The members were professionals equipped to solve contemporary problems; their attitude toward their assignment was forward-looking and ambitious, not nostalgic or self-aggrandizing, as some of their critics have suggested.

DESIGNING THE TRIANGLE

The board met in late May 1927 and immediately set about determining a final plot plan for the buildings within the Triangle. Ayres and Medary brought their recollections and sketches from their meetings with Charles Moore, and Bennett brought his first scheme and the sketches he had made with Brown in San Francisco. Brown and Delano also brought in a series of drawings, made the previous weekend while Brown stayed with Delano in New York.[30] Over the course of the first two days, the board drew up thirteen plot plans for the Triangle, designated schemes A–M. Within a week the board had chosen the parti it would follow throughout most of project, Scheme B, and had settled on a palette of materials and a set of cornice heights. The cornice heights are particularly significant; it seems to have been agreed upon from the beginning that the regulating elevations of the Natural History Museum would set the heights for the Triangle.[31] Although Bennett nominally chaired the meetings, Louis Simon really set the parameters within which the board was to design. As the treasury architect, he knew the programs required of each department and organization to be housed, the local conditions, and perhaps most importantly, the bureaucracy and procurement system.

The two immediately striking features of the ground plan proposed for the Triangle were the Great Plaza, fronting on Fourteenth Street and running back to an apse in the middle of the superblock, and the Circular Plaza that split Twelfth Street next to it (figs. 5.11, 5.12). Because the design of these two large open spaces was assigned to Brown and Delano, respectively, it may be presumed that these were the salient features of the scheme they had brought to Washington. These same two features were the most disruptive of the existing street pattern of the Triangle, and the most controversial aspects of the design. Brown and Delano presumed the incorporation or demolition of the existing structures along Pennsylvania Avenue, including the twenty-year-old District Building by Cope & Stewardson and the thirty-year-old Post Office by Willoughby J. Edbrooke. Conflict regarding the relationship between the Great Plaza and the Circle and between these open spaces and their neighbors would dominate the debate among the board's members and eventually doom the Triangle to incompletion.

The members of the board were assigned the buildings that they would eventually design as early as June 1927. Besides Ayres's and Simon's facilities, which were already in preparation, Delano was assigned the facility for independent establishments, later the Post Office Department, and Medary the Department of Justice. Brown received the buildings for the Department of Labor and later the Interstate Commerce Commission, the latter likely because of his friendship with and prior patronage from Herbert Hoover, the Secretary of Commerce.[32] Bennett was to coordinate all of the landscape elements of the design, and control the master plan. By late summer of 1927 each architect had laid out the general lines of his building, and the courts surrounding it, although only York & Sawyer and Louis Simon were authorized to proceed with their working drawings.

Over the course of the next four years the particulars of the other facilities would constantly change as the various government departments changed their programmatic requirements and location within the plan, disrupting the architects. However, the architectural language employed in each facility did not change; classical design dominated the composition throughout the design process. Its appropriateness was never questioned by the board—it was simply the style of the federal district. The minutes of the board suggest a general agreement about the question of architectural form for the Triangle; there is little discussion of "style" but a great deal of attention to sources. Much more contentious was the question of how to handle the enormous scale of the complex, which stretches almost three thousand feet along Constitution Avenue. Within the dynamics of the board, it was Brown who often sought to inspire the members to a unity and monumentality to which they were unaccustomed. In organizing the massing of the Triangle, for exam-

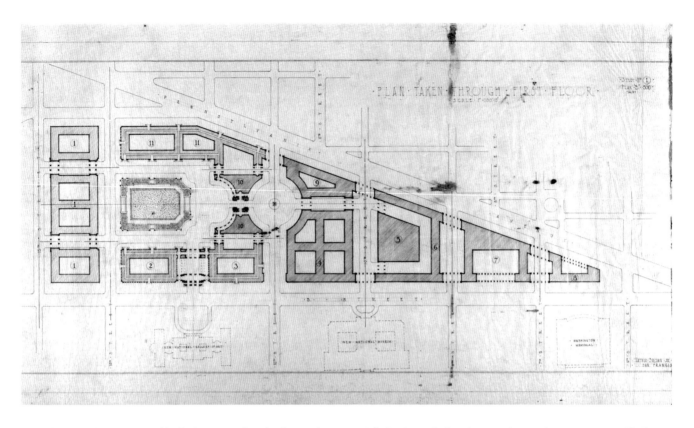

5.11 (*above*). Arthur Brown Jr., block plan proposal, Federal Triangle, July 6, 1927, indicative of "Scheme B" as interpreted by Brown. Drawing, Arthur Brown Jr. Collection, Bancroft Library.

5.12 (below). Board of Architectural Consultants, consensus block plan of Federal Triangle, July 1927. Papers of the Commission of Fine Arts, Prints and Drawings Collection of the National Archives.

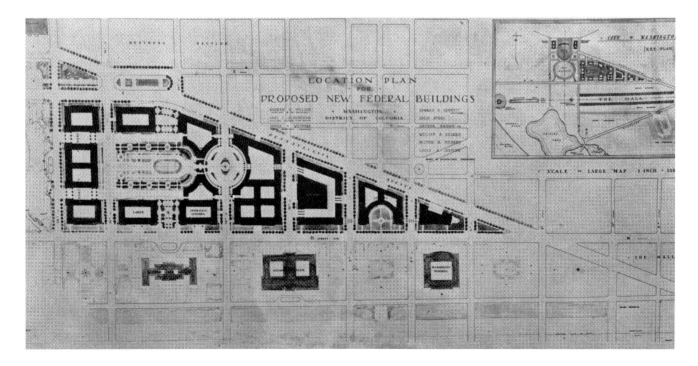

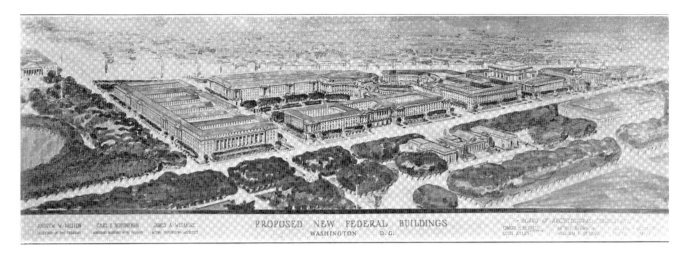

PROPOSED NEW FEDERAL BUILDINGS
WASHINGTON D.C.

5.13 (*above*). Perspective rendering of proposed Triangle, produced by the Office of the Architect of the Treasury, 1927. *Eleventh Report of the Commission of Fine Arts.*

5.14 (below).. Aerial photograph of the Federal Triangle upon the completion of all but the Apex Building. Photograph for the Department of the Treasury by the Commercial Photo Company, c. 1935, author's collection.

ple, Brown asked Simon to coordinate the Constitution Avenue side of his Internal Revenue Service Building with Ayres's largely designed Commerce Building (figs. 5.13, 5.14). This layout formed a group four blocks long that centered on a triumphal entry motif into the Great Plaza, which was flanked in turn by Brown's Labor–ICC buildings.[33] Despite a number of coordination successes such as this, there were trouble spots. The first was the Great Plaza, the second the tall massing and eccentric location of the National Archives Building and the General Accounting Office surrounding it, and the third the Department of Justice Building and its relationship to the cross-axis of the Mall. In time, the latter two problems would be amicably resolved, to the betterment of the entire Triangle. The Great Plaza, however, became the Achilles' heel of the project, exposing deep professional divisions among the members of the board.

At the very first meetings of the board Brown was charged with designing the facades of the buildings along the Great Plaza; this job put him immediately at odds with Delano, whose Independent Establishments building separated the Great Plaza from the Circle. Brown's initial design ignited the controversy. While the balancing north and south boundaries of the Plaza were somewhat conventional structures employing the neoclassical vocabulary of the rest of the Triangle (the south facade was eventually built as part of the Department of Labor block), the eastern, focal end of the Plaza was designed to an altogether different scale. Like his oversize dome for San Francisco City Hall, Brown desired a grand gesture, what he termed an "echelle," or overscaled element, which would control the entire Plaza and hold up against the enormous colonnade of the Commerce Building opposite.[34] He drew up a heroic triumphal arch, a full five stories high, over which a two-story attic and pediment would soar above the roofs of the surrounding buildings (fig. 5.15). This great arch was to be tied back to the flanking buildings with baroque quadrant hyphens, atop which statues of the great men of the Republic were to be installed. To lend further monumental quality to the plaza, the arch was to be dedicated to George Washington, father of the civil service as well as the country.

This enormous connector infuriated Delano because it cut his building in two and disrupted the flow of the colonnade around the circle on the Twelfth Street side. Although Delano realized the importance of the vista from the Commerce Building to the circular plaza, he did not feel that the architecture required to support such a vista should overwhelm the whole, and certainly not his plaza, which he hoped to be as understated as its model, the Place Vendôme (fig. 5.16). For over three years Brown and Delano submitted their respective designs for the connection of the two plazas to the board and to the Commission of Fine Arts. In the main, Delano wished to terminate the plaza with three single-story archways, which would not overemphasize the plaza at the expense of the circle. Brown remained convinced that some architectural elaboration of the end of the Great Plaza was necessary to relate it to the whole Triangle. Unfortunately, both designers were in the right, so no matter what negotiating strategy was utilized, Brown and Delano could not reach a compromise. Even the model crafted for Secretary Mellon's presentation of the Triangle to Congress in April 1929 reflected this ongoing conflict: both Brown's and Delano's schemes were constructed over interchangeable modules, so both could be presented (fig. 5.17). Eventually, Brown attempted to combine the best of both schemes into one that placed a portico over a triple-arched basement; this drawing won the support of a majority of the Board of Architectural Consultants on September 10, 1929, but not that of Delano, who prevailed when the design was presented to the Commission of Fine Arts the next day.[35]

The language of the commission's recommendations seemed to the board to allow for further study of the problem, which Brown did, submitting designs for the board's consideration at both its November 1929 and February 1930 meetings. During this time, too, the Department of the Post Office was finally designated as the tenant for the building behind the hemicycle, raising the stature of the facility and the corresponding architectural dignity of its principal entry. Thus Brown revised his design to emphasize the center of the east elevation of the Great Plaza as well as to simplify its sculptural program (fig. 5.18). He still brought a tetrastyle portico forward from the hemicycle and raised its entablature some 10 feet above the cornice line of the surrounding buildings. However, he deemphasized the end pavilions, narrowing them to one bay framed by coupled columns capped by a simple balustrade; this design addressed the commission's concern that the elevation was "crowded."

The new design was doomed from the start, no matter how significant its merits, for Delano would not support any large element at the end of the Great Plaza. Delano clearly stated his concerns about Brown's designs in a letter to Major Ferry K. Heath, Secretary Mellon's assistant: "My objections to the big motive there [at the east end of the plaza] have been based on the fact that it made our building [Independent Establishments/Post Office Department] seem wasteful in cubic contents, and that while the big motive might be effective, it was out of scale and savored more of an exposition group than governmental offices; and so I favored the hemicycle with a commemorative monument in the center."[36] Delano's assertion that Brown's design had the character of exposition architecture summed up the feeling of the Commission of Fine Arts. They felt that although Brown could compose technically correct architectural assemblages, he might not understand on which occasions a more sober architectural language was more suitable than an exuberant

5.15. Arthur Brown Jr., central motif of the grand plaza, Federal Triangle, 1927. The inscription and spandrel sculpture were a memorial to George Washington, founder of the federal civil service. From a diazo print of a lost original sketch, Arthur Brown Collection, Bancroft Library.

one. Implied in this criticism was perhaps a touch of metropolitan superiority over provincial naiveté; the votes within the Board of Architectural Consultants would suggest this, as the New Yorkers on the board voted en bloc whenever one of their number required their support. Once John Russell Pope was formally placed on the Board of Architectural Consultants in the fall of 1929, the voting majority tipped in favor of Delano's simpler scheme.[37] Brown's second design was also denied by the Commission of Fine Arts at a joint meeting of the board and commission on February 10, 1930.[38]

Brown and Delano worked together to create a final compromise scheme in March 1930, in which the portico followed the cornice height of the adjacent hemicycle, and the pediment was lowered to set below the ridge line of the attic story. This design was scrapped once it was learned that the commission would refuse to approve any scheme that included an accent of, or a break in, the cornice. Finally, at the April 10 meeting of the board, Brown's remaining supporters, Bennett and Simon, announced that they would support a motion adopting Delano's unbroken hemicycle in the interest of moving the project along and to avoid forcing a confrontation between Secretary Mellon and Charles Moore (fig. 5.19). Brown refused to make the motion unanimous.[39] As he had stated in at the board's previous meeting, the subordination of professional opinion to the whims of Charles Moore "is a question of the Board sacrificing a beautiful thing for the idea of a suitable thing."[40]

Brown was not the only member of the board to be manipulated by the Commission of Fine Arts. The landscaping plans for the Great Plaza became highly controversial, once a monument to former Secretary of Commerce Oscar Strauss was proposed for a place of honor on Fourteenth Street. Aesthetic and infrastructure decisions handed to the Board of Architectural Consultants by the Commission of Fine Arts

and the National Capital Park and Planning Commission delayed action on Bennett's landscape designs for the plaza until 1934.[41] The eventual removal of the sunken pool and most of the trees from the plaza design subordinated the open space to the masses of the buildings that enclosed it, and the delay in its construction fated it to become a parking lot.

The other contentious design questions that faced the Board of Architectural Consultants concerned the location of the Archives Building and the relocation of the Department of Justice Building. As originally planned, Justice was to occupy the position of honor on the cross-axis of the Mall, fronting both Pennsylvania and Constitution avenues between Eighth and Ninth streets. Archives was to occupy the center of the block to the west, between Ninth and Tenth streets, facing not onto one of the avenues but onto Tenth. Around the north, east, and south sides of the building was to be a shallow office building for the General Accounting Office. Initially Louis Simon produced some tentative elevations for the Archives Building, so that it could be featured in the

5.16. William A. Delano, circus at Twelfth Street, Federal Triangle, 1927–29. Because of the decision to retain the Post Office Building, the fountain and eastern third of the circle were not completed. *Eleventh Report of the Commission of Fine Arts.*

5.17 (*above*). Presentation model of the Federal Triangle for the Board of Architectural Consultants, 1929, view of east end of Great Plaza. *Eleventh Report of the Commission of Fine Arts*.

5.18 (*below*). Presentation rendering of second proposal for the east end of the great plaza, Federal Triangle, 1930. Arthur Brown Jr. Collection, Bancroft Library.

model. However, Secretary Mellon and Chairman Moore wished to consult John Russell Pope as to the final design of the building. With the death of Milton Medary and the need to formally invite Clarence Zantzinger to join the Board of Architectural Consultants, the opportunity arose in the autumn of 1929 to extend a second invitation to Pope to join the board, first as a consultant on the Archives Building and later as a full member. Immediately upon his arrival, Pope comprehended the fundamental planning problem facing the board. The high mass of the windowless Archives block called for a monumental treatment that was inappropriate off the Mall's cross-axis. At the same time, attempts by Medary and Zantzinger to place a forecourt in front of the Department of Justice Building had not allowed for a large enough ground plan for Justice's expanding program; to accommodate this forecourt and a square on the Pennsylvania Avenue elevation, Zantzinger's proposed building reached ten stories—as high as the Archives Building.

Earlier in the year Brown had suggested that a balancing device similar to those on the Commerce and IRS buildings be applied to the Constitution Avenue facades of the Apex Building and the Archives Building.[42] This desire to group the

apex of the Triangle into a three-block composition inspired Pope to request that Archives, with its need for a very tall cornice height, center the group on axis with the transept of the Mall. To this end he and Zantzinger presented several possible configurations of the Justice and Archives buildings to the board at its February 20, 1930, meeting. Pope's favored proposal, drawn the previous month in New York, transposed the sites of the two buildings, placing Archives on the axis of the Mall. The decision as to where to properly place Archives largely rested on the board's conception of the symbolic meaning of the Archives building. Pope said: "[I]f an architectural opportunity is to be made out of the building it [Archives] should be placed on the cross-axis of the Mall, but if not, and it is used as a store house for documents, it is proper in its present location."[43] By the end of the meeting, Zantzinger grudgingly accommodated this change in site for his Department of Justice Building, because it allowed him to scrap the awkward forecourt and domed pavilions he had inherited from Medary, and it gave him a larger ground plan in which to fit Justice's complex program. The change in site also permitted the board to group all of the departmental buildings together, further clarifying the layout of the Triangle. Finally, the completion of

5.19. Arthur Brown Jr. and William Adams Delano, east end of the great plaza as constructed, without accent in the hemicycle. Photograph courtesy of Henry Hope Reed.

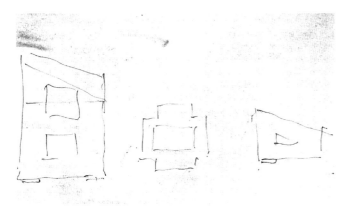

5.20. Arthur Brown Jr., sketch of proposed configuration of buildings at the east end of the Federal Triangle, on verso of Bennett, Parsons & Frost elevation for Apex Building, 1931. Arthur Brown Jr. Collection, Bancroft Library.

5.21. Bennett, Parsons, & Frost, print of rendering of proposal for Apex Building, Federal Triangle, c. 1931, following Brown's suggestion for end pavilion (not as built). Arthur Brown Jr. Collection, Bancroft Library.

Archives argued for the construction in 1936 of Bennett's Apex Building, which had been commissioned, but not funded, in 1930. The Apex Building, the home of the Federal Trade Commission, completed the three-part composition centered on Archives and brought the Triangle to a suitable termination (figs. 5.20, 5.21).[44]

This example of constructive cooperation should not imply that all discussions within the board were invariably cordial, or that cliques did not develop within the group. Dissension grew among the members of the board with the arrival of Pope, who was characteristically condescending and argumentative toward many members of the board, particularly Bennett.[45] As Brown's experience with the Great Plaza demonstrated, when disagreements over elements of the plan developed, those members of the board who were also current or former members of the Commission of Fine Arts tended to support each other, often putting the others, particularly Brown and Bennett, on the defensive. Because all design decisions ultimately had to be approved by the Commission of Fine Arts, the commissioners had considerable leverage over the other members of the Board of Architectural Consultants.

DEPARTMENT OF LABOR–INTERSTATE COMMERCE COMMISSION BLOCK

Brown's Labor–ICC composition was inspired by Bennett's first scheme, which placed two identical ranges of office buildings between Twelfth and Fourteenth streets, between which a plaza was to open out onto an anticipated national gallery. These office blocks not only framed this plaza, but related to the larger monumental core, mirroring the two Department of Agriculture office blocks across the Mall. Brown amended Bennett's concept by replacing the plaza with a central temple-front device that presented a continuous elevation 940 feet long along Constitution Avenue (figs. 5.22, C.20). Brown's enormous entry screen—an open portico over a rusticated, arcaded basement—was placed between the flanking office buildings to mirror the central block of the Agriculture Building then under construction and to recall the relationship of Gabriel's Palais de la Marine to the Church of the Madeleine in Paris. To strengthen this allusion, Brown terminated each office block with Roman Doric porticos, similar in form, if not in order or richness, to the pavilions on the Place de la Concorde. The board and Commission of Fine Arts felt his "Madeleine" placed too great a stress on an relatively minor axis, and asked Brown to revise the design. Instead, he later incorporated a departmental auditorium into the scheme, allowing him to retain the dramatic portico he desired while signifying an indisputably needed facility within the Triangle.

At this early stage of the design of the buildings, Brown was chiefly concerned with the exterior elevations, because the departments that were to occupy the facilities were not yet determined. According to June 1927 letters from Secretary Mellon, Brown was to design only the Department of Labor Building, whereas Delano was to design a facility for the Interstate Commerce Commission and a building for various "other independent establishments."[46] However, by the end of the summer, Delano had agreed that Brown should also design the ICC facility, because it required about 330,000 net square feet of assignable space, about 30 percent more than that of Labor, but half that of the Independent Establishments Building, which was at that time believed to be a very large element of the program. Yet, just as Delano's facility would finally be dedicated to the Post Office Department in 1930, the tenant for Brown's block changed a few times before being finalized at the last possible moment. Even after Brown had prepared full floor-plan layouts for the ICC from their formal program in 1929, the Treasury was still considering another tenant for the building. During the spring months of 1930 the Treasury officially designated the General Accounting Office as Brown's client, requiring him to reprogram the facility.[47] Soon thereafter, however, it was demonstrated that the GAO required too much space for the facility (for which working drawings were underway), and the ICC was again allotted the building.

Between 1929 and the final preparations of plans in late 1932, Brown worked with Samuel J. Gompers, chief clerk of the Department of Labor, and George McGinty, secretary of the ICC, to develop floor plans specific to each agency's detailed programs. The office blocks themselves were simple in their form (fig. 5.23). Each was a hollow block in which double-loaded corridors served an inner and outer ring of offices; vertical circulation was placed at the inside corners. Within each block a large light court, about one-third of the total area, was to be planted with formal gardens. At the ICC Building the gardens eventually gave way to a pair of hearing rooms, but the courts were otherwise left open. In section, two floors were placed within the rusticated basement of the elevation, four floors within the scope of the order, and one floor within the attic, which was set back of the main wall behind a balustrade on the exterior side of the building to emphasize the entablature (fig. 5.24). This accommodation of the classical facades of the exterior led to some compromises in utility. For example, although the primary public spaces of the complex were on the ground floor, the tallest story was the third floor, corresponding to a piano nobile of the palazzo form. On this floor Brown placed the senior administrative offices of the Department of Labor and the commissioner's suites for the ICC. The monumental entablature of the office blocks also meant that the entire outer ring of rooms on the sixth floor would be windowless. Although most of this space was relegated to files and service uses, Brown did have some trouble juggling space assignments within the ICC block.

One difficulty Brown encountered during the development of the design of the complex was a constant increase in the amount of space required by the ICC. By April 1929, the program for the ICC had grown to over 360,000 net square feet, serving a population of almost 1,600 employees.[48] This prompted Brown to request that 75,000 square feet of this space be housed in Delano's adjoining Independent Establishments Building.[49] The most significant change to the program, however, occurred two months later, when Louis Simon requested that Brown attempt to incorporate an 1,800-seat auditorium into the project.[50] As early as September 1927, Brown had proposed a large meeting room behind the central portico of his group (it appears in section on the right side of his elevation sketches for the Great Plaza, fig. 5.25). He was thus prepared to respond to Simon's request by inserting this large assembly space behind the portico, at once accommodating this new program requirement and suppressing any criticism that this large motif, like the large arch at the end of the Great Plaza, was architecture for its own sake.

5.22 (*above*). Arthur Brown Jr., first proposal for Labor–ICC block, Federal Triangle, July 1927, "Scheme B" with end pavilions. The center motif is an open screen to the great plaza beyond. Drawing, Arthur Brown Jr. Collection, Bancroft Library.

5.23 (*below*). Arthur Brown Jr., Labor–ICC Block, Federal Triangle, November 1929, presentation plan of Labor–ICC complex, showing office circulation and auditorium building. Photograph of drawing courtesy of Moulin Archives.

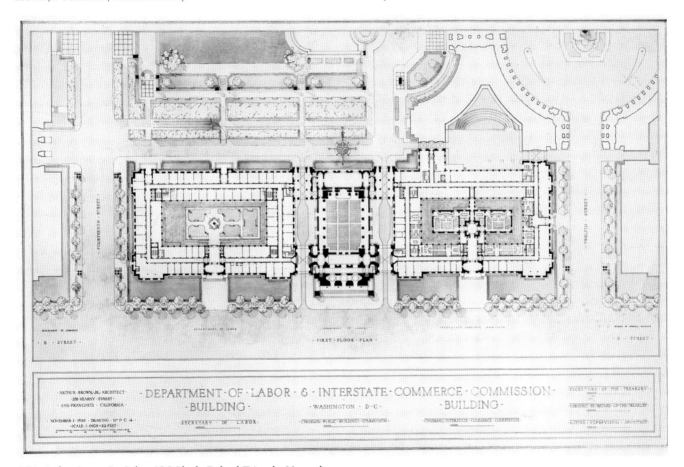

5.24. Arthur Brown Jr., Labor–ICC Block, Federal Triangle, November 1929, longitudinal section of Labor–ICC complex, delineating light court elevations and auditorium end wall. Photograph of drawing courtesy of Moulin Archives.

5.25. Arthur Brown Jr., Labor–ICC Block, Federal Triangle, 1927, detail of longitudinal section. The germ of the auditorium is present in this drawing, done to deflect criticism of the linking device between the Labor and ICC wings of the complex. Diazo print of a lost drawing, Arthur Brown Jr. Collection, Bancroft Library.

The auditorium was not as welcome to the Daughters of the American Revolution as it was to the executive branch officers whose staff was to use it.[51] It is unknown why the DAR's wishes were heeded in this regard, but many concessions were made to practicality in order to subordinate the Departmental Auditorium to the DAR's Constitution Hall on the west side of the White House. Brown was forbidden to introduce a sloped floor into the room, the seating was not to be fixed to the floor, the stage was to have no accommodation for cultural presentations, and even a cloak room was to be excised from the program; these mandates were communicated to Brown through the Treasury Department.[52] Despite these restrictions, Brown created one of the most sumptuous public facilities in the capital in this auditorium. This extraordinary building impresses the viewer with its overwhelming portico and its lavish polychromed interior; it has become a prestigious setting for social and governmental functions in the capital.

Originally, the exterior order of the auditorium was to be Corinthian, but because of cost considerations and a need to respect the superior status of Constitution Hall, the portico was executed in the Doric. Nonetheless, this central portico received the dominant share of the sculptural embellishment afforded the Labor–ICC group, including Edgar Walter's group Columbia in the pediment, Edmond R. Amateis's relief *George Washington Planning the Battle of Trenton with Generals Greene and Sullivan* above the door out to the

colonnade, and Leon Hermant's limestone eagles at the corners of the pediment and his figurative keystones over the entrance portals (figs. 5.26, 5.27).[53] The transitions between the auditorium block and the office buildings demonstrate Brown's deft handling of the Doric order (fig. 5.28). Brown adopted a device used by William Chambers at Somerset House in London to accommodate the different building lines of the two facilities; he also inserted an intermediate plane between that of the buildings and that of the archway and colonnade. This plane allowed the order to project the depth of one triglyph and metope from the archway as well as the two side walls, so that the entablature wrapped smoothly from the pediment and primary corner of the office block to the archway and into the higher end wall of the auditorium, without disrupting the Doric frieze or the intercolumniation over the arch.

The interior of the auditorium was formally worked out in a series of sectional presentation drawings presented to the Treasury to aid in the appropriation campaign for the complex (fig. 5.29).[54] The visitor entered a one-story vestibule and then walked into a vaulted cross-hall, at either end of which were entrances from the departmental office buildings and a pair of stairwells. Beyond this was another vaulted lobby, with entry to the auditorium proper, which ran on a transverse axis from the street. A full three stories high, the main room, the largest in the Triangle, was framed on three sides by screens of Doric columns, which defined the main space and filtered the light

5.26. Arthur Brown Jr., Labor–ICC Group, Federal Triangle, c. 1936. View of the auditorium portico and office-block end pavilions. Photograph by Theodor Horydczak, Library of Congress, Prints and Photographs Division.

5.27. Arthur Brown Jr., Labor–ICC group, Federal Triangle, c. 1936. Detail of entry to Auditorium Building; keystones by Leon Hermant, lighting fixtures designed by Brown. Photograph by Theodor Horydczak, Library of Congress, Prints and Photographs Division.

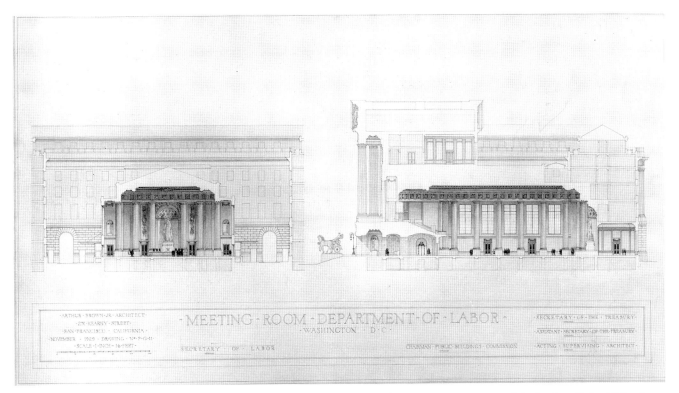

MEETING · ROOM · DEPARTMENT · OF · LABOR ·
· WASHINGTON · D · C ·

5.28 (*opposite*). Arthur Brown Jr., Labor–ICC group, Federal Triangle, c. 1936. Linking device between the Department of Labor block and the Auditorium Building. Photograph by Theodor Horydczak, Library of Congress, Prints and Photographs Division.

5.29. Arthur Brown Jr., Departmental Auditorium, Federal Triangle, November 1929. Sections detailing relationship between auditorium and portico. Photograph of drawing courtesy of Moulin Archives.

from the room's five bays of double-height windows (fig. 5.30). At the end of the room was a large exedra intended to receive an allegorical sculpture, which was soon removed from the program (fig. C.21). The entablatures, coffering, and rinceaux were all executed in plaster to save weight and expense; the metopes and spandrels of the entablature were polychromed in reds and blues, whereas the rinceaux were gilded. Behind the auditorium proper was a suite of conference rooms, a large meeting room directly behind the end wall of the auditorium, and two flanking square reception chambers to either side. These rooms faced the plaza and were lighted with nearly floor-to-ceiling windows. All of these rooms were paneled in hardwoods painted "water green," with the architectural embellishments picked out in gold leaf—the same color scheme as at the ballroom at Filoli.

The design, engineering, and construction of the Labor–ICC group was relatively trouble free once the final program was set and the funds appropriated. The preliminary cost estimates, prepared for approval with the formal presentation drawings at the end of 1929, describe the anticipated cost of the complex and the materials to be used. The initial cost of the Department of Labor Building was estimated at an even

$5 million, the Interstate Commerce Commission Building at $5.25 million, and the auditorium at $3.25 million.[55] These estimates were accepted as the approved expenditures in 1929, but actual authorizations for construction were lowered over 20 percent upon the award of the contracts. This sharp reduction in expenditures did not mean a proportionate reduction in the scope of the project or in the quality of the workmanship and finishes obtained, because many costs associated with the project likewise fell as the Great Depression worsened in the early 1930s.

Design development and the production of working drawings had to wait many months after the approval of the design by the Treasury and the Public Buildings Commission. By the spring of 1930, however, passage of the Elliott–Keyes Bill granted the Treasury authority to hire the Triangle architects to prepare detailed drawings of their projects, and it appropriated over $230 million toward the construction of hundreds of public buildings throughout the nation.[56] Within Brown's office Edward Frick served as the job captain for the entire course of the building campaign of the Labor–ICC block and supervised the design development process, the preparation of the working drawings and specifi-

5.30. Arthur Brown Jr., Departmental Auditorium, Federal Triangle, 1929–35, interior of main auditorium space. Photograph by Theodor Horydczak, Library of Congress, Prints and Photographs Division.

cations, and the construction of the buildings themselves. Frick made numerous trips to Washington for this latter purpose, often staying several weeks at a time to coordinate the work of local suppliers and specialties craftsmen. In 1931, Brown's most trusted engineer, Christopher Snyder, was brought onto the project team. Although most of the steel-frame construction of the Labor–ICC block was fairly straightforward, there were engineering challenges associated with the long span of the auditorium and the pier foundations, which had to be driven deep into the swampy soil under the former canal along Constitution Avenue (fig. 5.31).

Although the design development process was not completed until late 1931, detailed working drawings were begun as soon as possible, so that a contract set was available for bidding by April 1932. As was the case for San

Francisco City Hall, full-sized details were drawn after construction had begun, so these drawings date from as early as November 1932 to January 1934. In all of this in-house work Frick was assisted by John Baur, who had an independent practice throughout the 1910s and 1920s, but had fallen on hard times during the Great Depression, and Henry Howard, John Galen Howard's son, among others. The project specifications were largely prepared in-house by Brown's staff, then edited and amended by the Office of the Supervising Architect of the Treasury to ensure uniformity among the various buildings of the Triangle. As befitting such a large governmental project, the specifications were voluminous, running to 386 pages.[57]

The materials used in construction were common to most of the buildings in the Triangle: the exterior was faced in

Indiana limestone—except in the upper floors of the light courts, where pressed buff brick was substituted—and on all exterior wearing surfaces, such as at the entrance steps, which are granite (fig. 5.32). The roofs are clad in red Italian tile, as per Louis Ayres's recommendation. The windows and doors were hollow-core steel, although these have been replaced in places over the years. The interior structure demonstrates a similar concern for fireproof construction.

The floors were of composite concrete slab and hollow terra-cotta tile construction, over which marble, terrazzo, or ceramic tile finishes were floated, although some work areas were finished in cork (now carpeted), and some ceremonial rooms, such as the Secretary of Labor's office, received hardwood floors. Interior partitions were clay tile finished with marble veneer or hardwood paneling in public spaces and plastered elsewhere. Particular attention was given to hard-

5.31. Arthur Brown Jr. and William Adams Delano, Department of the Post Office and Labor–ICC group, Federal Triangle, c. 1932. Aerial photograph of construction in progress. The ICC and Post Office blocks were started first; the hemicyle and Department of Labor buildings have just been framed. The Auditorium Building was the last in the group to be constructed. Photograph by the Commercial Photo Company for the Department of the Treasury, author's collection.

ware and lighting fixtures, which were all designed for the buildings by Brown and his staff in full-size details, from which castings were made both in San Francisco and Washington (fig. 5.33).

In an unprecedented move, the Treasury decided to combine the contracts for the Labor–ICC complex with Delano's Post Office Building, creating the largest peacetime construction contract ever awarded by the United States government up to that time.[58] This tactic reduced the cost of some materials, owing to the very large quantities in which they were purchased, but it also limited the number of potential bidders for the job to only the largest national contracting firms. The winner was James Stewart & Company, which signed the combined contract on June 18, 1932; the bid for the Labor–ICC half of the contract came to $9,081,000. An estimate of total costs made in August 1934, at substantial completion of the project (only the artistic sculpture, lighting, and incidental finishes remained), came to $10,737,292, indicating that certain extras were added to the project, including an air conditioning system.[59] By January 1933, work had progressed

5.32. Arthur Brown Jr., Labor–ICC group, Federal Triangle, August 1933. hoisting of pedimental masonry. Photograph by the Commercial Photo Company for the Department of the Treasury, author's collection.

enough on the foundations of the complex to permit a cornerstone-laying ceremony with Herbert Hoover in attendance. Construction proceeded quickly enough that by the end of 1933 all the exterior work was completed, except for the art sculpture.[60]

Once interior finishing work began, however, the construction campaign was brought to a near halt by strikes brought against the project by trade unions competing for the same work. For example, the carpenters and steam fitters unions both claimed the right to install the radiator enclosures, shutting down the job for six weeks, and later the carpenters and cement workers argued over the installation of the mastic tile floors, again delaying the job for two weeks. Both disputes were settled once the contractor arranged for William Green, the president of the American Federation of Labor, to act as mediator.[61] The other delay in finishing the complex was perhaps less grim but far more frustrating to the architects. Upon the death of William N. Doak, Frances Perkins became Secretary of Labor—a groundbreaking appointment. In an effort to demonstrate safe working conditions, Perkins insisted on replacing any finish materials in the building that did not meet her standards, despite the fact that her predecessor had approved the materials and certified their installation. Thus many of the marble floors in the building were replaced with cork, custom-designed lighting was replaced with stock indirect fixtures, and additional restroom facilities were constructed for the department's more numerous female employees, including the secretary, who was horrified to learn that she was slated to share a washroom with her male chief counsel.[62] It is reported, however, that Perkins did find her four-room Louis XV office suite otherwise satisfactory. Finally, on February 25, 1935, Perkins dedicated the new Department of Labor facility with appropriate ceremony, several weeks after the completion of the rest of the complex.[63]

THE END OF THE TRIANGLE

As construction of the Triangle continued into the 1930s, support for the massive expenditures necessary to complete the complex dwindled. Although Charles Moore had close ties to the Coolidge administration, having been a personal friend of Grace Coolidge, he enjoyed less influence with Hoover. However, Hoover was an enthusiastic champion of the scheme—as Calvin Coolidge's Secretary of Commerce, he was a prime participant in the project from its inception. Brown was able to apply a personal touch when requiring presidential support for the project. Brown had known Hoover since he was appointed university architect by Stanford University's board of trustees. Hoover would remain an important patron for Brown, both during his presidency,

5.33. Arthur Brown Jr., Labor–ICC group, Federal Triangle, c. 1935, ironwork and lighting fixture at Labor rotunda. Photograph by Theodor Horydczak, Library of Congress, Prints and Photographs Division.

when Brown received the commission for the Federal Building in San Francisco's civic center, and afterward, when Brown designed the tower at Stanford for the Hoover Institution. FDR was more circumspect in his support than his predecessors, cutting back the scope of the construction effort and delaying the expenditure on much of the northern side of the Triangle.

After several aborted campaigns to complete the ensemble in the 1960s and 1980s, the Federal Triangle is now in what is considered to be its finished state. A decision to grant landmark status to the Old Post Office Building ensured that Delano's circular plaza would not be filled out,

and required that any effort to finish the Triangle would have to sensitively address this building. Pei-Cobb-Freed's enormous Ronald Reagan Building, completed in 1997, has filled in the Great Plaza, leaving very little open space within the Triangle itself. If Arthur Brown's monumental frontispiece for the plaza had been constructed, the plaza might have retained some meaning for official Washington and been completed. At the very least, such a device would have controlled enough space in front of the hemicycle to force the new construction into a less aggressive relationship with the rest of the Triangle, allowing for a more spacious and light-filled plaza in the center of the superblock. Yet

Pei-Cobb-Freed used bold, classically derived forms that relate to the scale of the entire complex, while recalling both the Triangle's past ambitions and contemporary technology and needs.

THE UNITED STATES CAPITOL

Brown's final work in Washington concerned the extension of the east front of the United States Capitol, proposed by Speaker of the House Sam Rayburn. Brown served on an advisory commission under Architect of the Capitol J. George Stewart, to evaluate plans to extend the front wall and steps of the Capitol 32 feet 6 inches further east (fig. 5.34). Although his death in July 1957 prevented him from cowriting the final report to Stewart with the others on the panel, Brown's opinion of the extension proposal became a contentious issue during subsequent Congressional hearings, and his views on the matter received attention in the architectural press.

Plans to extend the east front of the Capitol date as far back as the Civil War, when Thomas U. Walter constructed his monumental iron dome over the rotunda. In order to gain the silhouette Walter desired for the dome, he had to enlarge its diameter over 25 feet and cantilever it over the walls of the rotunda. This design anomaly went unnoticed from most vantage points around the Capitol, but it caused the dome and its base to project over the east portico (fig. 5.35). To remedy this condition Walter proposed an extension of the central block and portico 55 feet to the east, so that the central portico would align with those on the House and Senate wings.[64] This addition was not constructed because of the pressing demands of the Reconstruction economy, but the idea of an extension remained. By the turn of the century the need for additional office space on Capitol Hill was great enough to revive plans for an eastern extension, this time in the context of the same City Beautiful ethic that gave rise to the McMillan Plan. In 1904 the New York firm of Carrère & Hastings was selected to evaluate Walter's proposal, their own plan to move the east wall out 12 feet 6 inches in order to line up with the dome (Scheme A), and a third proposal to move the wall out 32 feet 6 inches (Scheme B). Carrère & Hastings rejected both Walter's plan and Scheme B, arguing that any long extension of the portico block would obscure the view of the dome from the street. In the end, no plan was passed by both the House and the Senate.[65]

Over the next fifty years, periodic attempts were made by Congress or the Architect of the Capitol to construct an addition modeled on Scheme B. Each time, the AIA and other groups lobbied successfully against it. Finally, in 1955 enabling legislation was passed as an amendment to an appropriations bill, allowing the Architect of the Capitol to begin plans for an extension "in substantial conformance with Scheme B."[66] Stewart appointed a committee of architects and engineers to design an extension the next year. In response to criticism from the AIA and some congressmen, Stewart also appointed a board of advisory architects, consisting of Henry R. Shepley, John F. Harbeson, Arthur Brown, and after Brown's death, Gilmore D. Clarke. The architects were charged with evaluating the planned extension but could not offer alternatives to the legislatively approved course of action.

The arguments for and against the extension were both compelling. Those in favor of the extension recalled Walter's intention to remedy the awkward relationship of the dome to the portico by such an extension; they also knew that the sandstone used in the portico was a "soft, friable material, difficult to work under the chisel and subject to damage by time and the elements."[67] Those demanding a new east front pointed to significant damage to the column capitals and entablature of the portico and a bulge in the walls of the old House and Senate chambers. The opponents of the extension, which included most of the membership of the AIA, noted that the east wall and portico comprised the only remaining substantially unaltered portion of Charles Bulfinch's exterior, and that a repair or even refacing of the structurally sound east wall could be undertaken for far less expense than the extension, the difference being put toward the construction of new office space on Capitol Hill. As Brown's friend and former AIA president Ralph Walker wrote at the time: "This, then, is one of the rare instances when we can have our cake and eat it as well. The Congress can easily restore the east front of the Capitol and still provide ample space for itself for less money than it would cost to betray the trust which history has given us."[68]

The advisory board was not free to consider alternatives but had to frame its report in terms of the legislative mandate for Scheme B. Thus, although the members of the board were not in support of an extension, their report described how to best mitigate the damage such an extension would cause, rather than to present another solution. Stewart used the report to claim that all of the advisors were unanimous in their approval of the extension. To bolster his claim, Stewart specifically reported that Brown was in favor of the plan, writing that "Mr. Arthur Brown, Jr., a member of the advisory group, died July 7, 1957, but concurred in these recommendations before his death."[69] Both Shepley and Harbeson denied that Brown favored the extension and, in fact, later admitted that neither Brown nor they supported Stewart's campaign for an extension. In fact, Shepley reported that "Brown was so wildly opposed to the idea that he didn't even want to work within the framework of the law."[70] However, Brown did feel duty

5.34. East front, United States Capitol, July 1956. Photo from the Office of the Architect of the Capitol.

5.35. Model of the United States Capitol, c. 1956, showing planned extension of the east front. Photo from the Office of the Architect of the Capitol.

bound to keep his feelings undisclosed for the sake of professional courtesy.

Brown did speak freely, off the record, about the Capitol and his role as an advisor. In an interview for *The Architectural Forum* in April 1957, just weeks before his last trip to Washington, Brown said that he "hoped to protect the Capitol from the bumbling milliners who think architecture is a fashion and who want to change it every year."[71] He also explained what he found significant about the dome: "As it now stands, the dome and its columns come down in a harmonious flow. This is very rare in domes, and very beautiful. It has a certain quality which would be lost if anything basic was changed." This "harmonious flow" was Brown's chief concern in all of his own domes. The dome must not only seem to be soundly supported by its base, but the lines of its elements must be carried down to the ground in a continuous, seemingly inevitable manner. For a dome set too far back from its base, this flow is cut off by a pediment or attic; the dome loses all sense of connection to the rest of the building. Michelangelo's dome at St. Peter's is an example of this difficulty: rarely is it satisfactorily viewed from St. Peter's Square. It was Brown's intention to maintain this relationship between dome and central block that compelled him to serve as an advisor. He summed up his view: "What we want to do is to keep the dignity, counterpoint and balance of the building. To the public as a whole it is very satisfying now. Trouble is, there are a lot of fellows with itchy fingers who want to monkey with it all."

Despite the publication of these views in October 1957, George Stewart persisted in characterizing Brown's recommendations to him as those of support for the extension. In that month the Joint Congressional Commission on the Capitol authorized Stewart to proceed with contract drawings for the extension, but by the following February the Senate Subcommittee on Public Buildings and Grounds was holding public hearings to rescind congressional approval for Scheme B. At these hearings, Stewart testified that Brown "sat in my office one day and said, 'Insofar as the court effect out front [is concerned], I know you want to move it out. I am here to help you move it out right away.'"[72] When Jessamine Brown heard this testimony she sent a telegram to Ralph Walker, leader of the effort to stop the extension: "Am greatly distressed by newspapers announcing imminent mutilation of the Capitol. Surely a way can be found to prevent this grievous error. Arthur made his last and fatal journey hoping to prevent it. The effort and the frustration cost his life."

In the end, the efforts to retain Bulfinch's walls and pediment were in vain. Although the Senate subcommittee voted to rescind the authorization and won Senate concurrence, the Speaker of the House would not allow any impediment to delay the Capitol building program and the extension. The east front of the Capitol now fully supports the dome, which appears much more structurally logical, but its drum is cut off from view, as expected (fig. 5.36). The real loss, however, is in the masonry: the new marble facade and entablature have no sense of history in them, and still look freshly carved after nearly forty years. It may be many years before the new east facade and Capitol steps carry the physical signs of history with which they are imbued in the popular imagination.

Despite this loss on Capitol Hill, Brown's legacy in the Capitol ended in a victory for the preservation of Washington's federal past. Through Brown's lifelong friendship with Marie Beale, he had always had an entrée into Washington society: indeed, he was entertained and lodged at Decatur House numerous times. Though he rarely capitalized on their close relationship (she was godmother to his daughter Victoria), on two occasions she did use her considerable influence to promote a historically sensitive solution to problems at the executive end of Pennsylvania Avenue; these campaigns resulted in commissions for Brown's associates. The first required little assistance from Brown, but nonetheless it was Brown who introduced Beale to William Adams Delano upon commencement of the Federal Triangle work in the late 1920s.[73] Delano became a frequent visitor to Decatur House, and it was no doubt helpful to him to have Mrs. Beale's recommendation when her close friends, the Trumans, were seeking an architect to design the reconstruction of the White House twenty years later.

Marie Beale's final campaign concerned the proposal to demolish the historic houses around Lafayette Square for federal office buildings. Beale fought to preserve the square's nearly unparalleled collection of row houses until her death in 1956. Eventually, the National Trust for Historic Preservation and other advocacy groups convinced officials in the Kennedy Administration, and the Kennedys themselves, to consider the preservation of the houses as office space, and to construct the tall office blocks behind the square.[74] The architects for both these tasks had close connections with Arthur Brown. The houses were rehabilitated by George Livermore, who had known Brown all his life and worked as an apprentice in Brown's office in the late 1930s; the office towers were designed by John Carl Warnecke, who had worked for Brown in the 1930s, and whose father (Carl) had studied in Brown's atelier at the San Francisco Architectural Club.[75]

Arthur Brown's life spanned the most critical period of Washington's growth and development since its beginnings. The transition of the city from a somewhat ramshackle, largely part-time, community into the capital city of a superpower required a corresponding architectural transformation. Brown was eager to participate in this transforma-

5.36. East front of the United States Capitol, 1997, showing Rayburn extension in place.

tion and willing to make personal and architectural sacrifices in the name of a more monumental and beautiful federal district that more closely fulfilled the vision documented in L'Enfant's plan. By the end of the 1950s, though, he began to believe that the new wave of post-war building had lost sight of the vision and was threatening to destroy all that was compelling about the place. Brown became a defender of the historic fabric of the city, however imperfect, not only on aesthetic grounds, but because it preserved an element of humanity that was fast giving way to modernization.

6.1. Arthur Brown Jr., schematic design for a capitol complex
at Monterey, December 1928, L. B. Miller, delineator. Drawing,
Arthur Brown Jr. Collection, Bancroft Library.

CHAPTER SIX

ARTHUR BROWN JR.
AND ASSOCIATES

Brown's placement on the Board of Architectural Consultants for the Federal Triangle was recognition that by the end of the 1920s he had become an architect of national importance. Although the vast majority of his work remained in California and particularly in the San Francisco Bay Area, with his independent practice Brown began to do work elsewhere on the Pacific Coast and throughout the nation. Brown was invited to serve as one of the design architects for the Century of Progress International Exposition in Chicago, which opened in 1933, and he collaborated with his friend Frère Champney on St. Mark's Episcopal Cathedral in Seattle. Although the work in Washington, DC, was time-consuming, it was immensely rewarding for Brown; he had hoped to do similar governmental work outside of California, but as the Great Depression worsened in the early 1930s he found building opportunities everywhere limited.

The work out of state meant that the structure of the new firm had to be more decentralized than Bakewell & Brown had been. Although Brown continued to be the unquestioned authority on all matters of design, he was not always immediately at hand because of his heavy travel schedule. A meeting of the Board of Architectural Consultants in Washington, DC, for example, required nearly two weeks of Brown's schedule. This meant that Brown's associates, J. S. Gould, Edward Frick, Lawrence Kruse, and at times John Baur, had to manage their projects autonomously, and as these projects went into construction, they were often called away to the job site for weeks at a time. The office could have descended into chaos in Brown's long absences, but Edith Fremdling,

Brown's administrative assistant, kept everything and everybody in line. Miss Fremdling did much more than screen Brown's calls and type correspondence. She coordinated the schedules of all the firm's associates, kept the accounts, did the firm's (and Brown's) banking, and kept Brown fully informed of the events of the day through long letters and telegrams.[1] Without her managerial skills, it is very unlikely that Brown would have had the success as an independent practitioner that he did.

The first half of Brown's independent practice was largely devoted to governmental work on both local and national scales. Between 1928 and 1935, Brown designed and reviewed the construction of the Labor–ICC block of the Federal Triangle, the San Francisco War Memorial, and the San Francisco Federal Building, important governmental buildings that cost over $20 million to construct. Brown was also invited to participate in several national projects and competitions in these years, the most important of which were designs for the Century of Progress exposition in Chicago and for the Federal Reserve Building in Washington, DC. Finally, Brown designed for the city of San Francisco the Coit Memorial Tower on Telegraph Hill and the Holly Courts housing development, and was one of the architects for the Bay Bridge and Transbay Terminal project and the Golden Gate International Exposition.

Through these years Brown's architectural aesthetic began to change. The ornamented baroque of the San Francisco City Hall had already given way in the 1920s to an interest in regional variations on the classical architectural tradition, such as the abstracted Byzantine he explored at Temple

Emanu-El, or the Spanish colonial he interpreted at Pasadena, San Diego, and with a proposed state capitol complex for Monterey (fig. 6.1). In most of his governmental projects Brown returned to eighteenth-century French classicism, but often sought ways to simplify the presentation of these buildings. The earliest of these commissions, the Labor–ICC block, is the most elaborate in its use of sculpted ornament and complex orders. Brown responded to the less-generous budgets of facilities such as the War Memorial and the Federal Building with a simplification of the classical elements. A strong Doric order was employed to unite these buildings with San Francisco City Hall and the rest of the civic center and to convey the militaristic or protectionist character of facilities. In the mid-1930s Brown's design stance transcended simplification and entered the realm of abstraction. This reduction of the canonical parts of the classical orders to their essential forms was the hallmark of Brown's last period, although it is difficult to be certain whether he designed in this manner because the market demanded it, because stylistic trends in the profession were calling for it, or because he himself desired a more direct architectural expression; there is evidence for all three.

ST. MARK'S CATHEDRAL

No project illustrates the contrast between the optimistic ambitions of the 1920s and the grim limitations of the 1930s better than Brown's involvement with the design of St. Mark's Episcopal Cathedral in Seattle. Brown undertook the project in 1926 as a favor to both his friend Frère Champney and his brother-in-law John Eddy.[2] By the time Brown ended his association with the diocese of Olympia, Champney was dead, the cathedral lay half constructed, and Brown had severed ties with his brother-in-law.

The project began in 1922, when the diocese hired parishioner Champney to draw up an image of a proposed cathedral, to be located at Tenth and Galer streets in Seattle (fig. 6.2). The project was delayed with the appointment of a new bishop, and by 1926 Champney's fortunes had taken a decided turn for the worse.[3] The building committee believed that Champney was not able to see a project as large as a cathedral through to construction because he did not have a great deal of experience with large projects, nor did he have a staff to work with him. Champney was, however, under contract, and the building committee felt obligated to honor his rights to the project. The committee approached several local Seattle architects in the hopes that one of them might associate with Champney, but his reputation for erratic behavior made this impossible. John Eddy, the treasurer of the vestry and a principal financial backer of the project, saw an opportunity for his brother-in-law. Brown was Champney's closest

6.2. Frère Champney, sketch for St. Mark's Cathedral, Seattle, late 1922. Arthur Brown Jr. Collection, Bancroft Library.

professional colleague, the most prominent architect working on the Pacific Coast, and the one person with whom Champney might be able to work. Eddy wrote his brother-in-law on July 19, 1926, proposing that Brown "rescue the church out of the difficulty" and accept Champney's proposal to associate on the cathedral, which he was to suggest to him in the next several days.[4]

Champney did indeed follow Eddy's suggestion and he soon proposed an association with Brown, who agreed to work with his Seattle colleague, although he did have reservations about the situation, given the difficulties he had had with Willis Polk on the San Francisco War Memorial project. The architects started with Champney's drawing of an English Gothic church, a sketch that captivated the imagination of the former bishop and many members of the building committee. Brown immediately saw that the scheme was not constructible, but he worked with Champney to derive a plan that was structurally possible. He also wrote to the head of the building committee, J. F. Duthie, to verify the program and the available budget for the complex. Champney had really only envisioned a church, but Brown understood that a

Sunday school, parish hall, rectory, and Episcopal offices should be designed for a master plan for the entire complex.

The team set to work in September 1926 and made good progress in developing the plans through the remainder of the year. Brown considered three cathedral projects, in particular, as models: Ralph Adams Cram's St. John the Divine in New York City, Sir Giles Gilbert Scott's Liverpool Cathedral, and Lewis Hobart's Grace Cathedral in San Francisco. All three of these structures attempted to reconcile traditional Gothic architectural forms with contemporary construction techniques, although to a varying degree. Grace Cathedral was most relevant to Brown, as Hobart's use of concrete and structural steel permitted the construction of the great church in a fraction of the time and budget that masonry construction would have required, and at the same time protected the structure against seismic forces. Bakewell, Brown, and Champney proposed a steel structure that was to be faced with stone, braced with concrete infill walls, and vaulted with concrete shells. The building was intended to evoke the architectural qualities of an English thirteenth-century cathedral church—through the use of the most modern materials available (fig. 6.3).

The church, as constructed, was square in plan, with nearly identical high bays that radiated from the crossing; the north and south bays were to serve as transepts, the east as a narthex, and the west as the choir. Each elevation was regulated by massive buttresses that framed large lancet windows. At each elevation a rose window with stone Gothic tracery was planned, but none was executed. The dominant visual feature of the building was to be the crossing tower, rising over 200 feet above the church floor. This tower and the subordinate transept and corner towers were to have been crowned with a myriad of pinnacles and arcaded screens, which would have given the building a highly active silhouette against the gray skies of Seattle.

Brown understood the great challenge he was undertaking in building a modern Gothic cathedral; the rector, John D. McLaughlan, and the building committee were less understanding of the extent of their ambition. In fact, it took the architects a full year to prepare an approved schematic design that reconciled the diocese's needs with its extremely tight budget. From October 1927 on, Brown's office prepared the construction documents for the first phase of the construction, the nave and Thomsen Chapel; these were delayed while additional land was purchased and critical engineering and materials choices were debated. During the delay the vestry grew impatient to break ground. Brown wrote Duthie in January 1928, urging him to look at the bigger picture:

> I think it might be well to impress upon the vestry that we are trying to produce a building of first class importance, and the time spent has not been abnormal compared with other buildings of the same type and aspirations. . . . As you will recall,

we decided sometime ago that in order to make a great Cathedral, it would be necessary to depart from the traditional methods of construction of the Gothic Architecture and apply the principles of modern construction to this problem. There is very little precedent for this method of attack. We are exploring in a new and unknown territory in working out the application of modern methods to this traditional and ancient form of architecture. It is difficult to visualize the magnitude of this undertaking, which, as I have said before, is of the first order.[5]

The vestry directed Brown to engineer the building as if the facing stone were to be used throughout the project. This design requirement delayed the completion of the working drawings, and to little effect, because the $1.2 million budget that Brown initially planned for shrank quickly as the Depression worsened. The vestry's insistence on designing for an ideal future church greatly alarmed John Eddy, who saw no way to reconcile the architectural plans with the

6.3. Hugh Ferriss for American Institute of Steel Construction, rendering for St. Mark's Cathedral, Seattle, c. 1929. Reproduced with permission of the AISC.

reduced budget. He threatened to resign unless the facing stone was excised from the program and a more realistic budget for the project was adopted.[6] Eddy's threat was taken seriously, and the vestry eventually finalized a construction budget of about $450,000 in October 1928.

As construction began early the following year, the builders, Henry & McFee Contracting Company, found that Brown's first phase could not be built for much less than $680,000. This news forced the vestry to finally explore the use of bare concrete on the building exterior. Eddy challenged Brown to make a concrete exterior aesthetically pleasing, telling him, "you must convince us that you can produce a more or less satisfactory outside appearance with plain concrete that will more or less satisfy people."[7] Still, members of the vestry held out for stone and directed Brown to engineer the building for that material. Finally, in the summer of 1929, as the building was going up, a decision had to be made. Brown supported the use of bare concrete and wrote Dr. McLaughlan a letter defending the use of concrete in this case: "I am inclined to believe that the use of concrete in Gothic form may very well be justified providing the forms themselves are pleasing and that the masses are impressive and well proportioned. It would seem to me that the use of granite would cripple the budget for many years to come without, perhaps, any real gain in appearance."[8]

Brown made his case, and the bare concrete was approved. But at the same moment a fresh controversy arose regarding Brown's fee, which came to over $40,000 by March 1929.[9] The secretary of the building committee, Horton Force, a lawyer, attempted to invalidate Brown's claims against the vestry to buy the group time to raise more funds for construction. The project was thrown into further turmoil in early June, when Champney died at his temporary home in Berkeley.[10] Brown now had to assume the entire cathedral project, which meant that he had to find a staff member who could travel to Seattle several times a month to observe the progress of the construction and answer questions. Brown himself went to Seattle in June 1929 and met with the building committee to evaluate the construction progress and to settle his claim against the vestry. During this trip the vestry passed a resolution acknowledging Brown's outstanding balance of $37,480.[11]

Brown's quick trip quelled criticism of his handling of the cathedral project, at least for a while. But by the beginning of 1930 there was growing discontent in Seattle about the costs associated with the church Brown had planned. Rather than blame the building committee, which had perhaps overestimated their means, the parishioners chose to blame the architect, who was safely out of town, for his "extravagance." Brown defended himself, reminding members of the vestry that he was following his clients' instructions. He wrote to Joshua Green:

At the time that I was instructed to go ahead with the monumental scheme of the church it was decided that this was only the beginning of a great scheme, and consequently, it should not be forgotten that it will take considerable courage during the incomplete stages. This, I believe, to be true in most similar cases and, therefore, I regret that there should be so much hostility felt by some of the members of the vestry toward me. I, after all, did not decide on this course of action and many times before it was adopted suggested a less ambitious building.[12]

Payments on the pledges the building committee had counted on to continue the construction of the building slowed with Black Tuesday and stopped altogether as the Great Depression took hold of the nation's economy; in the end, the vestry resorted to mortgaging the property for $250,000 to finance the project. Work on the cathedral finally stopped in the spring of 1931, when the building was hastily enclosed and consecrated in a largely unfinished condition. At that time, the vestry requested that John Eddy ask Brown to relinquish his lien rights against the parish property and to consider dropping his claim against them.[13] Brown refused, suspecting that the mortgagee, a St. Louis bank, was about to foreclose on the property. Brown retained a Seattle lawyer to enforce his rights, hoping to keep his claim alive in the event of foreclosure.[14]

The cathedral was eventually foreclosed upon, in 1941, but was recovered by the diocese in 1944. Funds were quickly raised for the buyout of the note after the war, and in 1947 the diocese claimed itself free of any debts associated with the building of the cathedral. Brown was quite surprised to hear this, as he had never been fully paid for his work, his account balance standing at nearly $20,000 when the work was suspended. He asked John Eddy to assist him in gaining a final settlement with the vestry, but Eddy believed that the vestry owed Brown nothing and refused to support his brother-in-law. In disbelief, Brown let his lawyers negotiate as good a settlement as they could get and ceased any direct communication with his brother-in-law. Finally, in 1948, Brown received a check for $8,000 to settle the account on work largely executed two decades earlier.

The Cathedral of St. Mark's is a fairly complete facility today. In 1958 the vestry constructed the Cathedral House, which houses the social hall, parish offices, classrooms, and meeting spaces. In 1965 the sanctuary was remodeled to permit the installation of a new organ.[15] Finally, an extensive enlargement and renovation of the building by Olson Sundberg Architects, begun in the mid-1990s, now permits the cathedral to seat over one thousand worshipers on Easter and other special occasions. The contemporary additions complement the rough concrete exteriors of the building quite well, and for the first time the building can be said to fulfill the diocese's ambitions for its great cathedral church.[16]

Emerging Modernism:
The Century of Progress Exposition

Brown experienced the "moderne" aesthetic in Paris first in 1924 and again in 1926. During the latter year Brown was in the French capital to be installed as a Membre Etranger of the Académie des Beaux-Arts of the Institut de France. The architectural tradition represented by that body had been boldly challenged the year before in the Exposition Internationale des Arts Décoratives et Industriels Modernes, from which art deco received its name. Brown saw much of the remnants of this influential event and must have wondered if the modernistic mode would take hold in America. He would soon participate in one of the great exhibitions of the early modern movement when he agreed to design several buildings for the Century of Progress exposition.

The idea of a second Chicago World's Fair, forty years after the World's Columbian Exposition of 1893, gradually gained interest in the mid-1920s. Finally chartered in January 1928,

this Chicago Second World's Fair Centennial Celebration was intended to commemorate the one-hundredth anniversary of the founding of the city, and to showcase American and world achievement in science and technology over that century. To emphasize this theme, exhibition chairman Rufus Dawes envisioned fairgrounds that would emphasize the contemporary and portend the future; the Century of Progress exhibition was to avoid the historicist architectural references of past American world's fairs.

Dawes selected Paul Cret and Raymond Hood, two East Coast architects with significant midwestern experience, to head the architectural commission. Both Cret and Hood were Beaux-Arts–trained architects whose work deviated from the historically inspired and heavily ornamented work associated with the school at the time of their attendance. Cret was famed for his "modern neoclassic" style, a stripped-down architecture that simplified the classical orders to bare essentials yet retained the clarity of circulation and careful proportioning of work produced a century earlier. Hood, initially

6.4. Arthur Brown Jr., proposal for the Century of Progress Exposition, 1929. Brown's skyscraper-based scheme was typical of most of the proposals made by the members of the Board of Architects, but they all proved impracticable. Photograph, Arthur Brown Jr. Collection, Bancroft Library.

CHICAGO WORLD'S FAIR 1933
ARTHUR BROWN JR. ARCHITECT. SAN FRANCISCO

known for his winning design for the Chicago Tribune Tower, designed office towers in New York with ever more abstract detailing. Hood and Cret were charged with selecting the other architects for the exhibition, and through a complex selection process they arrived at Ralph Walker, Harvey Wiley Corbett, Arthur Brown, and Edward Bennett. These architects then chose two Chicago architects, John Holabird and Hubert Burnham, sons of Columbian Exposition designers William Holabird and Daniel Burnham, to give the commission a local presence.

The commission met in 1928 and early 1929 to masterplan the site in South Park, now Burnham Park and McCormick Place. The site was long and narrow, squeezed between the Illinois Central rail yards and Lake Michigan, and bounded by institutional and recreational buildings of southern Grant Park to the northwest and Thirty-ninth Street to the southeast. The most prominent feature of the fairgrounds was Northerly Island, on which the Adler Planetarium was being constructed, and the lagoon that separated it from the shore. The commission first met on May 23, 1928, and over the course of the next few days considered the appropriate character of the exposition buildings and became acquainted with the site. They did this by walking the land and viewing it from an airplane (Brown's first and possibly only aircraft ride).[17] The commissioners then arrived at a vision statement that signaled their intentions. They reported this consensus in a letter to Dawes, which read, in part: "The architecture of the buildings and of the grounds of the Exposition of 1933 will illustrate in definite form the development of the art of architecture since the great Fair of 1893, not only as in America, but in the world at large. New elements of construction, products of modern invention and science, will be factors in the architectural composition. . . . The architects of the Chicago World's Fair Centennial Celebration of 1933 intend that the buildings of the Fair shall express the beauty of form and detail of both national and the international aspects of this creative movement."[18]

At the close of the first round of meetings, Edward Bennett was chosen to prepare an initial scheme for the exposition grounds that could be used for comment and elaboration. This scheme, prepared in just a few days, was relentlessly symmetrical and clearly grounded in the design principles of the first Chicago fair as much as the second.[19] At the next meeting, the commissioners developed a set of planning principles and a program for the buildings at the exposition.[20] From this foundation, each architect produced a plan of his own, exhibited and debated at the January 1929 meetings of the commission. The best features of each were to be melded by each architect into a compromise scheme that would become the guiding plan for the exposition. Although there were exceptions, most of these composite plans presented at the May 1929 meetings located

high, tower-like edifices along the shores of the lagoon in a formal Beaux-Arts ground plan (fig. 6.4). Brown's scheme regularized the lagoon and created a small island within it, on which he placed a grand square bisected by the major Twenty-third Street cross-axis of the exposition. To the south of the lagoon Brown placed a tall stepped skyscraper, the theme structure for the fair. On either side he laid out broad avenues and gardens lined by twenty eight-story towers that marked the entrance to the exhibit halls. Toward the north end Brown placed another bridge, elliptical in plan, guarded by two sixteen-story towers.

These formal plans were scrapped the next day when Raymond Hood presented his plans for an asymmetrical scheme. Hood had been in Paris and in Spain, where he visited the expositions in Barcelona and Seville. Accounts of the origins of his scheme vary, but, in any case, Hood's plan was drawn up by American architectural students in Paris so that it would be ready for his return to New York.[21] The scheme had considerable merit, including the practical point that it was far more flexible in accommodating change, if the amount of exhibit space needed to be altered or if an exhibitor dropped out. The commissioners discussed each proposal and eventually identified Hood's as the most promising. To ensure a balanced and independent development of it, the commission appointed Cret to refine it into the final layout for the exposition.[22] At the same time, the commissioners divided the primary exhibition grounds around the lagoon into eight precincts and assigned each member to design the buildings for one precinct. Although the locations and assignments changed for some commissioners, Brown was assigned the north half of Northerly Island; he saw his designs for the Hall of States and the Dairy and Agriculture buildings through to completion.

The architecture of the fair was to be decidedly novel and governed by modern construction and technology. The challenge for the commissioners was to identify which of several competing visions of the architectural future was the most appropriate for the exposition. While the rationalist white boxes of Walter Gropius, Ludwig Mies van der Rohe, and Le Corbusier would shortly be celebrated as the "International style," several other forms of nonhistoricist modern architecture were also vying for preeminence in the late 1920s and early 1930s. The commissioners' first thought was to use the skyscraper as the controlling visual cue for the exhibition. The skyscraper became a problematic form, though, because although a forty- or sixty-story exhibition hall would have been dramatic, it was impossible to design a structure that would be both structurally sound and temporary. Furthermore, by 1930 the financial exigencies of the Great Depression required that the commissioners look at less costly expressions of modernity. Most of the commissioners had seen the art deco exposition and were enthralled by the French abstraction of classical architecture. The frequent employment of

6.5. Aerial photograph of the Century of Progress Exposition, Chicago, 1933. Note the overwhelming scale of the Skyride and the integration of the fairgrounds into the Grant Park cultural district. Brown's Hall of States and Agriculture Building are at center, under the Skyride. Photograph by Harry Koss, courtesy of the Library of Congress, Prints and Photographs Division.

chevron and fountain motifs and the strong colorization of the French fair made a lasting impression on the commissioners and became important design elements in Chicago.

The commissioners also looked at Russian constructivist architecture of the 1920s. Although constructivism proved to be a short-lived movement, a number of creative designers explored the sculptural potential of steel and glass and new structural forms such as the catenary to create buildings that owed no obvious debt to the past. The commissioners were inspired by the constructivists' ability to improvise with new materials under difficult financial circumstances. They found themselves facing similar challenges, in that new materials such as aluminum and plywood were to be used as the basis for constructions that freed architectural space from the constraints of masonry-based form. Traditional design imperatives such as balance and symmetry were to be replaced with the efficient determinism of the engineered object. Harvey Corbett stated the exposition buildings' purpose: "The Fair stands as a symbol of the architecture of the future—icons of the past cast aside, the ingenuity of the designers of the present thrown on their own resources to meet the problems of the day—strengthened only by the background of scientific and engineering genius."[23]

The exposition's signature structure, the Skyride, exemplified the commissioners' debt to the constructivist spirit and the need to improvise with an ever-changing program, budget, and palette of materials. Now common in any theme park across the country, the concept of the Skyride was first presented to the fair's commissioners by inventor William Hamilton in the summer of 1931. Hamilton's idea was to shuttle passenger cabins across the fairgrounds high in the air on wires suspended from two towers over 600 feet high and one-third of a mile apart (fig. 6.5).[24] Although the Skyride was rejected initially by the commissioners as being impracticable, Nathaniel Owings, deputy director of design and future founder of Skidmore, Owings & Merrill, revived the idea and had it built in the first months of 1933.[25] Although the speed of the ride was not much faster than walking, the experience of floating above the lagoon was captivating and made the Skyride one of the fair's chief attractions.

The eight members of the architectural commission all agreed to work in the spirit described by the group's letter to President Dawes. The success of each contributing architect's work varied according to the zeal with which he took to the problem. Hood's Electrical Pavilion and Cret's Hall of Science received critical acclaim at the exposition's opening. Other buildings, such as Bennett's domed and towered United States Government Building, were half-hearted attempts at modernism that lacked conviction. Brown's Hall of States, which abutted Bennett's work, was a cellular building arranged so that each state would get only the exhibition space it required. From the triangular Court of the States a semblance of order prevailed, but from the rear the structure looked like a series of grain silos arranged about a concrete viaduct (fig. 6.6). Of all Brown's works, this building may well have been his least favorite.[26]

6.6. (*above*) Arthur Brown Jr. and Edward H. Bennett, Federal Government Building and Hall of States, Century of Progress Exposition, Chicago, 1933. Bennett's building is the towered structure to the left; Brown's facility spreads out to the right; the Agriculture Building is behind to the right center. Photograph by Kaufmann & Fabry, courtesy of the Chicago Parks District.

6.7. (*below*) Arthur Brown Jr., Agriculture Building, Century of Progress Exposition, Chicago, 1933. Photograph by Kaufmann & Fabry, courtesy of the Chicago Parks District.

Brown was more successful with his designs for the Dairy and Agricultural buildings. Although the drawings were done in San Francisco, he shared titular association with Bennett. In both cases he and his team produced credible modern buildings that effectively used new materials. Given how many projects were in the office as these buildings were designed, it is possible that one of Brown's younger associates took a leading role in the design development of these two progressive buildings. The Dairy Building, one of the smallest exhibit halls at the fair, was a study in asymmetry and somewhat resembled W. M. Dudok's town hall for Hilversum, the Netherlands, which had just been published. A series of increasingly tall masses was grouped around a five-story tower; fins further emphasized the verticality of the tower. Fairgoers could enjoy ice cream on the second-floor loggia, whose roof dramatically hovered over the space. The Agricultural Building was a long, streamlined structure organized along a dramatic vaulted circulation spine that was covered with a half-elliptical aluminum ceiling, onto which colored light was thrown. The result was a cavernous, atmospheric space quite unexpected in a building that housed farming and food-product exhibits. A series of terraces wrapped around the south side of the building, allowing visitors to view events and light shows over the lagoon (fig. 6.7).

All of the structures at the exposition attempted a constructivist aesthetic that emphasized the novel materials employed and the details used to connect them. This aesthetic imposed a sort of unity on the assemblage that was heightened by Joseph Urban's bold, even garish, color scheme. In fact, it was the colors to which the public reacted most, but the architecture also won its share of detractors among the public. Professional criticism of the exposition was mixed. Some noted architects, such as Albert Kahn, found the buildings appropriate and interesting as exposition architecture. Others were horrified. Ralph Adams Cram astutely recognized that the constructivist aesthetic was already dated by the exposition's opening; the European avant-garde had already abandoned it.[27] Frank Lloyd Wright was typically scathing, characterizing the architecture as "wholesale imitation, hit or miss, of the genuine new forms that occurred in our country in out of the way places many years ago."[28] It was typical of Wright to dismiss the work of others while at the same time glorifying himself, but here he may also have been voicing his distain for the work of a team from which he had been pointedly excluded.

COIT MEMORIAL TOWER

The Century of Progress demonstrated that designers trained to appreciate the set of architectural values taught at the Ecole des Beaux-Arts had difficulty creating work in the sup-

6.8. Arthur Brown Jr., Coit Tower, San Francisco, 1933. Photograph courtesy of Moulin Archives.

posed "scientific" culture of modernism as defined by the European avant-garde. Both Hood and Cret were regarded by modernist critics as having successfully made the transition in the following years, Hood with the *Daily News* and McGraw-Hill buildings in New York City, and Cret with his building for the Federal Reserve in Washington, DC. Other designers of this generation, such as Brown, explored the possibilities of abstraction but insisted on retaining the emphasis on mass and controlled proportions of the classical manner. Brown's design for the Coit Memorial Tower on Nob Hill is perhaps the most abstract of his permanent architectural creations, and also his most misunderstood work (fig. 6.8).

The flamboyant Lillie Hitchcock Coit was one of the colorful characters of the Barbary Coast days that San Franciscans were happy to have had in their past but whose exploits the citizenry was not eager to see repeated in the present. Coit was a child when brought to San Francisco, and she grew up revering the city's firefighters. In 1863, as a young woman, she was elected to fire company number five, not as a mascot but as a full-fledged firefighter. She thereafter answered every fire call to "Number Five" possible until the

6.9. Arthur Brown Jr., Coit Tower, September 1931, first presentation drawing, probably by Henry Howard. Arthur Brown Jr. Collection, Bancroft Library.

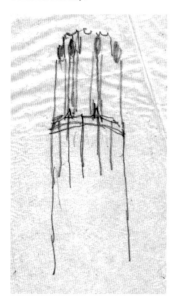 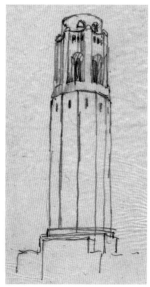

6.10 (*left*). Arthur Brown Jr., Coit Tower, San Francisco, c. 1931, initial design sketch depicting "sawed-off" crown. Arthur Brown Jr. Collection, Bancroft Library.

6.11 (*right*). Arthur Brown Jr., Coit Tower, c. 1931, refined design sketch. Arthur Brown Jr. Collection, Bancroft Library.

turn of the century. She lived in Europe for most of the years between 1903 and 1924 but she returned to San Francisco to spend her final years. Upon her death in 1929, Coit bequeathed nearly $100,000 to the City of San Francisco to "expend the same in an appropriate manner for the purpose of adding to the beauty of said city, which I have always loved."[29]

The city took some time in creating a vehicle to realize Coit's directive. Eventually Herbert Fleischhacker, president of the Board of Park Commissioners and city supervisor, formed a Coit advisory committee, which included William H. Crocker, executor of Coit's estate, and John McLaren, director of Golden Gate Park. This committee was to oversee the selection and construction of an appropriate monument, which Fleischhacker had determined should be sited in Pioneer Park on Telegraph Hill. The park, the site of an early semaphore that signaled the passage of ships through the Golden Gate, was associated with Lillie Coit's service to the fire department and seemed the natural place for a grand aesthetic gesture.[30] The site also offered unique design challenges. The perfect monument would have to be scaled to the city yet not overwhelm the hill; it would be viewed from below and also in elevation from nearby Russian Hill; and it would have to be constructed within a bare-bones budget.

The advisory committee decided that the responsibility to select a suitable design for the monument should fall upon the city's Fine Art Commission. The commission arranged a limited competition in the spring of 1931 among the city's architects and artists, and rather quickly dismissed as impracticable several overscaled proposals. Brown, a former chairman of the Fine Art Commission, had been contemplating the erection of a monument at Pioneer Park since 1905, when he designed a "pharos," or light tower, for the Burnham plan. So while the art commission debated various forms the memorial might take, Brown had his preferred solution in mind and knew exactly how to sell his concept to his former fellow commissioners. Brown also had considerable backing on the advisory committee. Herbert Fleischhacker was heavily involved with the War Memorial project, which Brown was completing at the civic center, and William Crocker had commissioned Brown to build his home on the peninsula.

Not surprisingly, the commission selected a poured concrete observation tower and lighthouse, which was designed and refined by Brown. The initial conception is definitely Brown's; sketches in Brown's papers demonstrate how he worked the tower into something like its final form. From April to September 1931, Brown and the project design manager, John Baur, refined the idea, which was rendered by Henry Howard for presentation to the art commission.[31] The presentation drawing illustrated all of the essentials of the built design, but none of the poetry (fig. 6.9). A three-stage tower rose from a square base, and an arcaded observation level was crowned by a circular attic, but the fluted shaft was only twice as high as the base, which gave the whole composition a rather stubby appearance. The tower form did not win unanimous approval from the art commissioners; the women members were particularly unimpressed. Gertrude Atherton, a member, recalled that "None [of the schematic designs] were adequate in my opinion nor in that of Mrs. Musante—the only other woman on the Commission—but the model of a tower by the eminent architect Arthur Brown met with the final approval of the men. Mrs. Musante and I protested in vain; men always stand by other men against women, and after days of wrangling the males of the Commission went into a huddle and emerged with the dictum that they were for the Coit Tower, and that was that."[32]

Brown was officially hired as the architect of the tower at a meeting of the advisory committee on September 2, 1931. At the same meeting Haig Patigian was commissioned to execute a statuary monument to the "Original Volunteer Fire Department of the City" (this work was a provision of Lillie Coit's will), and John McLaren was appointed the "landscape engineer" for the project. The budget was increased to $125,000, but only $100,000 was to be used for the tower.[33]

The design of Coit Tower became an exercise in pure aesthetics, albeit limited by a tight budget. The additional appropriation allowed Brown to raise the tower higher and gain a more dramatic silhouette. Working drawings were begun immediately in September 1931, and a bid set was completed by mid-December. This intermediate design presented the tower in nearly its final state. Its fluted concrete shaft, now approximately 100 feet high, emerged from a 25-foot-high cubic base that presented a segmental colonnade on three sides concentric with the tower (the base was originally unenclosed). The crown presented particular design problems, because it had to effectively terminate the tower when viewed from below as well as from head-on. As Henry Howard reported in his article on the tower in *The Architect and Engineer*, the arcaded loggia atop the shaft was "designed to provide protected observation points and at the same time a fine terminal for the shaft."[34] The entire piece was controlled with eight massive piers, which were repeated in the upper stage of the crown. The primary stage of the crown was concave in plan between these piers, and a set of three small arched openings punctuated the top of the stage. The smaller arcade of the upper stage is reminiscent in silhouette of the Tour de Buerre at Rouen, although there are no flyers. The top of the tower ended abruptly, in order to emphasize the proportions of the object over any terminating detail. George Livermore related Brown's recollection of the decision: "He said he didn't know how to end it, so he just sliced it off. It just looks that way, doesn't it? He just went up a couple of feet, and asked, 'What am I going to do now?' So, he just sliced it off." (figs. 6.10, 6.11)[35]

MONUMENT FOR TELEGRAPH HILL
SAN FRANCISCO
ARTHUR BROWN JR.
ARCHITECT

6.12. Arthur Brown Jr., Coit Tower, middle stage of tower design, December 15, 1931, Henry Howard delineator. Drawing, Arthur Brown Jr. Collection, Bancroft Library.

Although the firm of Young & Horstmeyer won the bid for the construction of the tower in the December 1931 round of bidding, many members of the art commission and the advisory board wanted the tower taller (fig. 6.12). The commission's ambivalence about the height of the tower is demonstrated by the bidding requirements themselves, which asked that bidders calculate the additional costs of raising the tower 26 feet, 3 inches as a bid alternate.[36] Eventually the tower was raised by 43 feet, 6 inches, to reach a total height of 172 feet, and an entirely new set of working drawings was required to accommodate this increased height; structural engineer Christopher Snyder had to recalculate all of the footing and structural pier dimensions to accommodate the enormous addition of weight to the foundation.

At this point, the tower suddenly encountered serious political opposition. A new city charter activated in 1932 was interpreted to transfer the authority for the tower project to a restructured Fine Art Commission, eliminating the Park Department's advisory board.[37] Angelo Rossi, San Francisco's new mayor, appointed a number of new members to the Fine Art Commission, and although some of the new members, including sculptor Edgar Walter and John Bakewell, were obvious allies of Brown, others were skeptical of the value of the tower project, given the financial crisis faced by the city and the nation as a whole.[38] The tower received a great deal of negative press in the spring and summer of 1932, and Brown was forced to defend the project anew to the Fine Art Commission and to "value-engineer" the project, removing any features that might be deemed excessive or unjustifiably expensive. To this end, Brown had a model of the tower built, then worked with it for several months to adjust the proportions and base of the tower; this model also served as a presentation piece to the art commission.[39] The tower scheme was once again put to a vote of the commission on August 22, 1932, and was initially defeated, four to three. However, all of the ex-officio members of the commission supported the tower, including Herbert Fleischhacker, who had the power to revoke Lillie Coit's bequest, and so the commission asked Brown to reduce the costs further and re-present the project later in the year.[40]

Finally, on November 17, 1932, Young & Horstmeyer was authorized to construct the tower for a cost of just over $100,000. The alterations to the tower design were many. A restaurant planned for the base of the tower was eliminated, simplifying the plumbing and heating requirements of the building, and permitting the terrace that surrounds the building to be cut back to a minimum for circulation. The entrance block was simplified, the vaulted porch giving way to a deep recess flanked by two fluted columns that mimicked the larger tower beyond. Inside, skylights that were to light the vestibule and the rest of the interior were eliminated, a decision later regretted by the architect and many others.[41] Some alterations were intended to improve the tower's aesthetics. The number of flutes around the shaft was reduced from thirty-two to twenty-four, not only to save expense, but also because the increased height of the tower reduced the need for as many verticals in the composition. In comparison with the early renderings of the project, the constructed tower appears stronger, more massive, and more primitive—qualities Brown was seeking in the abstracted vocabulary of the design. Brown also placed cast-stone fasces and a medallion of a phoenix, executed by Robert Howard, above the entry to represent the city's strength and recovery from the earthquake and fire.

Construction on the tower began in January 1933. The primary innovation utilized by Young & Horstmeyer in pouring the shaft of the tower was the reusable plywood formwork that held the curve of the fillets on the tower and resisted warping in the wet conditions of the pour. The use of plywood formwork was relatively new, and it speeded construction. Not only could it be reused as the tower rose, but the larger sheets of formed plywood reduced the amount of finishing required to achieve the smooth, unbroken surface the architect desired. By June the project was a full three months ahead of schedule, and it was certain that construction would be finished within the year.[42]

Even as the tower was under construction San Franciscans speculated about its symbolism. None of the oft-repeated stories are true; the tower was not intended to represent a fire nozzle or emulate a power plant, nor was it anatomical in any sense of the word. If any analogy were applicable to its design, it was that of medieval defensive structures, such as those at San Gimigniano; but the form was not intended to allude to anything other than what it was—a tower. Brown's construction manager, John Davis Hatch, wrote *Time* magazine on this question, stating, "The tower is not a lighthouse, or a bell tower. It is only incidentally an observation tower. It is a tower very pure and simple. Its design has been called 'modern.' Possibly primitive Gothic would be more suitable."[43] By the time of its dedication on October 8, 1933, most San Franciscans had become accustomed to the tower and were eager to share the view from the observation deck with the world (fig. C.22).

Although it took the public some time to get used to Coit Tower, the debate over its form and stripped character was soon forgotten in a controversy over the extraordinary suite of murals painted on its interior. At the time of the tower's dedication, there was no defined plan for the ground-floor spaces that surrounded the elevator. Some thought had been given to a museum to the pioneers, but no collection was ever moved to the tower, and for several months the space remained empty. Then in December 1933, two independent initiatives, one in Washington, DC, and one in San Francisco, converged to create at Coit Tower a federally funded art program that became a model for many others across the nation.

The Washington initiative came from George Biddle, a close friend of Franklin D. Roosevelt and an admirer of the mural art of Mexico that had blossomed under governmental sponsorship in the 1920s. Biddle proposed to Roosevelt that a similar program might be created in the United States, which would employ artists to embellish federal buildings. Roosevelt directed Biddle to Assistant Secretary of the Treasury Lawrence Robert, who in turn brought the idea to Edward Bruce, a financier and painter himself. Bruce immediately created within the Department of the Treasury the Public Works of Art Project (PWAP), which he envisioned would hire 2,500 artists across the country to create a renaissance in public art in the United States. Bruce introduced the concept of the PWAP at a meeting in Washington on December 8, 1933, with Eleanor Roosevelt in attendance. Within half a week, he had set up a central office in Washington to administer the program and a nationwide network of regional directorates that would identify projects and hire promising and needy artists.[44]

At the same moment, the fine artists of San Francisco

demanded relief work from the federal government. Called together by Bernard Zakheim, the artists met at the Whitcomb Hotel in mid-December to discuss how they might win a federal commission. Ralph Stackpole, a prominent sculptor and teacher, knew Edward Bruce, and suggested that the group contact him. They proposed that the group might decorate the band shell at Golden Gate Park. Unaware of the PWAP initiative, which had been launched only days before, the artists were shocked to receive a letter four days later promising them the work they had asked for![45]

Bruce selected Walter Heil, the director of the DeYoung Museum in Golden Gate Park, to lead the PWAP program in Northern California and Nevada. Heil met with an advisory committee of artists and laypersons on December 18, 1933, just one week after Bruce had contacted him about the project, with the express purpose of identifying Coit Tower as the site of the first PWAP project on the West Coast. Heil began by asking Brown if he would favor decorating the interior of the tower with murals. Brown concurred, but added, "[T]he primitive nature of the Coit Tower would lend itself to that sort of thing better than other public buildings, unless work can be confined to enclosed spaces such as rooms."[46] In other words, if one of Brown's buildings were going to be ornamented with murals, he felt it would be better that this "primitive" art form be showcased at Coit Tower than at the city hall or War Memorial Opera House. From the outset, Brown supported the aim of the project—to get artists working again—but he doubted the architectural appropriateness of the mural form and was concerned that a unified, coherent result be achieved. As he put it, the work "should be composed as a whole, [and] should not be done in patches or pieces."

The federal government gave little direction as to the theme or content of the murals, other than that they depict "American life." Brown suggested that the murals focus specifically on San Francisco, since the building was a municipal monument. The committee expanded on this idea and suggested a series of themes that described life in the city and beyond in the Bay Region. Brown called for a control over the themes and subject matter of the murals and desired that all work be approved by the Fine Art Commission before any paint touched the wall. This proved impossible, because the funding for the project required that the artists be working by mid-February, 1934, just two months off. The committee concluded that if anything did not meet the art commission's approval, it could be removed. As Harold Mack put it, "[T]he murals can't hurt Coit Tower. Let us paint Coit Tower and later whitewash it."[47] As it turned out, in at least one case, Mack's flip remark proved strikingly prophetic.

Twenty-six master painters and nineteen artist assistants were selected to decorate the tower. Victor Arnautoff was appointed the artists' director, responsible for ensuring conti-

6.13. Maxine Albro, *California*, 1934, detail.

nuity of program, scale, and coloration throughout the project.[48] The majority of the artists chose to work in fresco, applying ground pigments to wet plaster one small section at a time. Fourteen artists worked on the main floor of the tower, and six on the second-floor suite of rooms; Lucien Labaudt's double mural of Powell Street on the spiral stair was intended to join the two. The ground-floor frescos, the glory of the project, depict various scenes and people of Bay Area life. Ralph Stackpole's *Industries of California* and Maxine Albro's depiction of the Santa Clara Valley in *California* are hopeful images of ordinary people hard at work (fig. 6.13). Arnautoff's *City Life* depicts the San Francisco financial district of the 1930s, where throngs of people go about their daily business while avoiding a rather gruesome traffic accident and a fairly bold daylight mugging. Other muralists chose to comment more directly on the economic crisis of the Depression and the politics of the day. John Langley Howard, another son of John Galen Howard, illustrated in *California Industrial Scenes* the ecological and human toll that extractive industries took on the state. In the same work he pointedly contrasted a family of indigent migrant workers with a set of wealthy tourists and depicted a sea of grimly determined workers attending a May Day commemoration. Bernard Zakheim rather pointedly painted Howard reaching for a copy of Marx's *Das Kapital* in his mural *Library*, while others read leftist newspapers such as the *Western Worker*.

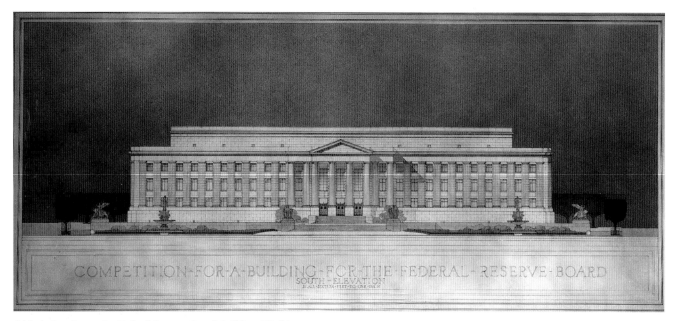

6.14. Arthur Brown Jr., Federal Reserve Board Building, Washington, DC, 1935, competition drawing, principal elevation. Copy photograph, author's collection.

The most controversial statement was made by Clifford Wight, a former assistant to Diego Rivera. Wight's subjects—surveyor, steelworker, cowboy, and farmer—were not inflammatory, but in the header above the west window, between the surveyor and the steelworker, Wight added the Communist hammer and sickle. Brown and many others objected. Frustrated by being shut out of the process, Brown seized the opportunity to demonstrate the precipitous nature of the mural project to Herbert Fleischhacker, president of the Board of Park Commissioners: "In making a casual visit to the Coit Tower on Saturday, I noticed that the emblem of the communist party with its slogan [Workers of the World Unite] was painted over the lintel of the window of the western wall of the first floor promenade. This emblem is accompanied by the N.R.A. emblem and also an emblem including a chain and 'E Pluribus Unum.' I think possibly some of the artists have been indiscreet in putting controversial political emblems in a public building of the character of the Coit Tower."[49]

Fleishhacker allowed Heil to try to settle the matter quietly. But with the San Francisco dockworker's strike precipitating an economic and social crisis in the Bay Area, the charged political atmosphere demanded that Heil's idealistic notions of artistic freedom give way to the pragmatic need to salvage the PWAP as a viable relief program. Heil wrote to Washington for guidance. Edward Bruce directed that the objectionable material be removed, if not by the artist responsible then by the group of artists working on the proj-

ect. The artists refused to alter their work, and the murals stayed as they were.[50]

The press was itching to make Wight's and Zakheim's political art public. On July 5, 1934, the San Francisco Examiner ran a composite picture of Wight's Communist insignia with Zakheim's Library scene. Under the pressure of the events of that day, on which two of the striking dockworkers were shot to death, Fleishhacker and the Board of Park Commissioners padlocked the entrance to the tower and posted a guard.[51] Anger over the death of the dockworkers and the importation of thousands of California National Guardsmen led to the general strike of July 16–19, 1934, which shut down most commercial activity within the city limits of San Francisco. In the chaos of the general strike, the situation at Coit Tower was forgotten, and after several weeks, the offending material in Wight's mural was removed by an unknown hand. The tower finally opened to the general public on October 20, 1934.[52]

The controversy over the Coit Tower murals was not the only pressing problem Brown faced with regard to the tower in 1934, but it left him with a distrust of painters for the rest of his career. As he feared, the painters began to look to his other buildings as targets of opportunity, and he had to protect several interiors from further embellishment. Henry Howard's wife, Jane Berlandina Howard, who had executed the egg tempera murals entitled Home Life at Coit Tower, wanted particularly to paint the arched panels in the auditorium of the War Memorial Opera House. Despite Brown's objections, in 1937 Mrs. Howard prepared a set of designs, which Brown finally repudiated. It is certainly not coincidental that Brown refused to allow any painting in his last projects.

Changing Practice in the 1930s

With the worsening of the Depression in the early 1930s, even Brown was forced first to reduce his employees' salaries and then his office staff. He did try to bring work into the office through invitational competitions, the most well known of which was that for the Federal Reserve Board in Washington, DC, conducted in June 1935. Most of the architects who entered believed that an abstracted classicism would succeed with the jury; Brown accordingly removed most of the details from the exterior of his proposal. It cannot be said, however, that he strayed very far from conventional academic classicism (figs. 6.14, 6.15). His entry did not have the usual forcefulness of his monumental designs because although the main facade presented an unornamented classicism, it provided little of interest except the spare portico at the center. Design sketches for the project illustrate what was discarded, including very promising end pavilions with a distyle-in-muris motif and an elevation that grouped the windows into tall banks of glass (fig. 6.16). The winning entry, by Brown's old friend Paul Cret, much more deftly straddled the line between the classic and the modern, and was constructed in the late 1930s.

When Bakewell & Brown dissolved in 1928, Brown's office had thirteen employees. The work in Washington allowed him to increase his staff at a time when other architects were laying off dozens of draftsmen. Just as suddenly, however, Brown's office shrank back to fourteen in 1933, and fell again to just six by 1935; only the work at Stanford remained. Brown used this lull in business to attend a congress of architects in Rome in the fall of 1935. Just as his parents had done forty-five years earlier, Brown took his wife and daughters

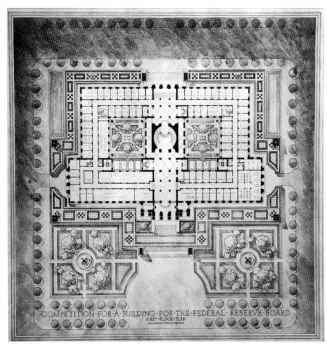

6.15. Arthur Brown Jr., Federal Reserve Board Building, Washington, DC, 1935, competition drawing, plan. Copy photograph, author's collection.

with him, to show his "girls" the sights of Europe. They visited Brown's old friends from the Ecole and called upon Victor Laloux in the Touraine. After a trip to Italy, including the congress, the Browns returned to Paris, where his elder daughter, Victoria, fell gravely ill with a viral infection. She lay in hospital for months, delaying the family's return to San Francisco until mid-1936. On his return to San Francisco, Brown entered the final phase of career, when he became the master planning architect for both Stanford and the University of California, as well as for the last large world's fair in San Francisco, the Golden Gate International Exhibition.

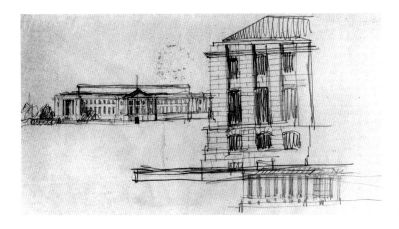

6.16. Arthur Brown Jr., Federal Reserve Board Building, Washington, DC, 1935, preliminary sketches. Arthur Brown Jr. Collection, Bancroft Library.

The Golden Gate International Exhibition

The Golden Gate International Exhibition (GGIE) was organized to celebrate the completion of the Golden Gate and Oakland–Bay bridges in the mid-1930s, but it was primarily a device to stimulate the local economy and to provide a western counterpart to the contemporaneous New York "World of Tomorrow" Exhibition in Flushing Meadows. Although its promoters expected to repeat the success of the Panama-Pacific International Exhibition of 1915, the press compared the GGIE unfavorably to that event and to the larger fair across the country in New York. Yet, when taken on its own terms, the GGIE was as successful as those expositions.

The GGIE was situated on Treasure Island, a man-made polder adjoining the natural Yerba Buena Island, midway between Oakland and San Francisco, and it was linked to these two cities by the Bay Bridge. The idea of filling in the dangerous Yerba Buena shoals was first proposed in 1931 by the aeronautics committee of the San Francisco Jaycees, which argued that an island at the shoals would be the perfect location for a regional airport. Three years later, the Bridge Celebration Founding Committee—the group responsible for planning the inaugural celebrations of the two bridges— suggested that a second world's fair be planned as the centerpiece of the events, and that the shoals be used to provide a spectacular setting to highlight the bridges and the bay itself. The two ideas gained momentum, and by the middle of 1935 the city of San Francisco had gained ownership of the site from the state of California and had ratified the chartering of the exposition and the new airport in a municipal election. The exposition was managed by an independent corporation that appointed Leland W. Cutler as president and Athol McBean, Brown's client and president of Gladding–McBean (a terra-cotta manufactory), as chairman of the board of directors. Will P. Day was named director of works and George Kelham, architect for the University of California at Berkeley, chairman of the board of architects.[53]

The design of the GGIE grounds was established by the architects in 1936. The commissioners, Lewis Hobart, William Merchant, Timothy Pflueger, Ernest Weihe, Kelham, and Brown, sought to create a place apart from the everyday world, while at the same time capitalizing on the island's views of the city and the Golden Gate. The architecture, inspired by the temples and gardens of southern Asia and Central and South America, was intended to keep the real world outside the gates of the exhibition. Within the walls of Treasure Island, pure fantasy was to rule the day, without consideration of serious purpose. As Talbot Hamlin noted in his preview of the exhibition in 1938, an analysis of the ensemble was akin to an "anatomy of play."[54] This insouciant stance on behalf of the organizers, and particularly on behalf of the architectural committee, was in contrast to the New York World's Fair, where every inch of the grounds was to prepare the fairgoer for the brave new future that the technological and commercial communities were creating for them. As George Kelham described the GGIE's aesthetic position:

> A great many people think of an exposition, and rightly, as a great educational and intellectual achievement, showing the world's serious thought and progress. From the standpoint of its exhibits and from many other angles this is true, but to me, its architecture must always be an appeal primarily to the senses. . . . [I]t must transport them into another and more joyous world where the everyday worries and problems do not, at least for a time, exist. It must stir in them a love of beauty, must make them appreciate that beauty—both of form and of color—can and does make life more worth while.[55]

Although the site was nearly ideal, the designers did have two significant factors to consider in their site planning. First, the site would have to be cleared and converted into a municipal airport within a year of the fair's closing. An airport terminal building and two large hangars, designed by Kelham and Day, were to be built in permanent materials on the eastern edge of the island, nearest the Bay Bridge. During the fair these buildings would serve as the administration building and exhibition halls, respectively.[56] Development of the rest of the island was also limited by the need to keep the site ready for air travel; it was to later serve as runway and taxi areas. Thus, no great changes in topography were allowed, and a proposed system of canals and lakes was abandoned early on to avoid the expense of later retrofitting the island to its new use.

The second constraint the architects faced was a familiar one—the ever-present western winds. To combat the cold winds of summer on the bay, they looked to the strategy that had worked so well in 1915 and designed a walled compound that protected most of the site from the prevailing winds. Visitors arrived by ferry or parked their automobiles at the western end of the island and worked their way into the walled compound of the exhibition proper through several enormous gates. Once inside, they traversed a series of exotic garden courts arranged on two unequal axes, around which was placed an outer series of courts and exhibition buildings that reflected the subtitle of the exhibition: A Pageant of the Pacific. Similar to the procedure at the Century of Progress, each of the principal architects was given a sector of the key plan to design. The northern court, the Court of Pacifica, was designed by Pflueger; the eastern two courts, the Court of Reflections and the Court of Flowers, by Hobart; the eastern lagoon and Pacific House by Merchant, in association with Bernard Maybeck; and the south gardens and Court of the Moon by Kelham.

6.17. Golden Gate International Exposition and Coit Tower, San Francisco, 1939. In this one image are two of Brown's towers of the 1930s, the Tower of the Sun, on Treasure Island, and Coit Tower, on Telegraph Hill. Photograph courtesy of Moulin Archives.

The western walls and triumphal entry gates, the "Portals of the Pacific," were designed by Ernest Weihe. The portals were large pyramidal-shaped masses that dominated the western flank of the exposition. The main entrance portals were particularly memorable—twin-stepped pyramids were crowned by a triplet of enormous abstract elephants. Weihe wrote later, "[T]he elephant forms were used sculpturally because of their universal association with pageantry and because they afford a broad use of planes and masses at a scale harmonious with facades a half-mile long." George Livermore, a summer intern in Brown's office at the time, remembers visiting sculptor Donald Macky's studio in San Francisco and observing Weihe, Brown, and Macky establishing the proportions for their prodigious pachyderms.[57]

Brown's Tower of the Sun and Court of Honor attempted to balance the constraints of monumentality and impermanent construction required of a world's fair. The tower was intended to serve as a counterpoint to the horizontal proportions of the rest of the fair complex, and was scaled to hold its own visually with the massive towers of the Bay Bridge (fig. 6.17). To Brown the tower was a natural centerpiece to the rest of the exposition: "Relations of mass, space, line and coherence have governed the composition of the tower. The vertical motif is inevitable as a contrast and foil to the essentially horizontal character of the Bay, the Island, and the intentionally parallel lines of the building groups. It has been the aim, in architectural expression, not to resort to visual shock or strange idiom, nor to seek to express ideas of either literary origin or those inappropriate to the medium."[58] Like Coit Tower, the Tower of the Sun is an abstraction of the medieval tower type. Brown's intention was to find a contemporary expression of a known form, rather than attempt to completely reinvent an architecture.

Nearly 400 feet high, the tower was octagonal in plan, its transparency emphasized through the use of open arcades of immense height. Originally, these arches were to soar over 200 feet to the crown of the steel-framed tower, but once exhibition engineer John E. Gould made his structural calculations, Brown found that he had to tie the piers together with a secondary arcade at the base. The crown of the tower rose in three stages. The first continued the verticals of the piers to abstracted finials about two-thirds of the way up. Within the arches of this stage Gordon Huff's figures of Industry, Agriculture, Science, and the Arts looked down upon assembled throngs of fairgoers. The second stage housed carillon bells, which were partially enclosed in the final design, to protect them. The third section, the spire, was decorated with a swirling ornamental relief representing flames, from which a gilded wrought-iron phoenix by O. C. Malmquist rose to the heavens.[59] The whole was best viewed from either just inside the Elephant Towers or from Kelham's Court of the Moon, where the arching jets of the fountains in the Court of the Sun repeated the parabolic curves of the crown. The Court of Honor was designed to set off the tower and to serve as the primary circulation node within the walled precinct of the grounds (fig. C.26). It was bounded at its edges by a circular arcade, broken at the major axes of the courts and main gate. Brown commissioned Adeline Kent to represent Air and Water in bas-relief at the main arches where visitors entered the court from the north and south.[60] Four domed entrance pavilions marked the principal entrances to the four exhibition halls that formed the court; within each Brown placed statuary representing Flora, Fauna, Land, and Sea.[61]

When George Kelham died unexpectedly in December 1936, Brown was chosen by the board of trustees to succeed him as chief of architecture, with the understanding that the basic outlines of the exposition's design would not change. Brown's primary task in the next two years was to work toward reducing the costs of the building program by $1.7 million, and to ensure that these cuts were made judiciously and equitably. Although this cost-control program had begun under Kelham, Brown confirmed the hard choices. Several major cuts were particularly difficult. The first was the exclusion of the principal music auditorium from the program of the fair. William Merchant and Bernard Maybeck had

designed an exotic Temple of Music that proved to be too costly for a temporary structure.[62] Significant elements were also removed from Hobart's Court of the Flowers and Pflueger's Court of Pacifica; the latter was redesigned nearly in its entirety to simplify its construction and gain additional exhibit space.

Brown's other great task was the coordination of the international, federal, state, and local pavilions with the exhibition's theme. As at the first San Francisco fair, the prospect of war drastically reduced the number of foreign participants. Many nations, particularly from East Asia and Europe, scaled back their exhibits or withdrew entirely. Nevertheless, the GGIE had a strong showing in its first year from Pacific Rim nations. As at past exhibitions, many of the foreign pavilions grouped around the Lake of Nations were designed in the vernacular style of the host nation and featured ethnographic and travel-related exhibits. The Japanese compound, for example, included a pagoda, a medieval castle, a "samurai house," and an extensive garden planted by the emperor's gardener. Colombia served coffee in a re-created Spanish colonial village. Other nations chose to emphasize their development and modernization: Italy erected a small modern travel information pavilion dominated by a gigantic vertical sign, and Argentina showcased its cultural and export artifacts behind an enormous quadrant of glass in Armando D'Ans's striking and sophisticated International-style pavilion. Several nations, such as Norway and China, lost their political independence by the end of the first season. Some pavilions were staffed in the second season by expatriates and second-generation Americans familiar with the culture of the nations under siege.[63]

The federal, state, and local pavilions were also generally modern in form. Timothy Pflueger's Federal Building was a light, airy structure that incorporated exhibition space within two colonnaded wings joined by a hypostyle Colonnade of the States, an open loggia whose soaring roof was supported by forty-eight lacy piers.[64] Pflueger also designed the California Auditorium and State buildings, which together with the Federal Building bounded the Court of the Nations. The auditorium employed a similar openwork steel colonnade as the Federal Building as well as large murals by Lucien Labaudt. The State Building served as the official reception area for the exposition and contained a suite of receiving rooms and a ballroom for evening functions. California's counties were represented by a number of smaller pavilions grouped behind the state buildings; these either evoked the traditional architecture of the region or took on progressive

6.18 (*opposite*). Arthur Brown Jr., Tower of the Sun, GGIE, San Francisco, 1939. Photograph courtesy of Moulin Archives.

forms that presented a forward-looking, contemporary appearance to the public.[65]

Landscape, color, and lighting were important design elements at the GGIE. The landscaping plan emphasized the color and variety of the Pacific Rim plants. The exposition's landscape program was designed and executed by the staff of horticulturalists and gardeners that maintained Golden Gate Park, with John McLaren as executive consultant. The plantings in the wind-protected courts were designed by several prominent Bay Area landscape architects, including Thomas Church, and changed constantly, ensuring that the flower beds were a riot of color throughout the exposition's run. The color scheme was keyed to the landscape designs and to the colors of the bay. Director of Color Jesse E. Stanton chose a palette of nineteen colors to be used throughout the exhibition. The bodies of the buildings were painted in tertiary shades, predominantly neutrals, but also pastel yellow, brown, and blue. Trim and accent colors were bolder and included reds, jades, yellows, apricot, and several blues.[66] These colors were heightened in the illumination scheme, which transformed the fairgrounds into a breathtaking wonderland of color. For the first time in an exposition, the vast majority of illumination was indirect; the lighting was hidden behind screens or within valances and bounced off the subject to be illuminated (fig. 6.18). The lighting at the Court of Pacifica was particularly inventive: the color in the fountain and that which lit Robert Stackpole's theme statue "Miss Pacifica" gradually changed every few minutes, controlled by a "thyratron" circuit.[67]

In addition to the palaces, the exhibition company had to build a great number of other structures to support the fair. Many private organizations and concessionaires also built on Treasure Island. To coordinate all of this construction and ensure some design harmony among the various concessionaires, W. P. Day appointed Edward Frick, Brown's principal associate in the mid-1930s, to the position of chief of architecture. Frick acted as a liaison between the director of works and the board of architects, working to ensure that each understood the needs of the other. He also designed a number of the exhibition's minor structures as well as the Western States Building, and was responsible for the efficient production of the working drawings required to construct each exhibition building. In addition, Frick coordinated the design and layout of the more purely entertainment exhibits. These diverse amusements were laid along the "Gayway;" their themes ranged from the educational, such as the extensive Chinese village built by San Francisco's Chinese community, and the "Better Babies" exhibit that displayed premature babies nursed in incubators, to the salacious. Sally Rand's "Nude Ranch" was particularly popular for its presumably fictional depiction of everyday life among a company of topless cowgirls. The

"Cavalcade of the Golden West" inhabited an open-air auditorium large enough to permit reenactments of Custer's Last Stand and the driving of the Golden Spike of the Transcontinental Railroad, replete with two steam locomotives.[68] In the exhibition's second season, Billy Rose brought his Aquacade, which featured performers Morton Downy, Johnny Weismuller, and Esther Williams swimming in a specially crafted pool that covered over a quarter of an acre.[69]

By the time the GGIE closed its second season in September 1940, over sixteen million visitors had passed through its gates. With American participation in the Second World War a near certainty, Treasure Island was leased to the War Department for use as a naval base; the planned municipal airport never materialized. The exposition buildings were painted a drab tan and converted to military uses—barracks, a dispensary, a machinist's shop, whatever was required. The base served as a receiving center for much of the war, and then the headquarters for naval operations for the Bay Area afterward. In 1947 a fire destroyed many of the buildings on the eastern side of the island, and by the end of that year the Navy had demolished all of the temporary exposition structures that remained.[70] Fifty years later, Treasure Island was returned to the city of San Francisco to be redeveloped as a low and moderate income residential community for municipal employees and the homeless.

HOLLY COURTS

Arthur Brown's residential work has received less notice than his city halls and his institutional work. Brown himself did not emphasize it and accepted only those residential commissions that he could not afford, socially, to turn down. For this reason his residences were usually built for the top Bay Area aristocrats—if you had an Arthur Brown house, you were probably the scion of one of the Big Four, the president of a bank, or perhaps controlled the region's utilities. Good examples of these "mandatory" mansions are the Timothy Hopkins house on Presidio Heights, San Francisco, of 1928, where Brown installed some of the Herter Brothers interiors from Sherwood Hall into a staid French classical townhouse (fig. 6.19); and the W. W. Crocker House in Hillsborough, constructed in 1930, which translated much of the Mediterranean renaissance detailing of Pasadena City Hall to a residential scale (fig. 6.20). Although Brown never apologized for his rich and powerful clients and friends, he was equally anxious to use his talents to socially responsible ends, just as he had been trained to do at the Ecole des Beaux-Arts. With the incorporation of the San Francisco Housing Authority, however, Brown got the opportunity to design Holly Courts, the first federally subsidized housing development west of the Rocky Mountains, and a model project to this day.

6.19. Arthur Brown Jr., Hopkins Residence, San Francisco, 1928.

6.20. Arthur Brown Jr., William W. Crocker House, Hillsborough, 1930. Photograph courtesy of Moulin Archives.

Subsidized low-rent housing was not a new idea in 1939 when Brown began work on Holly Courts. Several eastern and midwestern cities had municipal housing authorities dating back a decade or more. But with the passage of the United States Housing Act of 1937, the federal government directly funded and guaranteed bonding for state and municipal housing projects. California had no means by which a municipality could create an independent housing authority to qualify for the federal monies provided for by the act, so in 1938 the California legislature passed four pieces of enabling legislation that permitted the creation of housing authorities

and granted them tax-exempt status and the power of eminent domain. Once the state legislation was in place, the city and county of San Francisco founded its local housing authority by resolution of the Board of Supervisors. Formally created on April 18, 1938, the anniversary of the earthquake and fire, the housing authority quickly launched two development projects, Holly Park and Potrero Terrace, to bring 660 subsidized apartments onto the market.[71]

The Board of Supervisors demanded that the housing authority operate in the context of "equivalent elimination." For each housing unit it built, it was to purchase and destroy one unit of substandard housing. The philosophy was that although the new units necessarily had to be built on nonresidential land to avoid displacement of existing residents, they must not expand the inventory of low-cost housing or the existing stock of substandard housing would continue to contribute to the blight of its neighborhood.

Of course, much of the blight had little to do with the housing stock itself, and more to do with the overcrowding and disinvestment many of these areas faced in the Depression years. The neighborhoods targeted for removal and reconstruction were those that stood outside the fireline of 1906. These areas, such as the Inner Mission, the Geary–Filmore of the Western Addition, and Potrero Hill, received the bulk of working-class families displaced by the fire; the single-family Italianate and Queen Anne Victorian homes of these districts were converted into multifamily flats. Because the newer, post-fire construction was beyond the means of most of the residents of these close-in neighborhoods, the low-income residents stayed put, making permanent the high densities that had been considered temporary. With the policy of "equivalent elimination," rehabilitation of the existing housing stock was not usually an option; the housing authority had to prove that a given number of housing units had been demolished. Although twice as many projects were planned for the first phase of the authority's building campaign, it built five communities containing 1,741 units on 76 acres before the Second World War curtailed construction in 1943.[72]

The housing authority was concerned about public perception of subsidized housing communities, so it gave very careful consideration to the architects employed in its first projects. Eventually most of the city's prominent architects, including Lewis Hobart, Timothy Pflueger, Clarence Tantau, and William Wurster, designed for the housing authority. Brown was selected to design the first project because of his past record with public work and because the housing authority wanted to make a statement that its projects were as deserving of excellence in design as any private home for the wealthy. The site, next to Holly Park in Bernal Heights, was one contiguous parcel of land, already owned by the city of San Francisco. Thus, land acquisition was simple.

Brown was put under contract in January 1939; within a few weeks he had designed ten residential buildings with a total of 118 apartment units for the 2.68-acre site (fig. 6.21). The buildings were terraced in pairs down the sloped triangular site, affording the second floors of each building a view of Diamond Heights to the west, a reservoir or Holly Park to the north and east. Brown intended the buildings to cascade down the hillside, giving the effect of an Italian hill town or a Greek fishing village. Each building was broken down into two- or three-unit blocks, and one block was turned 90 degrees to the others to form an L-shaped structure, giving variety to the elevations and forming courts along each terrace. These courts were the heart of the complex. Opening one into the next, they provided security and also afforded space for a mix of community and private space, playgrounds and private gardens. The novel site planning needed some explanation to San Franciscans used to the 25-foot city lot; most prospective tenants were wary of the communal space of the courts. As Brown wrote in the introductory pamphlet issued by the housing authority: "Good living is not provided by the common narrow lot used in San Francisco and generally throughout the country. You have a chaotic city where each house is its own rare or extinct species. We are satisfied that for the people living there Holly works much better than the crowded city block."[73]

Holly Courts changed during the course of the design. Brown's initial schemes cast the buildings in a colonial-revival mode with hipped roofs and shutters flanking every window. The hipped roofs were replaced by flat roofs screened by a parapet, and the shutters were dropped altogether. The result was more International-style than Brown had intended, but it was important to the housing authority that the units convey "service and simplicity"—they should be easily maintained and look comfortable but not luxurious. To this end, the entire complex was constructed of reinforced concrete. The exterior walls were left fairly rough, with the lines of the formwork serving as a reminder of the clapboarded houses of the past. The only breaks in the wall surfaces came at the overhanging porch roofs at the entries and the sills of the windows. The divided-light steel casement windows retained some of the traditional feel of Brown's design, but also enhanced the modernist qualities of the construction.

The success of Holly Courts lies largely in its planning. Brown ensured that each unit had some private outdoor space and an individual entry porch. The one-bedroom corner units were flats, stacked one on top of the other, whereas the two- and three-bedroom units were two-story townhouses with a high degree of separation between the living areas and the sleeping quarters. In all of the units, a living room and eat-in kitchen form the living space of the unit; the kitchens were basic but included an adequate supply of cabinet and pantry space. The bedrooms all featured walk-in closets or wardrobe space, and were designed to afford a maximum of daylight and privacy. The bathrooms were small, but all had a built-in tub and a small linen closet.

Because public housing was new to San Francisco in the 1940s, the housing authority was sensitive to accusations that its projects would house only the most undesirable of tenants and degrade the neighborhoods around them. To counter the considerable opposition, its literature stressed that it intended to house working-class families already living within a mile or so of the project site. One promotional brochure for Holly Courts argued: "It cannot be doubted

6.21. Arthur Brown Jr., presentation rendering for Holly Courts housing development, San Francisco, c. 1939. Drawing, Arthur Brown Jr. Collection, Bancroft Library.

that the neighborhood community will be enriched by the addition of these new tenants—young and at the same time stable, and interested almost without exception in the wholesome values of family life. The accusation that this class of people is not our most needy and should therefore not be housed first in our federal and local program is untrue. This is the class in our society, if ever any was, that will respond most to the single factor of a decent home environment."[74]

The first residents of Holly Courts moved in on June 8, 1940.[75] Newspapers praised its "modern look" and carefully described the families who would live there. The "first family" of Holly Courts, Ethel and Thurman Rogers and their son Jerald, were portrayed as representative of the "worthi-

ness" of the new tenants and selected specifically because they were a "typical American Family."[76] It is a testament to the careful planning and sturdy construction of Holly Courts that it remains one of the most popular and viable of San Francisco's public housing. Projects decades newer than Holly Courts have been demolished for their unlivability and barren landscapes. In contrast, Holly Courts houses a fiercely loyal community that maintains many of the amenities planned into the complex in the 1940s.

Holly Courts marks the end of Brown's private practice outside of academic work. It is fitting that this last residential project was built not for the nabobs of Burlingame or Presidio Heights, but for people who had struggled a bit more in life than he had.

7.1. Shepley, Rutan & Coolidge and Frederick Law Olmsted, plan for the Leland Stanford Jr. University, 1888, detail of promotional literature, c. 1910. Arthur Brown Jr. Papers, Stanford University Archives.

CHAPTER SEVEN

DESIGNS FOR THE ACADEMY

Some of Arthur Brown's best opportunities to design within the context of the architectural ensemble came with his work for the two great universities of the San Francisco Bay Area, Stanford and Berkeley. Bakewell & Brown served as the design architect and master planner for the Leland Stanford Jr. University for nearly thirty years, from 1913 to 1942—by far the longest association the firm had with any client. In fact, the Stanford commissions continued the titular association of Bakewell & Brown long after the partnership's dissolution in 1928. Throughout this time, Brown strove to expand the campus largely as the original designers, Frederick Law Olmsted and Shepley, Rutan & Coolidge, had intended. Brown designed several landmark buildings for the campus, including the Hoover Institution Tower, which remains the university's chief architectural symbol. For a few years, between 1936 and 1942, Brown served as the campus architect at both Stanford and the University of California at Berkeley. As at Stanford, at Berkeley Brown attempted to enhance and continue the existing campus plan, which had been developed by John Galen Howard in the first decades of the twentieth century. Brown's principal structures for the campus, such as Sproul Hall, were designed relatively late in his career, and within the context of the Great Depression and the Second World War they are quiet and reserved rather than showy and exuberant.

STANFORD UNIVERSITY

Stanford University began as a memorial to Jane and Leland Stanford's son, Leland Stanford Jr., who died in 1883. In his grief Stanford resolved to his wife that "the children of California shall be our children," and together they planned to create a great university for the state.[1] The couple traveled east to interview the presidents of several great universities to learn what might be required to build, staff, and operate the finest university possible. They soon learned that the financing of their endeavor was the easiest part of it. Though the Stanfords could afford to hire the best academic talent in the world, they had great difficulty convincing that talent to leave the East to teach at a school in the Far West that had neither a building nor a student body. So the buildings came first, a president and faculty second, and a student body after that.

At first, Stanford intended to design the university buildings himself. He naturally thought of himself as a great builder—he had willed the transcontinental railroad into existence, after all—and he no doubt thought of the university facilities as a lesser task. He did have a vision for the campus. The buildings were to be arranged around a "parallelogram," that is, a rectangular courtyard, and the plan was to be extendable.[2] Yet as Stanford consulted with General Francis A. Walker, president of the Massachusetts Institute of Technology, he realized that professional assistance in the architectural and landscape planning of the university was necessary and inevitable. At Walker's suggestion, Stanford hired the biggest names in the architectural profession in 1886—Frederick Law Olmsted to design the master plan for the grounds, and Shepley, Rutan & Coolidge, the successor firm to Henry Hobson Richardson, to design the buildings.

Walker, Olmsted, and the Stanfords assembled in August 1886 for the first of several extended planning sessions that led to the "quad" concept for the university. During the next several months they established the location of the campus, the low, spreading massing of the buildings, the introduction of arcades as linking devices, and the use of native California plants as the dominant materials of the landscape.[3] Olmsted returned to Boston to locate the buildings. He eventually chose to arrange them in two ranks around a long, rectangular courtyard, so that one set of buildings, the inner quad, linked by an arcade, faced into the court, while the other group, the outer quad, faced outward onto a set of streets. Originally the long sides of the quads were to be oriented north and south, but Stanford insisted on rotating the scheme 90 degrees, so that as one entered from the north, one faced Memorial Church opposite, at the center of the long side. Once the general character of the buildings had been determined, Stanford then turned to Charles Coolidge of Shepley, Rutan & Coolidge, to design the buildings. Coolidge, who had visited the Palo Alto site in the summer of 1886 as planning was beginning, was able easily to collaborate with Olmsted; both lived in Brookline, Massachusetts.

Coolidge developed the low single-story buildings of the inner quad in the style of his mentor, H. H. Richardson, who had made his personal adaptation of southern French and Spanish Romanesque architecture the most celebrated American design statement of the second half of the nineteenth century. Like Richardson, Coolidge relied on massive stone walls and heavy, prominent roofs to convey the raw power and energy of his time; these qualities also suggested a permanence and heritage that was particularly necessary at a fledgling institution such as Stanford. Coolidge linked nearly anonymous buildings with an arcade around the inner quad, which only was broken at the four cardinal points of the scheme—the entry from the north, from the entrance gatehouses at the east and west, and the Memorial Church to the south. Although Coolidge appreciated the asymmetry of Olmsted's first proposal, Stanford wanted a more axial and monumental scheme. In 1887 he proposed several elements that reinforced this formality. The most visible was the Memorial Arch, 100 feet high, that marked the entry into the complex at the building line of the outer quad. Entry was through the arch, into Memorial Court, a mediating arcaded space between the inner and outer courts, and then through an archway into the inner quad, to confront the Memorial Church and its very tall tower (fig. 7.1).

The inner quad was largely completed by 1891, the year the university opened. Representatives of Shepley, Rutan & Coolidge ensured the conformance of the work to their drawings and specifications. The arch, Memorial Court, church, and the two- and three-story-high buildings of the outer court were also designed between 1887 and 1891, but these designs were executed under the supervision of other architects over a number of years, up to 1902. Because Leland Stanford had died in 1893, the larger part of this construction was overseen by Jane Stanford, who relied heavily on her brothers, Ariel

and Charles Lathrop, to superintend the day-to-day workings of the construction. At the same time, Jane Stanford commissioned several large structures in widely divergent architectural styles, including the university library, a chemistry building, a gymnasium, and the Leland Stanford Jr. Museum; these were sited along Palm Drive, in violation of Olmsted's intentions.[4] Of these structures, the museum is the most noteworthy, because Ernest Ransome's reinforced concrete structural system introduced several refinements now universally employed, including the lapping of the reinforcing bars and the twisting of the bars to create barbs that better gripped the concrete.[5]

In 1905 Jane Stanford died, and the leadership of the university's board of trustees was passed to Timothy Hopkins. Just a few months later the Stanford campus was rocked by the earthquake of 1906, which severely damaged, and in some cases completely destroyed, the buildings. The vast majority of the early sandstone buildings of the inner quad survived the temblor relatively well; the construction of these structures was supervised by Shepley, Rutan & Coolidge, under Leland Stanford's personal control. Conversely, almost every structure built after Leland Stanford's death suffered catastrophic damage, with the exception of Ernest Ransome's central block of the Leland Stanford Jr. Museum.[6] Thus, the first years of Hopkins's leadership were concerned with the salvage and repair of the university's buildings following the earthquake of 1906. The rebuilding campaign would last all of the next decade, but the siting and design of most of the new facilities at Stanford would be directed by Bakewell & Brown (fig. 7.2).

Bakewell & Brown came to Stanford in 1906, just as the reconstruction work was beginning in earnest. Although Brown hoped and expected that he would be tapped by his good friend Timothy Hopkins to do a number of buildings at Stanford, Hopkins was too responsible to entrust an important commission to a relatively untried architect, no matter who he was. Instead, Bakewell & Brown were given a tryout. They were commissioned to design several professors' houses on Alvarado Row and Salvatierra Walk; from the beginning the university constructed housing for some faculty in an effort to promote a scholarly community on campus. Bakewell & Brown's double houses are interesting for their variety—one is very much in the arts-and-crafts shingle mode, similar to the work of Bernard Maybeck, John Galen Howard, and Julia Morgan. Another house is a clapboarded English cottage with asymmetrical rooflines similar to those of Brown's MacDonald House, which was designed at the same time.[7]

Bakewell & Brown did not get another commission from Stanford until the eve of the First World War. By that time, the firm's successes at the Burlingame Country Club and in the San Francisco City Hall competition demonstrated to Hopkins and the trustees that the firm could handle a larger

7.2. Stanford University, aerial view, looking south, c. 1922.
Photograph, Arthur Brown Jr. Papers, Stanford University
Archives.

construction campaign. The partners' permanent association with Stanford began in 1913, when the Stanford Union and its alumni auxiliary, chaired by Herbert Hoover, hired them to prepare plans for a new student union on land leased for this purpose by the university. This commission required that the new building link the Charles Wittlesey's Men's and Women's Clubs into a unified composition, be constructed in reinforced concrete, and be "of the Mission style of architecture in thorough harmony with the buildings of the university."[8] Bakewell & Brown responded with a three-story building, flanked by twin bell towers, whose ground-floor arcade extended to either side to link up the existing clubhouses and then wrapped around the fourth side of the Union courtyard to a towered entry pavilion. In use as a student union until the construction of the Tressider Student Union in 1965, the Old Union is now administrative offices.[9]

Later in the year, in November 1913, Timothy Hopkins proposed retaining Bakewell & Brown as the university archi-

tects, a move that was widely supported by the university president, J. C. Branner, and the board of trustees. Bakewell & Brown entered into a contractual agreement with Stanford to provide consultative architectural services on either a time-and-material basis for planning and facilities work, or at the AIA-suggested fee of 6 percent of the cost of new construction. What began as a measure of convenience on Hopkins's part eventually led to twenty-five additional built commissions, both on the Stanford University campus proper and also at its satellite facilities in San Francisco and Monterey.

PLANNING THE EAST QUAD

By 1916, Bakewell & Brown had arrived at the first of several master plans they would design for Stanford. The direction of their efforts had been set as early as 1914, when James F.

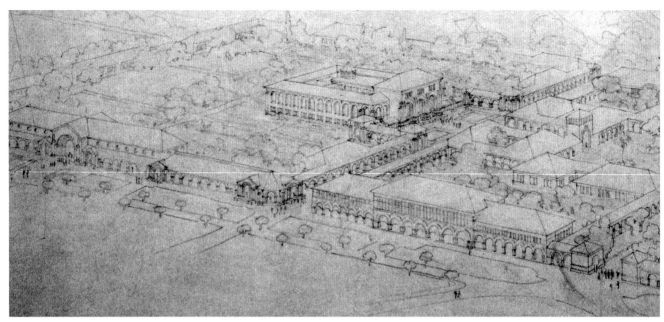

7.3. Arthur Brown Jr., plan for Stanford University, 1916, perspective view showing development plans for the east quad. The Green Library is set behind the plaza at the center of the picture and the art gallery is at the corner of the block in the lower left center. Drawing, Arthur Brown Jr. Papers, Stanford University Archives.

Dawson, of Olmsted Brothers, visited Stanford and issued a formal report entreating the university to adhere to the three-quadrangle plan proposed in 1887:

> It may be of interest to recall that the original preliminary general plan provided for the repetition of the big interior arcaded court idea, one west and another east of the central one. . . . The two front buildings of the central group were intended to be the Library and the Museum. It would certainly be convenient to have the Library centrally located. If neither of the existing buildings can be adapted for the Library, our next choice would be to place it either in the middle of the north part of the next block, in case it is a very large and imposing building, or in the west half of this frontage if it will fit in there, leaving a sufficient central entrance to the proposed east court. It should have embodied in it the arcaded walk adopted as the distinguishing characteristic of Stanford University, and this arcaded walk should line up with the northern one of the central group of buildings.[10]

Bakewell & Brown strove to develop the east quadrangle in a manner consistent with the initial master plan. For the 1916 master plan, Brown explored both of Dawson's suggestions for the position of the library. Although Brown attempted to retain an open axis into the lateral quads in most of his studies, the size of the library needed by Stanford at this time required a more central and monumental treatment than a subordinate location would allow. Bakewell & Brown's drawings of December 1916 place the library at the center of the quadrangle, but set back about 100 feet so as to form a plaza in front of the building (fig. 7.3).[11] Arcades connect the multistory library to one-story ranges on either side, which turn the corner of the block to connect with larger buildings at the centers of the adjacent sides. These new constructions would form a four-quad ensemble along Serra Way and connect Shepley, Rutan & Coolidge's men's dormitory, Encina Hall, with the main academic precinct.

Bakewell & Brown's proposals of 1916 were not so accommodating of Frederick Law Olmsted's landscape. James Dawson himself criticized the university's decision to plant the oval and its adjacent fields in thirsty turf rather than in a native ground cover. He also criticized the placement of a large statue in the center of the oval, where it obscured the view into the inner quad and beyond to Memorial Church.[12] In his redesign of the north side of the campus, Brown attempted to bring an expanded chemistry building and the art museum into some sort of relationship with the main quads. In most schemes he created a very large square or rectangular court, the width of the outer quad, which directed traffic to Lomita and Lasuen streets. A cross-axis aligned with the centerline of the chemistry building would have marked the center of the court, which would have been subdivided into geometric flower beds and shallow basins. A secondary courtyard to the east was planned alternately as an orchard or formal plaza; this space was to lead to playing fields and tennis courts farther east that occupied the lands between Encina Hall and a new men's gymnasium. Little of these schemes was realized, except some planting of trees along Lasuen Street. The oval remains a prominent feature of the campus, even as traffic is now largely diverted away from it.

With the library quad master plan approved by the university trustees in November 1914, many on campus expected that the initial structure in the new quadrangle would be the desperately needed library. However, in March 1915 it was decided that the university would first build an art gallery to house the collection of paintings granted to it by Thomas Welton Stanford, the founder's brother.[13] The northwest corner of the east quad was chosen as the site, allowing Bakewell & Brown to establish the regulating heights and bay widths for the new precinct. The building was designed to emulate the Romanesque character of the central quads and was constructed of the same San Jose sandstone (fig. 7.4). Almost all the embellishment of the small gallery was placed on the arcade and the corner entry portal, which Brown modeled on the great Romanesque churches of southern France. In fact, a large plaster model at one-eighth scale was crafted to study the ornament around the archivolts of the portal. Inside, the entry hall to the gallery was lighted with a high octagonal lantern, which was set on the square plan of the room with arched squinches. The rest of the interior was finished in a simpler manner, except for the dramatic skylights of the galleries.

CECIL H. GREEN LIBRARY

The other building of the east quad to be completed before World War I was the University Library, renamed the Cecil H. Green Library, now a special collections library. The need for a new library building was tremendous. Stanford's small collection of 3,000 volumes at the university's founding was at first housed in temporary quarters on the inner quad. In 1900, the collection, grown to 50,000 volumes and ever increasing, was housed in the Thomas Welton Stanford Library, the central building of the northeast grouping of the outer quad. In 1904 Jane Stanford directed the trustees to construct a new library building to the east of the oval, opposite the chemistry building, to the designs of San Francisco glassmaker Joseph Evan Mackay. This work was unfinished at the time of the earthquake, and the partially completed building crumbled into useless rubble within seconds.[14]

The university did not deem a replacement library to be of highest priority in the years after the earthquake. The library remained in the Welton Stanford space, although it became increasingly difficult to manage in this space as the library grew. Stanford hired George Thomas Clark, former chief librarian of the city of San Francisco, to manage the growing collection, by then at 300,000 volumes. Clark began to plan for a new library structure in 1913 and worked directly with Bakewell & Brown in a cooperative fashion. Their joint efforts produced a design for the building that was intended to accommodate the growth of the collections and the student body for fifty years. Construction on the new facility

7.4. Bakewell & Brown, Thomas Welton Stanford Art Gallery, Stanford University, 1915, view of entry. The art gallery was Brown's most serious attempt at continuing the Stanford arcade scheme through the new development in Quad III. *The Architect and Engineer* 59, no. 1 (October 1919): 46.

VNIVERSITY LIBRARY

L . S . J . V .

Bakewell and Brown 1917

7.5. Bakewell & Brown, University Library, Stanford University, 1917,
presentation rendering. Courtesy Stanford University Archives.

was delayed by the nation's entry into the First World War,
but the building was finally finished and dedicated at the end
of 1919.[15]

Whereas the art gallery was designed as a background
building that would be subordinate to the arcade in front of
it, the library was to terminate the east–west axis of the
inner quad in the same way that Memorial Church terminates the Palm Drive axis. In some of the 1916 master-plan-
ning schemes the women's gymnasium, eventually named
Roble Gym, was to terminate the transverse axis on the west;
in this way, the principal buildings of the university would
be located at the most significant locations in the plan and
reinforce the university's concern with cultivating the student's mind, body, and spirit. The rest of the library quad was
to be arcaded similar to the inner quad. As Bakewell and
Brown described their intent in the dedicatory pamphlet

about the building, "the remainder of the second quadrangle
will follow the same scheme of arcades which has been made
the feature of the general plan, and when the buildings adjacent to the library are completed the library will have a large
open court in front flanked with smaller buildings. . . . These
lower buildings are needed to complete the composition at
this point, and until they have been erected, the library must
of course be considered an incomplete structure."[16] The forecourt in front of the library was important to the architects
and to university president Ray Lyman Wilbur. It was to be a
gathering place for students, smaller than the inner quad, and
thus more conducive to interpersonal interaction.

In designing the exterior of the library Brown again turned
to Romanesque sources, but this time more for the structural clarity of eleventh-century forms than for specific detail.
The building comprised a monumental central block and two

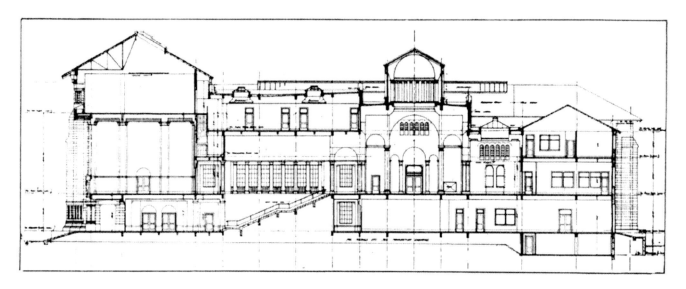

7.6. Bakewell & Brown, University Library, Stanford University, 1917, design development drawing: section. *The Architect and Engineer* 59, no. 1 (October 1919): 48–49.

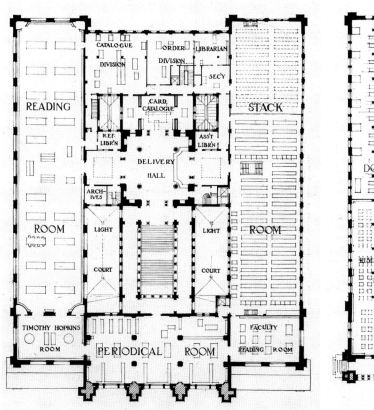

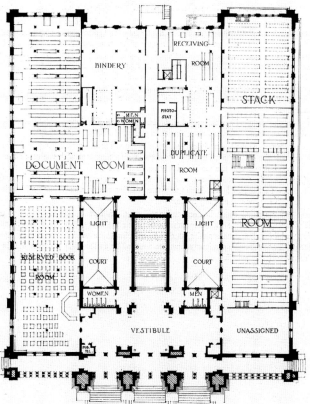

7.7. Bakewell & Brown, University Library, Stanford University, 1917, design development drawings: ground and main floor plans. *The Architect and Engineer* 59, no. 1 (October, 1919): 48–49.

7.8. Bakewell & Brown, Cecil H. Green Library, Stanford University, 1917, view from plaza.

side wings, through which a colonnade was threaded at the ground floor (fig. 7.5). The central block was composed around three high arched bays, with exaggerated buttresses; these elements were intended by Brown to "give a play of light and shade and also emphasize the massiveness of this central figure (fig. C.23)."[17] Sculptural representations of Art, Philosophy, and Science adorned the portals over the doors, but this was the only ornamentation on the building (figs. 7.6, 7.7). Brown appreciated the uniformity of line and material in the older quads, but he was also wary of monotony. At Green Library the main block of the building projects past the line of the arcades to avoid one unbroken line along the length of the quad. In deference to the old quads and the recently completed art gallery, Brown roofed the building in red mission tile and used the San Jose sandstone of the old quads for the facade, but he clad the other three sides of the building in a buff brick (fig. 7.8).

The parti for the plan was taken from George Kelham's San Francisco Main Library, which Brown admired so much that he wrote a review of it in *The Architect and Engineer*.[18] Entry to the Green Library was through a vestibule and then up a monumental stair to the delivery hall, where the card catalog and circulation desk were close at hand (fig. C.24). The stacks occupied the south wing of the building, the reading, document, and reserve rooms the north; to the west, over the entry, a double-height periodical room was set behind the arches of the main facade. A set of seminar rooms and a

"seminar library" were located on the top floor above the periodical room. These interiors were spare in their detailing; only a handful of beamed ceilings, "Byzantine" column capitals, and wrought-iron lighting fixtures provide ornamental touches. Brown intended the interiors to "evoke the monastic architecture of the early middle ages, which is the type used in the University buildings."[19] Thus there is little elaboration of the interiors except where utility might demand it, such as in the cabinetry.

Brown's plans for Green Library were generally successful, but the functional layout of the building became inconvenient when the University Library went to a circulating model for serving the student body. The university continued to develop specialized libraries for the professional schools as well as for many disciplines in the arts and sciences to accommodate the continuously escalating number of volumes held by its library system and delay the need for significant expansions of the central library. Brown had planned for an expansion of the facility to accommodate fifty years of growth, and, in fact, although the stacks were expanded over the years to their ultimate capacity and several satellite libraries were constructed in the 1960s and 1970s, an addition to the library was not planned or constructed until 1980.[20]

Bakewell & Brown's 1916 master plan for Stanford's new quads was well received. The revival of the quad plan perpetuated the best features of the campus, such as the arcades and the interior courtyards, while allowing some latitude in the massing and detailing of new facilities. As Irving Morrow wrote in his review of the new work for *The Architect and Engineer*, "the new quadrangle seems to contain the promise of a group with far more variety and interest than are possessed by the old, in each of proportion, mass, and handling; and this without the sacrifice of unity."[21] Unfortunately, the east quad would be added to piecemeal, and the connecting arcades that were to unify its component buildings were never constructed.

STUDENT HOUSING AND RECREATION SPACE

Stanford has always been a residential university. At first this was an absolute necessity, because Palo Alto was a small village at the time of the university's founding. As the university community grew, the town had difficulty housing both faculty and students, and most students continued to live on campus or very nearby. In the 1920s and early 1930s the university expanded its enrollment beyond the founder's original projections. By the beginning of the 1920s, two-thirds of Stanford's students were living in fraternities or off-campus housing. University president Ray Lyman Wilbur demanded that Stanford take the initiative in creating a more residential campus, necessitating a concurrent expansion of the dormitory, dining, and recreational facilities. The university ren-

ovated and expanded the Encina dormitory complex and erected the Branner, Toyon, Roble, Ventura, and Lagunita Residence Halls, constructed the Encina Commons dining complex, and built the Encina and Roble gymnasiums.[22] All of these projects, with the exception of Roble Hall, were designed by Bakewell & Brown or by the association of Brown and Bakewell & Weihe.

Branner and Toyon halls were the cornerstone of an ambitious building program that was to consolidate the men's housing at the university. In the early 1920s, Stanford had three men's dorms, which at capacity left at least five hundred men unhoused on campus. To meet this need the university planned a four-building residential quadrangle east of the Encina dormitory. Two of the four buildings, Toyon and Branner halls, designed to house 152 and 135 students, respectively, were constructed by 1923. The other two buildings, twins of the first two, mirrored in plan across the new quadrangle, were to have been built within the next few years.[23]

Both Toyon and Branner halls share a similar architectural parti and thus similar floor plans (figs. 7.9, 7.10). The students were housed in two-room suites; one room served as a study, the other as a bedroom. Four sitting rooms were located at the ends of the dormitory wings, where they would receive the most daylight and ventilation. At Toyon two of these wings formed a courtyard that was enclosed on the fourth side by two stair towers and an arcaded entry loggia.

7.9. Bakewell & Brown, Toyon Hall, Stanford University, 1923.

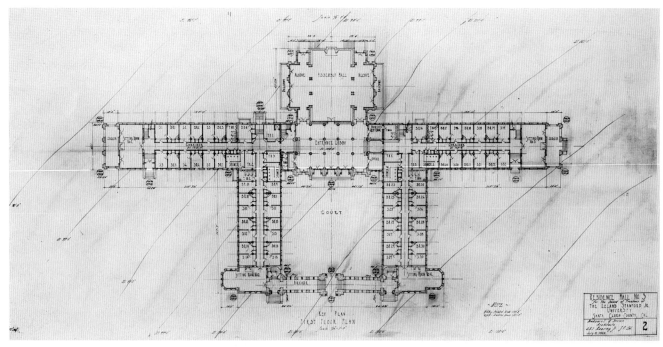

7.10. Bakewell & Brown, Toyon Hall, Stanford University, 1923, plan.

Toyon also featured a very large assembly hall that usually served as the primary social space in the group (fig. 7.11). This double-height space was focused on a baronial fireplace and high clerestory windows. An arcade on each side delimited the side alcoves, which were more intimate in scale and which let out to balconies through French doors. The entire space took on the austere character of a monastic refectory. The heavy concrete walls were relieved with only a bit of ornament in the beam ends of the ceiling, in the carvings of the Romanesque capitals of the fireplace and arcades, and in the decorative work of the wrought-iron lighting fixtures.

The twin dormitories that would have completed the Toyon/Branner quad were never built; sufficient funds were not raised before the Great Depression, and the Second World War limited the demand for dormitory space at Stanford for men. At the same time, the enrollment cap for women, which had restricted the number of women students to five hundred since Jane Stanford's time, was lifted in the early 1930s, and the university built an additional residential complex for the increased number of women. Lagunita Courts was located next to Roble Hall, on the shore of Lake Lagunita. Its form was similar to Branner and Toyon Halls, except that six dormitory buildings were arranged to form a T-shaped courtyard that was further enclosed by an assembly building at the street and a large dining hall and kitchen complex that overlooked the lake to the rear. Perhaps in defer-

ence to its female inhabitants, the architecture at Lagunita Courts is a bit more refined than at Branner; the exteriors are Spanish mission, and the interiors of the public rooms are lighter, airier, and a bit more ornamented than the men's dorms. This lighter character may be due to the lightweight prefabricated steel frame of the buildings, which was engineered by two Stanford faculty members.[24] All of Bakewell & Brown's dormitories share interesting vistas and views from the circulation. At Lagunita Courts the stepped transitions from one building to the next offer views into the courtyard and avoid the monotony of a long, uninterrupted corridor.

Bakewell & Brown's other large project for the residencial program at Stanford was its addition to Encina Hall, the Encina Dining Commons. This one-story building was intended to consolidate the food service required of Encina Hall into a modern and efficient structure. The building fronted Crothers Way, behind Encina Hall, but was tied back to the dormitory with a colonnade that wrapped around the three public sides of the building. A number of dining rooms fronted the street, separated from each other by open courtyards that served as exterior dining spaces in fine weather. A central kitchen and service wing occupied the center of the plan, so that each dining room was easily serviced. Architecturally, the one-story building derives its presence from the colonnade and from the two-story entry tower at the center of the principal elevation. This square block is pierced with a great arched entry and lit from an octagonal gallery above. Brown found this device so compelling that he used it on a number of structures at Stanford, including Toyon Hall, which he was designing at the same time.

Bakewell & Brown also designed a number of buildings for the athletic department and student recreational use at Stanford. The first building constructed following Bakewell & Brown's master plan of 1916 was Encina Gym (fig. 7.12). This brick structure, sited outside the academic precinct, attempted to respect the scale of the rest of the university while housing the large, high spaces required of its program. The surfaces of the exterior were treated very simply; Brown employed the barest hints of classical order in the handling of the fenestration and surface modeling. Encina was joined by the Burnham Pavilion, the campus's early basketball arena, in 1922. Brown again used simple brick construction for this building, which derives its interest largely from the exposed trusses that support the roof.

Throughout the 1920s Bakewell & Brown continued to design structures for the athletic department, including an administration building and a clubhouse for the campus golf course. Their best athletic facility may very well be Roble Gymnasiuim, which was originally constructed in 1931 to improve the recreational facilities for women (figs. 7.13, 7.14).

7.11. Bakewell & Brown, Toyon Hall, Stanford University, 1923, main lounge.

7.12. Bakewell & Brown, Encina Gym, Stanford University,
aerial view, c. 1919.

At Roble the two trussed gymnasium buildings were sited on either side of a landscaped court; to the rear Brown placed a locker room, and to the front, a large domed entry lobby. This lobby, where large trefoil windows throw light onto the Guastavino tile dome, is one of Brown's best spaces at Stanford.

STANFORD IN THE 1930S

Even after Bakewell & Brown dissolved, the two former partners continued to associate at Stanford. Brown's office became responsible for much of Stanford's medical and scientific facilities, as well as producing additions for Wright & Saunders' Lane Hospital in San Francisco and Stanford's medical complex in Palo Alto. Most of these hospital structures have been demolished or renovated beyond recognition, but the old surgical wing and the nurses' dormitories still stand as part of the Pacific Presbyterian Medical Center. Brown also designed several important facilities to house the university's scientific research program in the mid-1920s. These facilities included Ryan Electrical Laboratories, located south of the outer quad, and the Jacques Loeb Marine Research Center in Pacific Grove, which was partly funded by Timothy Hopkins. The latter facility, located just west of the Monterey Bay Aquarium, remains an important part of Stanford's program in biological research.

Bakewell & Brown's plans for a fully realized east quad were suspended in the 1920s, when the university's building priorities shifted to residential and athletic buildings. In the 1930s, however, President Wilbur directed Stanford's building energies to the completion of the library quad. Four projects were the focus of this work: a building for the School of Education, a new home for the School of Law, a new library building to house the Hoover War Library, and a war memorial to commemorate Stanford graduates who had given their lives in the First World War. As it happened, only two of these projects were realized within the bounds of the library quad—the other two were sited elsewhere, leaving the quad incomplete, in fact, abandoned—in the years after the Second World War.

The first building to be realized in this second phase of the library quad was the School of Education. This building

7.13 (*above*). Bakewell & Brown, Roble Gymnasium, Stanford University, presentation sketch, c. 1930. Photograph of drawing courtesy of Moulin Archives.

7.14 (*below*). Bakewell & Brown, Roble Gymnasium, Stanford University. Photograph courtesy of Moulin Archives.

was funded by a faculty member, Ellwood Cubberly, the first dean of the School of Education.[25] For years the department was housed in a single room on the inner quad. The department began to offer a Ph.D. in education in 1916, and the following year it was reorganized as a professional school; during the 1920s the faculty nearly doubled, and the number of students grew to over 500 by the end of the decade.[26] When Cubberly retired in 1933 he gave the university a sum that represented his outside earnings from lectures, consulting, and book royalties. By 1936 this sum had increased enough that Cubberly and Wilbur were able to dedicate the entire amount toward a building for the School of Education.

Cubberly became so involved with the design of the building that he is usually given joint credit for its design. The site, just south of Green Library, marked the southwest limit of the library quad and was reserved for just such a building, according to Bakewell & Brown's updated master plan. The building was pushed forward to the street line, so that it would form the south edge of the library courtyard. It took the form of an arcaded main block to which two files of lateral wings were joined; these separated to form a courtyard on either side. Thus the plan resembled a shallow H lying on its side. A physical connection was made with the University Library as well. A colonnade of paired columns connected the northeast wing of the education building to the rump arcade of the library; a terrace ran around the north and south sides of the building connecting the colonnade to the dominant arcade of the front (west) elevation. The massing of the front was kept at nearly the same height as the outer quad across the street; the apparent two stories of the composition were divided into bays by the arcade and heavy buttresses of the ground story.

The program of the building was primarily divided by floor. The ground floor contained four general classrooms and a large auditorium to be used by the entire university, as well as the School of Education's administrative offices and a small number of faculty classrooms. The second and third floors were devoted entirely to the School of Education. The school's library occupied the front range of spaces; a double-height reading room was positioned behind the large windows of the principal facade, and stacks occupied the second and mezzanine floors of the wings. The second floor also housed a number of teaching laboratories and seminar rooms, as well as a large number of faculty offices. The third floor housed research space, offices, and a student and faculty social hall. The interiors of the building were intended to be clean, unarticulated, and contemporary. There was very little architectural elaboration, except for a list of famous educators inscribed on the building's facade at the request of Dean Cubberly, and a set of fluted concrete columns in the entrance lobby. The primary works of art in the building are two mosaics in the entrance lobby by Roccheggiani, executed in 1876 and donated to Stanford by Timothy Hopkins's wife, Marie.[27]

Stanford's School of Law was also seeking larger quarters at the same time the School of Education was building its new facilities. Although law had been taught at the undergraduate level since 1893 and graduate course work was initiated in 1916, the school was not formally designated a graduate professional school until 1926. At this time, it was located on the inner quadrangle in very inadequate space. Lacking a single generous donor such as Ellwood Cubberly, the School of Law asked Bakewell & Brown develop the plans for a new complex to the east of Green Library as a means of raising funds for the new construction. The facility was to complete the fourth side of the library quadrangle and firmly reestablish the quad as the basic unit of campus space at Stanford. Unfortunately, the fundraising campaign ran into the teeth of the Great Depression, and the school was never able to raise enough funds to implement Bakewell & Brown's design.

The School of Law was to be a low-rise set of buildings joined by arcades set around a landscaped courtyard similar to the library group to its immediate west (fig. 7.15). Two nearly identical buildings, north and south, were planned to hold lecture auditoria and seminar rooms, and a longer range of buildings, two stories tall, was to bound the court to the west and house administrative and faculty offices. A fourth building, the law library, was to extend beyond the administration building to the west, nearly up to Green Library. In the early 1930s versions of the plan, the complex was to be bounded on the east with an arcade that connected the group to the rest of the quadrangle. By the 1940s, however, Brown had given up on completing the quadrangle as a series of interconnected structures, and Skidmore Owings & Merrill's law group, completed in 1975, stands free of the other structures, connected to everything else only by walks. The plan for the east quad was abandoned after the Second World War; new buildings for the Department of Art interrupted the links between the library and the art gallery, and Edward Durell Stone's Meyer Library straddled Escondido Road and destroyed its southern edge. Nevertheless, Bakewell & Brown managed to define three sides of the quad before their term as university architects expired, and the firm gave the institution its signature building, the Hoover Tower.

THE HOOVER TOWER

The Hoover Institution was the brainchild of its founder, Herbert Hoover. Born in 1874 in Iowa, Hoover came to California as a young man, and became a member of Stanford's first graduating class. While at Stanford, he met

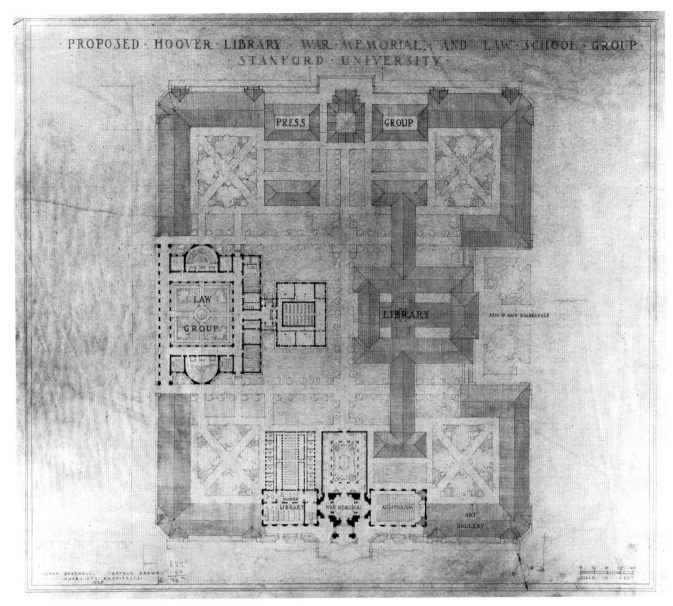

7.15. Arthur Brown Jr., master plan for the School of Law in the east quad, Stanford University, 1925. Arthur Brown Jr. Papers, Stanford University Archives.

his wife, Lou Henry Hoover, who had also been born in Iowa the same year and had independently found her way to Palo Alto. After graduation Herbert became a highly successful mining engineer and an internationally sought consultant on mineralogy and mining. With his success Hoover sought to return something to his alma mater, and he spearheaded the campaign to build men's and women's clubs at Stanford. In appreciation of his efforts, Hoover was asked to serve on the board of trustees of the University;

this began his lifelong association as a principal governor of the institution.

While engaged in relief work in Europe during the First World War, Hoover became aware of the need to collect the documents, letters, propaganda, and memorabilia pertaining to the causes and prosecution of the war. He encouraged hundreds of his colleagues and acquaintances to collect this material and send it to Stanford, where he had resided prior to the war. This collection, housed initially in Green Library, became the primary research collection dedicated to the study of the Great War and its aftermath. As the collection grew, its focus expanded to encompass the history of the Soviet Union and the consolidation of the Soviet Empire. Renamed the Hoover Institution of War, Revolution, and Peace, the library has become the nation's leading research center on foreign affairs, with particular emphasis on Eastern Europe and the former Soviet Union.

At the same time, a group of alumni sought to build a memorial to those Stanford graduates who had perished in the war. In 1925 Bakewell & Brown was asked to design a complex of buildings that would both honor the dead and house Hoover's ever-growing collection of documents pertaining to the war. The earliest schemes put the library in a modest two-story building behind the art gallery. A war memorial court in the Romanesque style of the art gallery arcade was to contain a contemplative garden and serve as an entry to the complex; a towered gatehouse would provide access to the group. For a few years, no funds were readily available for the project, and the plans languished; Hoover could not devote any attention to the affairs at Stanford while he was president. In the mid-1930s a student and alumni group requested that the war

memorial take a more pragmatic and useful form than a garden, and it was proposed that an auditorium building be constructed. The associated architects were called to design this structure, now known as Memorial Hall, which was placed directly across Serra Way from the site of the Hoover Library (fig. 7.16). Construction for this facility was begun in 1936, and completed the following year.

With the completion of Memorial Hall, the plans for the Hoover Institution could again be considered. By 1937 the collection of material on modern European political history had grown so much that the facility had to be radically expanded and redesigned. Although the commission could have been assigned to someone else, Brown was endorsed as the facility's architect. The Hoover Tower commission should have been a source of great satisfaction for Brown, but the project opened old wounds with John Bakewell, who demanded equal credit for the building and half the profit Brown earned from the project because it was initiated while Bakewell and Brown were still in partnership together. In fact, Bakewell & Brown's contract with Stanford was still enforceable, so the matter of attribution hinged on whether the commission was with the Hoover Institution—a private

7.16. Bakewell & Brown, Memorial Hall, Stanford University, 1937. Like the other work at Stanford after 1927, Memorial Hall was executed by Brown and Bakewell & Weihe as associated architects.

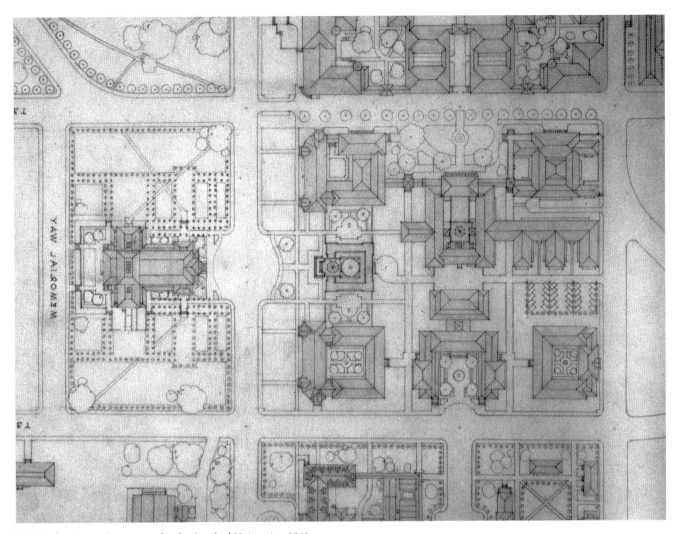

7.17. Arthur Brown Jr., master plan for Stanford University, 1941, detail of vicinity of the East Quad (north is down on this map). Brown retained all of his planning documents for Stanford in the event he was called back at the conclusion of World War II. Arthur Brown Jr. Papers, Stanford University Archives.

entity distinct from the university—or with the university itself. The architects appealed this question to Frederick Meyer, by then the vice-president of the AIA in Washington, who ruled that because the building was at Stanford, the commission was covered by the 1913 contract with Bakewell & Brown, and therefore Bakewell should receive attribution for the building, even if he contributed nothing to the project.[28] This outcome rankled Brown, who always considered the Hoover Tower a personal commission given him by Hoover himself, a close friend. Hoover apparently felt the same way, and in a letter dated August 3, 1960, he reiterated that he considered the commission to be Brown's: "Arthur

was the sole designer of the Hoover Tower, and . . . Mr. Bakewell had nothing whatever to do with it."[29] Nevertheless, it is correct to attribute the building to Bakewell & Brown.

Brown completely restudied the problem and eschewed the horizontal composition of the previous design. Instead, he enlarged the four-story entry monument into a fourteen-story tower. Brown chose the tower for both practical and symbolic reasons, perhaps mindful of the prominence of John Galen Howard's Sather Tower at the University of California at Berkeley. As the *President's Report* of 1939 stated:

7.18. Arthur Brown Jr. and Bakewell & Weihe, associated architects, Hoover Institution, c. 1938, first, Mediterranean design. Drawing by Francis Todhunter, Arthur Brown Jr. Papers, Stanford University Archives.

7.19. (*opposite*) Arthur Brown, Jr. and Bakewell & Weihe, associated architects, Hoover Institution, c. 1938, revised, domed design, which recalls other buildings by Brown on the Stanford campus. Drawing, Arthur Brown Jr. Papers, Stanford University Archives.

This building will be in the form of a tower, the central portion of which will house the collection under the most favorable condition of protection from light and undue moisture. Since the loss of the steeple of the Memorial Church and the Memorial Arch the University has lacked a building of sufficient height to provide adequate architectural expression to the whole plant. The problem of providing similar towers for other universities has been difficult since there is a large amount of waste space. In the new Hoover Library Building this space will be occupied by the main collection.[30]

The Hoover Tower was sited as a freestanding building, unconnected to the arcades proposed for the rest of the quad. Brown's 1941 master plan for Stanford demonstrates that he had begun to doubt Stanford's commitment to the connect-

ing arcades that had originally defined the campus (fig. 7.17). Instead, each group responds to the axis of the whole university and to the buildings directly across the street.[31] Projected buildings, such as the Law Group opposite the Green Library, still make provisions for an arcade but no longer presuppose the arcade in their design.

The design of Hoover Tower was relatively straightforward once the tower form was determined. The memorial court and arcade were simply transformed into the library. The entry pavilion was replaced with a domed reception hall, from which visitors moved to exhibition galleries in the wings, and the extent of the courtyard itself defined the base of the steel and concrete tower. The exterior forms of the base group boast little ornamentation, reflecting the limited budget for the project and Brown's emerging preference for cleaner lines that emphasized the proportions of the architecture. The shaft of the tower was ordered by a series of slightly projecting pilasters, which were resolved with arches at the top of the structure in the final design. Two distinct crowning motifs were designed for the building, which received an important function when the carillon from the Belgian Pavilion at the 1939 World's Fair in New York was donated to Stanford and intended for the tower.[32] The first carried the pilasters past a doubled arcade of tall windows to a hipped roof (fig. 7.18). Although the hipped roof was appropriate to Stanford and recalled the lost tower of Memorial Church, the roof itself seemed lost from the ground and was not deemed satisfactory by President Hoover.

Sometime in 1939 Brown took the drawings to Hoover's home, and while in discussion with him about how the tower might fit into the Romanesque campus, Lou Henry Hoover made the suggestion that Brown look at the New Tower at the Old Cathedral at Salamanca, Spain. Brown had already used the arcaded dome form at Pasadena City Hall and the AT&SF station at San Diego—but at Stanford the Salamanca motif was transformed into an entire building (fig. 7.19).[33] Eight blunt pilasters framed each corner of the octagonal drum, between which an arcade repeated the relieving arches of the story below. In the final design, which was validated with a wooden model, the pilasters are diminished and pyramidal pinnacles fill out the corners of the composition; the final result is close to Brown's towers at the Old Union, across the quad, and the western towers at San Diego.[34] This model was an extremely important design tool. It was photographed from many different angles so that the images could be superimposed on photographs of the campus. The photomontages demonstrated the effect the tower would have on the campus's skyline, and convinced Hoover and President Wilbur that the building would punctuate, but not dominate, the Stanford grounds.

The Hoover Institution on War, Revolution, and Peace was formally dedicated on June 20, 1941, in a grand ceremony that marked the conclusion of Stanford University's commemoration of its fiftieth anniversary (fig. 7.20). With a Second World War raging in Europe and the Pacific, the speeches given that day, including one by former President Hoover, could not help but highlight the need for research into the causes and effects of war in the hope that such work might lead to peace. Hoover recalled all of those who had helped to assemble the library's collection, remarked on its incomparable breadth and nonpartisan scope, and demanded that the lessons of war and peace be learned within its walls:

> [H]ere are the records of the world's effort to make peace. Here are the proofs of the highest idealism. And here are the records of selfishness and the lowest trickery. Here can be found the

record of the ideas and forces which made for failure of the last peace and the ideas and forces which might have made its success. Out of these files the world can get great warning of what not to do and what to do when it next assembles around the peace table. . . . And here are the documents which record the suffering, the self-denial, the devotion, the heroic deeds of men. Surely from these records there can be help to mankind in its confusions and perplexities, and its yearnings for peace.[35]

The entry of the United States into the war marked a watershed for the development of the Stanford campus. On February 26, 1942, the board of trustees formally revoked its resolution of November 28, 1913, which had appointed

Bakewell & Brown as the university architects. Since 1942 each building project at Stanford has been coordinated by a university planning office but designed by separately contracted architectural firms.[36] Although Brown struggled throughout his career to follow the Olmsted plan for the Stanford campus, post-war conditions made adherence to the design undesirable. The quadrangle schemes of the plan were abandoned in these years and in many places could not be restored without the demolition of structures now deemed historic in their own right. With the need to rehabilitate and expand its facilities following the 1989 Loma Prieta earthquake, the university embarked on an ambitious building campaign to reestablish the quad form in several new constructions for the School of Engineering in the western quad. Buildings by Robert A. M. Stern, Antoine Predock, and Pei-Cobb-Freed and Associates exploit the best architectural and planning features of the Olmsted plan while offering a contemporary interpretation of the Richardson Romanesque architectural forms of the old quads.

THE UNIVERSITY OF CALIFORNIA AT BERKELEY

The University of California owes its existence to the Morrill Act of 1862, which promised a steady stream of income from the sale of federal land grants to a set of public universities, if these institutions would offer course work and degree programs in agriculture and the mechanical arts. California enthusiastically chartered a new state-supported university in response. On March 23, 1868, Governor Henry H. Haight signed legislation creating a state university that was to be merged with, and supersede, the College of California, which had been chartered in 1855. This college had purchased a 140-acre parcel of land along the banks of Strawberry Creek north of Oakland that offered a beautiful setting and a spectacular view of the Golden Gate, directly west of the site across San Francisco Bay. Just after the Civil War the trustees had hired Frederick Law Olmsted to create a master plan for a university at the Berkeley site. Olmsted's plan envisioned a park-like setting in which curvilinear streets wound up the slopes of the hill to a high plateau, on which the first college buildings would be erected; a great axis, emphasized by an allée of trees, aligned these new structures with the Golden Gate. Olmsted's proposal was not realized, although his great axis and informal treatment of Strawberry Creek remained in many subsequent plans.

7.20. Arthur Brown Jr., Hoover Tower, Stanford University, 1940. Photograph courtesy of Moulin Archives.

The Organic Act of the University of California called for a master plan and specified that the regents of the new university should "adopt a plan as shall set aside separate buildings for separate uses and yet group all such buildings upon a general plan, such that a larger and central building hereafter erected may bring the whole into harmony as parts of one design."[37] The regents held a competition for a new master plan that would incorporate the larger system of professional schools and academic departments. Most of San Francisco's architectural firms entered the competition. The winning firm, Wright & Saunders, withdrew from the commission in a dispute over its fee, and the second-place finisher, Kenitzer & Farquharson, was hired to execute its six-building plan for the university. Two of the structures were built in the early 1870s. South Hall, a mansard-roofed French renaissance– revival building that housed the College of Agriculture, still stands. Its companion building, North Hall, housed the College of Arts; hurriedly constructed in wood, it was demolished in 1917 when the completion of Wheeler Hall made it redundant.[38]

THE HEARST COMPETITION AND THE BÉNARD PLAN

Development at Berkeley was somewhat haphazard in the 1880s and early 1890s. Indeed, as the university grew, its facilities were slow to keep pace. A number of buildings were quickly constructed as new programs were initiated or existing programs outgrew their space, but these were sited in comparative isolation, without regard for one another or the natural features of the site. It became clear first to Bernard Maybeck, and then to the regents, that the university needed a vision for development that would direct the growth of facilities as the university expanded its mission and student body in the twentieth century. Maybeck suggested a competition for a campus master plan in 1896, while Brown was still a student of his in the Department of Civil Engineering. In that year Maybeck's initiative gained the support of the board of regents and caught the imagination of Phoebe Apperson Hearst, who underwrote the cost of the entire enterprise with Maybeck serving as the competition director.

Over the next two years Maybeck traveled to the East Coast and Europe, where he assembled a prestigious jury that would ensure the competition gained the notice of the world. He based himself in Paris for much of 1897 and 1898 and met frequently with Julien Guadet, the professor of theory at the Ecole des Beaux-Arts and its pedagogical leader. Together with William Ware, the head of Columbia University's School of Architecture, Guadet and Maybeck wrote the competition program. This document summed up the aspirations of the university and the Beaux-Arts planning philosophy, in general. It read, in part:

7.21. Emile Bénard, competition drawing for the Hearst Memorial Competition, 1898. *Illustrated History of the University of California*, 1901, 234.

It is the desire of those who have charge of this enterprise, to treat the grounds and buildings together, landscape gardening and architecture forming one composition, which will never need to be structurally changed in all the future history of the University. . . . [The entrant] is asked to record his conception of an ideal home for a University, assuming time and resources to be unlimited. He is to plan for centuries to come. There will doubtless be developments of science in the future that will impose new duties on the University, and require alterations in the detailed arrangement of its buildings, but it is believed to be possible to secure a comprehensive plan so in harmony with the universal principles of architectural art, that there will be no more necessity of remodeling its broad outlines a thousand years hence, than there would be of remodeling the Parthenon, had it come down to us complete and uninjured.[39]

The Hearst competition was the most generous and noteworthy architectural competition of the nineteenth century.

Over one hundred entries were received in the first round of judging, which was held in the early days of October 1898. The authors of eleven schemes were awarded prizes and the right to continue to the second round. These eleven architects were invited to California to study the Berkeley campus site and to learn more about the university and its requirements. The brief for the second phase of the competition emphasized the need to minimize the amount of earthwork required to realize the competitor's designs, and asked the entrants to carefully consider the natural amenities the site had to offer, such as the views from the hillside of the Golden Gate and the scenic possibilities of Strawberry Creek.

In early September of 1898, nearly a year after the first round, the jury met again in San Francisco to declare a winner of the competition. Emile Bénard, winner of the Grand Prix de Rome in 1867, won the top prize for a scheme that grouped the university buildings around a number of large courts and a relentless main axis that sliced through the site from College Avenue on the west to the top of the hill at the eastern edge of the campus (fig. 7.21). However, Bénard proved to be a very uncooperative individual. He had underestimated the hilly nature of the site; his scheme would have required an immense amount of grading to execute, and then each structure would have to be raised on plinths several stories high. Thus, when Bénard came to California to collect his prize and to negotiate for his services in executing his plan, he was naturally asked to rework his designs substantially. At first he refused in such an emphatic manner that he alienated both Mrs. Hearst and university president Benjamin Ide Wheeler. Although Bénard agreed to work on the Berkeley project from Paris, he refused to move to Berkeley to oversee the implementation of his plan. Eventually, the regents looked to John Galen Howard, who placed fourth, to create a new plan that would incorporate the essential characteristics of Bénard's scheme into a new effort that would be achievable on the Berkeley site. By late 1901 the president and the regents had installed Howard as the supervising architect of the university and professor of architecture in the College of Engineering; he was tasked both to alter the Bénard scheme and oversee the erection of several new facilities.

THE HOWARD PLAN

Howard was a popular choice for the position of supervising architect. He was an easterner, born in 1864 and educated at MIT and the Ecole des Beaux-Arts. He had found employment with H. H. Richardson's firm in the mid-1880s, just as the firm gained the commission for Stanford University, and later with McKim, Mead & White, where he assisted White with the plans for the first Madison Square Garden.[40] Howard had lived in California in the late 1880s but, finding very little work there, had moved to New York and become a rising star, placing second in the New York Public Library competition. Thus it was not without some trepidation that he accepted the Berkeley position. For the first several years he attempted to work in both San Francisco and New York—this eventually became untenable in a time when the travel time between the two coasts was the better part of a week. Finally, in 1902, Howard closed down his New York practice and moved his family to Berkeley. He realized what an opportunity he had at Berkeley and dedicated the greater bulk of his career to it.

Howard's plan for the university evolved over the two decades he was in control of the planning at Berkeley (1901–24). His first few years at Berkeley were concerned with the design and construction of the Hearst Mining Building, perhaps Howard's most inventive work on campus.

At the same time, he began to make significant changes to Bénard's plan. By the end of his first decade, the master plan for the campus looked much more like Howard's entry in the competition than Bénard's (figs. 7.22, 7.23). What remained were the essentials: a wide, mall-like axis down the slope of the hill toward the bay; a campanile, Sather Tower, which punctuated a transverse axis and gave the university an architectural presence as far away as San Francisco; and a wooded zone along Strawberry Creek that separated town from gown.

Howard carefully planned new construction to reinforce the several transverse axes he created, such as the Esplanade, while respecting the topography of the site. Most of the twenty-five permanent buildings erected during his tenure were steel-framed structures clad in California granite and roofed with red tile. His best group, and the core of the campus, was Doe Library and Wheeler, California, and Durant halls. The library, in particular, acknowledged the open space of the glade to the north with the tall openings of the main reading room. Not all of Howard's work was classical, however. Several of his buildings along Strawberry Creek exhibit the more rustic and residential shingled mode, such as the "temporary" Ark, now North Gate Hall, and the Women's Faculty Club. The old student union, Stephens Hall, was collegiate Gothic, a form Howard thought appropriate for nonacademic buildings.[41]

Although Brown was close to Howard personally and professionally, Bakewell & Brown was invited to do only minor private work at the University of California during Howard's tenure there. The partners' first commission near the campus was an addition to the Beta Theta Pi House, completed in 1908. The firm's dining-room addition continued the medieval-inspired aesthetic of Ernest Coxhead's original design. (The building, completely renovated and expanded, now houses the Goldman School of Public Policy.) Bakewell & Brown next designed a memorial bridge across Strawberry Creek for the class of 1910. This new structure stepped down to the creek bank and then leapt over the water in a graceful span. It was ornamented with a triumphal arch simply framed with Doric pilasters that support a tablet and an Ionic cornice. The entire structure was constructed of poured-in-place concrete and was funded in part by Phoebe Apperson Hearst.

Howard was dismissed as university architect in 1924 in a dispute with the regents about his authority over his plan. He was eventually replaced by George Kelham, who designed much of the UCLA campus in Westwood and several buildings at Berkeley, most in conformance with Howard's plan, including the massive Valley Life Sciences Building in the southwestern corner of the campus and International House at the top of Bancroft Way. Kelham widened the range of architectural styles used for academic buildings at Berkeley, while generally following Howard's lead. At the same time,

BIRDS EYE VIEW
the
PHŒBE APPERSON HEARST
PLAN
UNIVERSITY OF CALIFORNIA

7.22. John Galen Howard, "Phoebe Apperson Hearst Plan," University of California, Berkeley, 1906. Original drawing in the Environmental Design Archives, University of California; engraving in author's collection.

7.23 (*opposite*). John Galen Howard, "Phoebe A. Hearst Architectural Plan," University of California, Berkeley, 1906. Howard's plan became the basis of development for the Berkeley campus until Brown's dismissal in 1948. Photostat of plan, Arthur Brown Jr. Collection, Bancroft Library.

the university administration took on a more active role in campus planning. President Robert Gordon Sproul formed an advisory committee on campus development and building location to work with the supervising architect in locating new facilities. The first chair of this powerful group was Warren C. Perry, John Galen Howard's successor as director of the School of Architecture.[42] Perry ensured continuity with the Howard plan, even as he sought new sites for development as the university grew.

Arthur Brown at Berkeley

The supervising architect had never had a monopoly on commissions at the university. Even during Howard's most productive years, some projects were commissioned to other architects. This policy was expanded during Kelham's tenure

as supervising architect, and several architectural firms were commissioned to do work that Kelham and his staff could not handle. Kelham selected Bakewell & Brown to design the campus infirmary, the Ernest V. Cowell Memorial Hospital. The firm had done several hospital buildings by that time, including additions to Stanford's Lane Hospital in San Francisco and St. Joseph's Hospital below Buena Vista Park. Cowell was a relatively small project, constructed in 1929 solely to meet the needs of the university population. The four-story hospital building was located west of Gayley Road, just south of California Memorial Stadium. Brown's design was politely neoclassical but astylar—it strove to match Howard's classical buildings across Strawberry Creek, yet not call too much attention to itself. Originally designed to provide quarantine facilities in the pre–World War II environment of infectious disease, Cowell eventually became the nation's first college residence for students with disabilities

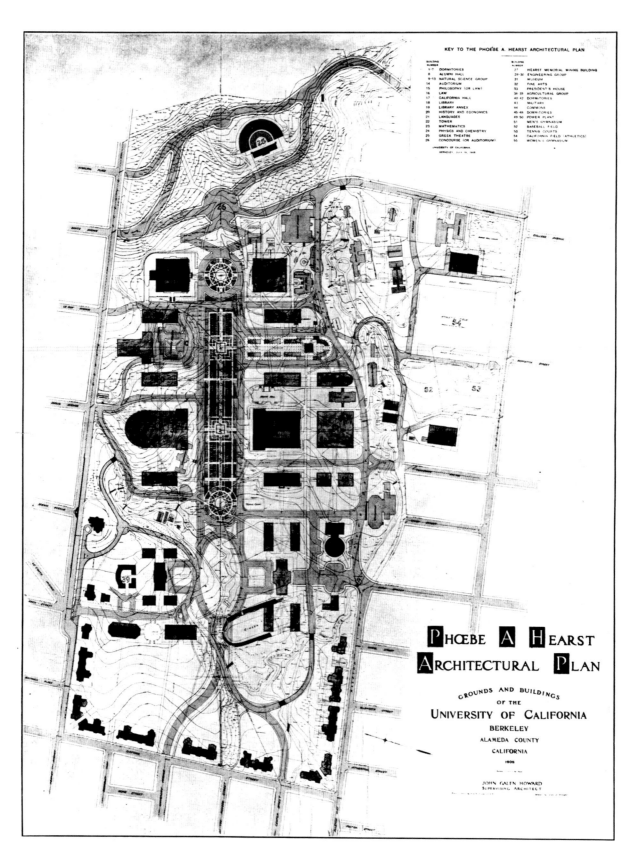

BUILDING NUMBER		BUILDING NUMBER	
1-7	DORMITORIES	27	HEARST MEMORIAL MINING BUILDING
8	ALUMNI HALL	29-30	ENGINEERING GROUP
9-13	NATURAL SCIENCE GROUP	31	MUSEUM
14	AUDITORIUM	32	FINE ARTS
15	PHILOSOPHY (OR LAW)	33	PRESIDENT'S HOUSE
16	LAW	34-39	AGRICULTURAL GROUP
17	CALIFORNIA HALL	40-42	DORMITORIES
18	LIBRARY	43	MILITARY
19	LIBRARY ANNEX	44	COMMONS
20	HISTORY AND ECONOMICS	45-48	DORMITORIES
21	LANGUAGES	49-50	POWER PLANT
22	TOWER	51	MEN'S GYMNASIUM
23	MATHEMATICS	52	BASEBALL FIELD
24	PHYSICS AND CHEMISTRY	53	TENNIS COURTS
25	GREEK THEATRE	54	CALIFORNIA FIELD (ATHLETICS)
26	CONCOURSE (OR AUDITORIUM)	55	WOMEN'S GYMNASIUM

UNIVERSITY OF CALIFORNIA
BERKELEY, JULY 15, 1908

PHŒBE A HEARST
ARCHITECTURAL PLAN

GROUNDS AND BUILDINGS
OF THE
UNIVERSITY OF CALIFORNIA
BERKELEY
ALAMEDA COUNTY
CALIFORNIA
1908

JOHN GALEN HOWARD
SUPERVISING ARCHITECT

and a landmark to the independent living movement.[43] Cowell Hospital also remained the home of the university student health program until its demolition in 1993, when its site was claimed for the Walter A. Haas School of Business Administration.

In 1938, two years after George Kelham's death, the university turned to Brown, on whom it had bestowed an honorary doctorate in 1931, to provide continuity in planning while it underwent the greatest enrollment growth in its history.[44] With the onset of World War II, much of Brown's work at Berkeley was of a temporary nature. For example, a large classroom building, now Minor Hall, was put up in a few months in order to handle the influx of servicemen sent through military schools housed at the university. Later, this building was given a third story, and it eventually housed the Department of Optometry because it was located next to Cowell Hospital.

Brown's immediate task in 1938 was to provide temporary and permanent quarters for the growing scientific community arriving to conduct defense-related research. The most famous of these researchers was Ernest Orlando

Lawrence, the Nobel prize–winning physicist whose development of the cyclotron and research into the production of radioactive isotopes had made him a world-renowned figure (J. Robert Oppenheimer, also "on the hill," would become at least as well known in a few years). As Lawrence garnered more grant money, he sought to build bigger and bigger cyclotrons; by 1938 they were large enough to require their own buildings, constructed to his specifications.[45] Brown provided Lawrence with these buildings, and, fellow Bohemians, they became close friends who often lunched together. Brown's family tradition holds that the object of these lunches was for Brown to teach Lawrence about art, and Lawrence to teach Brown about physics. Lawrence may have had the tougher assignment. In any case, when they were not lunching, Brown and Lawrence were creating the first purpose-built nuclear research compound and ushering in the age of Big Science.

The compound started with the building for the 180-inch cyclotron, now known rather ingloriously as Building Six at the Lawrence Berkeley Laboratory (figs. 7.24, 7.25). Lawrence and Oppenheimer had started their work in LeConte Hall,

7.24 (*opposite*). Arthur Brown Jr. with Ernest Lawrence, Cyclotron Building, 1940, Lawrence Berkeley Labs. Photograph courtesy of Lawrence Berkeley National Laboratories.

7.25. Arthur Brown Jr. with Ernest Lawrence, Cyclotron Building, 1940, Lawrence Berkeley Labs, construction photo. Photograph courtesy of Lawrence Berkeley National Laboratories.

the physics building. As their equipment grew larger, they needed more space. They first moved to a temporary structure east of the Esplanade, but as the world marched into war, it was clear that the nuclear labs would have to be relocated out of the main core of the campus. The cyclotron was the catalyst for this move, because Lawrence required a clear-span structure 160 feet in diameter to contain the fifth-generation device. The building was first assigned space in Strawberry Canyon, which would have required diverting the creek to bury the structure. Brown convinced Lawrence that the bucolic canyon would not remain so if Lawrence moved there. He suggested instead a bench in the hills high above the campus, at the eastern edge of the university tract, where the building would not have to be buried to provide the campus community protection from stray radiation.[46] Brown placed the structure perfectly on axis with Howard's main axis of the campus, in line with the Mining Circle, the Memorial Glade, and the Golden Gate.[47] With this move, the Berkeley Hill was crowned not by Howard's auditorium but by a temple to the science that would influence the destiny of humankind for decades thereafter.

The Cyclotron Building itself was not quite the high-tech marvel the cyclotron within it was, but it was an engineering and architectural challenge on its own. At first, Brown and Lawrence had difficulty obtaining the materials necessary to build the structure. The importance of Lawrence's research was lost on pre-war defense planners. Once the cyclotron was classified as an "instrument of war," however, it became possible to erect the structure at near record speed. The twenty-four-sided domed building was composed of heavy braced columns that supported twenty-four arched steel trusses; these were joined together in a compression ring at the center and by a web of concentric K-trusses and diagonal tie rods through the radius of the dome. The total weight of the roof steel came in at just eleven pounds per square foot, and the building was strong enough that Lawrence could support his equipment anywhere in it.[48] Much of the success of the building must be credited to San Francisco structural engineers Hall & Pregnoff, whom Brown used frequently in the years after Christopher Snyder's death.

Flexibility was the chief virtue of the Cyclotron Building. It was never intended to make a significant architectural statement, except in its siting; few of Lawrence's facilities were considered permanent enough to warrant formal architectural treatment, and Brown never was allowed to apply his artistic talents to any facility in the Lawrence Berkeley Laboratory. He did, however, design a medical-physics building, the Donner Laboratory, for the radiation therapy group led by Lawrence's brother, John. In this structure, atomic energy was first applied to the treatment of disease. Like Minor Hall, Donner Laboratory was treated very severely. Brown had found that with his research buildings at Stanford and Berkeley, the less elaboration, the better, because these facilities were not public buildings and required no public accommodation.

BERKELEY IN THE 1940S

During the 1940s Brown employed a simplified classicism that retained the proportions he had spent his life perfecting while presenting clean, uncluttered elevations. The most public of these buildings was Sproul Hall, a new administration building that was to be the key structure in an ensemble of formal buildings intended to occupy the site of the present student union (figs. 7.26, C.25). Completed in 1942, Sproul

Hall incorporated many of the architectural elements Brown most appreciated, such as a tetrastyle portico, projecting wings, and wrought-iron hardware and railings. Although the building uses the Ionic order, rare among Brown's works, every part of the composition is a reduction of the fully ornamented order. The portico itself, the most elaborated feature of the building, is unornamented except for the restrained capitals on the columns and a torus molding at their bases. Flat planes predominate, and no sculpture adorns the pediment or the entablature; even the dentils characteristic of the order have been omitted. The windows are punched and set deeply into the planar surface of the wall, without a surround or a pronounced sill. At the second floor of the pediment block and end pavilions, Brown allowed a slightly projecting shelf and simple wrought-iron balustrade, but none of the consoles or florid ironwork he had used two decades earlier.

Was the austere classicism of Sproul Hall imposed on Brown or a freely made response to the new architectural values espoused throughout the nation by the late 1930s? Given that Brown had proven his ability to construct a fully ornamented order in concrete at Pasadena, and because Sproul Hall was a monumental building for which a substantial appropriation was granted, it is likely that he consciously sought a middle way between the heavily ornamented

7.26. Arthur Brown Jr., Sproul Hall, University of California, Berkeley, 1942, elevation study. Drawing, Arthur Brown Jr. Collection, Bancroft Library.

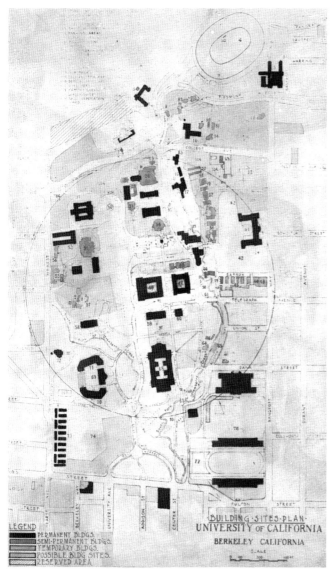

7.27. Arthur Brown Jr., plan for the University of California, Berkeley, c. 1940, existing layout of facilities. Brown sought to increase the density of development on the campus while maintaining the open-space corridors along Strawberry Creek. Drawing, Arthur Brown Jr. Collection, Bancroft Library.

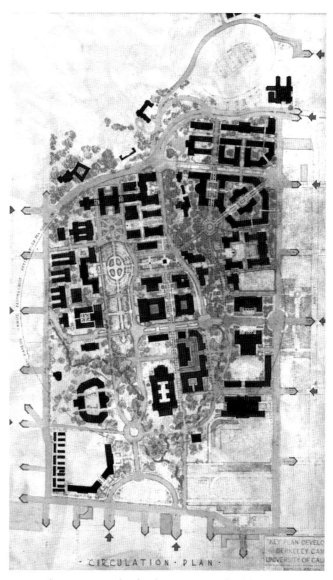

7.28. Arthur Brown Jr., plan for the University of California, Berkeley, c. 1940, circulation plan with footprints of planned new buildings and groups. Brown sought to increase the density of development on the campus while maintaining the open-space corridors along Strawberry Creek. Drawing, Arthur Brown Jr. Collection, Bancroft Library.

baroque of his earlier career and the abstracted functionalism of modernism. Sproul Hall was difficult: Brown had to build for fifty years into the future with the same palette of materials that had given the campus unity while Howard was supervising architect. At the same time, Brown had to acknowledge visually the austerity of the 1940s and work with the materials shortages that had halted most private building altogether and severely slowed most non-defense-related public build-

ing. With the formal declaration of war in December 1941, the task became more difficult. Brown designed and contracted for the interiors himself to ensure that the purpose-built furniture and finish materials would make it to Berkeley. The furniture for the regent's boardroom and President Sproul's office did not prove too difficult to obtain, but the "California blue" carpets were woven just in time, as nearly every carpet mill in America was converted to wartime use.

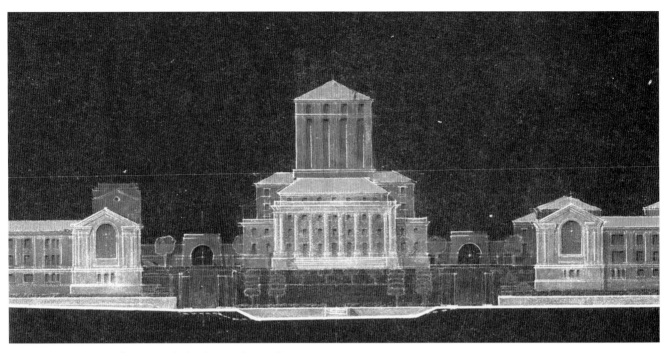

7.29. Arthur Brown Jr., planning study for the completion of Mining Circle, University of California Berkeley Campus, December 1943. Drawing, Arthur Brown Jr. Collection, Bancroft Library.

Brown spent a great deal of time studying the Howard plan. In 1940 and 1941 he drew up proposals for how the campus might look a generation later; he revised these drawings all through the war years. These studies culminated in the official plan of 1944, code-named K-18 (figs. 7.27, 7.28). As Brown saw it, the primary problem with the Howard plan was that it did not provide enough paths and roads through the campus. Brown sought to extend the axis between Doe Library and California Hall beyond Sather Gate to Bancroft Way. He widened Telegraph Avenue into a formal court; this extension was Sproul Plaza (later the staging ground for many political demonstrations). Brown's other interventions were further up the hill. At times in the planning process he proposed that a mathematics building be constructed to the west of Mining Circle, effectively terminating Howard's main axis at the Esplanade (figs. 7.29, 7.30). He also planned a diagonal axis from Sather Tower that would bisect a formal group of buildings in the southeast corner of the campus (later the site of Wurster Hall). The awkward intersection of College Avenue with Bancroft Avenue would be resolved with the introduction of a plaza at their junction. The structures placed along this new diagonal were to be mirrored across College Avenue to create a formal entrance corridor that would define the hillside edge of the campus.

The new four- and five-story buildings were to take their architectural cues from Howard. To Brown, nothing was more important than the maintenance of architectural unity. In a letter to the regents and President Sproul, Brown described his vision for the university:

> It may be safely assumed that the quality of unity dominates all artistic creations and in this case it is apprehended through the composition of space, mass and line. Unity is accentuated and enhanced by order and coherence. Coherence is partly attained by harmony of character, proportion and the discipline of architectural tradition. Full attainment of results worthy of admiration is, moreover, dependent on the innate taste of the Artist and his interpreters.
>
> Specifically, I suggest that the classical spirit already initiated in the most important existing buildings on the Campus (Library, California Hall, Wheeler Hall, etc.) be resolutely maintained for the sake of coherence. This should be simply and intelligently interpreted with sympathetic understanding of the character and possibilities of the classic approach. Appropriate character, homogenous scale, maintenance of the color of the existing granite and concrete walls and the general use of red tile roofs would effectively contribute to coherence.[49]

Here Brown flatly rejected the introduction of modernism into the campus. If unity and permanence are to be valued

7.30. Arthur Brown Jr., planning study for the completion of Mining Circle, University of California Berkeley Campus, December 1943. Drawing, Arthur Brown Jr. Collection, Bancroft Library

above all else, then there is no place for an architecture that has not proven itself over time. On this point, Brown may very well have had George Kelham's Life Sciences Building in mind: its neo-Babylonian ornamental motifs, although fresh at the building's opening, must have appeared very dated by the mid-1940s.

Brown knew the tide was turning against him. As the post-war development program gathered steam, he became unpopular on campus. Those buildings that had been programmed before the war, such as E. Geoffrey Bangs's Lewis Hall, Weihe, Frick & Kruse's Dwinelle Hall, and Miller & Warnecke's Mulford Hall, continued the classicizing proportions, granite-like exterior finishes, and red-tile roofs of pre-war construction. With completely new projects, however, there was considerable pressure to eschew Brown's insistence on monumentality and permanence in favor of modernism, which held the promise of quicker and less expensive building projects. Brown had a particularly difficult time with the departments of Theatre and Music, which were desperate for performance space and not at all sympathetic to Brown's traditional aesthetic sense. Each department wanted an overtly contemporary building, similar to those going up on campuses elsewhere. With a skyrocketing enrollment and fewer real dollars with which to build, Brown's appeal to build for the next century found less and less support.

Brown's greatest ally was Robert Gordon Sproul, who, like Lawrence, was a member of the Bohemian Club and a personal friend. As long as Sproul remained president, it seemed that Brown's agenda would be followed. This thesis was put to the test in the course of siting an addition to Howard's Doe Library, now the home of the Bancroft Library. Brown's greatest challenger on campus design matters throughout most of his tenure at Berkeley was William C. Hays, the chairman of the advisory committee on campus development and building location. Hays was a professor in the Department of Architecture and the designer of Giannini Hall. He wanted the library addition located north of the Doe Library, where there would be little restriction to its expansion. Brown wanted to keep Howard's axis open and preferred the site of North Hall, east of the library. For several years various campus committees studied the problem; then President Sproul created a Special Administrative Committee on University Library Problems. This committee generally favored an underground library, similar to the Gardner Stacks eventually constructed to the plans of Kaplan, McLaughlin & Diaz in the early 1980s. But Brown convinced Sproul and the regents that the North Hall site would ensure the maintenance of the Howard plan for another generation.

7.31. Arthur Brown Jr., Bancroft Library, University of California, Berkeley, 1949. The Bancroft building represents Brown's unornamented classicism in its final state.

7.32 (*opposite*). Arthur Brown Jr., Bancroft Library, University of California, Berkeley, 1949. Photograph by Sylvia Brown Jensen.

Brown's building, completed in 1949, presents an even more abstracted classicism than Sproul Hall, while it scrupulously adheres to the Howard plan (fig. 7.31). With the Bancroft, only the high water table, the quoining at the corners, and the cornice above the second floor define the building's patrimony—all else has been abstracted to the simplest forms possible. Whereas the east facade is simplicity itself, far more architectural interest is generated in the linking devices at the north and south ends of the building. There Brown deftly linked the new addition to Howard's library with connecting pavilions that mediate between the three-story addition and the much larger main library (fig. 7.32). Although there is no public access to the annex from Doe Library today, Brown's links are still the primary means by which students enter the main library.

Brown's victory with the library annex proved to be his last at Berkeley. By 1948, when plans were completed for the building, Brown was nearing his seventy-fifth birthday. The minimalist classicism he offered as a response to modernism seemed quaintly out of touch with the artistic currents of post–World War II America, and his buildings were proving expensive to build. Furthermore, he was constantly at odds with the university's Division of Architects and Engineers over contractual issues and building practices. On May 31, 1948, Brown was relieved of his duties as supervising architect for the university, although he continued to monitor the completion of the Bancroft for the next year.[50] Then William Wurster returned to Berkeley to chair the Department of Architecture and eventually to orchestrate the future development of the campus. It was time for a new generation to build at Berkeley and across California.[51]

8.1. Arthur Brown Jr., in his robes as a member of
the Institut de France. Photo in author's collection.

CONCLUSION

Arthur Brown's last years were not universally happy ones. Throughout the 1940s and 1950s he endured the loss of many of his friends and colleagues, at first due to the war, and later, old age. His own health declined as well, and he grew increasingly frail. As he put it in a letter to William Adams Delano, "My superstructure is gradually crumbling—that is, teeth, sinus and acid resisting plumbing—non-corrosive with regard to alcohol as well as lobster, cucumbers, and other comestibles."[1] Despite slow deterioration, Brown continued to work through the 1940s, and only semiretired at the completion of the Bancroft Library Annex in 1949. He took his last trip to Europe in 1950, when he toured the Romanesque abbeys of southern France and the baroque churches of Rome in the company of his family.

Once back home, Brown took up a number of causes. Professionally, he became active in the National Institute of Arts and Letters and the National Academy of Design—at least when it was time to elect new members or to award gold medals. He worked with a caucus of classically minded designers—Harrie T. Lindberg, Benjamin Wistar Morris, Horace Greenley, and especially Delano—to ensure a fair representation of traditionalists in these institutions. All of these men felt overwhelmed by the forces of the modern movement, which to them seemed a repudiation of all they loved about design. They spilled much ink lamenting the "incomplete" education then offered to aspiring architects in the newly "modernized" schools. The letters between them hold the greatest scorn for those who had been trained in the Beaux-Arts tradition but who had embraced the modern movement. To many, modernism was as much about generational change as architectural theory. Brown often forgot that the careers of those architects born around 1900 had often been postponed, first by the First World War, then by the Great Depression and the Second World War. By the later 1940s, these designers were nearly fifty years old, and most of them had never taken the lead role in a building. To this generation the modern aesthetic was a means of differentiating itself from its forebears.

Brown remained convinced that the formal principles he had learned in Paris were as applicable to twentieth-century building as they had been two millennia earlier, and that it was the job of the architect to apply this ethic of design to new programs, materials, and construction practices. The question for Brown was not whether architects should create an architecture that would respond to modern needs—that was precisely what the architect must do—but rather whether practitioners would continue to value that which made their profession an art as well as a science. In his final article for *The Architect and Engineer* in 1941, entitled, "Is Modern Architecture Really Necessary?" he wrote: "It can be easily shown by a definition and interpretation of what characterizes Architecture in relation to Engineering, that vastly too much weight is given the technical factor. Most of the new materials, so much talked of, are in reality in the nature of improvements on old materials, which do not affect the fundamentals of design. . . . I have felt, personally, that modern progress should be in the effort to eliminate abuses and to cultivate a clearer understanding of those fundamentals that have always guided the traditional current."[2] Although another set of architectural values held sway in Brown's declining years, he would have been heartened to know that his cherished fundamentals were not dead but simply in abeyance.

While Brown had little chance of stemming the tide of the modern movement in America's architectural community, he did feel that the forces of modernity were not completely unstoppable in San Francisco—he joined in several campaigns to limit the wholesale elimination of the city's historic fabric. His first campaign was to save Alfred B. Mullet's mint, a building that he felt was "designed in the excellent spirit of the old Federal buildings."[3] When he learned that Mullet's mint was to be superseded by a new one, he wrote a flurry of letters to his contacts in the Treasury Department, imploring them to consider an adaptive reuse of the building for federal office space, rather than demolishing it. Fortunately, the economic conditions of the Depression delayed demolition until the building was recognized as a landmark.

Brown's more vocal preservation campaign came very late in his life. Just months before his death, at a monthly meeting of the San Francisco chapter of the AIA, he lambasted the plans to build the Central and Embarcadero freeways through the heart of San Francisco. His remarks were picked up by the papers, and soon Brown was a chief spokesman for the anti-freeway movement.[4] The inquiries into Brown's statements were so numerous that eventually he had to have a public relations consultant work up his comments into a press release, which read in part: "Municipal and state authorities are sacrificing much that is good and beautiful in San Francisco in order to construct freeways across various parts of the City. Routes have been selected and designs for the elevated structures ruthlessly approved without regard to the effect, including aesthetics, in the areas where located. For example, the two-decked freeway now being constructed along the Embarcadero will obliterate all of the Ferry Building, except the Tower, and limit development of the potential within the immediate vicinity for years to come."[5] Brown's analysis proved to be correct: once the elevated freeways were constructed, development around them virtually halted. The removal of these unsightly constructions in the aftermath of the Loma Prieta earthquake has reconnected the city to the waterfront and the civic center and opened up many blocks of forgotten urban land to development.

Brown did not live to see the despised freeways constructed. He suffered a massive stroke in May 1957, in Washington, DC, where he was working with the Board of Advisory Architects on the Capitol. His wife arranged to have Brown transported by rail to their San Francisco home, where he lay until a heart attack took his life on July 7. Funeral services were held a few days later at Grace Cathedral, and Brown's body was interred at Cypress Lawn Cemetery when the sarcophagus was ready. Letters of condolence came to Le Verger from around the world as news of Brown's death spread to the scattered *anciens* of the Ecole des Beaux-Arts. Many of these shared William Adams Delano's sentiment that Brown was as beloved a friend as he was a respected colleague. Brown's former partner, John Bakewell, remembered him to Jessamine as "the greatest architect the United States has ever produced."[6]

Arthur Brown was increasingly concerned with his place in the history of American architecture as he grew older. He most wished to be remembered as an architect whose buildings supported the political and cultural life of the region, the nation, and the world. In this respect, he was eminently successful. Some of the most significant events in the history of the twentieth century have occurred within the architectural settings Brown created for the San Francisco Bay Area and for the federal government in Washington. It is ironic that the fissionable isotopes developed in Ernest Lawrence's Cyclotron Building were employed in the bombs that informally ended the Second World War, and that the treaty that formally ended it was signed in another Arthur Brown Jr. building, the War Memorial Opera House. Brown was able to attend many of the events associated with the founding of the United Nations, whose charter was signed at the War Memorial and celebrated under the dome of San Francisco City Hall.[7] A number of the events and organizations associated with the Cold War were also housed in Brown's buildings. NATO's charter was signed in Brown's Labor Auditorium on Consitution Avenue, and much of America's Cold War foreign policy toward the Soviet Union was formulated at the Hoover Institution at Stanford. The Free Speech Movement at Berkeley began on the steps of Brown's Sproul Hall and spread to encompass the student-led protest of the Vietnam War. Ironically, Joseph McCarthy had held a number of hearings of his House Committee on Un-American Activities at Brown's Veterans Building a decade earlier. As dubious as Brown would have thought some of these causes, he would have been pleased to know that his buildings were recognized as seats of collective authority.

Brown had a near-missionary zeal about classical architecture, and he used his considerable charm and skill to persuade doubters of the correctness of the classical taste. With San Francisco City Hall he demonstrated that it was entirely possible to translate the architectural tradition of the renaissance into the twentieth century and to continue this tradition in a "cultural outpost" such as California, just as others were bringing the French building traditions to locales as far-flung as Argentina and Indochina. The continuity with the past is manifest—as David Gebhard remarked, the building "succeeds so far beyond most such 20th-century efforts at Renaissance grandeur that it invites comparison with its models."[8] However, Brown did not ignore the social and environmental conditions in California; he adapted the classical language to these unique conditions. In buildings such as Pasadena City Hall and the Atchison, Topeka, & Santa Fe terminal for San Diego, Brown attempted a synthesis of the Mediterranean architectural tradition that has become part of the Southern California iconography.

Over the course of his career, Brown outgrew the French sources of his education and developed an architectural sensibility that was truly American. His work became bold, strong, and inventive, infused with a scale appropriate to the American nation and yet always controlled in its proportions and detail. The domes of San Francisco and Pasadena City Halls fairly shout the vigor and swagger of Theodore Roosevelt, to whose political philosophy they owe their existence. Yet the reflective mood of the nation in the 1930s is found in Brown's work as well. Toward the end of his career, he began to simplify the detail in his work and to reduce his classical vocabulary to its barest essences: logic, proportion, and repose.

The legacy of an architect is often quantified by the relative fame of his successors, the number of mentions given the designer in the standard survey texts, or in the imitations of the artist's work littering the countryside. In these respects Arthur Brown's legacy would be small indeed. His successor firm, Weihe, Frick & Kruse, formed during World War II, did significant work in the Bay Area, such as the completion of Grace Cathedral in San Francisco, and is known for its monuments at the Pacific National Cemetery on Oahu (the "Punch Bowl"). However, Weihe, Frick & Kruse did not make a national impact and did not carry Brown's aesthetic to a new generation. Brown is rarely mentioned as representative of his generation. There can be few imitations of such unique buildings as San Francisco City Hall or Temple Emanu-El, although Brown's French renaissance houses do have their progeny.

Brown may be better evaluated by the measure of esteem in which he was held by his peers. In his latter years he spent nearly as much time receiving awards and officiating at professional caucuses as he did designing buildings. Once he was installed as an Associé d'Etranger of the French Académie des Beaux-Arts in 1926 (the third American to be so honored), he always had a place in French artistic and intellectual circles.[9] In contrast, many of his American honors came later than might be expected. Brown was not elected as a Fellow in the American Institute of Architects until 1930. Memberships in other national artistic circles came much later; in 1940 he was made a member of the National Institute of Arts and Letters, and in 1953 was finally named a member of the National Academy of Design.

At his death Arthur Brown was one of the more decorated architects in the world, but he was as well known in France

as on the East Coast of the United States. Like many of the last in the unbroken line of American classicists, Brown's art had ceased to be relevant to the architectural community by the advent of World War II, although his buildings remained meaningful to the public they served. Through indifference, the reputations of these traditional American architects suffered well into the 1970s. Unlike those of his fellow classicists, Brown's reputation endured an additional misfortune—the preponderance of his work was on the West Coast, far from the consciousness of the professional tastemakers on the eastern seaboard. Without additional reinforcement from the architectural or scholarly presses, Brown's work quickly faded from memory.

Several of Brown's contemporaries with similar portfolios are today more well known to the architectural cognoscenti, largely due to the interest they have received from the scholarly community. Paul Cret, Auguste Perret, and John Russell Pope attended the Ecole des Beaux-Arts at the same time as Brown, and all conducted their careers within roughly the same time span. Cret, whom Brown befriended in Paris, has been renowned for his abstracted aesthetic since his own time. Likewise, Perret was noted early for his attempts to find an abstracted aesthetic well suited to ferro-concrete construction.[10] Pope is perhaps the closest to Brown in artistic temperament. Both men's work was highly praised in the 1910s and 1920s but called into question in the 1930s. For example, Pope's Jefferson Memorial, completed after his death in 1937 by Eggers & Higgins, was challenged in the architectural and popular press for its traditional vocabulary and formal, monumental qualities.[11] Because his classical architecture was often somber and scrupulously canonical, Pope is sometimes said to be the true heir to Charles Follen McKim.[12] Although Brown did at least receive a generous bequest from McKim, his work often deviates from the expected in inventive ways; at the same time, Brown's architecture always remains within the bounds of the classical tradition.

Brown was considered by most of his contemporaries as the best architectural designer of his generation. Certainly, few architects of the period put more effort into achieving as perfect a building as possible. Brown made many studies of each architectural element, until the perfect proportions and composition were found. Yet more studies were made to fully integrate the element into the whole building. The result of all this work was a fusion of intricately worked-out detail with absolute unity, even in a structure with as many diverse sources as Pasadena City Hall. In this respect, Brown built upon the considerable design skills of his heroes of the preceding generation. The dome at San Francisco City Hall, for example, is much more completely integrated into the rest of the building than McKim's dome at the Rhode Island State Capitol. Likewise, the detailing of a structure such as Temple Emanu-El has far more carefully considered proportions than

Richardson's Brattle Square Church.

Arthur Brown took the knowledge base of traditional American architecture handed down to his generation further than any predecessor. His best works extend the European traditions upon which they are based to another level—his forms are at once canonical, inventive, and distinctly American. Brown truly comprehended Guadet's theory on the use of precedent; he knew how to deftly interpret the forms of an archetype to a wholly new typology, and how to arrange those forms into a beautiful composition in both plan and silhouette. Brown's most memorable compositions are invariably big, because he understood the power of the overscaled motive. Yet he also assumed that the slightest adjustment to a detail could ensure the success of the entire building. In his exploration of the use of concrete in traditional building, Brown has few peers on either side of the Atlantic. Above all, Brown exemplified the fully formed professional architect; he was a gifted artist and a competent builder who also understood the larger social and political meaning of the built environment.

By the 1950s the classical tradition was deemed by most architectural critics to be irrelevant to modern society. To Brown, nothing could be farther from the truth. His education at the Ecole des Beaux-Arts had stressed the need for architecture to facilitate modern life and he fervently believed his work did precisely that. In "Is Modern Architecture Really Necessary?" he wrote: "I have felt, personally, that modern progress should be in the effort to eliminate abuses and cultivate a clearer understanding of those fundamentals that have always guided the traditional current. . . . Is it a valid postulate to assume that Tradition is essentially static? Progress, on the contrary, is one of the avowed aims of the tradition in which I was reared."[13] Brown truly believed that the transformation of American political, social, and material culture he had witnessed in his lifetime was more evolutionary than revolutionary, and that classical architecture should likewise be transformed to meet the demands of modern life; he saw absolutely no contradiction in this. Brown's public buildings emphasized both continuity and the contemporary, and many have become symbols of their respective communities, and by extension, embody the collective values and aspirations of the people. No higher compliment could be paid to him as a progressive classicist.

APPENDIX:
LIST OF WORKS

This catalog assembles key information on Arthur Brown's work both with Bakewell & Brown and as a sole practitioner. It is based on the firms' financial records and the drawing catalog assembled first in the 1930s and finalized during the Second World War. Only completed, built works and a few important competitions are included in this accounting; consultations, minor renovations, funereal memorials, and unbuilt projects are omitted with the exception of a few entries mentioned in the text—these are marked with an asterisk (*). Records for the period 1905–10 are not available, and many residential works from this period cannot be specifically attrib- uted to a given year or location because many drawings for these projects were lent to the owners or to subsequent architects to facilitate renovations; the dates and/or locations of these projects are marked by a question mark. Where a range of dates is given, the first date represents the first known work on the project and the second marks the completion of the building. Nearly all of Brown's built work survives in some form. Projects known to be demolished are marked with a double asterisk (**). If readers have more specific information on a given project than given here, the author invites corrections and elaborations to this listing.

PROJECT NAME	LOCATION	CLIENT NAME	DATES
BAKEWELL & BROWN—1905–27			
Hutchinson Residence	San Francisco	J. S. Hutchinson	1906
Rothermel Residence	San Francisco	Geo. Rothermel	1906
Macdonald House	Oakland	A. D. Macdonald	1907
Perry Residence	Piedmont?	Mrs. L. D. Perry	1907
Price Residence	Burlingame?	Mrs. Hugh Price	1907
Sloat Monument	Monterey		1907
Adams Residence	Oakland?	Lemuel Adams	1908
Braley Grote Building	Oakland		1908
Fireman's Fund Building	San Francisco?		1908
Hammer Residence	Oakland	George Hammer	1908
Mann Hotel	San Francisco?		1908
Martens Residence	Oakland	Frank C. Martens	1908
McKee Residence	Oakland	S. B. McKee	1908
Tucker Residence	Alameda?	M. E. Tucker	1908
Walker Residence	San Francisco?	Talbot Walker	1908
Berkeley City Hall	Berkeley		1907–1909
Beta Theta Pi Fraternity	Berkeley		1909
Campbell Double House	San Francisco?	Donald Campbell	1909
City of Paris Department Store**	San Francisco	Felix Verdier	1909

Bakewell & Brown—1905–27 *continued*

PROJECT NAME	LOCATION	CLIENT NAME	DATES
Leimart Residence	Piedmont?	Walter Leimart	1909
Miller Apartments	San Francisco?	H. M. Miller	1909
Redlands Station	Redlands	AT&SF	1909
Sanburn Residence	San Francisco?	Eliz. Sanburn	1909
Beale (Rosa) Residence	San Francisco	Rosa Beale	1910
Beale (Truxtun) Residence	San Rafael	Marie Beale	1909–1910
Brown (Arthur Sr.) Residence	Oakland	Arthur Brown, Sr	1910
Gallois Building★★	San Francisco	Eugene Gallois	1910
Josselyn Building	San Francisco	Charles Josselyn	1909–1910
Miller (Henry) Residence	Oakland	Henry East Miller	1910
Sacramento Valley Irrigation Co.	Sacramento		1910
Smith Residence	San Francisco?		1910
Touchard Residence	San Francisco?		1910
Waldron Residence	San Francisco?	Mrs. W. Waldron	1910
White Residence	San Francisco?	W. T. White	1910
Ashe Residence		Porter Ashe	1911
Baldwin Commercial Building	San Francisco	Eliz. Baldwin	1911
Beaver Residence	San Francisco?	Anna Beaver	1911
E. M. Pissis Apartments	San Francisco	E. M. Pissis	1911
Horton School	San Francisco?		1911
Sigma Nu Fraternity	Palo Alto		1911
Arnstein Residence	Hillsborough	Walter Arnstein	1912
Lent Residence	San Francisco?	Bessie Lent	1912
Oakland, Antioch & Eastern RR★	Oakland		1912
Pratt Residence	San Francisco?	Orville Pratt	1912–1913
Pratt Warehouse	San Francisco	Orville Pratt	1913
Avenali Residence★★	San Francisco	Mrs. E. Avenali	1914
Edoff Building	San Francisco?	J. D. Edoff	1914
Ellis Hotel & Stores	Oakland	G. & S. Ellis	1913–1914
Ghirardelli Chocolate Pavilion★★	San Francisco		1914
Palace of Horticulture★★	San Francisco	PPIE	1912–1914
Pope Residence★	San Francisco	George Pope	1911–1914
Weill Apartments	San Francisco	Michel Weill	?–1914
Welch's Grape Juice Pavilion★★	San Francisco	PPIE	1914
Miller Apartments	San Francisco	Horace Miller	1915
Pringle Residence	Woodside?	Covington Pringle	1915
Santa Fe Terminus	San Diego	AT&SF	1913–1915
Auzerais Residence	San Francisco	Mrs. L. Auzerais	1915–1916
Burlingame Country Club★★	Hillsborough		1911–1916
Miller (Horace) Residence	Piedmont	Horace Miller	1913–1916
Porter House	Berkeley	Warren Porter	1915–1916
San Francisco City Hall	San Francisco		1912–1916
State Building Competition★	San Francisco		1916
King (Frank) Residence	San Francisco	Frank King	1916–1917
Starr Residence★★	Grass Valley	George W. Starr	1916–1917
Dillman Residence	Oakland?	Charles Dillman	1919
Breeden Residence	Burlingame	E. B. Breeden	1920
Clark Residence	Pebble Beach	Mrs. C. Clark	1917–1920
Fitzhugh Building	San Francisco?	Mrs. W. Fitzhugh	1920
Lakeshore Highlands	Oakland?	Wickham Havens	1920
Meyer Residence	Menlo Park	J. H. Meyer	1920
Mills College Dormatories	Piedmont	Mills College	1918–1920

BAKEWELL & BROWN—1905–27 *continued*

Skewes-Cox Residence	San Francisco		1920–1921
Van Antwerp Residence	Hillsborough		1920–1921
Bakewell Residence	San Francisco	Holly Bakewell	1920–1922
Bourn Residence "Filoli"	Woodside	William B. Bourn	1916–1922
King (Hazel) Residence	Saratoga	Hazel King	1922
Parisian Dye Works**?	San Francisco	William Thomas	1922
Brown (Arthur Jr.) Residence	Hillsborough	Jessamine Brown	1922–1925
Chamberlain Residence	Woodside	S.Chamberlain	1925
Hibernia Bank (22nd & Valencia)	San Francisco	Richard Tobin	1923–1925
Stockton Comm. & Savings Bank	Stockton		1924–1925
YMCA Presidio	San Francisco		1923–1925
Chamberlain Building	San Francisco	S. Chamberlain	1924
Douglas-Everett School	San Francisco		1925–1926
Hibernia Bank (Mission & Norton)	San Francisco	Richard Tobin	1925–1926
Olympic Golf Clubhouse	San Francisco		1923–1926
Pacific Service Building	San Francisco	PG&E	1922–1926
Fuller Residence	San Francisco	Frank Fuller	1925–1927
California Academy of Fine Arts	San Francisco		1924–1928
Coyle Building	San Francisco	S. Chamberlain	1928
Hartford Fire Insurance Co.	San Francisco		1926–1928
Hearst (Phoebe A.) Memorial	San Francisco		1924–1928
Hibernia Bank (Geary & 10th)	San Francisco	Richard Tobin	1927–1928
Hopkins Residence	San Francisco	Timothy Hopkins	1927–1928
Pasadena City Hall	Pasadena		1923–1928
St. Joseph's Hospital Additions	San Francisco		1927–1928
Temple Emanu-El	San Francisco		1923–1928
Heller Residence	San Francisco	Walter S. Heller	1923–1929
Lilly Apartments	San Francisco		1927–1929
Volkman Residence	Hillsborough?	Mrs. D. Volkman	1927–1929
Crocker (Charles) Residence	Pebble Beach	Charles Crocker	1926–1930

ARTHUR BROWN JR. & ASSOCIATES—1928–50

Pacific Stock Exchange Comp.*	San Francisco		1928
Jewish Community Center**	San Francisco		1929–1930
Country School	San Mateo		1929–1931
Scott Residence	Hillsborough?	Lawrence Scott	1929–1931
Blyth Residence		Charles R. Blyth	1932
Coit Tower	San Francisco		1930–1932
War Memorial Opera House	San Francisco		1922–1932
War Memorial Veteran's Building	San Francisco		1923–1932
Century of Progress Exposition**	Chicago		1929–1933
Federal Triangle, Labor–ICC Group	Washington D.C.		1927–1934
St. Mark's Cathedral	Seattle		1928–1934
Bourn Building*	San Francisco	William B. Bourn	1928–1935
Crocker (William) Residence	Woodside	William Crocker	1928–1935
Cypress Lawn Cemetery	Colma		1934–1935
Federal Reserve Board Competition*	Washington D.C.		1935
Bethune Apartments	San Mateo		1935–1936
Federal Building	San Francisco		1930–1936
Oregon State Capitol Competition*	Salem		1936

Arthur Brown Jr. & Associates—1928–50 *continued*

Project Name	Location	Client Name	Dates
Sanctuary of Peace & Beauty*	Marin Co.	Mario Spagna	1936
Hooker Residence	San Francisco?	Osgood Hooker	1936–1938
Golden Gate International Expo.**	San Francisco		1936–1939
De Young Museum Alterations**	San Francisco		1941
Holly Park Housing Project	San Francisco		1938–1941

Stanford University—1913–41

Project Name	Location	Client Name	Dates
583–585 Salvatierra Road	Stanford		1906
612–614 Alvarado Road	Stanford		1908
611–613 Salvatierra Road	Stanford		1908
625–627 Salvatierra Road	Stanford		1909
Gates for Palm Drive	Stanford		1916
Thomas W. Stanford Art Gallery	Stanford		1913–1916
Lane Hospital Alterations	San Francisco		1916–1917
Green Library	Stanford		1916–1919
Burnham Pavilion	Stanford		1920–1921
Nurses' Home	San Francisco		1920–1921
Old Union	Stanford		1913–1921
Encina Hall Dining Commons	Stanford		1916–1922
Golf Club	Stanford		1922
Toyon Hall	Stanford		1921–1922
Branner Hall	Stanford		1922–1923
Children's Convelescent Home	Stanford		1923
Encina Gymnasium**	Stanford		1915–1925
Ryan Laboratories	Stanford		1925
University Hospital Additions	Stanford		1922–1925
Bakewell Hall	Stanford		1927
Carnegie Library	Palo Alto		1928
Loeb Laboratory	Monterey	Jacques Loeb	1925
Carnegie Chemical Lab	Stanford		1928–1929
University Press Shop	Stanford		1929
Roble Gym	Stanford		1931
Lagunita Court	Stanford		1934–1937
Memorial Hall	Stanford		1933–1937
Cubberly Education Building	Stanford		1927–1938
Law Group Proposal*	Stanford		1936–1938
Hoover Institution	Stanford	Herbert Hoover	1927–1941

University of California, Berkeley—1910–49

Project Name	Location	Client Name	Dates
Buckingham & Hecht Building**	San Francisco		1910
Hearst Memorial Bridge	Berkeley		1910
Cowell Hospital**	Berkeley		1928–1930
Classroom Building**	Berkeley		1938–1939
Sproul Hall	Berkeley		1938–1942
Minor Hall	Berkeley		1940–1943
Cyclotron	Berkeley	Ernest Lawrence	1939–1944
Donner Laboratory	Berkeley	Ernest Lawrence	1941–1947
Bancroft Library	Berkeley		1944–1949

NOTES

ABBREVIATIONS USED IN THE NOTES

ABJr   Arthur Brown Junior
ABSr   Arthur Brown Senior
AHHP   Office of Architectural History and Historic Preservation, Smithsonian Institution
BAC   Board of Architectural Consultants
BANC   Bancroft Library, University of California at Berkeley
EDA   Environmental Design Archives
JSAH   Journal of the Society of Architectural Historians
LOC   Library of Congress
PBS   Public Building Service

INTRODUCTION

1. Certainly other American architects were admired for their work, such as Louis Sullivan and Stanford White, but few would have suggested that their personal lives be held up for emulation!

2. See, for example, Henry Hope Reed's assessment of Brown in *The Golden City* (New York: W. W. Norton, 1971).

3. Arthur Drexler, ed., *The Architecture of the Ecole des Beaux-Arts* (New York: MOMA, 1977). Drexler considered the Beaux-Arts "reviled in the first quarter of the century" and thus past its prime by the time Brown attended (1897–1903). The essays concentrate on the work done between 1820 and 1870, the years between the revolt of the neo-Grecs and the completion of Garnier's Opera.

4. Richard Guy Wilson et al., *The American Renaissance 1876–1917* (New York: Brooklyn Museum, 1979).

5. Sally Kress Thomkins, *A Quest for Grandeur* (Washington, DC: Smithsonian Institution Press, 1991); George Guerny, *Sculpture and the Federal Triangle* (Washington, DC: Smithsonian Institution Press, 1985).

6. Richard Guy Wilson, "California Classicist," *Progressive Architecture*, December 1983, 64–71; David Gebhard, "Civic Presence in California's Cities: Where and How?," *Architectural Design* 57: 9/10 (1987): 74–80.

CHAPTER ONE

1. Many biographical details are found in "Death of Arthur Brown, Sr.," *The Architect and Engineer* 49: 1 (April 1917): 100.

2. John Debo Galloway, C.E., *The First Transcontinental Railroad* (New York: Simmons-Boardman, 1950), 90.

3. James McCague, *Moguls and Iron Men: The Story of the First Transcontinental Railroad* (New York: Harper & Row, 1964), 255.

4. McCague, *Moguls*, 203–204.

5. "The New Depot," Oakland *Tribune*, c. 1885. In Arthur Brown Sr. Scrapbook, Private Collection, San Francisco. The Mole was demolished in 1965 to provide a right-of-way for its successor, the Bay Area Rapid Transit District's Trans-Bay Tube.

6. Marriage certificate for Arthur Brown and Victoria A. Runyon, September 28, 1870, Sacramento County, California, Private Collection, San Francisco.

7. Both John Galloway and Oscar Lewis assert that Brown managed the construction of both the Stanford and Crocker houses on Nob Hill. Both houses were burned to the ground in the fire that followed the great earthquake of 1906. Galloway, 91; Lewis, 111–115.

8. This account of the design and construction of the Hotel Del Monte is taken from "The Renaissance of Monterey," San Francisco *Examiner* [?], 1880. In Scrapbook of Arthur Brown Sr., Private Collection, San Francisco.

9. William Henry Bishop, "Southern California," *Harpers Monthly Magazine* 65: 389 (October 1882): 727–728. To Bishop, "Southern California" began at the San Francisco county line!

10. David Gebhard et al., eds., *The Guide to Architecture in Northern California* (Salt Lake City, UT: Perigrine Books, 1973, rev. 1985), 461.

11. Crocker was charged with managing the Central Pacific's operations and was Brown's direct supervisor. Hopkins managed the company's budgetary concerns, so Brown also worked with him in accounting for the construction expenses. For more on the Big Four, see Oscar Lewis's definitive study, *The Big Four* (New York: Knopf, 1938).

12. Brown and Hopkins had traveled to Arizona to improve the latter's health, but Hopkins died in his sleep on March 29, 1878. Brown was the only person immediately present and reported Hopkins's final moments to his family and to the press. "How Mark Hopkins Died," Los Angeles *Herald*, March 30, 1878, in Arthur Brown Sr., Scrapbook, Private Collection, San Francisco.

13. Timothy Hopkins (né Nolan) was born about 1854 to a New England dockworker who subsequently died in San Francisco in

1862. His mother became the Hopkinses' domestic in Sacramento, but upon her remarriage and relocation to St. Louis, Timothy remained with the Hopkinses. In later years Timothy became his father's chief assistant and developed into a brilliant businessman. Upon Mark Hopkins's death, Timothy was formally adopted by his foster-mother, Mary. Over the next four decades, Timothy Hopkins acted as an important director of many charitable enterprises—most importantly for Brown's career, he acted as the chairman of the Board of Trustees at Stanford University from Jane Stanford's death in 1905 into the 1920s. See Lewis, 144–150, and Julia Cooley Altrocchi, *The Spectacular San Franciscans* (New York: Dutton, 1949): 231–232.

14. Travel Diary, May–December, 1889, Private Collection, San Francisco.

15. Brother Fidelis Cornelius, *William Keith: Old Master of California* (New York: Putnam 1942), 86. Photographs of the living room of the Brown's home in Oakland show several of these large canvases. Most of the family's collection of Keiths were loaned to Stanford University, where they inadvertently became part of that institution's permanent collection. One painting of Mt. Shasta, however, has remained in the family.

16. Cornelius, 535.

17. Richard Longstreth, *On the Edge of the World: Four Architects in San Francisco at the Turn of the Century* (New York: Architectural History Foundation, 1983), 273–275 and n. 28, p. 398. Edward R. Bosley, "A. C. Schweinfurth," *Toward a Simpler Way of Life: The Arts and Crafts Architects of California*, Robert Winter, ed. (Berkeley: University of California Press, 1997), 12–13.

18. Longstreth, n. 28, p. 398, and Bosley, "A. C. Schweinfurth," 21–32.

19. Brother Cornelius, 309.

20. Dimitri Shipounoff, "Introduction," *The Simple Home*, Charles Keeler (Santa Barbara: Peregrine Smith, 1979): xix, xxvii.

21. *Blue and Gold* 20 (1894). Because Keeler left Berkeley in 1893, he was listed as *Fratres in Urbe* from 1894 on, but still acted as the chapter's representative in legal and administrative affairs.

22. Richard Longstreth, *On the Edge of the World*, 158–159. Bakewell and Brown created an addition to the house in 1908.

23. *Blue and Gold*, 20 (1894): 39.

24. In March 1882 Maybeck passed the entrance examinations and enrolled formally in the school and into the Atelier André. Sally B. Woodbridge, *Bernard Maybeck: Visionary Architect* (New York: Abbeville Press, 1992).

25. During his stay in Paris, he spent much of his time studying the Romanesque and early Gothic monuments, and, thoroughly familiar with Ruskin, contemplating the possibility of medieval architecture as a source for modern architectural design.

26. Richard Chafee, "The Teaching of Architecture at the Ecole des Beaux-Arts," *The Architecture of the Ecole des Beaux-Arts*, Arthur Drexler, ed. (New York: MOMA, 1977), 65.

27. The number of students accepted to the school continued to increase up to the First World War and reached its peak at about 120 students. Julien Guadet, "L'enseignement de l'Architecture en France," *The Architectural Review* XIV: 82 (September 1903): 136–143.

28. Chafee, 83–84.

29. Egbert, Donald Drew. *The Beaux-Arts Tradition in French Architecture: Illustrated by the Grands Prix de Rome* (Princeton, NJ: Princeton University Press, 1980), appendix.

30. Guadet, "L'enseignement de l'Architecture en France."

31. A fine example of this sort of memoire is by Charles Collens, "The Beaux-Arts in 1900," *Journal of the AIA* 7: 2–4 (February–April, 1947).

32. Charles Collens, "The Beaux-Arts in 1900: Part I," *Journal of the AIA*, 7: 2 (February 1947): 82.

33. "Le Football Américain à Paris," *Le Temps* [Paris], November 27, 1897.

34. Aaron Betsky, *James Gamble Rogers and the Architecture of Pragmatism* (New York: Architectural History Foundation, 1994) 11.

35. James Gamble Rodgers, for example, had worked for Burnham and Root.

36. Brown's mother made sure no other foreign institution would have her son's affections; she refused Arthur's pleas to visit Oxford and Cambridge several weeks later when touring Britain. Arthur Brown Jr., Travel Diary, September 10 and 20, 1889.

37. Sara Holmes Boutelle, *Julia Morgan, Architect* (New York: Abbeville Press, 1988), 24.

38. Mrs. Brown reports on her work for Morgan with a great deal of pride in writing to her husband back in Oakland. She visited with Morgan as she opened her office in 1903 and was clearly living vicariously through her friends' talented daughter. Victoria Runyon Brown to Arthur Brown Sr., 1901–1902, Private Collection, San Francisco.

39. Bakewell had graduated from the University of California in 1893 with Loring Rixford. Both had been distinguished officers in the university's ROTC unit and were commissioned as officers in the United States Army, Bakewell as a first lieutenant and Rixford as a lieutenant colonel. Both served several years in the service before attending the Ecole. Corbett graduated from Cal in 1895 and went straight to Paris.

40. Details of Brown's career at the Ecole were summarized from Brown's transcript by Richard Chaffee in the 1970s; photocopies of these notes and of the transcript were sent to the author by Mr. Chaffee in 1997. The original *Feuilles de Valeurs* are now at the Archives Nationales, vol. AJ-52-402. Brown's student number was 4904.

41. "Concours á l'École des Beaux-Arts," *La Construction Moderne*, August 21, 1897, 564. Ecole des Beaux-Arts, *Feuilles des Valuers*, Arthur Brown Jr.

42. Musée d'Orsay, *Victor Laloux, l'Architecte de Gare d'Orsay* (Paris: Ministre de la Culture et de la Communication, 1987), 6.

43. Musée d'Orsay, *Victor Laloux*, 8.

44. "Hommage à Laloux," *Pencil Points* 18: 8 (October, 1937): 621–630.

45. Richard Chaffee, "Victor Laloux," *The AIA Gold Medal*, Richard Guy Wilson (New York: McGraw-Hill, 1984), 148–149.

46. Musée d'Orsay, *Victor Laloux*, 66, 70–71.

47. Chaffee, "Victor Laloux."

48. In fact, because his own robe did not arrive in time, Brown wore Laloux's robe for his induction ceremony.

49. "Hommage à Laloux."

50. Woodbridge, 77.

51. Brother Cornelius, 316.

52. See design drawings for this work reproduced in Musée d'Orsay, *Victor Laloux*, 46–47.

53. Cartoons and semifinished renderings of this project form part of an uncataloged collection of Brown drawings from the Ecole period at the Bancroft Library.

54. Brown told his daughters that he had the honor of carrying the funereal wreath from the École's American student body at Garnier's funeral procession in 1898. I have not been able to independently verify this assertion.

55. Brown and his mother both wrote detailed accounts of the Prix Godeboeuf situation in letters to Arthur Brown Sr., dated between December 20, 1900, and mid-January 1901. These letters are still in the possession of the Brown family.

56. Ecole des Beaux-Arts, *Feuille de Valuers*.

57. Brown discusses his thesis project in several letters to his father, dated between March and June 1901. These letters are still held by the family in San Francisco.

58. Colin Rowe, *As I Was Saying: Recollections and Miscellaneous Essays*, v. 1 (Cambridge, MA: MIT Press, 1996), 8.

59. Letter from Edward H. Bennett, Rome, to Phoebe Apperson Hearst, Pleasanton, April 20, 1902. In the Papers of Phoebe Apperson Hearst, MSS 85/3c, "Miscellaneous Correspondence," Bancroft Library. The trio arrived in Constantinople in mid-May. Brown's visas into Greece and Turkey are now also part of the Bancroft Collection.

60. For more on Brown's knowledge of the baroque see Rowe, 4–10. When Rowe writes of Brown as being in Gromort's atelier, he is, of course, mistaken. Brown and Gromort were contemporaries at the Ecole and retained a friendship well into their days as members of the Academie des Beaux-Arts.

61. Arthur Brown Jr. to Arthur Brown Sr., November 29, 1901. Letter in Private Collection, San Francisco.

62. The S.A.D.G. medal is still with the Brown family. A formal dinner was given in Brown's honor in December 1902, at which he was presented to all of the architectural members of the Academie des Beaux-Arts. Twenty-four years later, he was elected to join this august body as an Membre Etranger.

CHAPTER TWO

1. Brown had also been offered John Van Pelt's teaching position at Cornell, which he likewise turned down. Letters from Arthur Brown Jr. to Victoria Runyon Brown, May 3, 1904, ABJr Papers, Private Collection.

2. Letter from Arthur Brown Jr. to Arthur Brown Sr., July 31, 1904, ABJr Papers, Private Collection.

3. Schulze was first listed as a draftsman in the Oakland Bay Area directory in the late 1870s, and may have worked for Arthur Brown Sr. at some time in the 1870s and 1880s. Biographical information on Schulze is found in "Folger Building Listed on Register," San Francisco *Heritage Newsletter* 24: 5 (September/ October 1996): 5, 7. "The Folger House is documented in Michael R. Corbett's Nomination of the Folger Estate Stable Historic District to the National Register of Historic Places," 2004.

4. Brown's involvement with the Burnham plan is described in more detail in Chapter Three.

5. Gordon Thomas and Max Morgan Witts, *The San Francisco Earthquake* (New York: Stein & Day, 1971), 68–69, 271.

6. Cynthia Barwick Malinick, "*The Lives and Works of the Reid Brothers, Architects: 1852–1943*," MA Thesis, University of San Diego, 1992, 1–2.

7. Withey, *Biographical Dictionary*, 500.

8. Withey, *Biographical Dictionary*, 477–478.

9. Bakewell & Brown's early work was featured in a photo essay published as "Some of the Work of Bakewell & Brown, Architects," *The Architect and Engineer* 16: 1 (February 1909): 34–43.

10. Pergolas became such a characteristic of these early houses that the Hammer House and the F. C. Martens House were featured in an article on pergolas, published in *The Architect and Engineer* 20: 2 (March 1910): 37–43.

11. Roger Olmsted and T. H. Watkins's *Here Today: San Francisco's Architectural Heritage* (San Francisco: Chronicle Books, 1969) lists the Hutchinson House as having been constructed in 1905 but designed by Bakewell & Brown. Given that the terrace itself was not laid out until 1905, and Bakewell & Brown did not exist until very late in the year, it is far more likely that the house was begun in late 1905 and completed in 1906. *Here Today*, sponsored by the Junior League of San Francisco, was the first survey of historic San Francisco Bay Area architecture, covering San Francisco, Marin, and San Mateo Counties.

12. "Cornerstone of Berkeley's New Town Hall Laid with Fitting Ceremonies," Oakland *Enquirer*, June 27, 1908.

13. Ransome's work is briefly described in Michael R. Corbett's *Splendid Survivors*, 57.

14. Hennebique's system is described in every history of modern architecture. See, for example, Kenneth Frampton's *Modern Architecture: A Critical History* (London: Thames & Hudson, 1980), 38–39.

15. "Cornerstone," Oakland *Enquirer*.

16. A drawing titled "Front Elevation," dated October 1, 1907, not only illustrates the tower back in place, but lists Bakewell & Brown's new address on Montgomery Street. Although this drawing is not known to have survived, it was photographed for the firm in 1907, and the glass negatives now reside in the Arthur Brown Jr. Collection, BANC.

17. "The City of Paris Dry Goods Company Building," San Francisco *News Letter*, August 7, 1909; "City of Paris Back in Its Former Home," San Francisco *Chronicle*, July 22, 1909.

18. The decoration for the City of Paris, the Palace of Horticulture, and San Francisco City Hall are all largely the work of Brown's closest friend from Paris, Jean-Louis Bourgeois.

19. "City of Paris Back in Its Former Home," San Francisco *Chronicle*, July 22, 1909.

20. "The City of Paris Dry Goods Company Building," San Francisco *News Letter*, August 7, 1909, pasted into scrapbook, ABJr. Papers, Private Collection.

21. Neiman-Marcus bought the building in 1974. Preservationists attempted to have the building declared a city landmark at that time, but were thwarted by the city council, despite the landmark board's decision to designate the building. Activists then succeeded in listing the building on the National Register of Historic Places and as a California State Historic Landmark. "City of Paris Battle: Not Quiet on the Western Front," San Francisco *Examiner*, November 13, 1978.

22. Gerald Adams, "City of Paris Loss Triggers Backer's Tempers," San Francisco *Examiner*, January 12, 1979.

23. Gerald Adams, "City Planning Rules for City of Paris Building," San Francisco *Examiner*, December 22, 1978.

24. "Philip Johnson: Architecture or Sentiment?" *Preservation News*, April 1978, 12 ff.

25. Gray Brechin, *Imperial San Francisco: Urban Power, Earthly Ruin* (Berkeley: University of California Press, 1999), 93–96.

26. "Ingold Gets 40 Acres," San Francisco *Examiner*, May 12, 1954.

27. "Some of the Work of Bakewell & Brown, Architects," *The Architect and Engineer* 16: 1 (February 1909): 34–43.

28. "Competition for San Francisco Sub-Treasury Building," *The Architect and Engineer* 25: 2 (June 1911): 39–47.

29. "The City Hall Farce Competition," editorial, Oakland *Tribune*, April 18, 1910.

30. See "Result of Oakland City Hall Competition," *The Architect and Engineer* 21: 2 (June 1910): 48–49; "Judges Award First Prize of $10,000 to New York Architects," San Francisco *Chronicle*, June 23, 1910.

31. "Gotham Firm Receives Prize for City Hall," Oakland *Tribune*, June 23, 1910.

32. Ben Macomber, *The Jewel City: Its Planning and Achievement; Its Architecture, Sculpture, Symbolism, and Music; Its Gardens, Palaces, and Exhibits* (San Francisco: John H. Williams, 1915), 12–13. Macomber's guidebook to the exposition encapsulates the history of the event very well.

33. Macomber, *Jewel City*, 13.

34. Polk was deposed as chair shortly after the first meetings of the board; George Kelham replaced him as chair for the remainder of the exhibition.

35. Ben Macomber, *Jewel City*, 13–14.

36. Kenneth H. Cardwell, *Bernard Maybeck: Artisan, Architect, Artist* (Santa Barbara: Peregrine Smith, 1977), 141.

37. The design chronology of the architectural commission's work is recounted in Louis C. Mullgardt, "The Panama-Pacific Exposition at San Francisco," *The Architect and Engineer* 37: 3 (March 1915): 193–197. Preliminary plans were published as "An Early Glimpse of the Panama-Pacific Exposition Architecturally," *The Architect and Engineer* 30: (October 1912): 48–55.

38. Polk, "The Panama-Pacific Plan," 489.

39. William Woollett, "Color in Architecture at the Panama-Pacific Exposition," *Architectural Record* 45: 5 (May 1915): 437 ff.

40. W. D'Arcy Ryan, "Illumination of the Exposition," *California's Magazine*, Cornerstone Issue (1915): 317–320, and "Illuminations of the Panama-Pacific International Exposition," *Journal of the American Institute of Electrical Engineers* 25 (1916): 757–783.

41. Quoted in Louis Christian Mullgardt, *The Architecture and Landscape Gardening of the Exposition* (San Francisco: Paul Elder, 1915), 28.

42. Although no correspondence from the Redlands project remains, the letters from Storey to Brown regarding the San Diego terminal from 1913 to 1914 are exceedingly warm and always remember Arthur Brown Sr. See W. B. Story to Arthur Brown Jr. January 15, 1914, BANC.

43. City of Redlands, AT&SF Railroad Station, Redlands, California—Historic Resources Inventory, Department of Parks and Recreation, State of California, March 4, 1977.

44. John Bakewell Jr., "The Santa Fe Station, San Diego," *The Architect and Engineer* 41: 1 (April 1915): 40–46.

45. These drawings are not dated, but other material in the same set of drawings indicates that Bakewell & Brown was involved with the project by May 1916. The plans for the large version were abandoned in 1917, with American involvement in World War I. At that time, the garden was moved up the hill to the house. The drawing now resides in the ABJr Papers, BANC.

46. Polk either quit the job or was outright fired. Arthur Brown, as close friend to both Bourn and Polk, acted as intermediary and agreed to finish the work. The original drawings for Filoli were in Bakewell & Brown's papers, and electrical drawings modified by Bakewell & Brown demonstrate that they were involved with the construction from at least halfway through.

47. The Avenali House, at the top of Green Street, was demolished in the 1960s to clear a site for one of Russian Hill's residential towers.

48. Although he received many offers of employment, Weihe returned to San Francisco to work for Bakewell & Brown. Ernest Weihe to Arthur Brown Jr., February 12, 1923, BANC.

49. Frick was inducted into the U. S. Army and served until 1919, when he rematriculated into the school directly from the battlefield.

50. Preston Ames wrote many letters to Brown while in Paris. He later became Art Director Cedric Gibbon's chief assistant, eventually receiving set design credits for *An American in Paris* and *Gigi*.

51. A long series of letters from H. Langford Warren, professor of architecture, and A. Lawrence Lowell, president of Harvard University, to Brown in 1914 and 1915 survive and confirm Harvard's intense desire to hire Brown as an academic. However, Brown did not wish to give up the practice with Bakewell he had worked so long to establish. All of this correspondence is within the ABJr. Papers, BANC. For a richer discussion of Harvard's search for the right leadership, see Anthony Alofsin's *The Struggle for Modernism: Architecture, Landscape Architecture and City Planning at Harvard* (New York: W. W. Norton, 2002).

52. Brown was even deprived of his library of architectural books, which had been shipped in February and finally arrived the day Brown left Cambridge in May.

53. "Californians in Architecture and Landscape Architecture," *California Monthly*, November 1945 (University of California Alumni Association magazine): 8–11. Although it would be fascinating to know how well Brown and Wurster worked together, no records from Brown's tenure at Berkeley have been located.

CHAPTER THREE

1. Herb Caen, "Gloomy Sunday," San Francisco *Examiner*, October 28, 1952.

2. Contemporary historians have examined the social and political implications of the enterprise as well. See Judd Kahn, *Imperial San Francisco: Politics and Planning in an American City, 1897–1906* (Lincoln: University of Nebraska Press, 1979); Joan Elaine Draper, "The San Francisco Civic Center: Architecture, Planning, and Politics", Ph. D. dissertation, University of California, Berkeley, 1979.

3. Roger Olmstead and T. H. Watkins, *Here Today: San Francisco's Architectural Heritage* (San Francisco: Chronicle Books, 1968), 66–69.

4. Kahn, 68–69.

5. Kahn, 40.

6. *San Francisco Bulletin*, January 7, 1904. Reprinted in Mel Scott, *The San Francisco Bay Area: A Metropolis in Perspective* (Berkeley, University of California Press, 1959), 97–98.

7. Kahn, 81–82.

8. Richard Longstreth, *On the Edge of the World*, 299–300.

9. Daniel H. Burnham and Edward H. Bennett, *Report on a Plan For San Francisco* (San Francisco: Sunset Press, 1905), 211. Reprint: San Francisco: Urban Books, 1971.

10. In an article reviewing the plan for *The Architect and Engineer*, Brown hailed many aspects of the plan, including the civic center, but singled out the amphitheatre for particular emphasis and illustration (Arthur Brown Jr., "The Burnham Plan," *The Architect and Engineer* 29: 3 (September 1905): 29–31).

11. Daniel H. Burnham and Edward H. Bennett, *Report*, 36–37.

12. B. J. S. Cahill, "Adventurings in the Monumental," *The Architect and Engineer* 54: 2 (August 1918): 41–96.

13. Kahn, 108.

14. Gerstle Mack, *1906: Surviving San Francisco's Great Earthquake and Fire* (San Francisco: Chronicle Books, 1981), 49.

15. Sally Woodbridge, *California Architecture: Historic American Buildings Survey* (San Francisco: Chronicle Books, 1988), 76–77.

16. Kevin Starr, *Inventing the Dream: California through the Progressive Era* (New York: Oxford University Press, 1985), 199–203.

17. George E. Mowry, *The California Progressives* (New York: New York Times Book Co., 1963): 129–32. The best account of the San Francisco graft prosecutions is Walton Bean's *Boss Ruef's San Francisco: The Story of the Union Labor Party, Big Business, and the Graft Prosecution* (Berkeley: University of California Press, 1952).

18. For details of the Ruef prosecution, see the San Francisco *Call*, May 16, 1907, November 14, 1908, and December 11, 1908, and Bean's *Boss Ruef*.

19. James Rolph Jr., "Mayor's Inaugural Address," January 8, 1916, *San Francisco Municipal Reports—1915–1916* (San Francisco: City of San Francisco, 1918), 972–976.

20. "Rolph Asks Architects for Civic Center Ideas," San Francisco *Examiner*, c. December, 1911 (ABJr Scrapbook, Private Collection, San Francisco).

21. Journal Resolution 8, San Francisco Board of Supervisors, January 29, 1912, *San Francisco Municipal Reports—1915–1916* (San Francisco: City of San Francisco, 1918), 980.

22. Journal Resolutions 39 & 40, San Francisco Board of Supervisors, January 29, 1912, *San Francisco Municipal Reports—1915–1916*, (San Francisco: City of San Francisco, 1918), 980–981.

23. Reid was presumably placed on the board to act as the mayor's representative in the planning process, because the civic center was the linchpin of the early Rolph administrations. He would become San Francisco City Architect and would design many schools, libraries, and other civic buildings throughout Rolph's twenty-year long administration.

24. B. J. S. Cahill, "Adventurings in the Monumental," *The Architect and Engineer* 54: 2 (August 1918): 41–96.

25. Specifically, the vote tallied 45,133 votes in favor of the bond issue, 4,035 against. Representative of the press on the election is "Great Vote for Bond Issue," and "Women Electors Early at Polls," San Francisco *Call*, March 29, 1912.

26. "Eleven to One Bond Majority a Credit to the City," San Francisco *Call*, March 29, 1912.

27. "City Architectural Bureau Reorganized for Civic Center," San Francisco *Examiner*, March 29, 1912.

28. These estimates were based on a detailed survey of departmental needs made by Newton J. Tharp, the city architect from 1906 until his untimely death in 1909. Tharp is best known for his Hall of Justice south of Market ("Death of Newton J. Tharp," *The Architect and Engineer* 17: 2 [June 1909]: 110).

29. Consulting Architects, "Program of the Competition for the Selection of an Architect for the City Hall, San Francisco, California," Board of Public Works, City of San Francisco, April 6, 1912.

30. Architectural Consultants, "The Proposed Schemes for Civic Center," Board of Public Works, City of San Francisco, May 15, 1912, BANC; "Architects make Report on Civic Center," San Francisco *Call*, May 29, 1912.

31. Many of the prize-winning designs were pictured in the July 1912 edition of *The Architect and Engineer*.

32. The jury was composed of the three consulting architects, Commissioner of Public Works Daniel C. Fraser, Supervisor Paul Bancroft, President of the American Institute of Architects Walter Cook, and Mayor Rolph. See Jury, San Francisco City Hall Competition, "Judgment of the Competition for the Selection of an Architect for the City Hall," June 20, 1912; unpublished manuscript, City of San Francisco Archives.

33. "Plans for New City Hall Are Decided Upon," San Francisco *Call*, June 21, 1912.

34. B. J. S. Cahill, "The San Francisco City Hall Competition," *The Architect and Engineer* 29: 3 (July 1912), 53–78.

35. "Drawing of Large Domed Building," 1911, Arthur Brown Jr. Collection (uncatalogued), Prints and Photographs Division, Library of Congress.

36. Sketches of designs for San Francisco City Hall, c. March, 1912, BANC. The letter, from Brown's automobile insurance agent, is dated March 13, 1912, a week before the bond election. Although the sketches date from some time after this date, I believe them to be the earliest surviving drawings for the new city hall.

37. John Bakewell Jr., "The San Francisco City Hall Competition: How the Successful Architects Arrived at Their Solution," *The Architect and Engineer* 29: 3 (July 1912): 46–53. Note that the capitalization and punctuation of this excerpt are Bakewell's.

38. B. J. S. Cahill, "The San Francisco City Hall Competition."

39. B. J. S. Cahill, "The San Francisco City Hall Competition."

40. The form of the circular lantern in the model, too, is quite similar to Laloux's design, further indicating that this drawing was influential in the decision to enlarge the diameter of the dome.

41. Brown used the term "flow" in just this sense when discussing the dome and east portico of the United States Capitol Building in 1957.

42. "Report of the Civic Center Committee," San Francisco chapter, American Institute of Architects, March 1913; the only known copy of this document is listed as call number EvD NA4227 S4 .A6, California Historical Society Archives, San Francisco.

43. "Technicality Delays Contract with Architects," San Francisco *Examiner*, September 24, 1912. Bakewell & Brown were not confirmed as the superintendents of the construction phase of the project until April 28, 1913 [PR 10136, San Francisco Board of Supervisors].

44. George Wagner, interview by Bea Sebastian, March 13, 1978, transcript, Collection of the Friends of the San Francisco Library, San Francisco, 2–4.

45. Gould's close involvement with the development of the working drawings is documented in Bakewell & Brown's office log for the project. See Job Log #3 (1917–1920), Mss 1973.100.3, John Bakewell Jr. Collection, BANC.

46. Job Book #3, January 13, 1913.

47. Christopher H. Snyder, "Some of the Engineering Features of the San Francisco City Hall," *The Architect and Engineer* 46: 2 (August 1916): 79–80.

48. The recent retrofitting project strengthened the seismic resistance of the building by rebuilding the interior walls of the light courts with reinforced concrete shear walls and over six hundred base-isolated footings.

49. "City Hall Excavating Officially Begins," San Francisco *Call*, April 6, 1913.

50. Wagner, 11.

51. Wagner, 13.

52. "Editorial: Who Is It That Tries to Black Eye Our Home Industry?," San Francisco *Call*, February 8, 1913.

53. Descriptions of all of the major sculptural groups can be found in Michael R. Corbett, "National Register of Historic Places Nomination Form: San Francisco Civic Center," National Parks Service, Department of the Interior, 1976. This nomination was sponsored by the Foundation for San Francisco's Architectural Heritage.

54. "The Contractors Who Built the San Francisco City Hall," *The Architect and Engineer* 46: 2 (August 1916): 85. These foundries and most of the other suppliers of the specialty equipment for the building were local concerns.

55. "Magnificent New City Hall Is Dedicated: Mayor Rolph Moves into Fine New Office," San Francisco *Chronicle*, December 29, 1912.

56. Arthur Brown Jr., dedicatory speech at San Francisco City Hall, December 28, 1912, San Francisco (typescript in BANC).

57. Wagner, 17.

58. B. J. S. Cahill, "The New City Hall, San Francisco," *The Architect and Engineer* 46: 2 (August 1916): 38–77.

59. Cahill, "The New City Hall."

60. William L. Woollett, "Criticism of the San Francisco City Hall," *The Architect and Engineer* 46: 3 (September 1915): 70–71.

61. J. C. Branner, "The San Francisco City Hall," *The Architect and Engineer* 46: 2 (August 1916): 77.

62. Corbett, "San Francisco Civic Center," 18.

63. Willis Polk sent a letter to the governor and wrote newspaper articles voicing his and others' concerns about the intended design

(Willis Polk, "Civic Center Buildings Compared," *San Francisco Chronicle*, March 9, 1917). Brown, for his part, never forgave Faville for refusing to alter his design.

64. Corbett, "San Francisco Civic Center," 18.

65. Heiman's designs for the Public Health Building met with opposition from the architectural control board set up to ensure that buildings on the civic center would conform to the plan. Brown was head of the board at that time and required that Heiman submit his elevations to the critique of the board; the board then essentially designed the elevations for him (letters between Samuel Heiman and Arthur Brown Jr., 1929–30, BANC).

66. Resolution 10235, San Francisco Board of Supervisors, June 15, 1913, *San Francisco Municipal Reports—1915–1916* (San Francisco: City of San Francisco, 1918), 1003.

67. Corbett, "San Francisco Civic Center," 21.

68. The commission included Bernard Maybeck, John Galen Howard, Willis Polk, Ernest Coxhead, G. Albert Lansburgh, John Reid Jr., Frederick Meyer, and Arthur Brown. James Rolph Jr., *History of the San Francisco War Memorial* (San Francisco: City and County of San Francisco, 1930): 4.

69. Rolph, *History of the San Francisco War Memorial*, 6.

70. This bond was sent to the voters by resolution of the Board of Supervisors in early May, and passed by the electorate on June 14, 1927 (Rolph, *History of the San Francisco War Memorial*, 7–13).

71. Proposal for "Staffing the Office of the War Memorial," Alexander Wagstaff to John S. Drum, March 27, 1928; BANC.

72. Arthur Brown Jr. and G. Albert Lansburgh, "Report of Architects on the Estimate for the War Memorial," August 23, 1927, submitted to the Board of Trustees, San Francisco War Memorial; ABJr Papers, BANC. The substitution of terra cotta for granite saved almost $700,000 alone. Brown calculated the savings resulting from the reduction in the width of the buildings (naturally on both the north and south elevations) to over $500,000.

73. The meetings took place in July and September, 1927, and again in March and September 1928. These events are described in a letter from Alexander Wagstaff, San Francisco, to Arthur Brown Jr., San Francisco, November 7, 1929; BANC.

74. The total space in the 1923 program was 44,000 square feet, whereas the 1928 plans allotted over 108,000 square feet for the veterans' use. Alexander Wagstaff, San Francisco, to Supervisor Edward Rainey, San Francisco, November 20, 1928; BANC.

75. Memo from Mr. Otts, representing the Advisory Board of Veterans War Memorial Committee, San Francisco, to Arthur Brown Jr., San Francisco, February 28, 1928; BANC.

76. "Report of the Advisory Board of Veterans War Memorial Committee," March 20, 1929. Reprinted in Rolph, *History of the San Francisco War Memorial*, 66–69. Presumably the similar entrances across the street at San Francisco City Hall do not have this objectionable subterranean quality.

77. Arthur Upham Pope, San Mateo, to John S. Drum, San Francisco, November 7, 1927; BANC.

78. Upon meeting with Knudsen, Pope wrote Drum a report strongly urging the adoption of a two-gallery seating scheme. Knudson issued his formal report on several proposed designs in February 1929 and likewise advocated that the two-gallery schemes be given further study. Arthur Upham Pope, San Mateo, to John S. Drum, San Francisco, December 28, 1927; Vern O. Knudsen, "Report on the War Memorial Opera House," February 2, 1928; BANC.

79. Arthur Upham Pope, San Mateo, to Arthur Brown Jr., San Francisco, March 12, 1928; BANC. Swan graduated from MIT in physics in 1899 and received his doctorate from Harvard in 1908. He worked for Wallace Sabine from 1911 until Sabine's death in 1919.

80. Clifford M. Swan, San Francisco, to John S. Drum, San Francisco, May 1, 1928; BANC.

81. Brown wrote to Clifford Swan, "I am even more convinced after listening to the present season of Opera that even 3500 is much too large." Arthur Brown Jr. San Francisco, to Clifford M. Swan, New York, October 4, 1928; BANC.

82. Arthur Upham Pope, Chicago, to Arthur Brown Jr., San Francisco, October 5, 1928; Arthur Upham Pope, New York, to William H. Crocker, San Francisco, October 9, 1928; BANC.

83. Arthur Upham Pope, San Mateo, to John S. Drum, San Francisco, January 24, 1927, and February 12, 1928; BANC.

84. Christopher H. Snyder, "Structural Features of the San Francisco Opera House," *The Architect and Engineer* 111: 2 (November 1932): 43.

85. Dariel Fitzkee, "Opera House Stage Largest in America," *The Architect and Engineer* 111: 2 (November 1932): 45–46.

86. Arthur Upham Pope, San Mateo, to John S. Drum, San Francisco, August 1, 1928; BANC.

87. Arthur Upham Pope, San Mateo, to G. Albert Lansburgh, San Francisco, August 6, 1928; transcript by Rollin Jensen, original in BANC.

88. Richard M. Tobin, speech at the cornerstone ceremony for the San Francisco War Memorial, November 11, 1931; bound typescript presented to Arthur Brown Jr. BANC.

89. Such a facility was planned on this block at the same time the State Building was in competition. However, a federal building moratorium between the First World War and 1925 delayed work on the project. In March 1927, $2,500,000 was appropriated for the federal building, and the following year the city donated the site. Corbett, "San Francisco Civic Center," 24.

90. Corbett, "San Francisco Civic Center," 24.

91. David Gebhard et al. *The Guide to Architecture in San Francisco and Northern California* (Salt Lake City, UT: Peregrine Smith, 1985): 86–87.

CHAPTER FOUR

1. Harris Allen, "Three Country Houses by Bakewell & Brown," *The Building Review* 21: 1 (January 1922): 1–6.

2. For a discussion of the Hallidie Building and its precursors, see Michael Corbett, *Splendid Survivors* (San Francisco: Foundation for San Francisco's Architectural Heritage, 1979), 170.

3. The Chamberlain Building is illustrated and briefly described in Corbett's *Splendid Survivors*, 156.

4. The most detailed account of the competition is Katherine Solomonson's *The Chicago Tribune Tower Competition: Skyscraper Design and Cultural Change in the 1920s* (Cambridge: Cambridge University Press, 2001).

5. See Sullivan's 1896 essay, "The Tall Building Artistically Considered," first published in *Lippincott's Magazine*, but republished frequently and available in any collection of his writings. Sullivan actually identifies five subdivisions of the building, because he includes a mezzanine and the basement, but neither element was frequently expressed as an independent entity in most work.

6. Solomonson, *Chicago Tribune*, 172–195.

7. Frank M. Harris, "Pacific Service to Have New Home," *Pacific Service Magazine* 11: 6 (November 1922): 170–174.

8. Irving F. Morrow, "Recent San Francisco Skyscrapers," *The Architect and Engineer* 85: 2 (November 1923): 50–58.

9. John Bakewell Jr., "Architectural Treatment of the Building," *Pacific Service Magazine* 14: 5 (July 1925): 147–151.

10. "Pacific Service in Its New Home," *Pacific Service Magazine* 14: 5 (July 1925): 144–146.

11. Morrow, "Recent Skyscrapers."

12. Many of the drawings for the Bourn project are now housed in Tube 529, BANC. However, three presentation renderings are housed in the Environmental Design Archives, University of California at Berkeley.

13. Letter from Henry A. Schulze to Arthur Brown Jr., 1909, BANC.

14. Baur's and Bakewell & Brown's drawings are located in the archives of the Olympic Club. Many of these drawings are schematic sketches and are not dated. This collection has not been formally curated.

15. "Olympic Golf and Country Club," The Architect and Engineer 74: 2 (August 1923): 67–71.

16. One account of the building is Clay M. Greene's "After the Opening: An Appreciation and a Colloquy," The Olympian 13: 11 (November 1925): 7–12. The sculpture was moved to the south traffic circle at the time of the courtyard's enclosure.

17. The final project is well described in a prospectus mailed to Olympic Club members, titled "The New Olympic Club Building," January 1930. A copy can be found in the Olympic Club Archives, San Francisco.

18. "A Message of Felicitation: New Building Will Be Monument to Loyal Sons of the Olympic Club," The Olympian 18: 9 (September 1930): 7–10.

19. Mady Jones, "The San Francisco Art Institute," San Francisco Magazine (June 1980): 50–57.

20. Katherine Church Holland, "The San Francisco Art Association: 1871–1906," California History 76 (1997 Supplement): 17–20.

21. Chronicle of major real estate and facility events, ms., n.d., buildings and grounds miscellanea, Archives of the Art Institute of San Francisco.

22. Letter from John Bakewell Jr. to Arthur Brown Jr., May 29, 1924, BANC.

23. Letter from John Bakewell Jr. to Arthur Brown Jr., June 23, 1924, BANC.

24. Chronicle of major real estate and facility events.

25. Anthony W. Lee, Painting on the Left: Diego Rivera, Radical Politics, and San Francisco's Public Murals (Berkeley: University of California Press, 1999), 47–56. Lee gives a very clear and detailed account of Bender's, Gerstle's, Morrow's, and Pflueger's work to bring Rivera to the United States, which can only be outlined in this work.

26. Lee, 90.

27. This story was repeatedly told by family members for many years, and was relayed to the author by Brown's son-in-law, Rollin Jensen.

28. Fred Rosenbaum, Architects of Reform: Congregational and Community Leadership, Emanu-El of San Francisco 1849–1980 (Berkeley: Western Jewish History Center, 1980), 4–7.

29. Rosenbaum, 29–30.

30. Rosenbaum, 59.

31. Rosenbaum, 83.

32. "Sylvain Schnaittacher," obit., The Architect and Engineer 85: 1 (April 1927): 122.

33. Rosenbaum makes this claim. Although it is true that certain ornamental features in the Meyer Auditorium are not common in Bakewell & Brown's work, other parts of the building, such as the gymnasium, are very similar to the gyms Bakewell & Brown were building at Stanford University. Schnaittacher died in early 1926, when construction on the Temple House had not yet begun, so it is best to think of the whole project as a collaboration, with Brown acting as chief design architect.

34. Recall that this work at Emanu-El predates Brown's and Lansburgh's contentious association at the War Memorial Opera House.

35. Arthur Brown Jr., "The Temple Emanu-El, San Francisco," The Architect and Engineer 86: 2 (August 1926): 43–59; reprinted as "Building a Temple," Pacific Coast Architect 30: 3 (September 1926): 31 ff.

36. "Plans for New Synagogue in San Francisco Approved," San Francisco Chronicle, January 26, 1924, 7; "Work on New Synagogue to Begin Monday," San Francisco Chronicle, July 31, 1924, 5; "Ceremony Marks Laying of Cornerstone of Temple Emanu-El," San Francisco Chronicle, February 23, 1925, 5.

37. "New Temple Emanu-El Is Hallowed to Human Needs," San Francisco Chronicle, April 17, 1926, 16.

38. Rosenbaum, 97.

39. This and subsequent quotations from Lewis Mumford, "Towards a Modern Synagogue," The Menorah Journal 11: 3 (June 1925): 225–236.

40. Brown traveled to Constantinople in May 1902. His very elaborate visa, issued to him by the Ottoman Empire in old Turkish script, is now in BANC.

41. Rabbi Louis J. Newman, "The New Temple Emanu-El of San Francisco," Pacific Coast Architect 30: 3 (September 1926): 15 ff.

42. Brown, "Building a Temple."

43. Renowned artist Mark Adams designed the stained-glass windows that now enliven the sanctuary; these were installed in 1972. The east window depicts fire, and the west, water. The smaller south window retains the original glass.

44. Dennison (1872–1966) and Ingerson (1880–1968) were partners in life as well as in art. They shared a home and studio in Los Gatos, called "Cathedral Oaks," for well over fifty years, and created an artistic salon there that attracted many well-known artists and musicians. Bob Aldrich, "Renaissance Craftsmen," Los Gatos Weekly Times, February 19, 1997, 15.

45. Kevin Wallace, "San Francisco's 'Unknown' Art Treasure," San Francisco Chronicle, n.d. [1949].

46. Newman, "New Temple."

47. Harris Allen, "Sermons Cast in Stone," Pacific Coast Architect 30: 3 (September 1926): 10–13.

48. "San Francisco Structure Is Declared North's Best Architecture," San Francisco Chronicle, June 6, 1927, 10.

49. See the "Historic American Building Survey of the Jewish Community Center of San Francisco HABS CA-2724," prepared by BOLA Architecture + Planning in October, 2001, for more information on the JCC project.

50. For a brief description of the artistic and literary scene in Pasadena, see Kevin Starr, Inventing the Dream: California through the Progressive Era, (New York: Oxford University Press, 1985): 99–127.

51. The following discussion of Hale's sponsorship of the Pasadena city plan is carefully documented in Ann Scheid's "Pasadena's Civic Center: A Brief History—Part I," SAH/SCC Review: 2 (1984): 8–16.

52. Architectural Resources Group, Historic Structures Report: Pasadena City Hall, City of Pasadena, 1989, 11.

53. "[Civic Center Plan] Is Outgrowth of Need," Pasadena Star–News, March 28, 1923.

54. "Giant Stride Forward; No Wounds to Heal," Pasadena Star–News, June 8, 1923.

55. The nine firms were Alison & Alison; Bakewell & Brown; Bennett & Haskell with Edwin Bergstrom; Bliss & Faville; Johnson Kaufmann and Coate; Myron Hunt; Maston, Van Pelt and Maybury; Willis Polk & Company; and Carleton Winslow. Listed in "Civic Center Designs to Be Shown," Pasadena Star–News, March 1, 1924.

56. The jury was composed of Stuart French, chair of the Pasadena City Planning Commission, architects Robert Farquhar and Pierpont Davis of Los Angeles, astronomer George Ellery Hale, and tilemaker Ernest A. Batchelder. "Result of Competition for Pasadena Civic Center Buildings," *The Architect and Engineer* 76: 3 (March 1924): 77–80.

57. *Historic Structures Report*, 14–15.

58. "Result of Competition for Pasadena Civic Center Buildings," *The Architect and Engineer* 76: 3 (March 1924): 77–80.

59. "City Hall Is Picturesque Design," Pasadena *Star–News*, March 1, 1924.

60. "Firm Notable in Designing City Halls," Pasadena *Star–News*, January 9, 1926. This article included a lengthy biography of the two architects and a large photo of San Francisco City Hall.

61. Ann Scheid, "Pasadena Civic Center: A Brief History—Part II," *SAH/SCC Review* 2 (1985): 18–24.

62. Plans for the rear wing of Pasadena City Hall, along with Brown's other working drawings, are now at the Bancroft Library.

63. "New City Hall, Pasadena, Distinctive Southern California Type of American Architecture," *Plastide Progress* 3: 1 (October 1927): 3–7.

64. Harry C. Allen, *AIA Journal*, October 1928, quoted in *Monolithic Concrete Buildings* (Chicago: Portland Cement Association), 1930.

65. "City Hall Is Notable on Skyline," and "Embodied Best Features in Design," Pasadena *Star–News*, December 26, 1927.

66. See *The American Architect* 134 (September 5, 1928): 303–309, and *The Western Architect* 37: 7 (July 1928): pl. 122–126.

67. John Bakewell Jr., "The Pasadena City Hall," *The Architect and Engineer* 93: 3 (June 1928): 35–39.

68. Bakewell, "Pasadena City Hall."

69. James D. Van Trump, "Therefore with the Angels: An Architectural Excursion in Los Angeles," *Charette: Pennsylvania Journal of Architecture* 45: 6 (June 1965): 11 ff.

70. David Gebhard and Robert Winter, *A Guide to Architecture in Los Angeles and Southern California* (Santa Barbara: Peregrine Smith, 1977), 340, and David Gebhard, "Civic Presence in California's Cities: Where and How?," *Architectural Design* 57: 9/10 (1987): 74–80.

71. Once the end came, Jessamine Brown was very much involved; she reviewed the documents pertaining to the dissolution and insisted on corrections and changes in the terms of the agreements. Annotations in Jessamine Brown's hand are found in drafts of these papers still held by the family.

72. "With the Architects," *The Architect and Engineer* 90: 1 (July 1927): 111.

73. The final accounting of the partnership demonstrates that all continuing commissions went to Brown except the work done in association at Stanford and a commission from Genevieve King, Bakewell's sister-in-law. For some perspective on the success of the partnership, the net profit to be divided between the partners for 1927 was $55,265, a healthy sum for the time. Accounting statement for Bakewell & Brown, by Farquhar and Manners, San Francisco, May 3, 1928, BANC.

CHAPTER FIVE

1. Arthur Brown Jr. "Travel Diary—May–December 1889," Private Collection, San Francisco.

2. Andrew Jackson Downing, "Explanatory Notes to Accompany the Plan for Improving the Public Grounds at Washington, D.C.," March 3, 1851, Records of the Commissioners of Public Buildings, Letters Received, RG 42, LR, vol. 32, National Archives, Washington, DC.

3. David C. Streatfield, "The Olmsteds and the Landscape of the Mall," *The Mall in Washington, 1791–1991*, Richard Longstreth, ed., *Studies in the History of Art* 30 (Washington, DC: National Gallery of Art, 1991), 117–118.

4. Streatfield, 120. Olmsted also continued the didactic program of Downing's plans.

5. Thomas S. Hines, "The Imperial Mall: The City Beautiful Movement and the Washington Plan of 1901–1902," *The Mall in Washington, 1791–1991*, Richard Longstreth, ed., Studies in the History of Art 30, 86–93.

6. Theodore Roosevelt, address to the American Institute of Architects, January 11, 1905, Washington, DC. Transcribed by Charles Moore in *The Promise of American Architecture* (Washington, DC: American Institute of Architects, 1905), 15–18.

7. Glenn Brown, *Memories 1860–1930* (Washington, DC: W. F. Roberts, 1931), 274–280.

8. The details of the design of the National Museum are related in the author's article with Cynthia R. Field, "Creating a Model for the National Mall: The Design of the National Museum of Natural History," *JSAH* 63: 1 (March 2004): 52–73.

9. Philip Kent, "Catalog of the Hornblower and Marshall Drawings of the National Museum of Natural History, the Smithsonian Institution" (unpublished catalog in the archives of the Office of Architectural History and Historic Preservation, Smithsonian Institution, Washington, DC [hereafter AHHP] 1989), 9.

10. Ann E. Peterson, *Hornblower & Marshall, Architects* (Washington, DC: Preservation Press, 1978), 20.

11. Kent, 13, 25.

12. Peterson, 12.

13. Letter from Bernard R. Green, Washington, DC, to S. P. Langley, Washington, DC, January 23, 1904, and Certificate of Approval, signed Melville W. Fuller, J. B. Henderson, and S. P. Langley, January 27, 1904, Washington, DC. Photocopies in files of AHHP.

14. Letter from Bernard R. Green, Washington, DC, to S. P. Langley, Washington, DC, January 23, 1904. Photocopy in files of AHHP.

15. John Bakewell and Arthur Brown, "Memorandum Concerning Training and Work of Bakewell & Brown," March 17, 1910, ABJr Papers, BANC.

16. Letter from Arthur Brown Jr. to Arthur Brown Sr., December 3, 1903, Private Collection. Brown was staying in New York to procure a position in a large, nationally recognized firm. He received overtures from George Post and Carrère & Hastings, but had hoped to find a position at McKim, Mead & White. Brown knew nothing of Hornblower & Marshall until McKim told him of the National Museum project.

17. Arthur Brown Jr. to Arthur Brown Sr., February 14, May 3, and May 10, 1904. Letters are held in a private collection, San Francisco.

18. These cartoons are held in the Bancroft Library; they are not cataloged yet, but are kept in a folder marked "Smithsonian" within the "Student Drawings" collection.

19. This description is based on a two-point perspectival rendering produced by Hornblower & Marshall in 1906 and cataloged as "Design Drawing for the National Museum," Smithsonian Institution Archives, Catalog Number S04-I033, 1906, Washington, DC.

20. Joseph Hudnut, "Twilight of the Gods," *Magazine of Art* 10: 8 (August 1937): 484.

21. Contemporary treatments of the Triangle have either focused on its iconographic aspects, such as George Gurney's *Sculpture and the Federal Triangle* (Washington, DC: Smithsonian Institution Press, 1985) or spotlight the role of one of the project's protagonists, such as Sally Kress Tompkins's study of Charles Moore, *A*

Quest for Grandeur (Washington, DC: Smithsonian Institution Press, 1991).

22. Gurney, 48.

23. Draper, *Edward H. Bennett*, 40.

24. Letter from Charles Moore, Commission of Fine Arts, to Secretary of the Treasury Andrew W. Mellon, April 5, 1926, D. C. Building Program [Folder: General 1926], Public Building Service, Gen. Cors. 1926–1934, Entry 31, RG 121, Archives II.

25. Edward H. Bennett to Louis Simon, February 23, 1927, and Edward H. Bennett to Charles S. Dewey, April 22, 1927, Board of Architectural Consultants (hereafter BAC; [Folder: Feb.–Dec. 1927, Box 574]), Public Building Service (hereafter PBS), Gen. Cors., Entry 31, RG 121, Archives II.

26. Edward H. Bennett, Santa Barbara, to Charles Dewey, Washington, DC, Feb. 22, 1927.

27. Bennett, Brown, Delano, Medary, and Ayres were all born in 1874. Pope claimed to have been born in 1874, but was actually born in December 1873. Simon was slightly older.

28. Sandra L Tatman, "Milton B. Medary," in *The AIA Gold Medal*, Richard Guy Wilson, ed. (New York: McGraw-Hill, 1983), 158–159.

29. Letter from Edward H. Bennett, Chicago, to Arthur Brown Jr., San Francisco, May 13, 1927, ABJr Papers, BANC.

30. William Adams Delano, "A Letter from Mr. William Adams Delano," *Federal Architect* (January–April 1943): 19.

31. The story limit and floor heights were discussed from the first meeting. The Natural History Museum is cited as the model from the second meeting of the board. BAC, *Minutes*, May 24, 1927. *Project Files*, RG 121, National Archives.

32. Had the Commerce Department Building not been reserved for York & Sawyer, it is quite possible that Hoover would have lobbied for Brown's services for that facility instead of the ICC.

33. BAC, *Minutes*, July 11, 1927, and July 12, 1927.

34. Colin Rowe reported that in 1950 Brown meant the term *echelle* to describe an oversized architectural element intentionally placed within a composition to focus the attention of the viewer on an important space. Brown related that such mannerist usage was current at Laloux's studio and within the Ecole des Beaux-Arts, in general, during his tenure there. Colin Rowe, *As I Was Saying* (Princeton, NJ: Princeton University Press, 1996), vol. I, p. 10.

35. BAC, *Minutes*, September 10, 1927.

36. Letter from William A. Delano, New York, to Maj. Ferry K. Heath, Washington, DC, October 28, 1929, BAC [Folder: Jan.–Dec. 1929, Box 575], PBS, Gen. Cors. 1910–1939, Entry 31, RG 121, Archives II.

37. Pope was officially rendered a place on the board by Mellon in a letter dated September 17, 1929. He accepted the position the following week. Letter from Andrew W. Mellon, Washington, DC, to John Russell Pope, September 17, 1927, and letter from John Russell Pope, New York, to Andrew W. Mellon, Washington, DC, September 23, 1927, BAC [Folder: Jan.–Dec. 1929, Box 575], PBS, Gen. Cors. 1910–1939, Entry 31, RG 121, Archives II.

38. BAC, *Minutes*, February 10, 1930.

39. BAC, *Minutes*, April 10, 1930.

40. BAC, *Minutes*, February 12, 1930. Brown later had this statement struck from the official record.

41. The position of the Commission of Fine Arts is stated definitively in a letter from Charles Moore to Edward H. Bennett, November 20, 1929. General Correspondence, DC Building Program, RG 121, National Archives. Cited from photocopy made for Joan Draper; the file copy for the Commission of Fine Arts has been lost.

42. BAC, *Minutes*, April 24, 1929.

43. BAC, *Minutes*, February 20, 1930.

44. Gurney, 340. The Commission of Fine Arts demanded a revised elevation on Constitution Avenue that destroyed this framing effect. One presumes the present simplified elevation with a recessed colonnade was an attempt to save the cost of a formal pavilion with pediment.

45. Conversation with Stephen Bedford, March 8, 1997, Washington, DC.

46. Letters from Andrew W. Mellon, Washington, DC, to William Adams Delano, New York, and Arthur Brown Jr., San Francisco, June 21, 1927, BAC [Folder: Feb.–Dec. 1927, Box 574], PBS, Gen. Cors. 1910–1939, Entry 31, RG 121, Archives II.

47. Letter from Arthur Brown Jr., San Francisco, to William A. Delano, New York, June 7, 1930, BAC [Folder: Jan.–Dec. 1930, 1 of 2, Box 575], PBS, Gen. Cors. 1910–1939, Entry 31, RG 121, Archives II.

48. Program for the Interstate Commerce Commission Building, February 6, 1929, BAC [Folder: Jan.–Dec. 1929, Box 575] PBS, Gen. Cors. 1910–1939, Entry 31, RG 121, Archives II.

49. BAC, *Minutes*, April 24, 1929.

50. Arthur Brown Jr., San Francisco, to Louis A. Simon, Washington, DC, May 17, 1929, BAC [Folder: Jan.–Dec. 1929, Box 575] PBS, Gen. Cors. 1910–1939, Entry 31, RG 121, Archives II.

51. BAC, *Minutes*, September 11, 1929.

52. Conversation with Rollin Jensen, August 13, 1996.

53. Gurney, 242. Gurney details the entire sculpture program in his examination of the Labor–ICC block.

54. Presentation plans, elevations and sections of the Department of Labor and Interstate Commerce Commission Building, Arthur Brown Jr., architect, November 1, 1929: scale: 1/16″ = 1′-0″. Known from photostats in the ABJr Papers, BANC.

55. Sketch estimates of the Labor–ICC group, prepared by Arthur Brown Jr., architect, December 2, 1929, BAC [Folder: Jan.–Dec. 1929, Box 575] PBS, Gen. Cors. 1910–1939, Entry 31, RG 121, Archives II.

56. "Elliott-Keyes Bill Is Passed by Senate," *Daily Pacific Builder*, March 26, 1930. In Scrapbook, ABJr Papers, BANC.

57. A copy of the specifications can be found in Arthur Brown Jr. Collection, Carton 8 [Folder: Miscellaneous Data, Washington, DC, 1933–1937], Mss. 81/142c, Bancroft Library, Berkeley, CA.

58. "Four U.S. Building Jobs in One Here May Set Record," unidentified newspaper clipping, Scrapbook, ABJr Papers, BANC.

59. Arthur Brown Jr. Collection, Carton 5 [Folder: Miscellaneous Data, Washington, DC, 1933–1937], Mss. 81/142c, Bancroft Library, Berkeley, CA.

60. "Record Breaker," San Francisco *Chronicle*, Sept. 3, 1933, and photograph from Washington Monument, Harris & Ewing, photographers, *Mid-Week Journal*, December 9, 1933. Both found in Scrapbook, ABJr Papers, BANC.

61. "Labor–ICC Building Row up to Green," Washington *Post*, March 7, 1934. In Scrapbook, ABJr Papers, BANC.

62. "Labor Department to Be Model Structure," Washington *Daily News*, October 10, 1933; "When Perkins Bathes—She Asks Privacy," San Francisco *Chronicle*, Jan. 23, 1935. Both from Scrapbook, ABJr Papers, BANC.

63. "Perkins Opens Labor Building," Washington *Herald*, February 26, 1935. In Scrapbook, ABJr Papers, BANC.

64. Roscoe P. DeWitt, FAIA, "Extension of the East Front of the Capitol," *Journal of the AIA*, June 1958, 271.

65. "Chronology of Plans to Extend the East Front of the Capitol," *Journal of the AIA*, June 1958, 277.

66. "Chronology," 277.

67. DeWitt, 273.
68. Ralph Walker, "If This Be Sentiment . . . ," *Journal of the AIA*, June 1958, 284.
69. Quoted in "News," *Architectural Forum* 107: 10 (October 1957): 5.
70. "News," 5.
71. This and following quotes from "News," 6.
72. Walker, 282. One wonders if Brown ever used the word *insofar*.
73. Interview by Rollin Jensen of William Adams Delano, New York, February 17, 1958.
74. The first proposal to incorporate the row houses into the office complex north of Lafayette Square was presented to the Treasury in April, 1957. For details see Kurt G. F. Helfrich, "Modernism for Washington?" *Washington History* 8: 1 (Spring/Summer 1996): 16–37. Brown was in Washington at the time, working on the Capitol extension, and was likely aware of this proposal.
75. Livermore mentions both projects in his interview with the author, San Francisco, January 15, 1997. John Carl Warneke describes his work with the Kennedy administration in issue 13 of *White House History*, the Journal of the White House Historical Society, 2003.

CHAPTER SIX

1. Edith Fremdling's correspondence to Brown is found in the ABJr Papers, BANC.
2. Eddy's wife Ethel Garrett Eddy was Jessamine Garrett Brown's sister.
3. Champney had come to Seattle to work on the 1909 exposition. He stayed in Seattle for the rest of his life, building a moderately successful practice. In the 1920s he developed a severe chronic depression that rendered him incapable of any activity for weeks at a time. Champney gained a reputation for being difficult to work with, and by the middle of the decade he had lost his staff.
4. The letter explained the history of the commission and hinted at the difficulties that the vestry was having with Champney. Letter from John W. Eddy to Arthur Brown Jr., July 19, 1926, BANC.
5. Letter from Arthur Brown Jr. to J. E. Duthie, January 27, 1928, BANC.
6. Letter from John W. Eddy to J. E. Duthie, February 9, 1928, BANC.
7. Letter from John W. Eddy to Arthur Brown Jr., February 15, 1928, BANC.
8. Letter from Arthur Brown Jr. to Dr. McLauchlan, August 9, 1929, Carton 6, BANC.
9. Invoice from Arthur Brown Jr. to the rector, wardens, and vestry of St. Mark's Parish, March 14, 1929, BANC.
10. Champney died on June 4, 1929, under sudden and mysterious circumstances. His profound depression had not lifted and his unstable state of mind may very well have contributed to his death. Withey, *Biographical Dictionary*, 117.
11. Memorandum of Resolution, Horton Force, Vestry of St. Mark's Parish, Seattle, June 21, 1929, BANC.
12. Letter from Arthur Brown Jr. to Joshua Green, February 5, 1930, carton 6, BANC.
13. Letters from John W. Eddy to Arthur Brown Jr., June 12 & July 8, 1931, and Arthur Brown Jr. to John W. Eddy, June 26 and September 1, 1931, BANC.
14. Letters to Bronson, Jones & Bronson, December 5, 12, 19, 21, 1931, and January 12 and May 20, 1932; also Robert Bronson to Arthur Brown Jr., December 8 and 31, 1931, and January 21, 1932, BANC.
15. "The History of St. Mark's," St. Mark's Cathedral Parish website, www.saintmarks.org/history.htm, accessed October 12, 2003. Content adapted from material compiled by Thomas W. Huntley.
16. Sheri Olson, "West Wall, St. Mark's Cathedral, Seattle, Washington," *Architectural Record* 186: 7 (July 1998): 101–104.

17. John E. Findling, *Chicago's Great World's Fairs* (Manchester, UK: Manchester University Press, 1994), 61.
18. Letter from John A. Holabird for Harvey W. Corbett to Rufus C. Dawes, May 25, 1928, Century of Progress Archives, University of Illinois Chicago Special Collections. Quoted in Lisa Diane Schrank, "The Role of the 1933–1934 Century of Progress International Exposition in the Development and Promotion of Modern Architecture in the United States," Ph. D. dissertation (University of Texas at Austin, 1998), 128–129.
19. Schrank, 129–130.
20. Schrank, 129–134.
21. Walter H. Kilham Jr., *Raymod Hood, Architect: Form through Function in the American Skyscraper* (New York: Architectural Book Publishing Company, 1973), 108.
22. Joan Draper, *Edward H. Bennett: Architect and City Planner—1874–1954* (Chicago: Art Institute of Chicago, 1982) 34–36.
23. Harvey Wiley Corbett, "The Significance of the Exposition," *Architectural Forum* 59: 1 (July 1933): 20–28.
24. Findling, 67–68.
25. Nathaniel A. Owings, "Amusement Features of the Exposition," *Architectural Record* 75: 5 (May 1933): 355–362.
26. Brown reportedly described the fair as a lark and admitted that he gave the committee what it wanted, despite his misgivings concerning the superficiality of the architectural agenda. Interview by author with Rollin Jensen, San Francisco, January 1996.
27. Ralph Adams Cram, "Retrogression, Ugliness," *Architectural Forum* 59: 1 (July 1933): 24–25.
28. Frank Lloyd Wright, "Another 'Pseudo'," *Architectural Forum* 59: 1 (July 1933): 25.
29. "Lillie the Vamp," *Time* (October 9, 1933), n.p.
30. Masha Zakheim [Jewett], *Coit Tower, San Francisco: Its History and Art* (San Francisco: Volcano Press, 1984), 17–20.
31. Howard's drawing and his account (Henry T. Howard, "The Coit Memorial Tower," *The Architect and Engineer* 115: 3 [December 1933]: 11–15) have led some writers to attribute the design to Howard; however, Brown's records show that Howard was not involved with the project until September, 1931, and at no time was he a leading figure in its design. John Baur worked with Brown on the design and design development phases of the project and supervised the production of the construction documents, and John Davis Hatch administered the contract for the firm during construction. See Brown's accounting of the costs of working up the project, titled "Time on Coit Tower," prepared April 11, 1934, BANC.
32. Gertrude Atherton, *My San Francisco: A Wayward Biography* (Indianapolis: Bobbs-Merrill Co., 1946), 30.
33. Advisory committee for the expenditure of the bequest of the late Lillie Hitchcock Coit, Minutes, September 2, 1931, BANC.
34. Henry T. Howard, "The Coit Memorial Tower," The Architect and Engineer 115: 3 (December 1933): 11–15.
35. Interview by author with George Livermore, San Francisco, January 15, 1996.
36. Letter of transmittal of bid documents to San Francisco Park Commission, November 23, 1931, BANC.
37. Letter of Laurence I. Scott, president of the San Francisco Federation of Arts, to the editor, San Francisco News, May 26, 1932, BANC.
38. Letter from Arthur Brown Jr. to Herbert Fleischhacker, July 2, 1932, BANC.
39. Letter from Arthur Brown Jr. to Herbert Fleischhacker, July 2, 1932, BANC. Brown's daughter, Victoria Brown Polk, recalls Brown working with the model at Le Verger in the summer of 1932. Interview with Victoria Brown Polk, September 6, 2002.

40. Notes of meeting of the Fine Arts Commission by Arthur Brown Jr., August 22, 1932, BANC.

41. Letter of transmittal of Young & Horstmeyer's contract from John Baur for Arthur Brown Jr. to Capt. B. F. Lamb, December 19, 1932, BANC.

42. "San Francisco Contractors 90 Days Ahead of Schedule on Tower," *Daily Pacific Builder*, June 9, 1933.

43. John Davis Hatch to *Time* Magazine, October 11, 1933, BANC.

44. This entire series of events is best described by Zakheim, 27–32.

45. Zakheim, 32. Here Zakheim recounts the recollections of her father, Bernard.

46. This statement and all following discussion of the December 18, 1933, meeting are based on the "Minutes of the Second Meeting of the Regional Committee, District #15 of the Public Works of Art Project," December 18, 1933, Collection of Masha Zakheim.

47. "Minutes of the Second Meeting of the Regional Committee, District #15 of the Public Works of Art Project," December 18, 1933, Collection of Masha Zakheim.

48. Zakheim, 40–41.

49. Arthur Brown Jr. to Herbert Fleischhacker, June 25, 1934, ABJr Papers, BANC.

50. Zakheim, 47–51.

51. Zakheim, 51–54.

52. Zackheim, 53–54.

53. Will P. Day, "Birth of a Fair: How Treasure Island Was Conceived and Developed," *The Architect and Engineer* 136: 2 (February 1939): 23.

54. Talbot Hamlin, "The San Francisco Fair," *Pencil Points* 19 no. 11 (November 1938): 683–686.

55. Quoted in Paul Conant, "Never-Never Land in San Francisco," *Pencil Points* 20 no. 6 (June 1937): 377–388.

56. The administration building is the only major building from the exhibition to remain on Treasure Island. As it happened, it has served as a public airport terminal only on film, where it stood in for Berlin's airfield in George Lucas and Stephen Spielberg's *Indiana Jones and the Last Crusade.*

57. George Livermore, interview with the author, January 17, 1997.

58. Arthur Brown Jr., "The Architectural Planning of the Exposition," *The Architect and Engineer* 136: 2 (February 1939): 19–20.

59. This image was another reference to San Francisco's resurrection after the conflagration of 1906. Jack James and Earle Weller, *Treasure Island, "The Magic City"—1939–1940* (San Francisco: Pisani Printing, 1939), 32.

60. James and Weller, 33.

61. O. C. Malmquist executed "Fauna," Raymond Puccinelli modeled "Flora," Ettore Cadorin sculpted "Land," and Carlo Taliabue contributed "Sea." Eugen Neuhaus, *The Art of Treasure Island* (Berkeley: University of California Press, 1939), 44, BANC.

62. Letter from W. P. Day to George Kelham, July 3, 1936, BANC.

63. Patricia F. Carpenter and Paul Totah, eds. *The San Francisco Fair: Treasure Island 1939–1940* (San Francisco: Scottwall Associates, 1989), 83.

64. "United States Government Building," *The Architectural Forum* 70: 6 (June 1939): 474–475.

65. "County Buildings," *The Architectural Forum* 70: 6 (June 1939): 484–485.

66. J. E. Stanton, "Color and Light," *The Architect and Engineer* 136: 2 (February 1939): 39–40.

67. A. F. Dickenson, "Color: New Synthesis in the West," *Architectural Record* 85: 6 (June 1939): 75–90.

68. Carpenter and Totah, 124–127.

69. James and Weller, 191–192.

70. "Treasure Island Buildings Being Torn Down," San Francisco *Chronicle*, September 24, 1947.

71. *Second Annual Report of the Housing Authority of the City and County of San Francisco*, April 18, 1940, 4–5.

72. A brief survey of the entire SFHA program of the early 1940s may be found in "San Francisco Builds Low Rent Homes," *The Architect and Engineer* 150: 1 (July 1942): 18–29.

73. "Holly Courts: Special Bulletin of the San Francisco Housing Association," 3.

74. "Holly Courts: Special Bulletin of the San Francisco Housing Association," San Francisco Housing Association, 1940, 4.

75. *Fifth Annual Report of the Housing Authority of the City and County of San Francisco*, April 18, 1943, 18.

76. "Housing Project Homes All Ready to Greet 1st Tenants," San Francisco *Call-Bulletin*, April 27, 1940.

CHAPTER SEVEN

1. The early years of the university's founding are well documented in Edith Mirrielees, *Stanford: The Story of a University* (New York: Putnam, 1959), 13–31.

2. The history of Stanford's early years is documented in Paul Turner, "The Collaborative Design of Stanford University," *The Founders and the Architects: The Design of Stanford University* (Palo Alto: Stanford University Department of Art, 1976), 9–67.

3. Turner, *The Founders*, 26–27.

4. Turner, *The Founders*, 39–50.

5. Richard Joncas, David J. Neuman, and Paul V. Turner, *Stanford University* (New York: Princeton University Press, 1999), 34–35.

6. Turner, *The Founders*, 54–57.

7. Therese Degler has documented these houses for the Stanford Historical Society.

8. F. H. Fowler, chair of the Building Committee of the Stanford Union, San Francisco, to the Stanford Board of Trustees, Palo Alto, March 25, 1913, Stanford University Archives, Board of Trustees Supporting Documents, SC 27, Box 9 [Folder 1: March 28, 1913].

9. Joncas, Neuman, and Turner, *Stanford University*, 59–60.

10. James F. Dawson, report to the trustees of Leland Stanford Jr. University, May 8, 1914, Stanford University Archives, Campus Planning Documents, Ref 0220/2.

11. Photographs of these drawings survive in the ABJr. Papers. These drawings have been donated to the Stanford University Archives but were not cataloged at the time of this writing.

12. Dawson, "report to the trustees."

13. Marcia E. Vetrocq, "Stanford before 1945: The Fate of the 'Olmsted Plan,'" *The Founders and the Architects: The Design of Stanford University* (Palo Alto: Stanford University Department of Art, 1976), 85–87.

14. Joncas, Neuman, & Turner, *Stanford University*, 36–37.

15. John Maxon Stillman, "The University Library," *New Building of the Stanford University Library and a History of the Library, 1891–1919* (Palo Alto: Stanford University, 1919), 9–17.

16. John Bakewell Jr. and Arthur Brown Jr., "As Described by the Architects," *New Building of the Stanford University Library and a History of the Library, 1891–1919* (Palo Alto: Stanford University, 1919), 19–25. Although this article is credited to both architects, the language in this passage is very consistent with Brown's usage.

17. Bakewell and Brown, "As Described," 21.

18. Arthur Brown Jr., "The New San Francisco Public Library," *The Architect and Engineer* 49: 1 (April 1917): 40–49.

19. Bakewell and Brown, "As Described," 25.

20. Joncas, Neuman, & Turner, *Stanford University*, 58–59.

21. Irving K. Morrow, "Leland Stanford Junior University," *The Architect and Engineer* 59: 1 (October, 1919): 43–67.

22. J. Pearce Mitchell, *Stanford University: 1916–1941*, (Palo Alto: Stanford University Press, 1958), 12–13.

23. "Housing of Students at Stanford University" (Palo Alto: Stanford University, c. 1925), 2. This pamphlet was found in the ABJr Papers; copies exist in the Stanford University Archives.

24. Professors J. B. Wells and A. S. Niles exploited the Soule Steel Company's Unibuilt prefabrication system. Joncas, Neuman, & Turner, *Stanford University*, 69–70.

25. *President's Report*, Leland Stanford Jr. University, August 31, 1939, 14–15; *President's Report*, August 31, 1937, 27; *President's Report*, August 31, 1933, 49.

26. Ellwood Cubberly, "Education at Stanford: A History," *New Building of the School of Education and a History of the Work in Education: 1891–1938* (Palo Alto: Stanford University Press, 1938), 9–13.

27. Ellwood Cubberly, "Description of the Building," *New Building of the School of Education and a History of the Work in Education: 1891–1938* (Palo Alto: Stanford University Press, 1938), 17–27.

28. Frederick H. Meyer to John Bakewell Jr. and Arthur Brown Jr., March 18, 1938, ABJr Papers, University Archives, Stanford University.

29. Letter from Herbert Clark Hoover to Jessamine Garret Brown, August 3, 1960, ABJr. Papers, Bancroft Library and Stanford University Archives.

30. *President's Report*, Leland Stanford Jr. University, August 31, 1939, 14–15.

31. Marcia E. Vetrocq, "Stanford before 1945: The Fate of the 'Olmsted Plan,'" 89–96.

32. George Nash, *Herbert Hoover and Stanford University* (Stanford: Hoover Institution Press, 1988), 106–109.

33. Herbert Hoover described Lou Henry Hoover's involvement with the design: "Arthur made the original suggestion that the library building should be a tower for good working purposes. One day when he and I were discussing how a tower could fit into the Romanesque motif of the University Mrs. Hoover suggested that he might find justification in the towers of the Cathedral at Salamanca. He at once rejoiced and that is its dome." Letter from Herbert Clark Hoover to Jessamine Garret Brown, August 3, 1960, ABJr Papers, Bancroft Library and Stanford University Archives.

34. This model is the only known maquette to survive from Brown's studio.

35. Herbert Clark Hoover, dedication speech for the Hoover Library of War, Revolution, and Peace, June 21, 1941, published in *The Dedication of the Hoover Library* (Palo Alto: Stanford University Press, 1941), 36–39.

36. Vetrocq, "Stanford Before 1945: The Fate of the 'Olmsted Plan,'" note 89.

37. Harvey Helfand, *The Campus Guide: University of California, Berkeley* (New York: Princeton Architectural Press, 2002), 6.

38. Helfand, 41–43, 70.

39. Bernard Maybeck and Julien Guadet, "Program for the Hearst Competition for the University of California," 1897. Quoted in Loren W. Partridge, *John Galen Howard and the Berkeley Campus: Beaux-Arts Architecture in the "Athens of the West"* (Berkeley: Berkeley Architectural Heritage Association, 1978), 11–12.

40. Woodbridge, *John Galen Howard*, 1–13.

41. Woodbridge, *John Galen Howard*, 161.

42. Helfand, *University of California*, 20–21.

43. Helfand, *University of California*, 199.

44. Brown was presented with an honorary Doctorate of Laws at the same ceremony as Willa Cather, the Pulitzer Prize-winning novelist.

45. J. L. Heilbron and Robert W. Seidel, *Lawrence and His Laboratory*, vol. 1 (Berkeley: University of California Press, 1989), 484–488.

46. "Domed Building Fitted to Research Needs," *Engineering News Record*, April 9, 1942, 64–66.

47. Brechin, *Imperial San Francisco*, 315.

48. "Domed Building Fitted to Research Needs."

49. Arthur Brown Jr., "Progress Report to the Regents: Architectural Considerations," August 14, 1944, revised March 25, 1946, ABJr Papers, BANC.

50. J. H. Corley to Arthur Brown Jr., April 20, 1948, ABJr Papers, BANC. Corley was the university comptroller. This letter informs Brown that the regents cancelled his contract at their meeting of April 16, 1948.

51. Wurster had also designed Stern Hall in 1942, which was sited in clear defiance of Brown's master plan of the previous year. Eugenie L. Birch, "William Wilson Wurster," *Macmillan Encyclopedia of Architects*, vol. 4, Adolf K. Placzek, ed. (New York: Free Press, 1982), 450–451.

CONCLUSION

1. Arthur Brown Jr. to William Adams Delano, November 17, 1946, ABJr Papers, BANC.

2. Arthur Brown Jr., "Is Modern Architecture Really Necessary?," *The Architect and Engineer* 147: 1 (October 1941): 27–29.

3. Arthur Brown Jr. to Florance P. Kahn, December 16, 1933, ABJr Papers, BANC.

4. "Architect: S. F. Defaced by Freeways," San Francisco *Chronicle*, January 23, 1957; "'Freeways Deface City': Architect," San Francisco *Daily News*, January 23, 1957; Royce Brier, "An Aqueduct Is Like a Freeway," San Francisco *Chronicle*, January 25, 1957.

5. Arthur Brown Jr., "Statement on Freeways," press release through the Northern California Chapter, AIA, January 1957. Photostat in ABJr Papers, BANC.

6. John Bakewell, Jr. to Jessamine Garrett Brown, July [8], 1957, ABJr Papers, BANC. Bakewell's retirement was not, unfortunately, a happy one. He lost his sight shortly after World War II and his wife, Hazel, died at about the same time. He retreated to his home on Chestnut Street, where he enjoyed quiet afternoons in his gardens in the company of his niece. Bakewell died in 1963.

7. Brown and his wife both served as translators and volunteer aides to the French delegation to the United Nations' organizing convention.

8. David Gebhard, *The Guide to Architecture in San Francisco and Northern California* (Salt Lake City, UT: Peregrine Smith, 1985), 86.

9. Brown took John Singer Sargent's seat at the Institut de France. Brown had been made a corresponding member of the Institut in 1920. In 1932 he was also made an Officier of the Legion d'Honneur, a dignity he considered somewhat less significant than membership in the Institut.

10. Both Brown and Perret built in concrete when it was a relatively new material; Perret's apartment building at 25b rue Franklin precedes Brown's Berkeley City Hall by only three years.

11. Perhaps the most famous of these articles was Joseph Hudnut's "Twilight of the Gods," *Magazine of Art* 10: 8 (August 1937): 484–488.

12. Richard Chafee, "John Russell Pope," *Macmillan Encyclopedia of Architects*, vol. 3, Adolf K. Placzek, ed. (New York: Free Press, 1982), 450.

13. Arthur Brown Jr., "Is Modern Architecture Really Necessary?," 27.

BIBLIOGRAPHY AND SOURCES

ARCHIVES

Brown anticipated a biography and retained and cataloged his papers and drawings from the beginning of his career. These papers, which include the architect's original drawings and specifications for the preponderance of his oeuvre, have been turned over to the Bancroft Library at the University of California; these papers had not yet been cataloged at the time of this writing. In addition, there are significant repositories of material concerning Bakewell & Brown at the University Archives of the Leland Stanford Jr. University. A small collection of drawings by Brown has been assembled at the Prints and Drawings unit of the Library of Congress, and Brown's work at the Federal Triangle is well documented at the National Archives in College Park, Maryland.

California Historical Society
    Manuscripts Collection
    Photograph Collection
San Francisco Heritage
GSA Historic Preservation Division
Margaret Jensen
    Arthur Brown Jr. Papers
Library of Congress
    Prints and Photographs Division
National Archives
    RG 66 and 121
National Trust for Historic Preservation
    Western Regional Office
    Filoli
Victoria Brown Polk
City of San Francisco
    Department of Public Works
    Landmarks Advisory Board
    Public Library Arts and Music Dept.
    San Francisco War Memorial
San Francisco Architectural Club
California Institute of Fine Art
Stanford University
    University Archives
    Office of Facilities/Project Mgmt.
Temple Emanu-El

Treasure Island Museum
University of California at Berkeley
    The Bancroft Library
    Environmental Design Archive

PUBLISHED SOURCES

Adams, Gerald. "City of Paris Loss Triggers Backer's Tempers." San Francisco *Examiner*, 12 January 1979.

———. "City Planning Rules for City of Paris Building." San Francisco *Examiner*, 22 December 1978.

Aldrich, Bob. "Renaissance Craftsmen." Los Gatos *Weekly Times*, 19 February 1997, 15.

Allen, Harris. "Sermons Cast in Stone." *Pacific Coast Architect* 30, no. 3 (September 1926): 10–13.

Allen, Harris. "Three Country Houses by Bakewell & Brown." *The Building Review* 21, no. 1 (January 1922): 1–6.

Alofsin, Anthony. *The Struggle for Modernism: Architecture, Landscape Architecture and City Planning at Harvard.* New York: Norton, 2002.

Altrocchi, Julia Cooley. *The Spectacular San Franciscans.* New York: Dutton, 1949.

American Institute of Architects, San Francisco Chapter. *Report of the Civic Center Committee, San Francisco Chapter of the American Institute of Architects, and Reply of the Consulting Architects, City of San Francisco.* San Francisco: American Institute of Architects, 1913.

American Institute of Architects. *Journal of Proceedings.* 44th Annual Convention, San Francisco, 1910. Washington, DC: American Institute of Architects, 1910.

"Among the Architects." *The Architect and Engineer* 2, no. 3 (October 1905): 75.

"Architect: San Francisco Defaced by Freeways." San Francisco *Chronicle*, 23 January 1957.

"Architects Make Report on Civic Center." San Francisco *Call*, 29 May 1912.

Association for the Improvement and Adornment of San Francisco. *First Annual Report of the President.* San Francisco: Association for the Improvement and Adornment of San Francisco, 1972.

Atherton, Gertrude. *My San Francisco: A Wayward Biography*. Indianapolis: Bobbs-Merrill, 1946.

Bakewell, John Jr. "Architectural Treatment for the Building." *Pacific Service Magazine* 14, no. 5 (July 1925).

———. "The Pasadena City Hall." *The Architect and Engineer* 93, no. 3 (June 1928): 35–39.

———. "The San Francisco City Hall Competition: How the Successful Architects Arrived at Their Solution." *The Architect and Engineer* 29, no. 3 (July 1912): 46–53.

———. "The Santa Fe Station, San Diego. *The Architect and Engineer* 41, no. 1 (April 1915): 40–46.

Bakewell, John Jr., and Arthur Brown Jr. "As Described by the Architects." *New Building of the Stanford University Library and a History of the Library, 1891–1919* (Palo Alto: Stanford University, 1919), 18–25.

Bancroft, Hubert Howe. *Retrospection*. New York: Hubert Howe Bancroft, 1915.

Barry, John Daniel. *The City of Domes*. San Francisco: Newbegin, 1915.

Bean, Walton. *Boss Ruef's San Francisco: The Story of the Union Labor Party, Big Business, and the Graft Prosecution*. Berkeley: University of California Press, 1952.

Bernhardi, Robert. *The Buildings of Berkeley*. Berkeley: Lederer, Street, & Zeus, 1971.

———. *The Buildings of Oakland*. Oakland: Forest Hill Press, 1979.

Betsky, Aaron. *James Gamble Rogers and the Architecture of Pragmatism*. New York: Architectural History Foundation, 1994.

Bishop, William Henry. "Southern California." *Harper's Monthly Magazine* 65, no. 389 (October 1882): 720–745.

Blair, Walter D. "Student Life at the Ecole des Beaux-Arts." *The Brickbuilder*. XVIII (March 1909): 52–54.

Blomfield, Arthur. *Fifty Years of the San Francisco Opera*. San Francisco: SFO Opera, 1972.

Blue and Gold. Berkeley: University of California, 1893–1897.

Bosworth, F. H. Jr., and Roy Childs Jones. *A Study of Architectural Schools*. New York: Association of Collegiate Schools of Architecture, 1932.

Boutelle, Sarah Holmes. *Julia Morgan, Architect*. New York: Abbeville Press, 1988.

Branner, J. C. "The San Francisco City Hall." *The Architect and Engineer* 46, no. 2 (August 1916): 77.

Brechin, Gray. *Imperial San Francisco: Urban Power, Earthly Ruin*. Berkeley: University of California Press, 1999.

Brier, Royce. "An Aqueduct is Like a Freeway." San Francisco *Chronicle*, 25 January 1957.

Brown, Arthur Jr. "The Architectural Planning of the Exposition." *The Architect and Engineer* 136, no. 2 (February 1939): 19–20.

———. "The Burnham Plan." *The Architect and Engineer* 29, no. 3 (September 1905): 29–31.

———. "Christopher Henry Snyder—Civil Engineer." *The Architect and Engineer* 129, no. 3 (June 1937): 44.

———. "Is Modern Architecture Really Necessary?" *The Architect and Engineer* 147, no. 1 (October 1941): 27–29.

———. "The New San Francisco Public Library." *The Architect and Engineer* 49, no. 1 (April 1917): 40–49.

———. "The Temple Emau-El, San Francisco." *The Architect and Engineer* 86, no. 2 (August 1926): 43–59.

Brown, Glenn. *1860–1930 Memories*. Washington, DC: W. F. Roberts, 1931.

Burner, David. *Herbert Hoover: A Public Life*. New York: Knopf, 1979.

Burnham, Daniel Hudson and Edward H. Bennett. *Report on a Plan for San Francisco*. San Francisco: City of San Francisco, 1905. Reprinted in facsimile in Berkeley, Urban Books, 1971.

Bushong, William, et al. *A Centennial History of the Washington Chapter of the American Institute of Architects, 1887–1987*. Washington, DC: Washington Architectural Foundation Press, 1987.

Caen, Herb. "Gloomy Sunday." San Francisco *Examiner*, October 28, 1952.

———. *Only in San Francisco*. Garden City: Doubleday, 1960.

Cahill, B. J. S. "Adventurings in the Monumental." *The Architect and Engineer* 54, no. 2 (August 1918): 41–96.

———. "The New City Hall, San Francisco." *The Architect and Engineer* 46, no. 2 (August 1916): 42–77.

———. "The San Francisco City Hall Competition." *The Architect and Engineer* 29, no. 3 (July 1912): 53–78.

———. "Winning Design Suggests Rational Style." *The Architect and Engineer* 92, no. 3 (March 1928): 43–51.

California at the World's Columbian Exposition, 1893. Sacramento: State of California, 1894.

"Californians in Architecture and Landscape Architecture." *California Monthly* (November 1945): 8–11.

Cardwell, Kenneth H. *Bernard Maybeck: Artisan, Architect, Artist*. Santa Barbara: Peregrine Smith, 1977.

Carpenter, Patricia, and Paul Totah. *The San Francisco Fair: Treasure Island, 1939–1940*. San Francisco: Scottwall Associates, 1989.

"Ceremony Marks Laying of Cornerstone of Temple Emanu-El." San Francisco *Chronicle*, 23 February 1925, 5.

Cigliano, Jan, and Sara Bradford Landau, eds. *The Grand American Avenue, 1850–1920*. San Francisco: Pomegranate Artbooks, 1994.

"City Architectural Bureau Reorganized for Civic Center." San Francisco *Examiner*, 29 March 1912.

"City Hall Excavation Officially Begins." San Francisco *Call*, 6 April 1913.

"City Hall Farce Competition." Oakland *Tribune*, 8 April 1910.

"City Hall is Noble on Skyline." Pasadena *Star–News*, 26 December 1927.

"City Hall Plans Given Formal Approval." San Francisco *Examiner*, 29 June 1912.

"City Hears 'Kicks' on Steel." San Francisco *Examiner*, 29 January 1914.

"City of Paris Back in its Former Home." San Francisco *Chronicle*, 22 July 1909.

"City of Paris Dry Goods Company Building." San Francisco *News Letter*, 7 August 1909.

"City of Paris Battle: Not Quiet on the Western Front." San Francisco *Examiner*, November 13, 1978.

"Civic Center Designs to Be Shown." Pasadena *Star–News*, 1 March 1924.

Collens, Charles. "The Beaux-Arts in 1900." *AIA Journal* VII (1947): 80–86, 144–151, 187–197.

"Competition for San Francisco Sub-Treasury Building." *The Architect and Engineer* 25, no. 2 (June 1911): 39–47.

"Competition for a Building for the Federal Reserve Board." *The Architectural Forum* 65, no. 7 (July 1935): 6–12.

Conant, Paul. "Never-Never Land in San Francisco." *Pencil Points* 18, no. 6 (June 1937): 376–390.

"Concours à l'Ecole des Beaux-Arts." *La Construction Moderne* (August 21, 1897): 564.

"Contractors who Built City Hall." *The Architect and Engineer* 46, no. 2 (August 1916): 85.

Corbett, Harvey Wiley. "The Significance of the Exposition." *The Architectural Forum* 59, no. 1 (July 1933): 20–28.

Corbett, Michael R. *Splendid Survivors: San Francisco's Downtown Heritage*. San Francisco: California Living Books, 1979.

Cornelius, Br. Fidelius. *William Keith, Old Master of California*. New York: Putnam, 1942.

"Cornerstone of Berkeley's New Town Hall Laid with Fitting Ceremonies." Oakland *Enquirer*, 27 June 1908.

Cram, Ralph Adams. *My Life in Architecture*. Boston: Little, Brown, 1936.

———. "Retrogression, Ugliness." *The Architectural Forum* 59, no. 1 (July 1923): 24–25.

Cubberly, Ellwood. *New Building of the School of Education and a History of the Work in Education: 1891–1938*. Palo Alto: Stanford University Press, 1938.

Day, Will P. "Birth of a Fair: How Treasure Island Was Conceived and Developed." *The Architect and Engineer* 136 no. 2 (February 1939): 23.

"Death of Arthur Brown, Sr." *The Architect and Engineer* 49, no. 1 (April 1917): 100.

"Death of Newton J. Tharp." *The Architect and Engineer* 17, no. 2 (June 1909): 110.

Delaire, E. *Les Architectes Elèves de l'Ecole des Beaux-Arts*. Paris: Librairie de la Construction Moderne, 1907.

Delano, William Adams. "A Letter from Mr. William Adams Delano." *Federal Architect* (January–April 1943): 19.

DeWitt, Roscoe P. "Extension to the East Front of the Capitol." *AIA Journal* (June 1958): 268–274.

Dickenson, A. F. "Color: New Synthesis in the West." *Architectural Record* 85, no. 6 (June 1939): 75–90.

Dobie, Charles Caldwell. *San Francisco: A Pageant*. New York: Appleton-Century, 1933.

"Domed Building Fitted to Research Needs." *Engineering News Record*, 9 April 1942, 64–66.

Draper, Joan. *Edward H. Bennett: Architect and City Planner—1874–1954*. Chicago: Art Institute of Chicago, 1982.

Drexler, Arthur, ed. *The Architecture of the Ecole des Beaux-Arts*. New York: Museum of Modern Art, 1977.

Duffus, R. L. *The Tower of Jewels: Memories of San Francisco*. New York: Norton, 1960.

"Early Glimpse of the Panama-Pacific Exposition Architecturally." *The Architect and Engineer* 30, no. 3 (October 1912): 48–55.

Ecole des Beaux-Arts. *Les Medailles des Concours d'Architecture, 1898–1905*, 7 vols. Paris: Ecole des Beaux-Arts, 1899–1905.

Egbert, Donald Drew. *The Beaux-Arts Tradition in French Architecture: Illustrated by the Grands Prix de Rome*. Princeton, NJ: Princeton University Press, 1980.

"Eleven to One Bond Majority a Credit to the City. San Francisco *Call*, 29 March 1912.

"Elliott-Keyes Bill Is Passed by Senate." *Daily Pacific Builder*, 26 March 1930.

Ferriss, Hugh. *The Metropolis of Tomorrow*. New York: Ives Washburn, 1929. Reprinted by Princeton, NJ: Princeton Architectural Press, 1986.

Field, Cynthia R., and Jeffrey T. Tilman. "Creating a Model for the National Mall: The Design of the National Museum of Natural History," *JSAH* 63, no. 1 (March 2004): 52–73.

Fielding, Mantle. *Dictionary of American Painters, Engravers, and Sculptors*. Stratford, CT: John Edwards, 1971.

Findling, John E. *Chicago's Great World's Fairs*. Manchester, UK: Manchester University Press, 1994.

"Firm Notable in Designing City Halls." Pasadena *Star–News*, 9 January 1925.

Fitzkce, Dariel. "Opera House Stage Larges in America." *The Architect and Engineer* 111, no. 2 (November 1932): 45–46.

"Folger Building Listed on Register." San Francisco *Heritage Newsletter* 24, no. 5 (September/October 1996): 5, 7.

Frampton, Kenneth. *Modern Architecture: A Critical History*. London: Thames & Hudson, 1980.

Frankenstein, Alfred. "Pageant of the Pacific." *Magazine of Art* (May 1939): 132–133.

Galloway, John Debo. *The First Transcontinental Railroad*. New York: Simmons-Boardman, 1950.

Gebhard, David. "Civic Presence in California Cities." *Architectural Design* 57 (September/October 1987): 74–80.

———. *Santa Barbara: The Creation of a New Spain in America*. Santa Barbara: University Art Museum, 1982.

Gebhard, David, et al. *Architecture in San Francisco and Northern California*. Salt Lake City, UT: Peregrine Smith, 1985.

Gebhard, David, and Robert Winter. *A Guide to Architecture in Los Angeles and Southern California*. Santa Barbara: Peregrine Smith, 1977.

"Giant Stride Forward: No Wounds to Heal." Pasadena *Star–News*, 28 March 1923.

"Gotham Firm Receives Prize for City Hall." Oakland *Tribune*, 23 June 1910.

"Great Vote for the Bond Issue." San Francisco *Call*, 29 March 1912.

Green, Clay M. "After the Opening: An Appreciation and a Colloquy." *The Olympian* 13, no. 11 (November 1925): 7–12.

Guadet, Julien. *Elements et Theories de l'Architecture, Cours Professé à l'Ecole Nationale et Speciale des Beaux-Arts*, 4 vols. Paris: Librairie de la Constuction Moderne, 1902.

———. "L'Enseignment de l'Architecture en France." *The Architectural Review* 14, no. 82 (September 1903): 136–143.

Guédy, Henry. *L'Enseignement à l'Ecole Nationale et Speciale des Beaux-Arts: Section d'Architecture*. Paris: Ecole des Beaux-Arts, 1899.

———. *La Section d'Architecure à l'Ecole Nationale et Speciale des Beaux-Arts: Programme pour l'Admission*. Paris: Ecole des Beaux-Arts, 1894.

Guérinet, Armand. *Ecole Nationale des Beaux-Arts: Les Grands Prix de Rome de 1850 à 1900*, 4 vols. Paris: Guérinet, n.d.

———. *Les Grands Prix de Rome: 1901–1910*. Paris: Guérinet, n.d.

Guerny, George. *Sculpture and the Federal Triangle*. Washington, DC: Smithsonian Institution Press, 1985.

Gutheim, F. A. "The Buildings and the Plan." *Magazine of Art* (May 1939): 134–138.

Hamilton, Frederick. "The New Office Building of the Pacific Gas and Electric Company, San Francisco." *The Architect and Engineer* 82, no. 1 (July 1925): 50–68.

Hamlin, Talbot F. "The San Francisco Fair." *Pencil Points* 19, no. 11 (November 1938): 683–686.

Hamlin, Talbot F. "Some Fair Comparisons." *Pencil Points* 20, no. 10 (October 1939): 641–648.

Harris, Frank M. "Pacific Service to have New Home." *Pacific Service Magazine* 11, no. 6 (November 1922): 170–174.

Hartman, Chester, with Sarah Carnochan. *City for Sale: The Transformation of San Francisco*, 2nd ed. Berkeley: University of California Press, 2002.

Hegemann, Werner, and Elbert Peets. *The American Vitruvius: An Architect's Handbook of Civic Art*. New York, 1922.

Heilbron, J. L., and Robert W. Seidel. *Lawrence and His Laboratory*, vol. 1. Berkeley: University of California Press, 1989.

Helfand, Harvey. *The Campus Guide: University of California, Berkeley*. New York: Princeton Architectural Press, 2002.

Helfrich, Kurt G. F. "Modernism for Washington?" *Washington History* 8, no. 1 (Spring/Summer 1996): 16–37.

Himmelwright, A. L. A. *The San Francisco Earthquake and Fire: A Brief History of the Disaster*. New York: Roebling Construction Company, 1906.

Hitchcock Jr., Henry-Russell, and Philip C. Johnson. *The International Style*. New York: W. W. Norton, 1966.

Holland, Katherine Church. "The San Francisco Art Association: 1871–1906." *California History* 76 (1997 Supplement): 17–20.

"Homage à Laloux." *Pencil Points* 18, no. 10 (October 1937): 620–628.

Hood, Raymond M. "Exterior Architecture of Office Buildings." *The Architectural Forum* 41, no. 9 (September 1924): 97–99.

Hoover, Herbert Clark. "Dedication Speech for the Hoover Library of War, Revolution, and Peace." *The Dedication of the Hoover Library*. Palo Alto: Stanford University Press, 1941.

"Housing Project Homes All Ready to Greet First Tenants." San Francisco *Call–Bulletin*, 27 April 1940.

Howard, Henry T. "The Coit Memorial Tower." *The Architect and Engineer* 115, no. 3 (December 1933): 11–15.

Howe, Kathrine S., Alice Cooney Freylinghuysen, and Catherine Hoover Voorsanger. *Herter Brothers: Furniture and Interiors for a Gilded Age*. Houston: Harry N. Adams, 1994.

"How Mark Hopkins Died." Los Angeles *Herald*, 30 March 1878.

Hudnut, Joseph. "Twilight of the Gods." *Magazine of Art* 10, no. 8 (August 1937): 484–488.

"Ingold Gets 40 Acres." San Francisco *Examiner*, 12 May 1954.

Jackson, Joseph Henry, ed. *The Western Gate: A San Francisco Reader*. New York: Farrar, Straus & Young, 1952.

Jacques, Annie, and Riichi Miyaké. *Les Dessins d'Architecture de l'Ecole des Beaux-Arts*. Paris: Arthaud, 1987.

James, George Wharton. *Through Ramona's Country*. Boston: Little, Brown, 1909.

James, Jack, and Earle Weller. *Treasure Island, "The Magic City"—1939–1940*. San Francisco: Pisani Printing, 1939.

James, Juliet Helena Lumbard. *Palaces and Courts of the Exposition*. San Francisco: California Book Company, 1915.

"Jean Louis Bourgeois." Obituary. *The Architect and Engineer* 40, no. 3 (April 1915): 108.

Joncas, Richard, David J. Neuman, and Paul V. Turner. *The Campus Guide: Stanford University*. New York: Princeton Architectural Press, 1999.

Jones, Mady. "The San Francisco Art Institute." *San Francisco Magazine* (June 1980): 50–57.

"Judges Award First Prize of $10,000 to New York Architects." San Francisco *Chronicle*, 23 June 1910.

Kahn, Judd. *Imperial San Francisco: Politics and Planning in an American City, 1897–1906*. Lincoln: University of Nebraska Press, 1979.

Kidney, Walter C. *The Architecture of Choice: Eclecticism in America 1880–1930*. New York: Braziller, 1974.

Kirker, Harold. *California's Architectural Frontier*. Santa Barbara: Gibbs Smith, 1973.

Kohler, Sue. *The Commission of Fine Arts: A Brief History 1910–1995*. Washington, DC: Commission of Fine Arts, 1995.

Koyl, George S., ed. *American Architects Directory*. New York: Bowker, 1955.

Keeler, Charles. *San Francisco and Thereabout*. San Francisco: California Promotion Committee, 1903.

———. *The Simple Home*. Edited by Dimitri Shipounoff. Santa Barbara: Peregrine Smith, 1979.

Kilham, Walter H. Jr. *Raymond Hood, Architect: Form Through Function in the American Skyscraper*. New York: Architectural Book Publishing, 1973.

"Labor–ICC Building Row Up to Green." Washington *Post*, 7 March 1934.

"Labor Department Building to Be Model Structure." Washington *Daily News*, 10 October, 1933.

LaFarge, C. Grant. *The American Academy in Rome*. New York: American Academy in Rome, 1920.

Lee, Anthony W. *Painting on the Left: Diego Rivera, Radical Politics, and San Francisco's Public Murals*. Berkeley: University of California Press, 1999.

"Le Football Américain à Paris." *Le Temps* [Paris]. 27 November 1897.

Le Guide Patrimoine Paris. Paris: Hachette, 1992.

Lewis, Oscar. *Bay Window Bohemia*. New York: Doubleday & Company, 1956.

———. *San Francisco: Mission to Metropolis*, 2nd ed. San Diego: Howell-North Books, 1980.

———. *The Big Four*. New York: Knopf, 1938.

"Lilly the Vamp." *Time*, 9 October 1933.

"Local Demonstration of the Practical Control of Concrete." *Plastide Progress* 3, no. 1 (October 1927): 11–12.

Longstreth, Richard. *On the Edge of the World: Four Architects in San Francisco at the Turn of the Century*. New York: Architectural History Foundation, 1983.

Longstreth, Richard, ed. *The Mall in Washinton, 1791–1991: Studies in the History of Art*. Washington, DC: National Gallery of Art, 1991.

Mack, Gerstle. *1906: Surviving the Great Earthquake and Fire*. San Francisco: Chronicle Books, 1984.

Macomber, Ben. *The Jewel City*. San Francisco: Williams, 1915.

"Magnificent City Hall Is Dedicated: Mayor Moves into Fine New Office." San Francisco *Chronicle*, 29 December 1912.

Maybeck, Bernard R. *Palace of Fine Arts and Lagoon*. San Francisco: Elder, 1915.

McGruder, Charles. "San Francisco Salutes Pacifica." *Pencil Points* 20, no. 2 (February 1939): 67–90.

McCague, James. *Moguls and Iron Men: The Story of the First Transcontinental Railroad*. New York: Harper & Row, 1964.

McCoy, Esther. *Five California Architects*. Los Angeles: Hennessey & Ingalls, 1960.

McGloin, John Bernard. *San Francisco: The Story of a City*. San Rafael, CA: Presidio Press, 1978.

Mead, Christopher Curtis. *Charles Garnier's Paris Opera: Architectural Empathy and the Renaissance of French Classicism*. New York: Architectural History Foundation, 1991.

"A Message of Felicitation: New Building Will Be Monument to Loyal Sons of the Olympic Club." *The Olympian* 18, no. 9 (September 1930): 7–10.

Meyer, Robert, ed. *San Francisco: A Chronological and Documentary History, 1542–1970*. Dobbs Ferry, NY: Oceana Publications, 1974.

Middleton, Robin D., ed. *The Beaux-Arts and Nineteenth-Century French Architecture*. Cambridge, MA: MIT Press, 1982.

Mirrielees, Edith. *Stanford: The Story of a University*. New York: Putnam, 1959.

Mitchell, J. Pearce. *Stanford University: 1916–1941*. Palo Alto: Stanford University Press, 1958.

Moore, Charles. *Daniel H. Burnham: Architect, Planner of Cities*, 2 vols. Boston: Houghton Mifflin, 1921.

Moore, Charles, ed. *The Promise of American Architecture: Addresses at the Annual Dinner of the American Institute of Architects*. Washington, DC: American Institute of Architects, 1905.

Morrow, Irving K. "Leland Stanford Junior University." *The Architect and Engineer* 59, no. 1 (October 1919): 43–67.

———. "Recent San Francisco Skyscrapers." *The Architect and Engineer* 85, no. 2 (November 1923): 50–58.

Mowry, George E. *The California Progressives*. New York: New York Times Book Co., 1963.

Mullgardt, Louis Christian. *The Architecture and Landscape Gardening of the Exposition*. San Francisco: Elder, 1915.

———. "The Panama-Pacific Exposition at San Francisco." *The Architect and Engineer* 37, no. 3 (March 1915): 193–197.

Mumford, Lewis. "Towards a Modern Synagogue." *Menorah Journal* 11, no. 3 (June 1925): 225–236.

Musée d'Orsay. *Victor Laloux 1850–1937: L'Architecte de la Gare d'Orsay*. Paris: Ministre de la Culture et de la Communication, 1987.

Nash, George. *Herbert Hoover and Stanford University*. Stanford: Hoover Institution Press, 1988.

National Commission of Fine Arts. *The Plan of the National Capital*. Washington, DC: United States Government Printing Office, 1923.

———. *Eleventh Report of the National Commission of Fine Arts, January 1, 1926–June 30, 1929*. Washington, DC: United States Government Printing Office, 1930.

Neuhaus, Eugen. *The Art of Treasure Island*. Berkeley: University of California Press, 1939.

"New City Hall, Pasadena, Distinctive Southern California Type of American Architecture." *Plastide Progress* 3, no. 1 (October 1927): 3–7.

Newman, Louis J. "The New Temple Emanu-El of San Francisco." *Pacific Coast Architect* 30, no. 3 (September 1926): 15–63.

"News." *The Architectural Forum* 107 no. 10 (October 1957): 5–6.

"New Temple Emanu-El is Hallowed to Human Needs." San Francisco *Chronicle*, 17 April 1926, 16.

Noffsinger, James Phillip. *The Influence of the Ecole des Beaux-Arts on the Architects of the United States*. Washington, DC: American Institute of Architects Press, 1955.

"Notes." *American Architect* XXVIII (May 31, 1890): 126.

"Notes." *The Architectural Journal* (April–June) 1920: 640.

"Notice to Architects Calling for Plans and Specifications in Detail for a Town Hall for the Town of Berkeley." Oakland *Tribune*, 16 April 1907.

Olmstead, Roger, and T. H. Watkins. *Here Today: San Francisco's Architectural Heritage*. San Francisco: Chronicle Books, 1968.

Olson, Sheri. "West Wall, St. Mark's Cathedral, Seattle, Washington." *Architectural Record* 186, no. 7 (July 1998): 101–104.

"Olympic Golf and Country Club." *The Architect and Engineer* 74: 2 (August 1923): 67–71.

Owings, Nathanial A. "Amusement Features of the Exposition." *Architectural Record* 75, no. 5 (May 1933): 355–362.

"Pacific Gas and Electric Building." *The American Architect* CXXVIII, no. 2485 (20 November 1925): Pl. 304–310.

"Pacific Service in its New Home." *Pacific Service Magazine* 14, no. 5 (July 1925): 144–146.

Partridge, Loren W. *John Galen Howard and the Berkeley Campus: Beaux-Arts Architecture in the "Athens of the West."* Berkeley, CA: Berkeley Architectural Heritage Association, 1978.

"Pergolas." *The Architect and Engineer* 20, no. 2 (March 1910): 37–43.

"Perkins Opens Labor Building." Washington *Herald*, 26 February 1935.

Perry, Warren C. "The San Francisco Stock Exchange Competition." *The Architect and Engineer* 92, no. 3 (March 1928): 35–43.

Peterson, Anne E. *Hornblower & Marshall, Architects*. Washington, DC: Preservation Press, 1978.

"Philip Johnson: Architecture or Sentiment?" *Preservation News* (April 1978): 12.

Polk, Willis. *A Matter of Taste: Willis Polk's Writings on Architecture in "The Wave."* Edited by Richard Longstreth. Reprinted in Berkeley, CA: Book Club of California, 1979.

———. "Civic Center Buildings Compared." San Francisco *Chronicle*, 9 March 1917.

———. "The Panama-Pacific Plan." *Sunset* 13, no. 4 (April 1912): 487–492.

"Plans for New City Hall Are Decided Upon." San Francisco *Call*, 21 June 1921.

"Plans for New Synagogue in San Francisco Approved." San Francisco *Chronicle*, 26 January 1924, 7.

Potter, Elizabeth Gray. *The San Francisco Skyline*. New York: Dodd, Mead, 1939.

"Railway Terminal Designed to Speed Commuter Traffic." *Architectural Record* 79, no. 7 (July 1939): 30–32.

Reed, Henry Hope. *The Golden City*. New York: Norton, 1971.

Regnery, Dorothy F. *An Enduring Heritage: Historic Buildings of the San Francisco Peninsula*. Stanford, CA: Stanford University Press, 1976.

Reps, John W. *Monumental Washington: The Planning and Development of the Capitol Center*. Princeton, NJ: Princeton University Press, 1967.

"Result of Competition for Pasadena Civic Center Buildings." *The Architect and Engineer* 76, no. 3 (March 1924): 77–80.

"Result of Oakland City Hall Competition." *The Architect and Engineer* 21, no. 2 (June 1910): 48–49.

Rivoalen, E. "Le Concours du Prix de Rome." *La Construction Moderne* (22 August 1902): 557–560.

Robertson, Michael. "Philip Johnson: Making His Mark on City Skyline," San Francisco *Chronicle*, 20 May 1982.

Robinson, Charles Mulford. *The Improvement of Towns and Cities: The Practical Basis of Civic Aesthetics*, 3rd ed., revised. New York: Putnam's Sons, 1907.

Rolph, James Jr. "Mayor's Innaugural Address" [8 January 1916]. *San Francisco Municipal Reports—1915–1916*. San Francisco: City of San Francisco, 1918.

Rosenbaum, Fred. *Architects of Reform: Congregational and Community Leadership, Emanu-El of San Francisco 1849–1980*. Berkeley: Western Jewish History Center, 1980.

Rowe, Colin. *As I Was Saying: Recollections and Miscellaneous Essays*, v. 1. Cambridge, MA: MIT Press, 1996.

Ryan, W. D'Arcy. "Illumination of the Exposition." *California's Monthly Magazine*, Cornerstone Issue (1915): 317–320.

Saarinen, Eliel. "A New Architectural Language for America." *The Western Architect* 32, no. 1 (January 1923): 37–38.

"San Francisco Builds Low-Rent Homes." *The Architect and Engineer* 150 no. 1 (July 1942): 18–29.

"San Francisco Contractors 90 Days Ahead of Schedule on Tower." *Daily Pacific Builder*, 9 June 1933.

San Francisco Housing Authority. *Fifth Annual Report of the San Francisco Housing Authority of the City and County of San Francisco*. 18 April 1943.

———. "Holly Courts: Special Bulletin of the San Francisco Housing Association." San Francisco Housing Association, 1940.

———. *Second Annual Report of the San Francisco Housing Authority of the City and County of San Francisco*. 18 April 1940.

San Francisco Municipal Reports—1915–1916. San Francisco: San Francisco Board of Supervisors, 1918.

Saylor, Henry H. "Make No Little Plans . . . " *AIA Journal* 27, no. 3 (March 1957): 95–99.

Scheid, Ann. "Pasadena's Civic Center: A Brief History—Part I." *SAH/SCC Review* 1: (1984): 8–16.

———. "Pasadena's Civic Center: A Brief History—Part II." *SAH/SCC Review* 2: (1985): 18–24.

Schrank, Lisa D. "The Role of the 1933–1934 Century of Progress International Exposition in the Development and Promotion of Modern Architecture in the United States." Ph.D. dissertation, University of Texas at Austin, 1998.

Schuyler, Montgomery. *American Architecture and Other Writings.* Cambridge, MA: MIT Press, 1961.

Scott, Mel. *The San Francisco Bay Area: A Metropolis in Perspective.* Berkeley, CA: University of California Press, 1959.

"Second Annual Report of the Housing Authority of the City and County of San Francisco." City of San Francisco, 18 April 1940.

Silverman, Deborah L. "The 1889 Exposition: The Crisis of Bourgeois Individualism." *Perspecta* 2 (1975): 71–91.

Snyder, Christopher Henry. "Some of the Engineering Features of the San Francisco City Hall." *The Architect and Engineer* 46, no. 2 (August 1916): 79–80.

———. "Structural Features of the San Francisco Opera House." *The Architect and Engineer* 111, no. 2 (November 1932): 43.

Solomonson, Kathleen. *The Chicago Tribune Tower Competition: Skyscraper Design and Cultural Change in the 1920s.* Cambridge, MA: Cambridge University Press, 2001.

"Some of the Work of Bakewell and Brown, Architects." *The Architect and Engineer* 16, no. 1 (February 1909): 34–43.

Stanton, J. E. "Color and Light." *The Architect and Engineer* 136, no. 2 (Febrary 1939): 39–40.

Starr, Kevin. *Americans and the California Dream, 1850–1915.* New York: Oxford University Press, 1973.

———. *Inventing the Dream: California Through the Progressive Era.* New York: Oxford University Press, 1985.

———. *Material Dreams: Southern California Through the 1920s.* New York: Oxford University Press, 1990.

Statts, H. Philip, with Charles H. Cheney. *California Architecture in Santa Barbara.* New York: Architectural Book Publishing Company, 1929.

Stillman, John Maxon, "The University Library," *New Building of the Stanford University Library and a History of the Library, 1891–1919* (Palo Alto: Stanford University, 1919), 9–17.

Stowell, Kenneth Kingsley, ed. "A Century of Progress." *The Architecural Forum* LIX, no. 1 (July 1933).

Sullivan, Louis. "The Chicago Tribune Competition." *Architectural Record* 53, no. 2 (February 1923): 151–157.

Swan, Clifford. "The Acoustics of the San Francisco Opera House." *The Architect and Engineer* 111, no. 2 (November 1932): 44, 59.

"Sylvain Schnaittacher." *The Architect and Engineer* 85, no. 1 (April 1927): 122.

"Technicality Delays Contract with Architects." San Francisco *Examiner,* 24 September 1912.

Temko, Allan. *No Way to Build a Ballpark.* San Francisco: Chronicle Books, 1993.

Thomas, Gordon, and Max Morgan Witts. *The San Francisco Earthquake.* New York: Stein & Day, 1971.

Tompkins, Sally Kress. *A Quest for Grandeur.* Washington, DC: Smithsonian Institution Press, 1991.

"Treasure Island Buildings Being Torn Down." San Francisco *Chronicle,* 24 September 1947.

Turner, Paul V. *Campus: An American Planning Tradition.* Cambridge, MA: MIT Press, 1984.

———. *The Founders and Their Architects: The Design of Stanford University.* Stanford: Stanford University Press, 1976.

"Two-story Rows and Flats." *The Architectural Forum* 73, no. 11 (November 1940): 45.

"United States Government Building." *The Architectural Forum* 70, no. 6 (June 1939): 474–475.

"USHA—San Francisco Housing Project." *Architectural Record* 88, no. 10 (October 1940): 46–49.

Van Trump, James D. "Therefore With the Angels: An Architectural Excursion in Los Angeles." *Charette: Pennsylvania Journal of Architecture* 45 no. 6 (June 1965): 11–60.

Van Zanten, David. "Nineteenth-century French Architectural Services and the Design of the Monuments of Paris." *Art Journal* 48, no. 1 (Spring 1989): 16–22.

———. "Felix Duban and the Buildings of the Ecole des Beaux-Arts, 1832–1840." *JSAH* vol. 37, no. 3 (October, 1978): 161–174.

Walker, Ralph T. "A New Architecture." *The Architectural Forum* 48, no. 1 (January 1928): 3–4.

———. "If This Be Sentiment…" *Journal of the AIA* (June 1958): 284.

Warnecke, John Carl. "The Rescue and Renaissance of Lafayette Square," *White House History* 13 (Summer 2003): 30–45.

"War Takes Noted Californians—Bourgeois and Breece Are Killed." San Francisco *Examiner,* 18 March 1916.

White, Theo B. *Paul Phillipe Cret: Architect and Teacher.* Philadelphia: University of Pennsylvania Press, 1973.

"Who is it that Tries to Black Eye our Home Industry?" San Francisco *Call,* 8 February 1913.

"When Perkins Bathes—She Asks Privacy." San Francisco *Chronicle,* 23 January 1935.

Wilson, Richard Guy. *The AIA Gold Medal.* New York: McGraw-Hill, 1980.

———. "California Classicist." *Progressive Architecture* (December, 1983): 64–71.

Wilson, William H. *The City Beautiful Movement.* Baltimore: Johns Hopkins University Press, 1989.

Winter, Robert, ed. *Toward a Simpler Way of Life: The Arts and Crafts Architects of California.* Berkeley, CA: University of California Press, 1997.

"With the Architects." *The Architect and Engineer* 90, no. 1 (July 1927): 111.

Withey, Henry F., Elise Rathburn Withey. *Biographical Dictionary of American Architects (Deceased).* Los Angeles: New Age Publishing, 1956.

"Women Electors Early at Polls." San Francisco *Call,* 29 March 1912.

Woodbridge, Sally B. *Bernard Maybeck: Visionary Architect.* New York: Abbeville Press, 1992.

———. *John Galen Howard and the University of California.* Berkeley: University of California Press, 2002.

Woodbridge, Sally B., ed. *California Architecture: Historic American Buildings Survey.* San Francisco: Chronicle Books, 1988.

Woollett, William L. "Color in Architecture at the Panama-Pacific Exposition." *Architectural Record* 45, no. 5 (May 1915): 437–444.

———. "Criticism of the San Francisco City Hall." *The Architect and Engineer* 46, no. 8 (September 1916): 70–71.

Wright, Charles H. C. *A History of the Third French Republic* (1916). Reprinted in facsimile. New York: Books for Libraries Press, 1970.

Wright, Frank Lloyd. "Another 'Psuedo.'" *The Architectural Forum* 59, no. 1 (July 1923): 25.

Young, Andree, and Noel Young. *Santa Barbara Architecture: From Spanish Colonial to Modern.* Santa Barbara: Capra Press, 1975.

Zakheim, Masha [Jewett]. *Coit Tower, San Francisco: Its History and Art.* San Francisco: Volcano Press, 1984.

Unpublished Material

Architectural Resources Group. "Historic Structures Report: Pasadena City Hall." City of Pasadena, 1989.

Bakewell, John Jr. "Architecture is for Everybody." Bancroft Library, 1920.

Bennett, Edward H. "The New Departmental Buildings in Washington, D.C." Manuscript of address given c. 1932, Art Institute of Chicago.

BOLA Architecture & Planning, "Historic American Building Survey of the Jewish Community Center of San Francisco HABS CA-2724." BOLA Architecture & Planning, Seattle, WA, October 2001.

City of Redlands, CA. "AT&SF Railroad Station, Redlands, California—Historic Resources Inventory." Department of Parks and Recreation, State of California, 4 March 1977.

Consulting Architects of San Francisco. "Program of the Competition for the Selection of an Architect for the City Hall, San Francisco, California." Board of Public Works, City of San Francisco, April 6, 1912.

———. "Proposed Schemes for the Civic Center." Board of Public Works, City of San Francisco." May 15, 1912.

Corbett, Michael. "San Francisco Civic Center." National Register of Historic Places Nomination, December 2, 1974.

Delano, William Adams. "A Letter to My Grandson." Privately printed, New York: 1944. In possession of Richard Delano. Quoted by Chaffee, 94.

Draper, Joan. "The San Francisco Civic Center: Architecture, Planning, and Politics." Ph.D. dissertation, University of California at Berkeley, 1979.

_____. "John Galen Howard and the Beaux-Arts Movement in the United States." Master's thesis, University of California at Berleley, 1972.

Goss, Gary A. "Index to *The Architect and Engineer*, 1905–1928." California Historical Society, Sacramento, 1982.

Howard, John Galen, trans. *Elements et Theories de l'Architecture* by Julien Guadet. College of Environmental Design, University of California, Berkeley, 1910.

Jury, San Francisco City Hall Competition. "Judgement of the Competition for the Selection of an Architect for the City Hall," June 20, 1912.

Kahn, Judd. "Imperial San Francisco: History of a Vision." Ph.D. dissertation, University of California at Berkeley, 1971.

Lee, Portia. "Victorious Spirit: Regional Influences in the Architecture, Landscaping, and Murals of the Panama-Pacific International Exposition." Ph.D. dissertation, George Washington University, 1984.

Malinick, Cynthia Barwick. "The Lives and Works of the Reid Brothers, Architects: 1852–1943." Master's thesis, University of San Diego, 1992.

Markwart, Arthur Herman. "Building an Exposition, Report of the Activities of the Division of Works of the Panama-Pacific International Exposition." 4 vols., 1915, Special Collections, Stanford University Library.

Moore, Charles. "Memories." Autobiographical manuscript, National Archives, RG 66.

Nelson, Christopher H. "Classical California: The Architecture of Albert Pissis and Arthur Brown, Jr." Ph.D. dissertation, University of California at Santa Barbara, 1986.

Page, Edward B. "Concerning the Architecture of Arthur Brown, Jr." Page, Anderson, & Turnbull, San Francisco, 1975.

Page, Anderson, & Turnbull. "The W. P. Fuller Building." San Francisco, n.d.

President's Report—1912–1942, Leland Stanford Jr. University.

"Report of the Civic Center Committee." San Francisco Chapter, American Institute of Architects, March 1913.

Rolph, James Jr. "History of the San Francisco War Memorial: Message to the Board of Supervisors and the People of San Francisco at a Special Meeting of the Board of Supervisors." San Francisco, February 18, 1930.

San Francisco Board of Public Works. "Program of the Competition for the Selection of an Architect for the City Hall, April 6, 1912." San Francisco, 1912.

Sebastien, Bea. "Interview with George Wagner," March 13, 1978. Transcript in collection of the Friends of the San Francisco Library.

Tobin, Richard M. "Dedicatory Speech for the San Francisco War Memorial," November 11, 1931.

INDEX

Note: Page numbers in *italic* type indicate illustrations.
Color plates are indicated by "C."
Architectural works are in San Francisco unless otherwise noted.

THE CLASSICAL AMERICA SERIES
IN ART AND ARCHITECTURE:

The Golden City by Henry Hope Reed
The American Vignola by William R. Ware
The Architecture of Humanism by Geoffrey Scott
The Decoration of Houses by Edith Wharton and Ogden Codman, Jr.
Italian Villas and Their Gardens by Edith Wharton
The Classic Point of View by Kenyon Cox
What is Painting? by Kenyon Cox
Man As Hero: The Human Figure in Western Art by Pierce Rice
Greek and Roman Architecture in Classic Drawings by Hector d'Espouy
Monumental Classic Architecture in Great Britain and Ireland by Albert E. Richardson
Monograph of the Work of McKim, Mead & White, 1879–1915, Student Edition
The Library of Congress: Its Architecture and Decoration by Herbert Small
Letarouilly on Renaissance Rome by John Barrington Bayley
The New York Public Library: Its Architecture and Decoration by Henry Hope Reed
The Elements of Classical Architecture by Georges Gromort
Palaces of the Sun King: Versailles, Trianon, Marly, The Chateaux of Louis XIV by Berndt Dams and Andrew Zega
Bricks and Brownstone: The New York Row House 1783–1929 by Charles Lockwood
The Architecture of the Classical Interior by Steven W. Semes
Classical Architecture for the Twenty-First Century: An Introduction to Design by J. Francois Gabriel

The Institute of Classical Architecture & Classical America
is the organization dedicated to the classical tradition
in architecture and the allied arts in the United States.
Inquiries about the mission and programs of the organization are welcome and should be addressed to:

The Institute of Classical Architecture and Classical America
www.classicist.org